Y0-EIA-908

Microsoft®
PowerPoint® 2000
Bible

Microsoft® PowerPoint® 2000 Bible

Faithe Wempen

IDG Books Worldwide, Inc.
An International Data Group Company

Foster City, CA ✦ Chicago, IL ✦ Indianapolis, IN ✦ New York, NY

Microsoft® PowerPoint® 2000 Bible

Published by

IDG Books Worldwide, Inc.

An International Data Group Company

919 E. Hillsdale Blvd., Suite 400

Foster City, CA 94404

www.idgbooks.com (IDG Books Worldwide Web site)

Library of Congress Catalog Card Number: 98-73782

ISBN: 0-7645-3252-9

Printed in the United States of America

10 9 8 7 6 5 4 3 2 1

1B/SW/QT/ZZ/FC

Distributed in the United States by IDG Books Worldwide, Inc.

Distributed by CDG Books Canada Inc. for Canada; by Transworld Publishers Limited in the United Kingdom; by IDG Norge Books for Norway; by IDG Sweden Books for Sweden; by IDGBA Ltd. for Australia; by IDGBA (NZ) Ltd. for New Zealand; by TransQuest Publishers Pte Ltd. for Singapore, Malaysia, Thailand, Indonesia, and Hong Kong; by Gotop Information Inc. for Taiwan; by ICG Muse, Inc. for Japan; by Norma Comunicaciones S.A. for Colombia; by Intersoft for South Africa; by Le Monde en Tique for France; by International Thomson Publishing for Germany, Austria and Switzerland; by Distribuidora Cuspide for Argentina; by Livraria Cultura for Brazil; by Ediciones ZETA S.C.R. Ltda. for Peru; by WS Computer Publishing Corporation, Inc., for the Philippines; by Contemporanea de Ediciones for Venezuela; by Express Computer Distributors for the Caribbean and West Indies; by Micronesia Media Distributor, Inc. for Micronesia; by Grupo Editorial Norma S.A. for Guatemala; by Chips Computadoras S.A. de C.V. for Mexico; by Editorial Norma de Panama S.A. for Panama; by American Bookshops for Finland. Authorized Sales Agent: Anthony Rudkin Associates for the Middle East and North Africa.

For general information on IDG Books Worldwide's books in the U.S., please call our Consumer Customer Service department at 800-762-2974. For reseller information, including discounts and premium sales, please call our Reseller Customer Service department at 800-434-3422.

For information on where to purchase IDG Books Worldwide's books outside the U.S., please contact our International Sales department at 317-596-5530 or fax 317-596-5692.

For consumer information on foreign language translations, please contact our Customer Service department at 800-434-3422, fax 317-596-5692, or e-mail rights@idgbooks.com.

For information on licensing foreign or domestic rights, please phone +1-650-655-3109.

For sales inquiries and special prices for bulk quantities, please contact our Sales department at 650-655-3200 or write to the address above.

For information on using IDG Books Worldwide's books in the classroom or for ordering examination copies, please contact our Educational Sales department at 800-434-2086 or fax 317-596-5499.

For press review copies, author interviews, or other publicity information, please contact our Public Relations department at 650-655-3000 or fax 650-655-3299.

For authorization to photocopy items for corporate, personal, or educational use, please contact Copyright Clearance Center, 222 Rosewood Drive, Danvers, MA 01923, or fax 978-750-4470.

ABOUT IDG BOOKS WORLDWIDE

Welcome to the world of IDG Books Worldwide.

IDG Books Worldwide, Inc., is a subsidiary of International Data Group, the world's largest publisher of computer-related information and the leading global provider of information services on information technology. IDG was founded more than 30 years ago by Patrick J. McGovern and now employs more than 9,000 people worldwide. IDG publishes more than 290 computer publications in over 75 countries. More than 90 million people read one or more IDG publications each month.

Launched in 1990, IDG Books Worldwide is today the #1 publisher of best-selling computer books in the United States. We are proud to have received eight awards from the Computer Press Association in recognition of editorial excellence and three from Computer Currents' First Annual Readers' Choice Awards. Our best-selling *...For Dummies®* series has more than 50 million copies in print with translations in 31 languages. IDG Books Worldwide, through a joint venture with IDG's Hi-Tech Beijing, became the first U.S. publisher to publish a computer book in the People's Republic of China. In record time, IDG Books Worldwide has become the first choice for millions of readers around the world who want to learn how to better manage their businesses.

Our mission is simple: Every one of our books is designed to bring extra value and skill-building instructions to the reader. Our books are written by experts who understand and care about our readers. The knowledge base of our editorial staff comes from years of experience in publishing, education, and journalism — experience we use to produce books to carry us into the new millennium. In short, we care about books, so we attract the best people. We devote special attention to details such as audience, interior design, use of icons, and illustrations. And because we use an efficient process of authoring, editing, and desktop publishing our books electronically, we can spend more time ensuring superior content and less time on the technicalities of making books.

You can count on our commitment to deliver high-quality books at competitive prices on topics you want to read about. At IDG Books Worldwide, we continue in the IDG tradition of delivering quality for more than 30 years. You'll find no better book on a subject than one from IDG Books Worldwide.

John Kilcullen
Chairman and CEO
IDG Books Worldwide, Inc.

Steven Berkowitz
President and Publisher
IDG Books Worldwide, Inc.

Eighth Annual Computer Press Awards ≥1992

Ninth Annual Computer Press Awards ≥1993

Tenth Annual Computer Press Awards ≥1994

Eleventh Annual Computer Press Awards ≥1995

IDG is the world's leading IT media, research and exposition company. Founded in 1964, IDG had 1997 revenues of $2.05 billion and has more than 9,000 employees worldwide. IDG offers the widest range of media options that reach IT buyers in 75 countries representing 95% of worldwide IT spending. IDG's diverse product and services portfolio spans six key areas including print publishing, online publishing, expositions and conferences, market research, education and training, and global marketing services. More than 90 million people read one or more of IDG's 290 magazines and newspapers, including IDG's leading global brands — Computerworld, PC World, Network World, Macworld and the Channel World family of publications. IDG Books Worldwide is one of the fastest-growing computer book publishers in the world, with more than 700 titles in 36 languages. The "...For Dummies®" series alone has more than 50 million copies in print. IDG offers online users the largest network of technology-specific Web sites around the world through IDG.net (http://www.idg.net), which comprises more than 225 targeted Web sites in 55 countries worldwide. International Data Corporation (IDC) is the world's largest provider of information technology data, analysis and consulting, with research centers in over 41 countries and more than 400 research analysts worldwide. IDG World Expo is a leading producer of more than 168 globally branded conferences and expositions in 35 countries including E3 (Electronic Entertainment Expo), Macworld Expo, ComNet, Windows World Expo, ICE (Internet Commerce Expo), Agenda, DEMO, and Spotlight. IDG's training subsidiary, ExecuTrain, is the world's largest computer training company, with more than 230 locations worldwide and 785 training courses. IDG Marketing Services helps industry-leading IT companies build international brand recognition by developing global integrated marketing programs via IDG's print, online and exposition products worldwide. Further information about the company can be found at www.idg.com. 1/24/99

Credits

Acquistions Editor
Andy Cummings

Project Coordinator
Tom Debolski

Cover Design
Murder By Design

Graphics and Production Specialist
Stephanie Hollier

Graphic Techicans
Sarah Barnes
Linda Marousek

Quality Control Specialists
Mick Arellano
Mark Schumann

Proofreading and Indexing
York Production Services

About the Author

Faithe Wempen is an A+ Certified hardware guru and software consultant with over 30 computer books to her credit. When she's not writing, she runs Your Computer Friend, a PC consulting company that specializes in helping beginning users get the most out of their PCs, and teaches classes in PowerPoint and other Microsoft Office products to individuals and groups. She also has a master's degree in rhetoric and composition and has taught writing courses at Purdue University.

To Margaret, who makes it all possible.

Foreword

Success often depends on a presentation. The company that assembles well-organized, persuasive presentations is the one that wins new contracts. The department head with the powerful presentation gets the sought-after budget increase.

Presentations are communications, and communicating is a complex process. Misunderstandings are common. Wise presenters understand that what they think they told their audiences does not matter. What matters is what the audience thinks the presenter said. This is where visual aids come into play. Effective visual aids facilitate the communication process, visually reinforce the presenter's message, and minimize the chances for misunderstanding.

Visual aids have another role as well: They aid in the retention of information. People remember 20 percent of what they hear, 30 percent of what they see, and 50 percent of what they see and hear. And because seeing is believing, a sprinkling of appropriate graphics adds credibility to a presentation.

As executive director of the world's leading organization devoted to public speaking, I've been looking for a good book on the topic of preparing visual aids for presentation. This one is terrific. PowerPoint is one of the most popular, easy-to-use presentation packages available. It helps presenters produce visual aids that are clear, direct, visually appealing, and memorable.

Most people today were raised on television. They are visually oriented and want their information presented in convenient, efficient "sound bites" and graphics. Although the latest presentation technologies make it possible for you to amaze your audiences with all kinds of electronic wizardry, proceed with caution. Too much dazzle can detract from your message while poorly prepared and designed visuals can muddy it and confuse your audience.

This book offers everything you need to know to effectively use PowerPoint to create powerful visuals. Whether you're preparing visuals for your first presentation or your five-hundredth, you'll find this book invaluable. If you're a beginner, you'll learn the basics of PowerPoint and proceed step by step through the creation process. If you're more experienced, you'll discover how to improve your visual materials to increase their impact. And everyone will learn various tricks and tips to make the preparation and presentation of effective visuals fast and easy.

Terrence J. McCann
Executive Director
Toastmasters International

About Toastmasters International

Even the best visual aids can lose their impact if the presenter has poor speaking skills. You've probably experienced presentations where the speakers mumbled, were so nervous that every other word was "ah" or "um," fumbled with their visual aids, or had other nervous habits that detracted from the presentation and message. Fortunately, Toastmasters International offers a safe, inexpensive way for presenters to practice and improve their skills in a supportive environment. More than three million people have become clear, confident speakers through their participation in Toastmasters Clubs. You'll find Toastmasters Clubs in more than 65 countries around the world. They meet at different times and locations — one is sure to be convenient for you. If you are interested in joining or forming a Toastmasters Club in your community or company write Toastmasters International: P.O. Box 9052, Mission Viejo, CA 92690. Or visit the Web site at www.toastmasters.org.

Preface

Some books zoom through a software program so fast it makes your head spin. You'll come out dizzy, but basically able to cobble together some sort of result, even if it doesn't look quite right. This is not one of those books.

The Microsoft PowerPoint 2000 Bible is probably the only PowerPoint book you will ever need. In fact, it may even be the only book on giving presentations you'll ever need. No, seriously! I mean it.

As you probably guessed by the heft of the book, this is not a quick-fix shortcut to PowerPoint expertise. Instead, it's a thoughtful, thorough educational tool that can be your personal trainer now and your reference text for years to come. That's because this book covers PowerPoint from "cradle to grave." No matter what your current expertise level with PowerPoint, this book brings you up to the level of the most experienced and talented PowerPoint users in your office. You may even be able to teach those old pros a thing or two!

But this book doesn't stop with PowerPoint procedures. Creating a good presentation is much more than just clicking a few dialog boxes and typing some text. It requires knowledge and planning—lots of it. That's why this book includes a whole chapter on planning a presentation, and another whole chapter on the practical issues involved in presenting one. You learn things like the following:

- ✦ How to select the best color schemes for selling and informing
- ✦ How to gauge the size of the audience and the meeting room when selecting fonts
- ✦ How to arrange the tables and chairs in the meeting room to encourage (or discourage) audience participation
- ✦ How to choose what to wear for a live presentation
- ✦ How to overcome stage fright

And lots more! When you finish this book, you will not only be able to build a presentation with PowerPoint, but you'll also be able to explain why you made the choices you did, and you'll deliver that presentation smoothly and with confidence.

If you are planning a presentation for remote delivery (for example, posting it on a Web site or setting up a kiosk at a trade show), you'll find lots of help for these situations too. In fact, an entire section of the book is devoted to various nontraditional presentation methods, such as live Internet or network delivery, trade show booths, and interactive presentation distribution on a diskette or CD.

How This Book Is Organized

This book is organized into parts, which are groups of chapters that deal with a common general theme. Here's what you'll find:

✦ **Part I: Creating Your First Presentation.** Start here if you have never used Windows-based programs before or if you are completely new to PowerPoint. If you have created presentations, but have not been happy with the results, make sure you read Chapter 6, which deals with planning.

✦ **Part II: Building Your Presentation.** In this part, you start building a robust, content-rich presentation by choosing a template, entering your text, and applying some basic text formatting.

✦ **Part III: Improving the Visual Impact.** This part teaches you all about formatting, graphics, backgrounds, and other features that can show off your presentation content to best advantage.

✦ **Part IV: Multimedia.** Here you learn how to include sounds, videos, animation effects, and transitions to jazz up a live presentation.

✦ **Part V: Presenting Speaker-Led Presentations.** If you expect to stand in front of a live audience giving the presentation, this part is for you. You learn about creating support materials, running a live show, and running a real-time show across a network or the Internet.

✦ **Part VI: Distributing Self-Serve Presentations.** If the presentation will take place without a live speaker, see this part to learn how to time the transitions between slides, prepare a presentation for Internet distribution, and set up a secure kiosk at a trade show.

✦ **Part VII: Cutting-Edge Power.** In this final part, you learn some noncomputer presentation skills that can help make your live shows more professional and compelling. You also find out about advanced features like team collaboration and macros.

Special Features

Every chapter in this book opens with a quick look at what's in the chapter and closes with a summary. Along the way, you also find icons in the margins to draw your attention to specific topics and items of interest.

Here are what the icons mean:

Notes provide extra information about a topic, perhaps some technical tidbit or background explanation.

Tips offer shortcuts and special helps to make the most of PowerPoint.

Cautions point out how to avoid the pitfalls that beginners commonly encounter.

Cross-references point to more complete discussions in other chapters of the book.

These icons highlight information for readers who are following the examples and using the sample files on the CD-ROM accompanying this book.

This icon calls attention to new features of PowerPoint 2000.

Good luck with PowerPoint 2000! I hope you have as much fun reading this book as I had writing it. If you would like to let me know what you thought of the book, good or bad, you can e-mail me at fwempen@iquest.net. I'd like to hear from you!

Acknowledgments

A big thanks to the IDG Books Worldwide team for making the production of this book go so smoothly. This is my first big project with IDG Books, and I have been extremely impressed by the professionalism and overall good cheer of the team. Thanks to Andy Cummings, Kathleen McFadden, Ken Brown, Kristen Tod, Anne Friedman, and Amy Asbury, and to the folks on the layout and proofreading team, who do such a great job and receive too little recognition.

Contents at a Glance

Contents

Part III: Improving the Visual Impact 193

Chapter 11: Changing the Presentation's Look....................................195

Chapter 12: Adding Clip Art and other Imagers 205

Part IV: Multimedia 325

Creating Your First Presentation

A First Look at PowerPoint

This chapter provides some background information about PowerPoint and shows you several practical applications for the materials you can create. When you're ready to forge ahead, turn to Chapter 2 to get started using the program.

PowerPoint 2000 is a member of the Microsoft Office 2000 suite of programs. (A *suite* is a group of programs designed by a single manufacturer to work well together.) Like its siblings Word (the word processor), Excel (the spreadsheet), Outlook (the personal organizer and e-mail manager), and Access (the database), PowerPoint has a well-defined role. It creates materials for presentations.

A *presentation* can be any kind of interaction between a speaker and audience, but it usually involves one or more of the following visual aids: 35mm slides, overhead transparencies, computer-based slides, hard-copy handouts, and speaker notes. PowerPoint can create all of these types of visual aids, plus many other types that you learn about as we go along.

Because PowerPoint is so tightly integrated with the other Microsoft Office 2000 components, you can easily share information among them. For example, if you have created a graph in Excel, you can use that graph on a PowerPoint slide. It goes the other way, too. You can, for example, take the outline from your PowerPoint presentation and copy it into Word, where you can dress it up with Word's powerful document formatting commands. Virtually any piece of data in any Office program can be linked to any other Office program, so you never have to worry about your data being in the wrong format.

How Will You Deliver?

Whether you give presentations for a living or you merely create them for others to give, you should be aware of the various delivery methods at your command. Of course, some of them require special equipment — for example, you can't give a computer-based show unless the appropriate computer equipment is available at the meeting site.

The most traditional kind of presentation is a live speech presented at a podium. For live presentations, you can use PowerPoint to create overhead transparencies, 35mm slides, or a computer-based show that can help the lecturer emphasize key points.

Over the last several years, advances in technology have made it possible to give several other kinds of presentations, and PowerPoint has kept pace nicely. You can use PowerPoint to create kiosk shows, for example, which are self-running presentations that provide information in an unattended location. You have probably seen such presentations listing meeting times and rooms in hotel lobbies and sales presentations at trade show booths.

The Internet also has made several other presentation formats possible. You can use PowerPoint to create a show that you can present live over a network or the Internet, while each participant watches from his or her own computer. You can even store a self-running or interactive presentation on a Web site and make it available for the public to download and run on their own PCs.

When you start your first PowerPoint presentation, you may not be sure which delivery method you will use. However, it's best to decide the presentation format before you invest too much work in your materials, because the audience's needs are different for each medium. You learn a lot more about planning your presentation in Chapter 6.

Real-Life PowerPoint Uses

Most people associate PowerPoint with sales presentations, but PowerPoint can be useful for people in many other lines of work as well. The following sections present a sampling of how real people just like you are using PowerPoint in their daily jobs.

Sales

More people use PowerPoint for selling goods and services than for any other reason. Armed with a laptop computer and a PowerPoint presentation, a salesperson can make a good impression on a client anywhere in the world. Figure 1-1 shows a slide from a sample sales presentation.

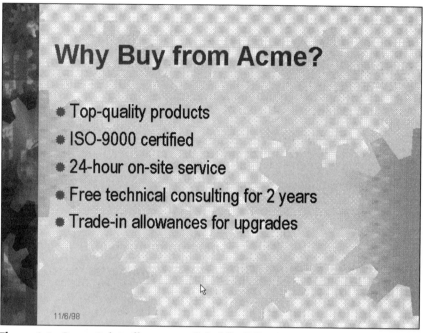

Figure 1-1: PowerPoint offers unparalleled flexibility for presenting information to potential customers.

Sales possibilities with PowerPoint include the following:

✦ Live presentations in front of clients with the salesperson present and running the show. This is the traditional kind of *sales call* pitch that most people are familiar with. See Chapter 22 to learn about controlling a live presentation.

✦ Online presentation broadcasts, where potential customers tune in with their Internet browsers from all over the world to see and hear the sales pitch. If all your customers are Internet savvy, your company can save a lot of money by sending the presentation to the client instead of paying for a salesperson's airfare. Presentation broadcasting is covered in Chapter 23.

✦ Self-running presentations that flip through the slides at specified intervals so that passersby can read them or ignore them as they wish. These types of presentations are great for grabbing people's attention at trade show booths. You create this kind of show in Chapter 25.

✦ User-interactive product information demos distributed on CD or diskette that potential customers can view at their leisure on their own PCs. This method is very inexpensive, since you can create a single presentation and distribute it by mail to multiple customers. You learn how to create a user-interactive show in Chapter 26.

Marketing

The difference between sales and marketing can be rather blurred at times, but marketing generally refers to the positioning of a product in the media rather than its presentation to a particular company or individual. Marketing representatives are often called upon to write advertising copy, generate camera-ready layouts for print advertisements, design marketing flyers and shelf displays, and produce other creative selling materials.

PowerPoint is not a drawing program per se, and it can't substitute for one except in a crude way. However, by combining the Office 2000's clip art collection with some well-chosen fonts and borders, a marketing person can come up with some very usable designs in PowerPoint. Figure 1-2 shows an example. You learn about clip art in Chapter 12.

Overwrought by technology?

Computer glitches giving you fits?

Don't despair!

Your Computer Friend can help. It's not easy being a computing beginner these days, but we can help you get up to speed with word processing, the Internet, or any other aspect of computing that you want to learn more about. We can even fix your current computer's ailments and recommend upgrades that will give you the most bang for the buck. And our rates are reasonable too, starting at just $45 for a one-hour residential house call.

Your Computer Friend
123 Main St.
Franklin, IN 46002
317-555-0594

Figure 1-2: PowerPoint can be used to generate camera-ready marketing materials, although they can't substitute for the tools used by professional advertising companies.

Status Reports

You have already seen how PowerPoint can generate presentations that sell goods and services, but it's also a great tool for keeping your internal team informed. For example, perhaps the vice president wants to know how many units your department has sold over the past six months. You can impress the heck out of the boss with a good-looking informational presentation that conveys all the pertinent details. You can even generate handouts to pass out to the meeting attendees. Figure 1-3 shows a slide from an informational presentation. As you can see, it contains a graph. PowerPoint can generate its own graphs with its Microsoft Graph module, or you can import graphs from another program, such as Excel. You learn about graphing in PowerPoint in Chapter 14.

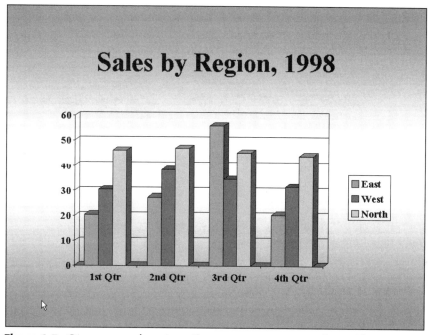

Figure 1-3: Convey your department's progress to your superiors with an informational presentation.

Human Resources

Human resources personnel often find themselves giving presentations to new employees to explain the policies and benefits of the company. A well-designed, attractive presentation gives the new folks a positive impression of the company they have signed up with, starting them off on the right foot.

One of the most helpful features in PowerPoint for the human resources professional is Microsoft Organization Chart. With it, you can easily diagram the structure of the company and make changes whenever necessary with a few mouse clicks. Figure 1-4 shows an organization chart on a PowerPoint slide. Organization charts are covered in Chapter 15.

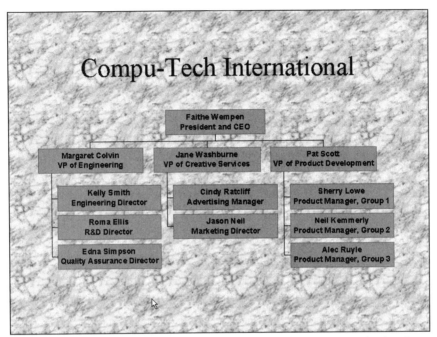

Figure 1-4: Microsoft Organization Chart lets you easily create organizational diagrams right from within PowerPoint.

Education and Training

Most training courses include a lecture section in which the instructor outlines the general procedures and policies. This part of the training is usually followed up with individual, hands-on instruction. PowerPoint can't help much with the latter, but it can help make the lecture portion of the class go smoothly.

PowerPoint accepts images directly from a scanner, so you can scan in diagrams and drawings of the objects you are teaching the students to use. You can also use computer-generated images, such as screen captures, to teach people about software.

PowerPoint's interactive controls even let you create quizzes that each student can take onscreen to gauge his or her progress. Depending on the button the student clicks, you can set up the quiz to display a "Yes, You're Right!" or "Sorry, Try Again" slide. See Figure 1-5. I explain this procedure in more detail in Chapter 26.

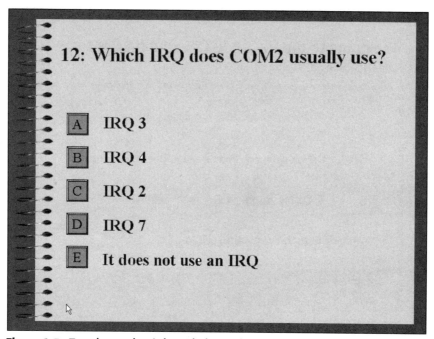

Figure 1-5: Test the student's knowledge with a user-interactive quiz in PowerPoint.

Hotel and Restaurant Management

Service organizations such as hotels and restaurants often need to inform their customers of various facts, but need to do so unobtrusively so that the information will not be obvious except to those looking for it. For example, a convention center hotel might provide a list of the meetings taking place in its meeting rooms, as shown in Figure 1-6, or a restaurant might show pictures of the day's specials on a video screen in the waiting area.

In such unattended situations, a self-running (kiosk) presentation works best. Typically the computer box and keyboard are hidden from the passersby, and the monitor displays the information. You learn more about such setups in Chapter 25.

Figure 1-6: Information kiosks can point attendees to the right meeting rooms from public lobbies.

Clubs and Organizations

Many nonprofit clubs and organizations, such as churches and youth centers, operate much the same way as for-profit businesses and need sales, marketing, and informational materials. But clubs and organizations often have special needs too, such as the need to recognize volunteers for a job well done. PowerPoint provides a Certificate template that's ideal for this purpose. Figure 1-7 shows a certificate generated in PowerPoint.

Even More Ideas

As you learn in Chapter 7, you can create presentations in PowerPoint based on a wide variety of predesigned templates. Many of these templates include not only design schemes but also sample content structures, into which you can plug your own information for a good-looking, quickly generated end result.

Broadway United Methodist Church
Certificate of Excellence

is hereby granted to:

Faithe Wempen

for outstanding performance and lasting contribution to the

Chancel Handbell Choir
Granted: November 6, 1998

Michael Hayden Director of Music

Figure 1-7: With PowerPoint, you can easily create certificates and awards.

With some of these templates, you can create all of the following documents:

✦ Business plans

✦ Company handbooks

✦ Web pages

✦ Employee orientation briefings

✦ Financial overviews

✦ Speaker introductions

✦ Marketing plans

✦ Team motivational sessions

✦ Technical reports

✦ Project post-mortem evaluations

Summary

Now that you have a hint of what PowerPoint can do, you are probably eager to get started. So turn the page to Chapter 2, where you begin learning all about this fascinating, powerful program.

✦   ✦   ✦

Learning Your Way Around PowerPoint

PowerPoint is one of the easiest and most powerful presentation programs available. As you can see from the QuickStart booklet that you received with this book, you can knock out a passable presentation in a shockingly short time with it. Or, as you learn in the remainder of this book, you can use some of PowerPoint's advanced features to make a complex presentation that looks, reads, and works exactly the way you want.

This chapter is primarily for those who have not had a lot of experience with Windows 95/98 or other programs. People who know all about menus, dialog boxes, and toolbars may find this chapter boring. If that description fits you, by all means feel free to skip it! But if you are still a little shaky on using Windows and applications in general, come on in.

Starting PowerPoint

You can start PowerPoint just like any other program in Windows: from the Start menu. Follow these steps:

1. Click the Start button.
2. Point to Programs. A submenu appears. See Figure 2-1.
3. Click Microsoft PowerPoint. The program starts.

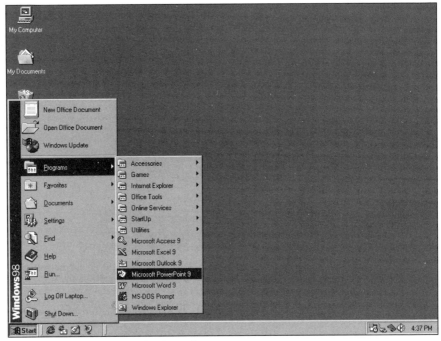

Figure 2-1: Start PowerPoint from the Start menu.

Tip   Another way to start PowerPoint is to click the Start button and choose New Office Document. Then click the Presentations tab and choose a presentation template on which to base your new presentation. But that method jumps ahead a little bit — you learn about creating new presentations a bit later. For now, just know that this method is there and that you might want to use it in the future.

Working with the PowerPoint Dialog Box

The first thing you see when you start PowerPoint is the PowerPoint dialog box (Figure 2-2). This dialog box appears only at program startup; if you close it, you can't reopen it without quitting and restarting the program.

In this dialog box, you have these choices:

✦ **AutoContent Wizard** — This option starts a question-and-answer session between you and PowerPoint that helps you build a presentation, complete with sample slides.

✦ **Design Template** — This option lets you choose from among dozens of formatting schemes for starting a new presentation.

✦ **Blank presentation** — This option starts a new, blank presentation with no sample slides and no special formatting.

✦ **Open an existing presentation** — This option opens a presentation file that you have previously created and saved.

Figure 2-2: The PowerPoint dialog box greets you each time you start the program.

You learn a lot more about starting new presentations in Chapter 7, and you learn about saving and opening them in Chapter 4. For now, though, all you need to do is start a dummy presentation so you can get a look at the screen. That being the case, do the following:

1. Click Blank presentation.

2. Click OK. The New Slide dialog box appears.

3. Click OK to place a new title slide.

Now you see the PowerPoint screen in front of you, and you're ready to learn about its interface in the remainder of this chapter.

Understanding the Screen Elements

PowerPoint is a fairly typical Windows-based program in many ways. It contains the same basic elements that you expect to see: a title bar, a menu bar, window controls, and so on. Figure 2-3 points out these generic Windows controls.

✦ **Title bar:** Identifies the program running. If the window is not maximized, you can move the window by dragging the title bar.

✦ **Menu bar:** Provides drop-down menus containing commands.

✦ **Minimize button:** Shrinks the application window to a bar on the taskbar; click its button on the taskbar to reopen it.

✦ **Maximize/Restore button:** If the window is maximized (full screen), changes it to windowed (not full screen). If the window is not maximized, clicking here maximizes it.

✦ **Close:** Closes the application. You may be prompted to save your changes, if you made any.

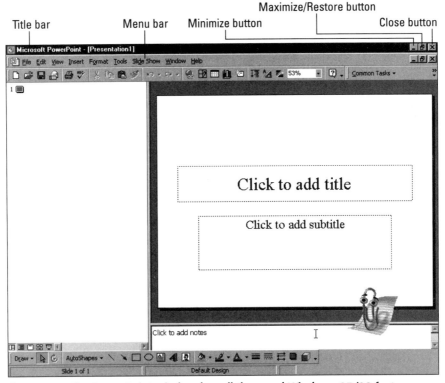

Figure 2-3: The PowerPoint window has all the usual Windows 95/98 features.

Note   I don't dwell on the Windows controls in detail because this isn't a Windows book, but if you're interested in learning more about Windows-based programs in general, pick up *Windows 98 For Dummies*, also published by IDG Books Worldwide.

The PowerPoint screen starts out in Normal view, which contains an outline pane on the left, a slide pane on the right, and a notes pane at the bottom as shown in

Figure 2-4. The slide and the outline are tied together; you can type text on one, and it appears on the other. To test this function, click where it says *Click to add title* and type your name. Your name appears both in the Outline pane and in the Slide pane. Chapter 8 covers text entry in more detail.

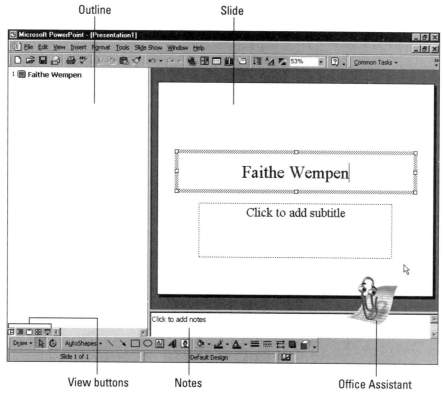

Figure 2-4: PowerPoint's Normal view lets you see the slide, the outline, and the notes all at once.

You may be wondering about the paperclip on the screen. That's Clippit, the Office Assistant, and he's there to answer your questions and provide suggestions. You can drag him out of your way if needed, or get rid of him by right-clicking him and choosing Hide the Office Assistant. Click him and type a question if you want to try him out now, or wait until Chapter 4 where you learn about the Help system in detail.

The view buttons in the bottom-left corner of the screen switch among the available views. The default one, shown in Figure 2-5, is Normal, but there are also buttons for Outline, Slide, Slide Sorter, and Slide Show. You learn more about changing views in Chapter 5.

Working with Menus

Menus are the primary means of selecting commands in PowerPoint. To open a menu, click its name on the menu bar and then click the command you want to select. In this book, such actions are written in a kind of shorthand. For example, if you are supposed to open the File menu and choose the Save command, it appears in this book like this: Select File ⇨ Save.

PowerPoint has the usual drop-down menus on the menu bar that you expect with Windows-based programs, but with a little twist. When you first open a menu, not all the commands appear — only the most commonly used ones. If you pause a moment with the menu open, or click the down arrow at the bottom of it, the rest of the commands come into view. Figures 2-5 and 2-6 show the Format menu, for example, when it is first opened and after it has been fully extended.

Figure 2-5: When you first open a menu, certain commands appear; and more pop up in a few seconds.

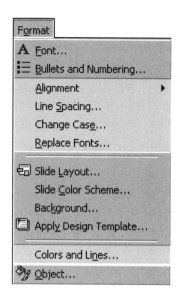

Figure 2-6: The secondary commands appear pressed in.

 Tip The menus show recently used commands first, and then the others, but if you are just starting out using PowerPoint, you don't really have any recently used commands yet. Therefore, the program shows a default set of common commands. As you use PowerPoint more, the recently used commands begin to be more meaningful. To reset the calculation of which commands qualify as *recent*, select Tools ⇨ Customize, click the Options tab, and then click the Reset my usage data button.

PowerPoint's new two-level menu opening seems like a great idea, but some people may find it annoying. To turn it off, follow these steps:

1. Select Tools ⇨ Customize. The Customize dialog box appears.

2. Click the Options tab. See Figure 2-7.

3. In the Personalized Menus and Toolbars section, deselect the checkbox next to the option called Menus show recently used commands first.

4. Click OK.

You can also customize each menu to show different commands or delete commands entirely from a menu, but that gets a bit hairy. Best to wait on that until Chapter 30. You don't really need to do that now anyway.

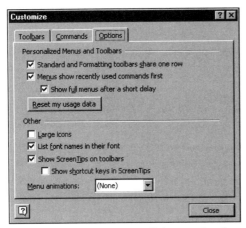

Figure 2-7: You can turn off the two-level menu system by deselecting the Menus show recently used commands first checkbox.

Some menus have submenus that fly out when you point to a certain command. For example, as shown in Figure 2-8, the Alignment command has a submenu.

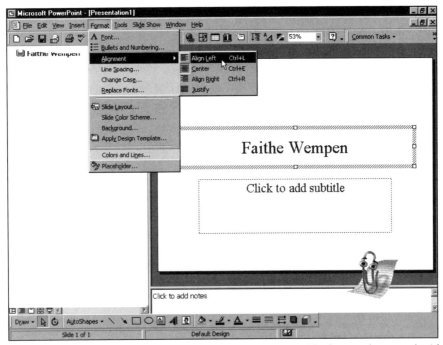

Figure 2-8: This menu has commands with submenus, with shortcut keys, and with ellipses.

Some commands have keyboard combinations listed next to them, such as Ctrl+L next to Align Left in Figure 2-8. These are shortcut keys. You can use the shortcut key combinations on the keyboard instead of opening the menu and choosing the command. Of course, it's kind of a Catch-22; you don't know the shortcuts without reading them on the menu, and once you've got the menu open, it is no longer more convenient to use the shortcuts. Still, over time you will memorize certain shortcuts and find that it is easy to use them.

Some commands have ellipses (three dots) after them. Such commands open dialog boxes, which are windows that request more information before executing a command. Figure 2-7 shows an example of a dialog box. You learn more about dialog boxes in the next section.

Some commands have icons to their left. This points out that there is a toolbar button equivalent for that command. You may not always see the button on one of the displayed toolbars, however, because there are over a dozen toolbars, and some appear only when you are performing certain tasks. You learn more about toolbars later in this chapter.

Sometimes a command appears in gray lettering rather than black; that's called *grayed out*, and it means the command is unavailable at the moment. For example, the Copy command on the Edit menu is grayed out unless you have selected something to copy. (There aren't any grayed-out commands in Figure 2-8.)

Working with Dialog Boxes

Dialog boxes are PowerPoint's (and Windows') way of prompting you for more information. When you issue a command that can have many possible variations, a dialog box appears so you can specify the particulars.

The Print dialog box (File ➪ Print) is an excellent example of a dialog box because it has so many different kinds of controls. Here are some of the controls you see on the Print dialog box shown in Figure 2-9:

- ✦ **Checkbox** — These are individual on/off switches for particular features. Click to toggle them on or off.

- ✦ **Option buttons** — Each section of the dialog box can have only one option button chosen at once. When you select one, the previously selected one becomes deselected, like on a car radio. Click the one you want.

- ✦ **Text box** — Click in a text box to place an insertion point (a vertical line) there and then type.

- ✦ **Increment buttons** — Next to a text box, these increment the number in the box up or down by one digit per click.

✦ **Drop-down list**—Click the down arrow next to one of these to open the list, and then click your selection from the menu that appears.

✦ **Command button**—Click one of these big rectangular buttons to jump to a different dialog box. OK and Cancel are also command buttons; OK accepts your changes and Cancel rejects them.

When you are finished looking at this dialog box, click Cancel to close it.

You may also sometimes see tabs at the top of a dialog box; this occurs when the dialog box has more controls than will fit on one screen. To move to a tabbed page, click the tab.

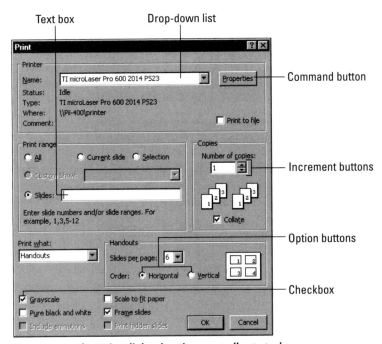

Figure 2-9: The Print dialog box is an excellent study in dialog box controls.

Dialog boxes that open or save files have some special controls all their own, but you learn about those in more detail in Chapter 4 when you learn to open and save.

Working with Toolbars

Toolbars are rows of icons (pictures) that represent common commands. You can click a toolbar button instead of opening a menu and clicking a command. They're purely a convenience; you don't have to use the toolbar buttons if you prefer the menus. Throughout this book, whenever there is a toolbar button equivalent for a command, I try to mention it.

Tip   To find out what a toolbar button does, point the mouse at it. A ScreenTip pops up explaining it to you.

PowerPoint displays three toolbars by default in Normal view: Standard, Formatting, and Drawing. The Standard toolbar contains commands that work with files (save, open, print) and insert elements in your presentation (slides, graphs, hyperlinks). The Formatting toolbar applies formatting (font changes, bold, underline, and so on.) The Drawing toolbar, at the bottom of the screen, contains commands that draw and format lines, shapes, and other artwork. You can display or hide toolbars by right-clicking any toolbar to get a pop-up menu that lists them, and then just click one to toggle it on or off.

New in PowerPoint 2000, the Standard and Formatting toolbars are displayed on the same row by default. This is supposed to save screen space for you, but not all the buttons can fit. To use one of the undisplayed buttons on a toolbar, you must click the > button at the right end to open a pop-up list of the remaining buttons, as shown in Figure 2-10.

Many people find this scrunching up of the toolbars inconvenient and want to go back to the old way, where each toolbar appears on its own line. To do so, you can either drag the Formatting toolbar (by its left end) down below the Standard one, or you can follow these steps:

1. Select Tools ➪ Customize. The Customize dialog box opens.

2. Click the Options tab.

3. Deselect the Standard and Formatting toolbars share one row checkbox. See Figure 2-11.

4. Click Close.

Click here

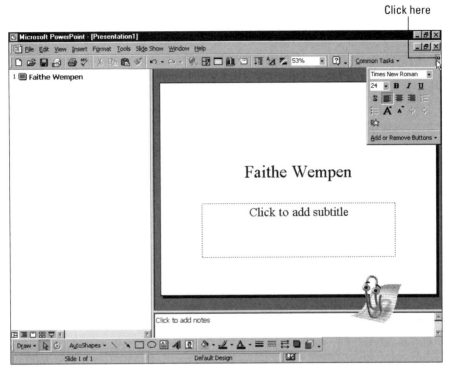

Figure 2-10: To access a toolbar button that does not appear due to screen space limitations, click the > button.

Clear this checkbox

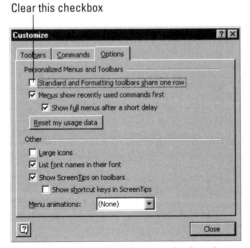

Figure 2-11: Deselect the Standard and Formatting toolbars share one row checkbox to put the toolbars in separate rows, as in previous versions of PowerPoint.

All the rest of the figures in this book show the toolbars on separate rows so you can more clearly see the buttons that I am pointing out to you along the way.

All of the toolbar buttons may look more or less equal, but there are several different types:

✦ Some buttons are toggle switches that turn on/off a feature. Examples include the Bold and Italic buttons.

✦ Some buttons open drop-down lists that give you a menu of selections, such as the Font and Font Size drop-down lists.

✦ Some buttons open dialog boxes. The Save button does this, as does the Open button.

✦ Some buttons perform an action right away, without waiting for a dialog box or confirmation. The New button, for example, starts a new, blank presentation.

✦ Some buttons are actually a set of options, and when you select one, another becomes deselected. Examples are the Left, Centered, and Right alignment buttons.

✦ Some buttons can be clicked normally, but they also have a down arrow that opens a drop-down list for additional controls. A good example is the Undo button. Click it once to undo the last action or open its drop-down list for a list of previous actions to undo.

✦ Some buttons perform a function every time you click them and the effect is cumulative. For example, every time you click the Increase Font Size button, the selected text grows by one size.

I won't go into every single button on these two default toolbars right now, but you learn what most of them are as you go along in this book.

Exiting PowerPoint

When you are ready to leave PowerPoint, select File ⇨ Exit or click the Close (X) button in the top-right corner of the PowerPoint window. If you have any unsaved work, PowerPoint asks if you want to save your changes. Since you have just been playing around in this chapter, you probably do not have anything to save yet. (If you do have something to save, see Chapter 4 to learn more about saving.) Otherwise, click No to decline to save your changes, and you're outta there.

Summary

This chapter offered a basic overview of PowerPoint's interface and controls for a beginner. You learned how to start PowerPoint, how to open menus and select commands, how to work with dialog boxes, and how to use toolbar buttons. So much for the warm-up! In the next chapter, you will discover the PowerPoint Help system, a surprisingly rich source of program information.

✦   ✦   ✦

Getting Help

C H A P T E R

The PowerPoint Help system is like a huge instruction book in electronic format. You can look up almost any PowerPoint task you can imagine and get step-by-step instructions for performing it.

There are two ways to use the Help system: with or without the Office Assistant. The Office Assistant is the little cartoon character running around on your screen. The default character is Clippit the paperclip. When you need something, you ask Clippit, and he goes into the Help system and brings back what you want. If you're not in the mood for cartoon characters, you can turn off the Office Assistant and search the Help system yourself. This is a faster and more powerful method for people who are more experienced and know what they are looking for.

Tip   If you don't like Clippit, you can choose a different character. Right-click Clippit and select Choose Assistant. Pick a different character from the Gallery by clicking the Back and Next buttons until you find the one you want. Click OK to change the character.

Asking the Office Assistant a Question

The best place to start is with the Office Assistant, since that's what most beginners use. To begin, open PowerPoint and click the Office Assistant. A box pops up asking what you would like to do. See Figure 3-1. Type your question and click Search.

In This Chapter

Understanding the PowerPoint Help system

Asking the Office Assistant

Finding help with onscreen elements

Accessing help on the Internet

Downloading patches and add-ons

Contacting technical support

Figure 3-1: Ask the Office Assistant a question by typing it in the box and clicking Search.

Note   If you don't see an Office Assistant character, select Help ➪ Show the Office Assistant. This command always produces the Office Assistant character, even if the feature has been turned off.

If the Office Assistant feature is already turned on (the default), you can also call the Office Assistant by pressing F1 or clicking the Help button on the toolbar. If the feature is turned off, however, these two methods open the full Help system instead. You learn to turn off the Office Assistant feature and use the full Help system in the following section.

The neat thing about the Office Assistant is that you can phrase questions in natural language. For example, you might type, **How do I save?** Figure 3-2 shows the answer that you would receive.

From the list of found topics shown in Figure 3-2, you can click the one you want, you can click See more to view additional topic matches, or you can rephrase your question by retyping it and clicking Search again.

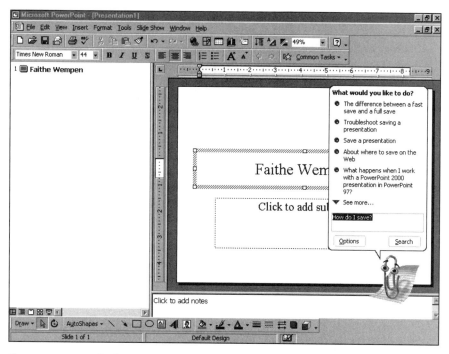

Figure 3-2: Here is the response to the question "How do I save?"

Assume for now that you found the topic you wanted on the list. For example, in Figure 3-2, assume that Save a presentation is what you want. Click it, and the full Microsoft PowerPoint Help system opens, alongside your regular PowerPoint window. See Figure 3-3. If the Office Assistant's bubble still appears, click anywhere away from it to close it.

Several underlined phrases appear in the Help window. Each of these represents a set of instructions you can view. Click the one that best matches your goal. For example, in Figure 3-3, you might choose Save a copy of a presentation. When you click it, the specific instructions appear, as shown in Figure 3-4.

PowerPoint window   Help window

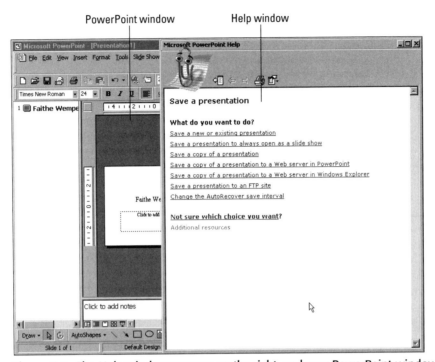

Figure 3-3: The Help window appears on the right, and your PowerPoint window scrunches up to make room.

Tip   If you want to switch to the full Help system controls, like the ones shown later in Figure 3-5, click the Show button at the top of the Help window. This is a good way to take advantage of the Office Assistant and still be able to use the full Help system functionality, too.

You can either perform the steps yourself by following the instructions on the list or, for some steps, you can click a Show Me link to have the Help system perform that step for you. For example, in Figure 3-4, you can click Show Me under Step 1 to open the Save As dialog box.

You can ask the Office Assistant another question at any point; just click him again, and the new topics you select appear in the Help window just like the others.

When you are finished working with Help, click the Close (X) button in the corner of the Help window to return to working normally in PowerPoint. You learn more about the additional options and controls in the Help system later in this chapter.

Show button

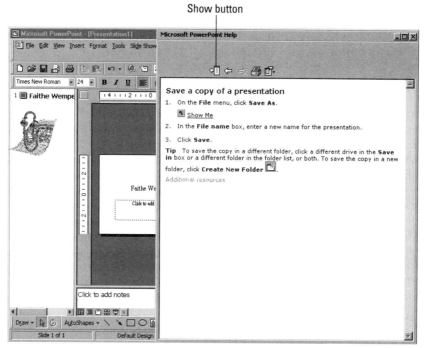

Figure 3-4: The step-by-step directions appear.

Using the Help System without an Office Assistant

If you don't want to use an Office Assistant, you can harness the Help system yourself. More experienced users may prefer this method; it's like the difference between having someone else do research in a library for you and actually slogging through the stacks yourself. Some people love slogging through the stacks, and find more information there that they wouldn't have thought to ask an assistant to look for.

Unlike in previous versions of PowerPoint, there is no separate command that accesses the Help system without an Assistant. Instead, you must turn the Assistant off so that the Help system opens without it. To do so, right-click the Office Assistant and choose Options. Then, in the dialog box that appears, deselect the Use the Office Assistant checkbox and click OK.

Caution

Turning off the Office Assistant, as you just did, is different from simply hiding it. When you hide it (with the Help ➪ Hide the Office Assistant command), it reappears the next time you press F1 or choose Help ➪ Microsoft PowerPoint Help. That is *not* what you want now; you want it completely disabled.

To get the Office Assistant back again after either turning it off or hiding it, the command is the same. Select Help ➪ Show the Office Assistant.

After you have disabled the Office Assistant, you can access the Help system by pressing F1 or choosing Help ➪ Microsoft PowerPoint Help. When you do, the Microsoft PowerPoint Help window appears, as shown in Figure 3-5. Notice that it looks different from the window in Figure 3-4; it is larger, and it has a three-tabbed section to the left that was missing before. This extra section contains the tools you use to browse or search the Help system.

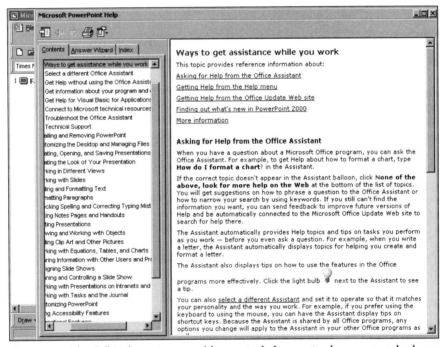

Figure 3-5: The full Help system provides controls for you to do your own lookups.

Each tab—Contents, Answer Wizard, and Index—provides its own method of looking up the same articles in the Help system. You should experiment with all three to find the method that best suits your style.

You can read about the Help system on the initial screen, as shown in Figure 3-5. When you are finished reading about it and ready to actually use the Help system, turn to one of the following sections.

Browsing Help Contents

The Contents tab provides a series of *books* on various broad subjects, such as Clip Art, Copying Objects, and so on. You can browse through these books, narrowing down your interest until you arrive at a particular set of steps or explanation.

For example, suppose you wanted to find information about placing a graph on a slide. You would follow these steps:

1. Click the Contents tab in the Help window.
2. Double-click the Charts book. It opens to show the list of articles it contains.
3. If necessary, use the scroll bar at the bottom of the book list to bring the titles of the articles into view, or enlarge or maximize the Help window.
4. Click the article you want to read (for example, Add a chart to a presentation). It appears in the right pane. See Figure 3-6.

This is the chosen article   To jump to a related topic, click here

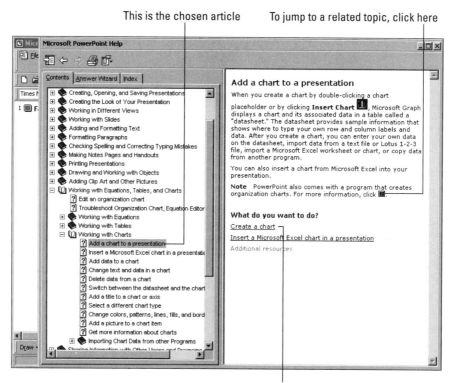

For step-by-step instructions, click here

Figure 3-6: You can choose a Help article from a book on the Contents tab.

5. If there are linked (underlined) phrases in the information, click any of them that interest you. For example, in Figure 3-6, after you have read the conceptual information, you can click <u>Create a chart</u> to jump to the step-by-step instructions.

6. When you are finished with that article, choose another. Or, if you are finished with the Help system, click its Close (X) button to exit.

Querying with the Answer Wizard

The Answer Wizard is essentially the same feature as the Office Assistant, except without the cartoon character. On the Answer Wizard tab, you can type a question in your own words and find articles that might contain the answer.

To use the Answer Wizard, follow these steps:

1. Click the Answer Wizard tab.

2. Type your question in the What would you like to do? text box.

3. Click Search. A list of topics appears in the Select Topic to display box. The first article on the list appears in the right pane. See Figure 3-7.

4. Click the article that you want to read. It appears in the right pane.

5. When you are finished, click a different article, type a new question in the text box to perform a new search, or close the Help system.

Looking Up Topics in the Index

Just as this book has an index, so does the Help system. It lists every topic in alphabetical order. If you know the name of the topic you want to find, you can easily look it up by using the Index tab.

To look up a topic in the index, follow these steps:

1. Click the Index tab.

2. Type a keyword in the Type keywords box. For example, if you want to know about inserting video clips, type **video**. Alternatively, you can choose a keyword from the Or choose keywords list.

3. Click the Search button.

4. Click one of the found topics on the Choose a Topic list. Its article appears in the right pane. See Figure 3-8.

5. When you are finished reading the article, click a different topic, perform another index search, or click Close (X) to exit the Help system.

Choose the article that best answers it   Type your question

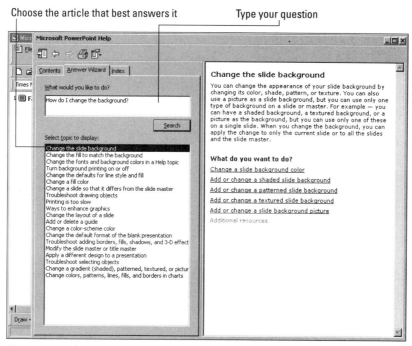

Figure 3-7: The Answer Wizard accepts plain-English questions just | like the Office Assistant does.

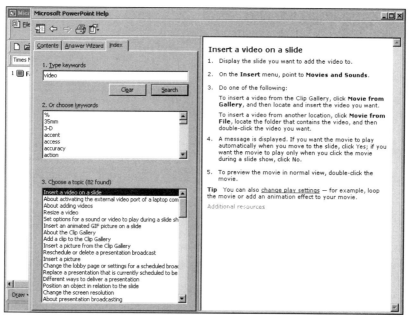

Figure 3-8: The Index helps you look up topics alphabetically by keyword.

Working with a Found Topic

So far in the preceding sections, I have led you to a topic and dropped you there. Now it's time to look at what you can do once you find an article:

✦ Underlined words and phrases are hyperlinks, just like on a Web page. Click one of them to jump to a related topic.

✦ Show Me links actually perform PowerPoint tasks for you. For example, some steps in numbered procedures are Show Me links, as you saw in the discussion of the Office Assistant earlier in this chapter. See Figure 3-9.

✦ Jump buttons (>) jump you to a related topic, the same way as a hyperlink does. See Figure 3-9.

Caution   Toolbar button pictures may appear in the article; these pictures are not live, and clicking them does nothing. They are simply for reference.

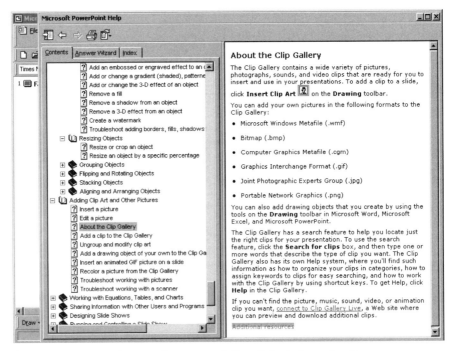

Figure 3-9: Help topics contain steps to follow, links to jump to other topics, and Show Me links that perform tasks for you.

To print an article, click the Print button at the top of the Help window. If a box appears asking whether you want to print the current topic or all topics in the current heading, make your selection and click OK. (Printing everything in the current heading can use a lot of paper; do this only when really necessary.)

Moving Among Articles You Have Found

Just like in a Web browser, you can move back to previous pages you have seen in the Help system by clicking the Back button. Once you have gone back, you can go forward again by clicking Forward. When the Back button becomes grayed out (unavailable), it means you have backed up as far as you can go, back to the first article you displayed in this session.

Using What's This? Help

What's This? Help is extremely useful when you don't know the function of an onscreen element. For example, suppose you notice a mysterious button with a picture on it. You don't know the function or name of the button, so you can't look it up in the Help system normally or ask the Office Assistant about it. What to do? Press Shift+F1. The mouse pointer gains a question mark next to it. Click the object you want to know about, and a box pops up with the information. Figure 3-10 shows the info popping up for the Increase Font Size button.

 Tip

You don't have to use What's This? just to get the name of an onscreen element. One way to find the name of a button is to point at it and wait a few seconds for a ScreenTip to pop up telling you the button's name.

If a dialog box is open, you can access What's This? Help for the dialog box controls. Just click the ? button in the top-right corner of the dialog box, then click the control that you are wondering about. See Figure 3-11.

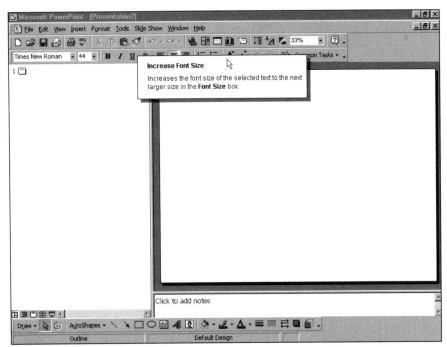

Figure 3-10: What's This? Help displays a brief explanation of whatever button or other screen element you click.

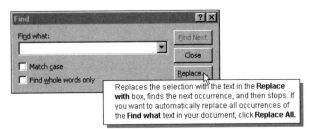

Figure 3-11: To get help in a dialog box, click the ? to activate What's This? Help and then click the dialog box control.

Getting Help from the Microsoft Search Page

When using the Office Assistant to search for help, you may have noticed that the last choice always gives you the option to look for more help on the Web. If you have an Internet connection, you can choose that option to access Microsoft's Search page and look for the information you want.

Caution
If you are paranoid about Internet security, you should know that by accessing online help, you are sending information to Microsoft about what you were searching for. Yes, I know this is harmless, but some people don't want to give any shred of information to any company.

When you choose the Web option, a Finding Help Topics window appears. From there, you can enter a description of your topic, click Send, and go to the Web. Internet Explorer opens (or whatever Web browser is set as your default), and you are prompted to start your Internet connection if it is not already running.

Once you are connected to the Internet, Internet Explorer displays the Search page at Microsoft's Web site. A list of Help articles appears based on the description you entered, as shown in Figure 3-12. When the list of articles appears, click an article title to read it, or type a new search phrase in the Start your search box and click Search.

 Note
If a registration page appears, fill in the required fields to identify yourself as a registered user. You must go through several screens of information; just follow the prompts. You only have to register the first time.

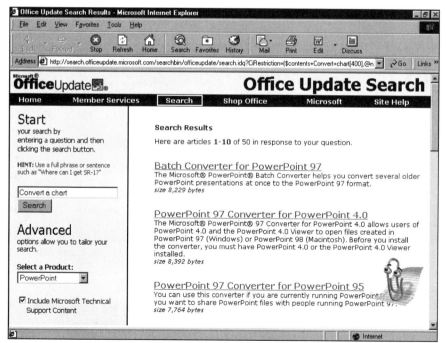

Figure 3-12: Articles appear based on your initial question; to search for other answers, enter a new question in the Start your search box.

Exploring the Microsoft Office Web Site

To keep up with the latest information about Microsoft Office products (of which PowerPoint is one), you can visit the Microsoft Office Update on the Internet. To access it with your Internet connection, select Help ➪ Office on the Web. Internet Explorer opens and you are prompted to establish your Internet connection if it is not already running.

On the Microsoft Office Update page, you find links to product news, common questions, and free downloads that can update and enhance your software. Figure 3-13 shows what it looked like the day that I visited, but it changes all the time, so what you see may be different.

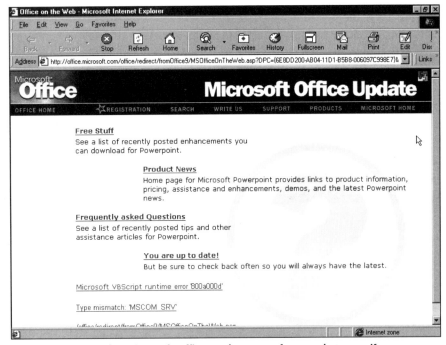

Figure 3-13: Visit the Microsoft Office Update page frequently to see if any new extras or articles are available.

Tip   If you aren't familiar with Internet Explorer, check out the Help system in the Internet Explorer window (Help ➪ Web Tutorial is a good place to start).

Downloading Patches and Add-Ons

Microsoft makes lots of extras available for free to PowerPoint users. To check out what's available, click the Free Stuff link on the Microsoft Office Update page. The freebies available when you visit may be slightly different, but Figure 3-14 shows the ones I found on the day I visited.

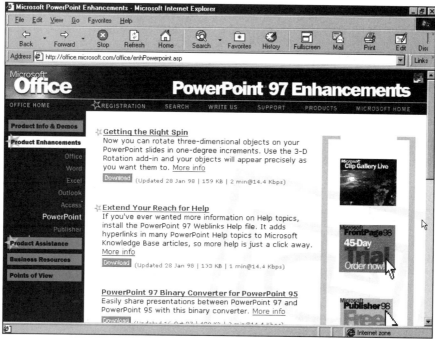

Figure 3-14: The Office Update page offers many free extras for you to use with PowerPoint.

To download and install an update, follow these steps:

1. Click the Download button under the description.

2. If a registration page appears, fill in the required fields to identify yourself as a registered user. You must go through several screens of information; just follow the prompts. You only have to register the first time; the next time you access the Web site, you can skip directly to Step 3.

3. A File Download box appears, as shown in Figure 3-15. Click Run this program from its current location. This selection starts the installation automatically after the download is complete. Then click OK.

Note   What's the difference between saving it to disk and running it from its current location? If you save the file to disk, you must choose a destination for it. Then the downloaded file is placed there, and you must go to that folder (using Windows Explorer) and double-click it to run the installation program. That's a lot of work. If you choose to run the program from its current location, the program is copied to a temporary folder on your hard disk and run from there automatically.

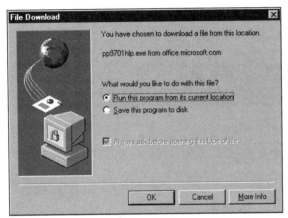

Figure 3-15: Choose to run the program from its current location.

4. If you see a Security Warning dialog box asking whether you want to install the update, click Yes. To avoid the security warning in the future, click the Always trust content from Microsoft Corporation checkbox before clicking Yes.

5. When you see a box asking if you want to install the add-in or update, click Yes to continue. The installation program runs.

6. When you see a message that the installation completed successfully, click OK.

Using Online Technical Support

If you are having a problem with PowerPoint that none of the sources mentioned so far can help with, you might want to visit PowerPoint's technical support page on the Internet. It's at `http://www.microsoft.com/support`. From there, click the Support Online hyperlink. Or, just click the Support button on the Microsoft Office Update page that you were working with in the preceding section.

When you arrive at the Search page, shown in Figure 3-16, follow these steps:

1. Under number 1, open the My search is about drop-down list and choose PowerPoint for Windows.

2. Under number 2, leave Keywords marked in the options list.

3. Under number 3, type the keywords you are interested in in the My question is text box.

4. Click Find.

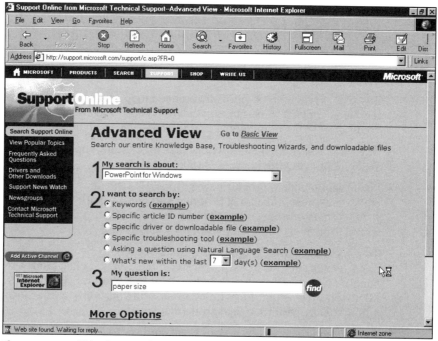

Figure 3-16: Fill in the search form to indicate the question or problem you want to look up, then click Find.

5. On the Search Results screen, click the article that most closely matches what you want. The article appears.

6. After reading the article, use the Back button to return to the preceding screen and select another article, or close Internet Explorer and your Internet connection if you are finished.

Ten Places to Get Help with PowerPoint

Need more help but don't know where to turn? Here are ten places to start.

1. Use the Online Help system in PowerPoint. Choose Help ⇨ Microsoft PowerPoint Help or press F1.

2. Search for help through Microsoft's online support page at `http://www.microsoft.com/support`.

3. Ask a question with the no-charge Web Response system on Microsoft's Web site. Go to `http://support.microsoft.com/support/contact` and click See Support Options and Telephone Numbers. Click Desktop Applications, and then click Standard No-Charge Web Response.

4. Ask a question over the phone for free. PowerPoint's Standard No-Charge technical support number is (425) 635-7145 in the United States or (905) 568-3503 in Canada.

5. Buy pay-per-incident support if you need help other than during regular technical support phone hours. Call (800) 936-5700 and charge it to your credit card ($35 per incident) or (900) 555-2000 to charge it to your phone bill.

6. Buy a Priority Annual Support package for 24-hour support. It costs $295 per 10 incidents, and the number is (800) 936-4700.

7. Post questions in Microsoft newsgroups. Use the news reader that comes in Outlook Express, the e-mail program you got free with Internet Explorer. Use `msnews.microsoft.com` as the news server. The newsgroup you want is `microsoft.public.powerpoint`.

   To avoid having to configure your news reader, visit `http://support.microsoft.com/support/news`, click Microsoft Office Family of Products, and click PowerPoint for Windows. Then, click the Microsoft PowerPoint for Windows link, and your news reader program opens automatically with that newsgroup displayed.

8. Join a computer society in your town, and try to locate other people who have an interest in PowerPoint. Large clubs often have special interest groups (SIGs) that include graphics and desktop publishing enthusiasts.

9. Contact a local computer training company and find out what PowerPoint classes are being offered.

10. Use a search engine on the Internet (such as `http://www.yahoo.com`) to search for the keyword PowerPoint. You can locate hundreds of Web pages related to PowerPoint.

Summary

In this chapter, you learned how to get help with PowerPoint through built-in Help, through the Internet, and through other sources, too. With all that help behind you, you can't help but succeed, right?

In the next chapter, you learn all about managing files. If you are an old hand at Windows 95/98 file management, this information may be a review for you, but beginners can benefit greatly from taking the time to learn about files, folders, drives, and the other mysteries of the filing system.

✦　　✦　　✦

Managing Presentation Files

Saving Your Work

In Chapter 2, you created your first presentation. But when you exit PowerPoint, that presentation will disappear forever — unless you save it. Saving a presentation copies it from your computer's memory onto a disk, where it is safely stored until the next time you want to open it.

Your first presentation is probably just a practice one, nothing that you need to keep. However, before you start creating valuable presentations, you should learn how to save your work.

The first time you save a presentation, PowerPoint opens the Save As dialog box, prompting you for a name and location. Thereafter, when you save that presentation, PowerPoint uses the same settings and does not prompt you for them again.

Saving for the First Time

If you haven't saved the presentation you are working on before, the File ⇨ Save command and the File ⇨ Save As command both do the same thing: they open the Save As dialog box. From there, you can specify a name, file type, and file location. Follow these steps:

1. Choose File ⇨ Save. The Save As dialog box appears.

2. Enter a filename in the File name box. You do not have to type .ppt at the end; the extension is added automatically for you. See Figure 4-1.

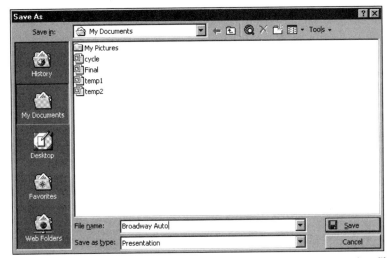

Figure 4-1: Save your work by specifying a name for the presentation file.

3. You can change the drive or folder location if you want. See the "Changing Drives and Folders" section later in this chapter for details.

4. Click Save. Your work is saved.

Filenames can be up to 255 characters. For practical purposes, however, you should keep the names short, such as Acme Marketing 1999 or Henson Sales. You can include spaces in the filenames and most symbols (although not < > ? or *).

Tip

If you are planning to transfer this presentation file to a different computer and show it from there, and that other computer does not have the same fonts as your PC, you should embed the fonts in your presentation so the fonts needed for the show are available on the other PC. To embed fonts from the Save As dialog box, click the Tools button and choose Embed TrueType Fonts. This makes the saved file much larger than normal, so do it only when necessary.

Saving Subsequent Times

After you have once saved a presentation, you can resave it with the same settings (same file type, name, and location) in any of the following ways:

✦ Choose File ➪ Save.

✦ Press Ctrl+S.

✦ Click the Save button on the Standard toolbar.

If you need to save under a different name, as a different type, or in a different location, use the Save As command instead. This reopens the Save As dialog box, as in the preceding steps, so you can save differently.

Saving in a Different Format

You can save your PowerPoint work in a variety of other formats for sharing with other people who may not have access to PowerPoint 2000. The available formats are shown in Table 4-1. Simply choose a file format from the Save as type drop-down list in the Save As dialog box shown in Figure 4-2.

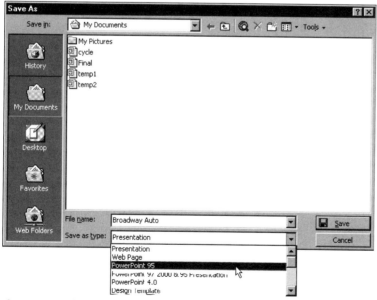

Figure 4-2: Choose a different format, if needed, from the Save as type drop-down list.

Table 4.1
PowerPoint Save As Formats

Presentations:

Format	Extension
Presentation (PowerPoint 2000)	PPT
Web Page	HTM, HTML
PowerPoint 95	PPT
PowerPoint 97-2000 & 95 Presentation	PPT
PowerPoint 4.0	PPT
Design Template	POT
PowerPoint Show	PPS

Graphics/Other:

PowerPoint Add-In	PPA
GIF Graphics Interchange Format	GIF
JPEG File Interchange Format	JPG, JPEG
PNG Portable Network Graphics Format	PNG
Device Independent Bitmap	BMP
Windows Metafile	WMF
Outline/RTF	RTF
Tagged Image File Format	TIF, TIFF

When you save in an alternate presentation format, the saved file is still a presentation; it's just designed to work with a different version of PowerPoint.

The newest version is the one you have: 2000. Before that was 97, and before that 95; the earliest supported version is 4.0. All versions of PowerPoint can open their own version files plus any versions earlier than themselves. For example, PowerPoint 95 can open PowerPoint 95 or PowerPoint 4.0 files. Therefore, if you are not sure what version someone has, save in an early version. However, early versions like 4.0 do not support many of the cool features that are available in more recent versions, so you should not automatically save in 4.0 in all cases or you will lose some of your animations and special effects.

Tip If you consistently want to save in a different format than PowerPoint 2000, choose Tools ➪ Options and click the Save tab. Then, choose a different format (for example, PowerPoint 95 Presentation) from the Save PowerPoint files as drop-down list. This makes your choice the default in the Save as type drop-down list in the Save As dialog box.

You may have noticed in Table 4.1 an oddly named format called PowerPoint 97-2000 & 95 Presentation. This format is very flexible; files saved in this format can be opened equally well in PowerPoint 95, 97, and 2000. If you are not sure what PowerPoint version the person you are giving the file to has, this is the best format to save in.

If you save the presentation in certain formats shown in Table 4.1, the file ceases to be a presentation and becomes a series of unrelated graphic files, one per slide. If you choose one of these formats, you're asked whether you want to export the current slide only or all slides. If you choose all slides, PowerPoint creates a new folder in the selected folder with the same name as the original presentation file and places the graphics files in it.

If you save in one of the other formats, what happens depends on the format you choose:

✦ **Design template:** Your presentation's formatting settings are saved as a new design template that you can apply to other presentations.

✦ **PowerPoint show:** Your presentation is saved as an uneditable show file that can be shown using either PowerPoint or the PowerPoint Viewer. See Chapter 22.

✦ **Web page:** Your presentation is saved in HTML format for Internet use. A better way to save in this format is to use the File ➪ Save as Web Page command, because it gives you access to more saving options. You learn about these in Chapter 27.

✦ **Outline/RTF:** The text from Outline view is saved in an outline that you can open in a word processor such as Word.

✦ **PowerPoint Add-in:** The macros and special capabilities of your presentation are saved as an add-in that you can attach to other presentations. This is an advanced feature, and is rarely used by average PowerPoint users. See Chapter 31 for information about macros.

Caution When you save a file under a different location or name, the original file remains intact, and you create a copy of it. However, if you save as a different format but keep the same name and location, PowerPoint overwrites the original file if the file extensions for both the old and new file types are the same. (For example, all versions of PowerPoint use the extension .ppt.) Be careful not to accidentally overwrite work that you want to keep.

Closing and Reopening Presentations

You can have several presentation files open at once and switch freely between them, but this can bog down your computer's performance somewhat. It's best to have only one presentation file open—the one you are actively working on. Luckily, it's easy to close and open presentations as needed.

Closing a Presentation

When you exit PowerPoint, the open presentation file automatically closes, and you're prompted to save your changes if you have made any. If you want to close a presentation file without exiting PowerPoint, follow these steps:

1. Choose File ➪ Close or click the Close (X) button for the presentation. (Note that there are two sets of window controls; the top set is for PowerPoint itself. You want the X in the lower of the two sets. See Figure 4-3.)

   If you have not made any changes to the presentation since the last time you saved, you're done.

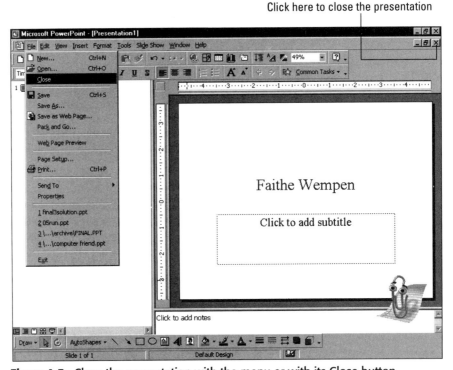

Figure 4-3: Close the presentation with the menu or with its Close button.

2. If you have made any changes to the presentation, you're prompted to save them. If you don't want to save your changes, click No and you're done.

3. If you want to save your changes, click Yes. If the presentation has already been saved once, you're done.

4. If the presentation has not been saved before, the Save As dialog box appears. Type a name in the File name text box and click Save.

Opening a Presentation

One way to open a presentation is from the PowerPoint dialog box that appears when you start PowerPoint. To do so, follow these steps:

1. From the PowerPoint dialog box, click Open an existing presentation.

2. If the presentation you want appears on the list, click it, then click OK, and you're done. See Figure 4-4.

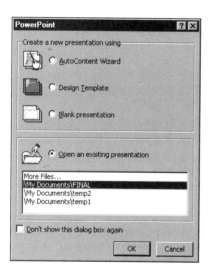

Figure 4-4: Select the presentation from the list if it appears there. If not, double-click More Files.

3. If you don't see the presentation you want, double-click the More Files entry on the list, and the Open dialog box appears. See Figure 4-5.

4. Choose the file you want from the Open dialog box and click the Open button. The presentation opens.

Views button

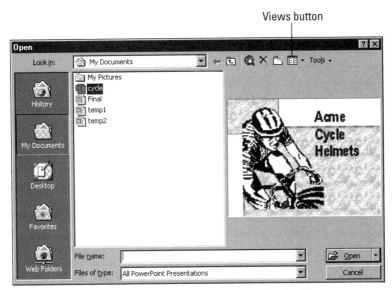

Figure 4-5: Use the Open dialog box to browse for the file you want.

If the PowerPoint dialog box is not currently open, you can display the Open dialog box (Figure 4-5) by choosing File ➪ Open or by clicking the Open button on the Standard toolbar. Then, select the file and click Open.

Here are some tips for opening files:

✦ If you need to change to a different location to find the file to open, see the "Changing Drives and Folders" section later in this chapter.

✦ If you need help locating the file to open, see "Finding a Presentation File," also later in this chapter.

✦ The default view in the Open dialog box is Preview, as shown in Figure 4-5. It lets you see a sample of the presentation you have chosen. You can choose a different view by clicking the Views button and selecting a different one (for example, Details, which shows each file's size and date last modified.) Or, you can click the Views button to cycle through the available views without bothering with its drop-down list.

✦ To open more than one presentation at once, hold down the Ctrl key as you click each file you want to open. Then, click the Open button and they all open, each in their own windows. See the "Working with Multiple Presentations" section later in this chapter.

✦ The Open button in the Open dialog box has its own drop-down list that you can open by clicking its down arrow. On that list, you can choose from Open (the default), Open Read-Only (which prevents changes from being saved), and Open as Copy (which creates a copy, leaving the original untouched). Most people will not use these options very often.

Opening a File from a Different Program

Just as you can save files in various program formats, you can also open files from various programs. This feature is handy, for example, if you are converting from some other presentation program, such as Lotus Freelance Graphics, to PowerPoint.

 Caution   If you want to include graphics, tables, charts, and so on from another program in a PowerPoint presentation, insert them using the Insert menu command. Do not attempt to open them with the Open dialog box.

PowerPoint can detect the type of file and convert it automatically as you open it. The only problem is that you can't open a file unless you can see it on the list of files in the Open dialog box, and by default only PowerPoint files appear there (that is, files with a .ppt extension).

To change the types of files displayed in the Open dialog box, open the Files of type drop-down list and choose the format. This filters the file list to show only files that have that particular extension. (This change is valid for only this one use of the Open dialog box; the file type reverts to All PowerPoint Presentations, the default, the next time you open it.)

Changing Drives and Folders

If you are a computing beginner, the concept of drives and folders may seem a little foreign at first. Here's a quick review.

Each drive has a letter, and your main hard disk customarily is C:. Your floppy disk drive is A:, and any other drives are lettered D: through Z:. When you save your work in PowerPoint, if you do not change the drive, the file is saved on C:, your hard disk.

Within a drive, files are organized into folders. These are like folders in a filing cabinet drawer that organize individual sheets of paper into categories. There is a folder for your Windows system files, one for PowerPoint program files, and so on. There is also a folder called My Documents, where your PowerPoint presentations are saved, along with data files from any other Microsoft Office applications that you use. Sometimes there are folders within folders, several levels deep.

Most people store their documents in My Documents, which is the folder displayed by default in the Save As and Open dialog boxes. Therefore, they never have to worry about changing the drive or folder. But you may occasionally want to save in a different location for some reason. Perhaps you need to save a copy onto your company's network drive or on a floppy disk.

Tip   If you consistently want your PowerPoint files saved into a different folder than My Documents, change the default file location. Choose Tools ➪ Options and click the Save tab. Then type a new file location in the Default file location text box. You cannot browse for it; you must know the full path name. For example, if you want to save by default in a folder called PPT, which is in a folder called Books, which is on drive E, the path would be E:\PPT\Books.

To change the drive and/or folder where saving or opening occurs, follow these steps:

1. In the Save As or Open dialog box, open the Save in or Open from drop-down list and choose the drive you want to save to or that contains the file you want to open. See Figure 4-6.

Up One Level button

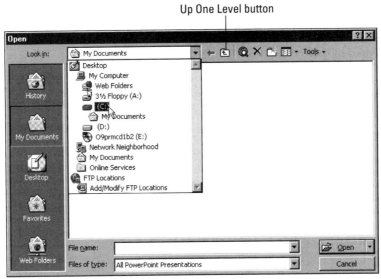

Figure 4-6: Select the drive containing the folder where you want to save or that contains the file you want to open.

2. All the top-level folders on that drive appear. Double-click the one you want to save in. (If it's a floppy, it may not have any folders. If so, skip this step.)

3. If you need to navigate through additional levels of folders, double-click them as necessary. For example, if you want to save in C:\IDG\Books\PowerPoint Bible, you would double-click the IDG folder, double-click the Books folder, and then double-click the PowerPoint Bible folder.

4. Finish saving the file normally if you are saving. (See the preceding set of steps.) If you are opening, double-click the file you want to open.

You've just learned one way to navigate to a different location for file saving and opening, but the Save As and Open dialog boxes also provide many alternative navigation methods that may sometimes be easier.

One way is to navigate from folder to folder. As you just learned, you can begin your navigation by selecting the drive. This places you at the top level, and you can wade through the folders from there. But if you are already several levels deep in folders, it can sometimes make more sense to go up one level at a time rather than jump all the way to the top. For example, suppose the default Save As folder is C:\IDG\Books\PowerPoint Bible and you want to save something in C:\IDG\Books\Teach Yourself Office. You can click the Up One Level button on the Save As toolbar (the icon is a folder with an up arrow on it) to change to C:\IDG\Books. From there, you can double-click the Teach Yourself Office folder.

Another way to navigate is to use the *Places Bar*. Along the left side of the Save As and Open dialog boxes are five special folders. This area is called the Places Bar, and it's a new feature in Office 2000. You can click one of these folders to jump there immediately to save or open a file. Here's an explanation of these folders and their functions:

✦ **History.** This folder contains shortcuts to the presentations and folder locations you have used most recently in PowerPoint. If you want to open a recently used file, you can select its shortcut from the History folder without having to locate it in its real location.

Note

Shortcuts are pointers that point to the original files. You probably have several shortcuts on your Windows desktop; when you click one, the program opens. The program itself is not located on your desktop, but the shortcut points to the program's actual location.

✦ **My Documents.** This is your regular My Documents folder where files are stored by default. If you navigate elsewhere, you can return to My Documents by clicking this button.

✦ **Desktop.** This is a special folder containing all the shortcuts that you have on your Windows desktop. If you save a file here, the file is saved on your desktop, rather than in one of the regular folders on your hard disk. I don't recommend saving to your desktop.

Note

The Desktop folder is actually a folder in the Windows folder on your hard disk, but for file management purposes, it appears on lists as separate from any particular disk drive.

✦ **Favorites.** The Favorites folder contains shortcuts that you place in it. You can use the Favorites folder to give yourself easy access to the presentation files that you use most frequently. To add a file to the Favorites folder, click it in the Save As or Open dialog box, click the Tools button, and then choose Add to Favorites.

✦ **Web Folders**. If you save Web presentations directly to the Internet, you can access those Internet locations from this folder. You learn more about this in Chapter 27.

Finding a Presentation File

If you have forgotten where you saved a particular presentation file, you're not out of luck. PowerPoint includes a search system that can help you locate it, and you don't even have to know the name. PowerPoint can find files by using many criteria. To use the search system, follow these steps:

1. Choose File ➪ Open to display the Open dialog box.

2. Click the Tools button to open its drop-down list and click Find. Alternatively, just press Ctrl+F.

3. In the Find dialog box (Figure 4-7), open the Property drop-down list and select a fact that you know about the missing file. For example, if you know its name, choose File name.

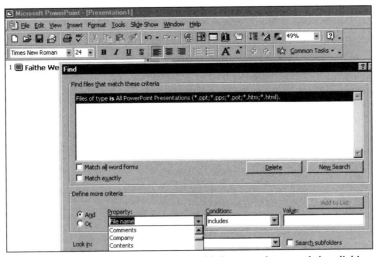

Figure 4-7: Set up criteria and then add them to the search by clicking Add to List.

4. Open the Condition drop-down list and choose the condition for that property. For example, if you know that the filename begins with F, and you chose File name in Step 3, choose begins with here.

Tip You can search based on presentation content, too. Just use Content for the Property criterion and enter a text string in the Value field that you know the presentation contains. Use this method to find, for example, a presentation that contains the words John Smith. This kind of search takes longer than other kinds because PowerPoint has to go through every word of every presentation in the specified location.

5. In the Value field, enter the value for the criterion. (For example, to continue the example of finding files beginning with *F*, enter *F* here.)

6. Click the Add to List button.

7. If you want an additional criterion in the search, click the And or Or button, and then repeat Steps 3 through 6. Use And if both criteria must match; use Or if either of them can be used.

8. If you know that the file is on a certain drive, choose it from the Look in drop-down list. Otherwise, choose My Computer from that list to search your entire system.

9. Make sure the Search subfolders checkbox is marked.

10. Make sure you have clicked Add to List after adding your last criterion.

11. Click Find Now to locate files based on your criteria. The Open dialog box reappears, with only the found files listed.

12. Locate the file you want on the list and open it in the usual way.

Tip Windows 95/98 also offers a good file-finding utility that doesn't have anything to do with PowerPoint. Find it by clicking the Start button and choosing Find; then choose Files or Folders. Many people prefer it to the Find feature built into PowerPoint.

Using Other Controls for Saving and Opening Files

Besides saving and opening files, you can do quite a few other file management functions from the Save As and Open dialog boxes. To finish off the discussion of these dialog boxes, take a look at the other tasks you can do within them:

✦ **Delete a file.** Select a file and press the Delete key on the keyboard or click the Delete button at the top of the dialog box. Alternatively, right-click the file and choose Delete. You cannot delete a file that is currently open.

✦ **Create a new folder.** Navigate to the drive and folder where you want to place it and then click the New Folder button. A new folder appears. Type a name for it and press Enter.

✦ **Rename a file.** Press F2 or right-click the file and choose Rename, then type a new name.

✦ **Print a file.** Click the Tools button and choose Print from the menu, or right-click the file and choose Print.

✦ **Add a file to your Favorites list.** Click the Tools button and choose Add to Favorites. This action creates a shortcut to the selected file in the Favorites folder.

✦ **Map a network drive.** Click the Tools button and choose Map Network Drive. This opens a dialog box that lets you associate a drive letter with a drive on your local area network, if you have one.

✦ **Set file properties.** With the appropriate file selected, click the Tools button and choose Properties or right-click the file and choose Properties. This action opens a Properties dialog box for the selected file. You learn about properties later in this chapter.

PowerPoint is also automatically set up to use AutoRecover. That means if a system error or power outage causes PowerPoint to terminate unexpectedly, you do not lose all the work you have done. The next time you start PowerPoint, it opens the recovered file and asks if you want to save it. The default save interval for AutoRecover files is 10 minutes; that means the most work you would ever lose due to system problems would be 10 minutes' worth. To change the interval at which the AutoRecover information is saved, or to turn the feature off completely, select Tools ⇨ Options, click the Save tab, and change or disable the AutoRecover setting.

Caution   AutoRecover is not a substitute for saving your work the regular way. It does not save in the same sense that the Save command does; it only saves a backup version as PowerPoint is running. If you quit PowerPoint normally, that backup version is erased. It is available for recovery only if PowerPoint terminates abnormally (such as due to a system lockup or the power going off).

Managing Files with File Properties

File properties are facts about each file that can help you organize them. If you have a lot of PowerPoint files saved, using file properties can help you search intelligently for them using the Find feature you learned about earlier in this chapter. For example, you can specify an author, a manager, and a company for each file, and perform searches that display the presentations for a certain author, manager, and/or company.

Tip   By default, PowerPoint does not prompt for properties when you save a file. If you are planning to use properties to manage your filing system, you can ask PowerPoint to open the Properties dialog box whenever you save a new file. To do so, select Tools ⇨ Options and click the Save tab. Then select the Prompt for file properties checkbox.

You can set file properties only for files that are *not* open. The best time to set the properties is right before you open a file. Follow these steps:

1. Choose File ⇨ Open.

2. Locate the file you want to set properties for and select it.

3. Click the Tools button and choose Properties from its menu. A Properties dialog box appears for that file. See Figure 4-8.

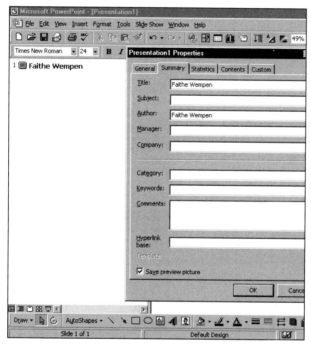

Figure 4-8: Specify values for these properties to help you find a presentation file more easily.

4. On the Summary tab, fill in any information about the presentation that you think can help you maintain your filing system. The Title and Author fields are already filled in for you.

5. On the Custom tab, choose any additional fields you need and set values for them. For example, click the Checked by field on the Name list, and type a value for it in the Value text box. Repeat this for any of the other custom fields.

6. Review the information on the Statistics and Contents tab if desired. (You can't change it.)

7. Click OK.

Now you can use the contents of the properties fields when performing a search in the Find dialog box (Figure 4-7).

Working with Multiple Presentations

You will usually work with only one presentation at a time. But occasionally you may need to have two or more presentations open at once — for example, to make it easier to copy text or slides from one to the other. You learn about copying in Chapter 10.

To open another presentation, choose File ⇨ Open and select the one you want, the same as usual. When more than one presentation is open, you can switch among them by selecting the one you want to see from the Window menu. Figure 4-9 shows that three presentations are currently open in PowerPoint.

Figure 4-9: Choose from among the open presentations on the Window menu.

Here's a feature that is very different from the way Windows usually operates, and it's brand-new in PowerPoint 2000. When you have multiple presentations open, each one has its own button on the Windows taskbar, so you can switch among the presentations by clicking the names on the taskbar. In most other Windows programs, a running program has only one button on the taskbar, regardless of how many files are open in it. Even though it looks as if three instances of PowerPoint are running in Figure 4-10, if I were to exit PowerPoint, all three instances would disappear.

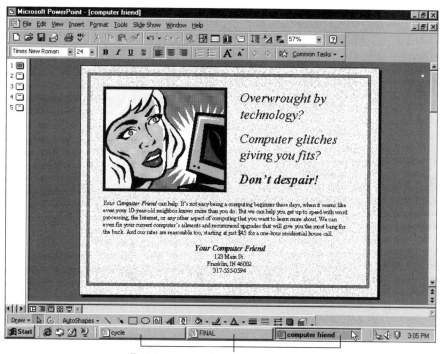

Task bar buttons for each open presentation

Figure 4-10: In PowerPoint 2000, each open presentation file gets its own taskbar representation.

There are many tricks to arranging multiple windows so that you can see what you need to see. Chapter 5 goes into them in detail.

Duplicating a Presentation

Sometimes it is useful to duplicate an existing presentation rather than create a new one from scratch. For example, if you created a presentation last year for your company's annual review, you might want to duplicate that presentation and then modify it for this year's review.

There are several ways to duplicate a presentation. One way, of course, is to copy it using Windows Explorer, which has nothing to do with PowerPoint. Since the PowerPoint presentation is just an ordinary file, and Windows lets you copy files, you can make a copy that way. (For more information about using Windows, check out *Windows For Dummies* or *Windows 98 Secrets*, both published by IDG Books Worldwide.)

You can also duplicate a presentation from within PowerPoint by using File ➪ Save As to save it under a different name. (You learned to do this earlier in this chapter.)

Here's a way to make a copy from within PowerPoint without opening the file:

1. From the Save As or Open dialog box, select the file you want to copy.

2. Right-click the file and choose Copy from the shortcut menu.

3. If necessary, change to a different drive and/or folder.

4. Right-click an empty area in the list of files.

5. Choose Paste from the shortcut menu. The file appears. If you pasted it into the same folder as the original, the new one has the words Copy of at the beginning of its name to differentiate it. You can rename it by pressing F2 and typing a new name.

6. Click Cancel to close the dialog box.

Deleting a Presentation

Just as you can copy a file, you can delete a presentation file from Windows itself, bypassing PowerPoint altogether. Just select the file in Windows Explorer or My Computer and press the Delete key, or drag it to the Recycle Bin on the Windows desktop.

To delete a file from within PowerPoint, select it from the Save As or Open dialog box and press the Delete key on the keyboard, or click the Delete button at the top of the dialog box.

Caution Be careful when deleting presentations! Make sure that the presentation contains nothing that you want to keep. Do not confuse deleting a presentation with deleting a single slide (covered in Chapter 7).

If you make a mistake in deleting, you can get it back if you deleted from Windows; just open the Recycle Bin and drag it back out. However, if you delete from within PowerPoint, it does not go through the Recycle Bin and it is gone forever.

Summary

This chapter made you a master of files. You can now confidently save, open, close, and delete PowerPoint presentation files. You can also save files in different formats, search for missing presentations, and lots more. This is rather utilitarian knowledge and not very much fun to practice, but you will be glad you took the time to learn it later when you have important files you need to keep safe.

In the next chapter, you learn a little bit more about the PowerPoint 2000 interface. You explore views and windows, learn how to select the best view for each situation, and discover how to zoom in or out to change your perspective on each slide.

✦   ✦   ✦

Controlling the Onscreen Display

A *view* is a way of displaying your presentation onscreen. PowerPoint comes with several views because at different times during the creation process it is helpful to look at the presentation in different ways. For example, when you are adding a graphic to a slide, you want to be able to work closely with that slide, but when you need to rearrange the slide order, you need to see the presentation as a whole.

PowerPoint offers the following views:

- ✦ **Normal:** A combination of Outline, Slide, and Notes page views. Normal is the default view.

- ✦ **Slide Sorter:** A light-table-type overhead view of all the slides in your presentation, laid out in rows, that is suitable for big-picture rearranging.

- ✦ **Slide Show:** The view you use to show the presentation onscreen in which each slide fills the entire screen in its turn.

- ✦ **Notes Page:** A view with the slide at the top of the page and a text box below it for typed notes. (You can print these notes pages to use during your speech.)

- ✦ **Slide:** A view of the selected slide with editing controls around it. This view is the upper-right pane of Normal view at its maximum size, with the Outline and Notes panes at their minimum sizes.

- ✦ **Outline:** A view that includes only the text from each slide displayed as an outline. This view is the left pane of Normal view at its maximum size, with the Slide and Notes panes at their minimum sizes.

Changing the View

There are two ways to change a view: open the View menu and select one there, or click one of the view buttons in the bottom-left corner of the screen. The catch is, not all views are available in both places. You can access Normal, Slide Sorter, and Slide Show views in either way, but Notes Page view is available only from the View menu, and Outline and Slide views are available only from the buttons. See Figure 5-1.

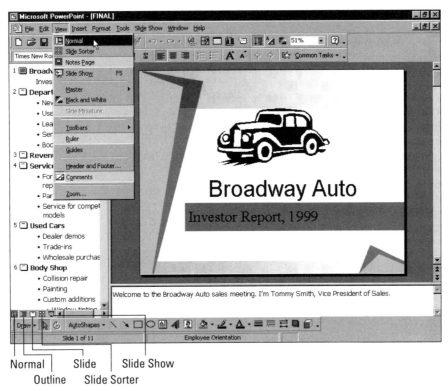

Figure 5-1: You can change the view from the view buttons or the View menu.

Normal View

PowerPoint 2000 comes with this brand-new view called Normal that includes windows for the outline, the currently selected slide, and the speaker notes. Normal view is the default, so it's the view you probably see right now on your screen. It's shown in Figure 5-2.

Outline pane   Slide pane

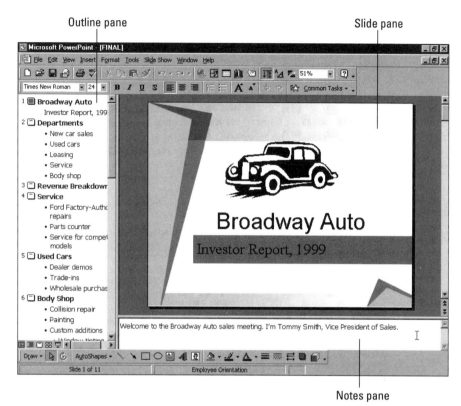

Notes pane

Figure 5-2: Normal view, the default, offers access to the outline, the slide, and the speaker notes all at once.

Each of the panes in Normal view has its own scroll bar, so you can move around in the outline, the slide, and the notes independently of the other panes. You can resize the panes by dragging the dividers between the panes. For example, to give the notes area more room, point the mouse pointer at the divider line between it and the slide area so that the mouse pointer becomes a double-headed arrow, and then hold down the left mouse button as you drag the line up to a new spot.

Note

In earlier versions of PowerPoint, all the views showed only one thing: the outline *or* the slide *or* the speaker notes. These single-faceted views are still available, but you may need them less frequently because Normal view is so flexible and useful.

As you can see, Normal view provides the best of several other single-purpose views. I talk more about the sorts of things you can do in the outline and slide panes later when I tell you about Outline and Slide views.

Slide Sorter View

Slide Sorter view, shown in Figure 5-3, is great for when you want to see an overview of the presentation. If you have ever worked with 35mm slides, you know that it can be helpful to lay the slides out on a big table and plan the order in which to show them. You rearrange them, moving this one here, that one there, until the order is perfect. You might even start a pile of backups that you will not show in the main presentation, but will hold back in case someone asks a pertinent question. That's exactly what you can do with Slide Sorter view. It lays out the slides in miniature, so you can see the big picture. You can drag the slides around and place them in the perfect order.

Slide Sorter view has its own toolbar

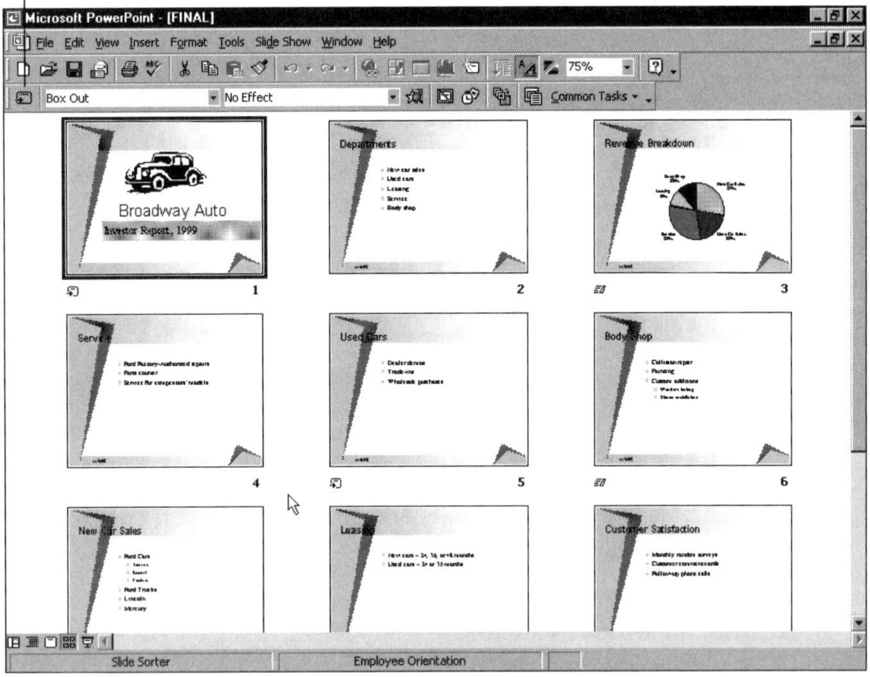

Figure 5-3: Use Slide Sorter view for a birds-eye view of the presentation.

Slide Show View

When it's time to rehearse the presentation, nothing shows you the finished product quite as clearly as Slide Show view does. In Slide Show view, the slide fills the entire screen (see Figure 5-4). You move from slide to slide by pressing the Page Up or Page Down keys, or by using one of the other movement methods available. (You learn about these in Chapter 22.)

You can right-click in Slide Show view to display a menu that enables you to control the show without leaving it. To leave the slide show, choose End Show from that menu or just press Esc.

Right-click to display a menu

Figure 5-4: Slide Show view lets you practice the presentation in real life.

Notes Page View

When you give a presentation, your props usually include more than just your brain and your slides. You typically have all kinds of notes and backup material for each slide — figures on last quarter's sales, sources to cite if someone questions your data, and so on. In the old days of framed overhead transparencies, people used to attach sticky notes to the slide frames for this purpose, and hope that nobody asked any questions that required diving into the four-inch-thick stack of statistics they brought.

Today, you can type your notes and supporting facts directly in PowerPoint. In Notes Page view, you see a single slide with a text area, called the notes pane, below it for your notes. See Figure 5-5. You can refer to these notes as you give an onscreen presentation, or you can print notes pages to stack neatly on the lectern next to you during the big event.

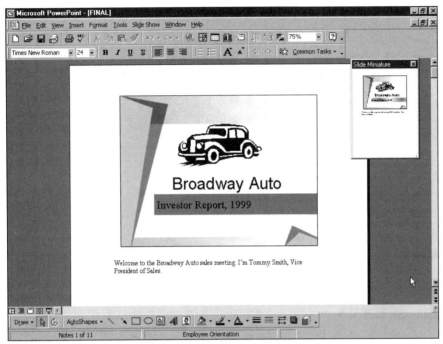

Figure 5-5: Notes Page view offers a special text area for your notes, separate from the slides themselves.

Slide View

Slide view is actually just Normal view with a few pane size changes. As you can see in Figure 5-6, in Slide view the divider between the slide and outline panes has been moved as far as possible to the left so that only the slide numbers appear. (You can jump to other slides by clicking one of those slide numbers.) The divider between the slide and notes panes has also been moved as far as possible to the bottom, so that the notes pane is not visible. These changes combine to display the slide pane as large as possible. If you drag the dividers so that the outline and/or notes panes become usable, you've just changed to Normal view.

So what's the point? Well, sometimes you might want the maximum screen space for your slide pane. You could drag the pane dividers in Normal view to achieve that, but it's easier to just click the Slide view button.

Figure 5-6: Slide view is just like Normal view except the notes and outline panes are at their minimum sizes.

Slide view is great for adding objects to slides. Normal view is good too, but by scrunching up the outline and hiding the notes pane, Slide view shows the slide slightly larger, and so it's a little better for precise positioning of objects. For example, when you want to place a piece of clip art precisely on the slide, Slide view shows you the slide large enough that you can get the placement just right.

Note

Most of the time, the text, graphics, or whatever you add to a slide applies only to that slide, not to all the slides in the presentation. However, sometimes you may want an object — such as a company logo or motto — repeated on every slide in the presentation. You could add this object to each slide manually, but a much better way is to add the object to the Slide Master.

The Slide Master is a special, hidden slide that every presentation has. Anything you add to the Slide Master appears on every slide in the presentation. To display the Slide Master, select View ➪ Master ➪ Slide Master. To return to working with an individual slide, click the Close button that floats above the Slide Master. You learn more about the Slide Master in Chapter 11.

Outline View

Outline view, shown in Figure 5-7, has the same three panes as the Normal and Slide views, but in different proportions. The slide pane is very small, so you see only a miniature of how the slide looks. The notes pane is underneath it. The bulk of the screen is taken up by the outline pane.

Just as with Slide view, you can create Outline view yourself by manually resizing the panes in Normal view. However, it is much easier to switch to Outline view with a single click of an onscreen button.

Tip   When working with an outline, whether in Outline or Normal view, you might want to display the Outlining toolbar. It does not automatically appear when you switch to a view that includes an outline, but you can display it by right-clicking one of the other toolbars and choosing Outlining. Figure 5-7 shows it displayed; as you can see, it runs along the left edge of the screen. The Outlining toolbar includes tools you can use to promote, demote, and move items in your outline. If you've worked with outlines in Word, these tools will seem familiar to you because they're very much the same.

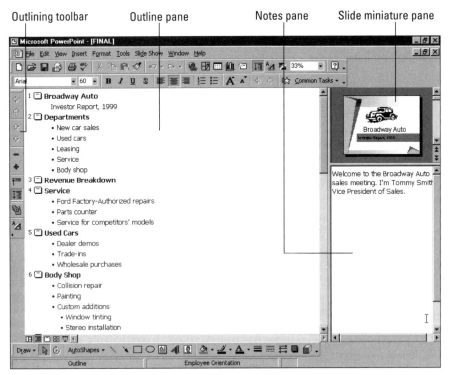

Figure 5-7: Outline view is good for adding and organizing lots of text.

Zooming In and Out

If you need a closer look at your presentation, you can zoom the view in or out to accommodate almost any situation. For example, if you have trouble getting a graphic object placed exactly at the same vertical level as some text in a box next to it, you might zoom in for more precision. You can view the presentation window at various magnifications onscreen without changing the size of the surrounding tools or the size of the print on the printout.

The easiest way to set the zoom level is to open the Zoom drop-down list on the Standard toolbar and choose a new level. Figure 5-8 shows the Zoom drop-down list open and the display zoomed to 100%. You can also type a specific zoom percentage into that box; you aren't limited to the choices on the list.

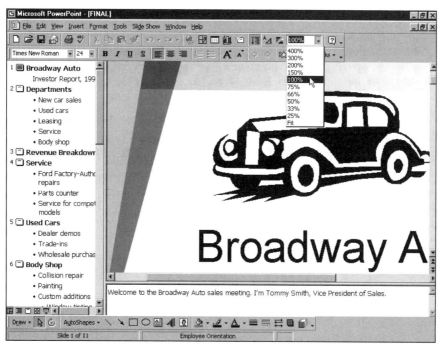

Figure 5-8: Choose a specific zoom percentage from the Zoom drop-down list if you need to zoom in or out.

The larger the zoom number, the larger the details on the display. A zoom of 10% would make a slide so tiny that you couldn't read it. A zoom of 400% would make a few letters on a slide so big they would fill the entire pane.

The default zoom setting for the slide pane (in Normal, Outline, or Slide view) is Fit, which means the zoom adjusts so that the entire slide fits in the slide pane and is as large as possible. If you drag the dividers between panes to redistribute the screen space, the size of the slide in the slide pane adjusts too, so that you continue to see the whole slide. (Compare the slides in Figures 5-6 and 5-7; in each case, they exactly fill the space allotted for the slide pane.) You can change the zoom to whatever you like, and then return to the default by choosing Fit as the zoom amount.

The Zoom controls are not available for all views. In Normal, Slide, and Outline views, you can change the zoom only if the slide or notes pane is the active pane. (To make a pane active, click it.) If your insertion point is in the outline pane, the Zoom drop-down list on the toolbar is grayed out and unavailable. The Zoom is set separately for the slide and notes panes; zooming in for one does not alter the other.

Zooming out goes the other way — it decreases the zoom, making everything smaller onscreen. The main advantage to zooming out is to fit more on the screen at once. For example, if you're working with a lot of slides in Slide Sorter view and normally can see three slides on each row, zooming out to 33 percent might let you see eight or more slides on each row, for a total of 40 or more slides per screen. The disadvantage, of course, is that if the slides get too small, as in Figure 5-9, you can't read the text and so you can't tell them apart.

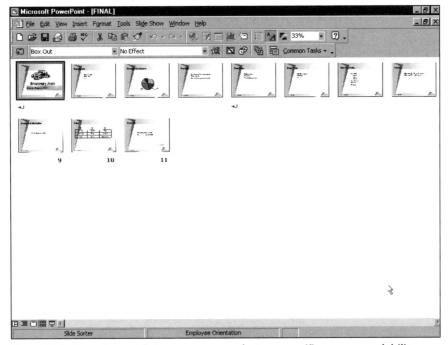

Figure 5-9: Zooming out lets you see more, but you sacrifice some readability.

Another way to control the Zoom is with the Zoom dialog box. Select View ➪ Zoom to open it. Make your selection, as shown in Figure 5-10, by clicking the appropriate button, and then click OK. Notice that you can type a precise zoom percentage in the Percent text box. This is the same as typing a percentage directly into the Zoom text box on the Standard toolbar.

Figure 5-10: You can zoom with this Zoom dialog box rather than the control on the toolbar if you prefer.

If the Zoom command is unavailable on the View menu, the outline pane is probably active. Click the slide pane to make the command available.

Displaying and Hiding Screen Elements

PowerPoint has lots of optional screen elements that you may (or may not) find useful, depending on what you're up to at the moment. In the following sections, I tell you about some of them and explain how to toggle them on and off.

The Ruler

Vertical and horizontal rulers around the slide pane can help you place objects more precisely. The rulers aren't displayed by default, however; you have to turn them on. To do so, select View ➪ Ruler. Do the same thing again to turn them off. Rulers are available only in the views that show an editable slide: Normal, Slide, Outline, and Notes Page.

Notice that each ruler starts with 0 in the middle, and runs 1, 2, 3 in both directions away from that midpoint. The rulers are just for positioning; you can't do anything to them by clicking them as you can in Word. See Figure 5-11.

Guides

Guides are onscreen dotted lines that can help you line up objects on a slide. For example, if you want to center some text exactly in the middle of the slide, you can place the object exactly at the intersection of the guide lines. Guides are available in the same views as rulers: Normal, Slide, Outline, and Notes Page. They aren't available in views that don't allow you to edit objects on individual slides.

To turn Guides on, select View ➪ Guides. Repeat the step to turn them off. Once Guides are on, you can drag the lines to reposition them. As you drag, a box pops up telling you the line's exact position, as shown in Figure 5-11.

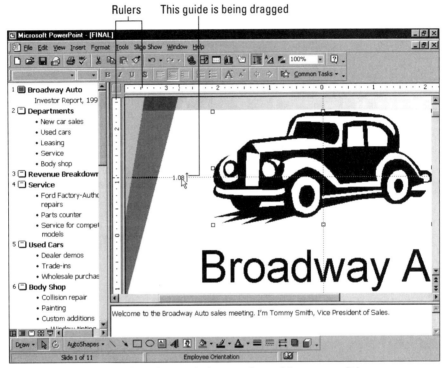

Figure 5-11: Rulers and guides can help you place objects on a slide.

Slide Miniature

The Slide Miniature window is available only when the entire slide (or page, in the case of Notes Page view) does not appear onscreen. It shows the entire slide or page in Zoomed-Out view (see Figure 5-12), which can be useful if you are working on the page in a Zoomed-In Detail view. To turn it on/off, select View ➪ Slide Miniature. (Note that the Slide Miniature command is not among the ones that appear immediately on the View menu; you must pause a moment for the less common commands to appear, as you learned in Chapter 2.)

Note
If you have used previous versions of PowerPoint, you may remember that the Slide Miniature view used to be available in Outline view, too. But in PowerPoint 2000, Outline view already contains a zoomed-out version of the slide, so the Slide Miniature would be redundant.

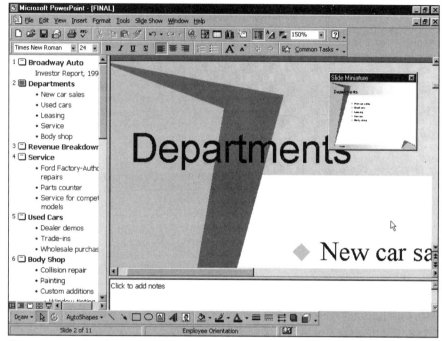

Figure 5-12: The Slide Miniature window helps you see the overall picture of a slide while working in Notes Page view.

Toolbars

PowerPoint comes with over a dozen toolbars, but only three are displayed by default in Normal view: Standard and Formatting at the top, and Drawing at the bottom.

 Note
Your Standard and Formatting toolbars may appear on the same line together; I showed you in Chapter 2 how to fix them so that they appear on separate lines, as they do in the figures in this book.

Some of the toolbars appear automatically whenever they are needed. (The Picture, WordArt, and Animation Effects toolbars are like that.) Other toolbars never appear unless you specifically call for them. (Outlining is a good example.) However, you can display other toolbars by right-clicking any displayed toolbar and choosing the one you want to see from the list. See Figure 5-13. You can also select View ⇨ Toolbars for the same list.

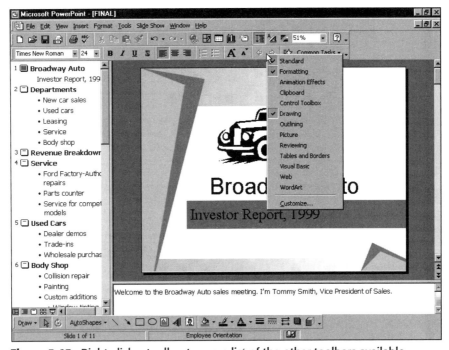

Figure 5-13: Right-click a toolbar to see a list of the other toolbars available.

Toolbar display and availability in Slide Sorter view are a little different from the other views. When you're in Slide Sorter view, you see only the Standard and Slide Sorter toolbars, and the list of available toolbars is decidedly shorter there. (That's because many of the toolbars, such as Picture, apply to individual slides, and you can't edit individual slides in Slide Sorter view.)

You can customize the toolbars as well as turn them on/off. You learn about that in Chapter 30.

Other Elements

PowerPoint has a few more elements you can choose to hide or display. Some of them aren't really screen elements, but rather dialog boxes at certain points in the program. To turn these options on/off, follow these steps:

1. Select Tools ➪ Options. The Options dialog box appears.

2. Click the View tab. See Figure 5-14.

3. Select or deselect the checkbox for the option you want to display or hide.

4. Click OK.

Figure 5-14: Set viewing options for PowerPoint here.

The View tab is divided into two frames: settings for all the working views (that is, all the views except Slide Show) and settings for the Slide Show view itself.

Here are the options that affect all views except Slide Show:

✦ **Startup dialog.** When you opened PowerPoint, recall that a PowerPoint dialog box appeared to help you get started. You can turn off this dialog box so that an empty work area appears when you start the program.

✦ **New slide dialog.** When you add new slides to a presentation, the New Slide dialog box appears, prompting you to select the slide layout you want to use. You can turn off this dialog box, signaling PowerPoint to add a totally blank slide each time you call for a new slide.

✦ **Status bar.** You can save about half an inch of onscreen space by turning off the status bar. This enables you to make the Zoom setting about 3 percent larger. Is it worth it? You decide.

✦ **Vertical ruler.** You saw earlier in this chapter that you can turn the rulers on or off; and you can deselect the vertical ruler here so that only a horizontal one appears when you turn the ruler on.

✦ **Windows in taskbar.** If you don't like the fact that PowerPoint 2000 places a separate bar on the taskbar for each open presentation file, deselect this checkbox to make PowerPoint 2000 display a single bar on the taskbar, just as it did in previous releases.

The following options affect only the Slide Show view:

✦ **Popup menu on right mouse click**. Normally, as you've seen, you can right-click elements in PowerPoint to make shortcut menus appear. You can disable this capability in Slide Show view if you want. It may deter a capricious user from tampering with your presentation if it is self-running.

✦ **Show popup menu button**. When you move your mouse in Slide Show view, an arrow appears in the bottom-left corner. You can click it to open the same menu that you get when right-clicking. You can disable it here to deter tampering.

✦ **End with a black slide**. If you want your presentation to end by displaying a black screen, leave this option selected. (It's a nice touch.)

Controlling Windows

If you are familiar with Windows 95 or 98 already, you can skip this section. It's all about controlling the windows. I've included it here because without a basic knowledge of how to control a window, your PowerPoint productivity can be severely hampered, especially when you begin working with more than one presentation at a time.

Working with Window Controls

Each window has three control buttons in its top-right corner. They are Minimize, Close, and either Maximize or Restore, depending on the window's current state:

Click the Minimize button to minimize a window. A minimized window is reduced to an icon or a small rectangle.

Click the Maximize button to maximize a window. A maximized window fills the entire screen or the entire space of the window in which it resides, if it's a window in a window.

Click the Restore button to restore a window to the size and shape that it was before it was maximized.

Click the Close button to close a window.

Understanding How PowerPoint Uses Windows

PowerPoint uses windows within windows, just like most Windows applications do. The outer window is PowerPoint itself. The inner windows are any presentations you have open. In Figure 5-15, for example, the PowerPoint application window is maximized; it fills the entire computer screen. Within it, three presentation windows are open: Final, Computer Friend, and Cycle. The Computer Friend and Cycle windows are minimized, and the Final window is restored (that is, not maximized). Contrast this to the maximized presentation in Figure 5-16. Notice that when a presentation window is maximized, it shares a title bar with the PowerPoint application window; when it's restored, it has its own title bar. Notice also in Figure 5-16 that when a presentation is maximized within the PowerPoint window, its window control buttons appear directly below those for the PowerPoint window itself rather than in the title bar.

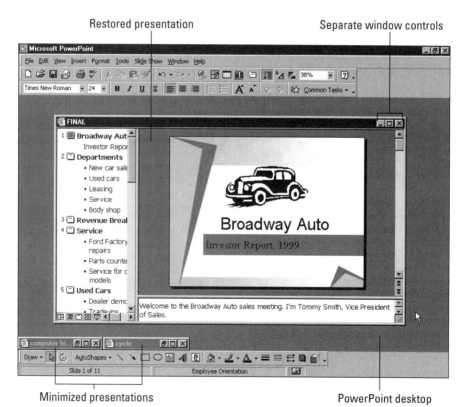

Figure 5-15: This PowerPoint window has three open presentations: two minimized and one restored.

Presentation title bar
combined with the PowerPoint title bar

Maximized presentation
window controls

PowerPoint
window controls

Figure 5-16: This PowerPoint window has a maximized presentation.

When a presentation window is minimized, it sits as a rectangular icon on the PowerPoint window's desktop, the gray area behind the presentations. To reopen a minimized presentation, double-click it. If another window is obscuring it, press Ctrl+Tab until it appears.

Caution

When you double-click a minimized presentation to open it, click the letters of the name, not the right end of the rectangle. With your first click on the rectangle, the window controls appear at the right end, and you may accidentally click one of those controls with the second click of your double-click.

Moving and Resizing Windows

You can move and resize windows that aren't minimized or maximized. You can move and resize the PowerPoint window itself too, or any window for that matter. To move a window, drag its title bar. To resize a window, position the mouse pointer over any border of the window so the pointer changes to a double-headed arrow. Then, drag the border until the window is the size you want it to be.

Opening a New Display Window

Have you ever wished you could be in two places at once? Well, in PowerPoint, you actually can. PowerPoint provides a way to view two different spots in the presentation at the same time by opening a new window.

To display a new window, select Window ⇨ New Window. You can use any view with any window, so you can have two different slides in Normal view at once, or Slide and Slide Sorter view, or any other combination. Both windows contain the same presentation, so any changes you make in one window are reflected in the other window.

Arranging Windows

When you have two or more windows open, whether they are for the same presentation or different ones, you need to arrange them for optimal viewing. You saw earlier in this chapter how to resize a window, but did you know that PowerPoint can do some of the arranging for you?

Almost all Windows-based programs have a Window menu with some commands that help you arrange the windows. When you want to arrange the open windows, do one of the following:

✦ Select Window ⇨ Arrange All to tile the open windows so there is no overlap. See Figure 5-17.

✦ Select Window ⇨ Cascade to arrange the open windows so the title bars cascade from upper left to lower right on the screen. Click a title bar to activate a window. See Figure 5-18.

These commands do not apply to minimized windows. If you want to include a window in the arrangement, make sure you restore it from its minimized state first.

Switching Among Windows

If you have more than one window open and can see at least a corner of the window you want, click it to bring it to the front. If you have one of the windows maximized, on the other hand, or if another window is completely obscuring the one you want, you must open the Window menu and choose the window to display.

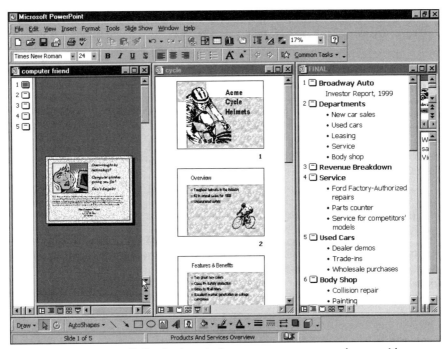

Figure 5-17: Arrange All tiles in the windows so you can see each one with no overlap.

Title bars

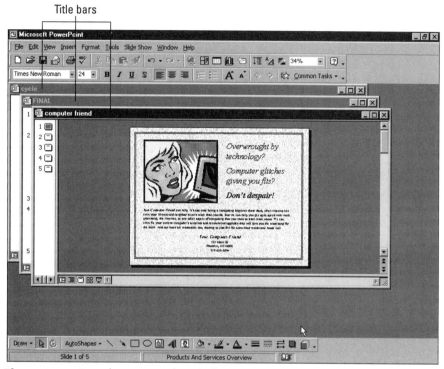

Figure 5-18: Cascade arranges the windows so that you can see all of the title bars.

Summary

In this chapter, you learned about PowerPoint's views, which are rather different in PowerPoint 2000 than they were in previous versions of the program. You also learned how to zoom in and out, display and hide onscreen tools, and control multiple windows. Now you're ready to tackle your first real presentation!

The next chapter is a *thinking* chapter, not a *doing* one. In it, you learn how to plan your presentation carefully from the ground up so you don't waste time. By taking the time to go through it, you can save yourself lots of time and frustration later.

✦ ✦ ✦

Developing Your Action Plan

Can you guess what the single biggest problem is when most people use PowerPoint? Here's a hint: It's not a problem with the software at all. It's that they don't think things through carefully before they create their presentation, and then they have to go back and make major modifications later. You've probably heard the saying, "If you don't have time to do it right, how are you going to find time to do it over?" This sentiment is certainly applicable to creating presentations.

In this chapter, I outline a nine-point strategy for creating the appropriate PowerPoint presentation right from the start. By considering the issues addressed here, you can avoid making false assumptions about your audience and their needs and avoid creating a beautiful presentation with some horrible flaw that makes it unusable. Spend a half hour or so in this chapter and you can save yourself literally days in rework later.

Step 1: Identifying Your Audience and Purpose

Before you can think about the presentation you need to create, you must first think of your audience. Different audiences respond to different presentation types, as you probably already know from real-life experience. A sales pitch to a client requires a very different approach than an informational briefing to your coworkers. Ask yourself these questions:

✦ **How many people will be attending the presentation?** The attendance makes a difference because the larger the group, the larger your screen needs to be so that everyone can see. If you don't have access to a large screen, you have to make the lettering and charts big and chunky so that everyone can read your presentation.

✦ **What is the average age of the attendees?** While it's difficult to generalize about people, it's especially important to keep your presentation light and entertaining when you're presenting to a very young audience (teens and children). Generally speaking, the older the audience, the more authoritative you need to be.

✦ **What role will the audience take in relation to the topic?** If you are rolling out a new product or system, the managerial staff will likely want a general overview of it, but the line workers who will actually be operating the product need lots of details. Generally speaking, the higher the level of managers, the more removed they will be from the action, and the fewer details of operation they need.

✦ **How well does the audience already know the topic?** If you are presenting to a group that knows nothing about your topic, you want to keep things basic and make sure that you define all the unfamiliar terms. In contrast, with a group of experts you are likely to have many follow-up questions after the main presentation, so you should plan on having some hidden backup slides ready in anticipation of those questions. See "Hiding Slides for Backup Use" in Chapter 24.

✦ **Does the audience care about the topic?** If the topic is personally important to the attendees (such as information on their insurance benefits or vacation schedule), they will likely pay attention even if your presentation is plain and straightforward. If you must win them over, however, you need to spend more time on the bells and whistles.

✦ **Are the attendees prejudiced either positively or negatively toward the topic?** Keeping in mind the audience's preconceived ideas can make the difference between success and failure in some presentations. For example, knowing that a client hates sales pitches can help you tailor your own to be out of the ordinary.

✦ **Are the attendees in a hurry?** Do your attendees have all afternoon to listen to you, or do they need to get back to their regular jobs? Nothing is more frustrating than sitting through a leisurely presentation when you're watching precious minutes tick away. Know your audience's schedule and their preference for quick versus thorough coverage.

Next, think about what you want the outcome of the presentation to be. You might want more than one outcome, but try to identify the primary one as your main goal. Some outcomes to consider include the following:

✦ **Audience feels good about the topic**. Some presentations are strictly cheerleading sessions, designed to sway the audience's opinion. Don't discount this objective — it's a perfectly legitimate reason to make a presentation! For example, suppose a new management staff has taken over a factory. The new management team might want to reassure the workers that everything is going to be okay. A feel-good, Welcome to the Team presentation, complete with gimmicks like company T-shirts or hats, can go a long way in this regard.

✦ **Audience is informed**. Sometimes you need to convey information to a group of people and no decision is involved on their part. For example, suppose your company has switched insurance carriers and you want to let all the employees know about their new benefits. An informational presentation can cover most of the common questions and save your human resources people lots of time in answering the same questions over and over.

✦ **Audience members make individual decisions**. This presentation is a kind of sales pitch in which you are pitching an idea or product to a group but each person says yes or no individually. For example, suppose you are selling timeshare vacation condos. You may give a presentation to a group of 100 in an attempt to sell your package to at least a few of the group.

This presentation type can also have an informational flavor; you are informing people about their choices without pushing one choice or the other. For example, if your employees have a choice of health plans, you might present the pros and cons of each and then leave it to each employee to make a selection.

✦ **Audience makes a group decision**. This is the kind of presentation that scares the bejezus out of a lot of people. You face a group of people who will confer and make a single decision based on the information you present. Most sales pitches fall into this category. You might be explaining your product to a group of managers, for example, to try to get their company to buy it.

Think about these factors carefully and try to come up with a single statement that summarizes your audience and purpose. Here are some examples:

✦ *I am presenting to a group of 6 to 10 midlevel managers, trying to get them to decide as a group to buy my product.*

✦ *I am presenting to 200 factory workers to explain their new health insurance choices and teach them how to fill out the necessary forms.*

✦ *I am presenting to a group of 20 professors to convince at least some of them to use my company's textbooks in their classes.*

✦ *I am presenting to individual Internet users to explain how my company's service works.*

Step 2: Choosing Your Presentation Method

You essentially have three ways to present your presentation to your audience, and you need to pick which way you're going to use up front. They include speaker-led, self-running, and user-interactive.

Speaker-Led

The speaker-led presentation is the traditional type of presentation: you stand up in front of a live audience (or one connected through teleconferencing) and give a speech. The slides you create in PowerPoint become your support materials. The primary message comes from you; the slides are just helpers. The special factors involved in this kind of presentation are covered in Part V of the book (Chapters 21 through 24).

With this kind of presentation, your slides don't have to tell the whole story. Each slide can contain just a few main points, and you can flesh out each point in your discussion. In fact, this kind of presentation works best when your slides don't contain a lot of information, because people pay more attention to you, the speaker, if they're not trying to read at the same time. For example, instead of listing the top five reasons to switch to your service, you might have a slide that just reads, "Why Switch? Five Reasons." The audience has to listen to you to find out what the reasons are.

This kind of presentation also requires some special planning. For example, do you want to send each audience member home with handouts? If so, you need to prepare them. They may or may not be identical to your PowerPoint slides; that's up to you. Handouts and other support materials (like notecards for yourself) are covered in Chapter 21.

You also need to learn how to control PowerPoint's presentation controls, which is the subject of Chapter 22. It can be really embarrassing to be fiddling with the computer controls in the middle of a speech, so you should practice, practice, practice ahead of time.

If you're not going to be physically in the same room with the audience, there are additional concerns. Will your PowerPoint presentation play on the video teleconferencing equipment you'll be using? If not, you may have to print the slides or convert them to 35mm slide format to be shown.

With PowerPoint, you can also present a live show from the Internet or a company intranet. (This process is explained in Chapter 23.) Basically, each audience member sits at his or her own PC and watches the show onscreen. You can use a telephone conference call to narrate, or you can let the slides speak for themselves.

Self-Running

With a self-running presentation, all the rules change. Instead of using the slides as teasers or support materials, you must make the slides carry the entire show. All the information must be right there, because you won't be looking over the audience's shoulders with helpful narration.

In general, self-running presentations are meant to be presented to individuals or very small groups. For example, you might set up a kiosk in a busy lobby or a booth at a trade show and have a brief (say, five slides) presentation constantly running that explains your product or service.

Because there is no dynamic human being keeping the audience's attention, self-running presentations must include attention-getting features. Sounds, video clips, interesting transitions, and prerecorded narratives are all good ways to attract viewers. Part III of this book explains how to use sounds, videos, and other moving objects in a presentation to add interest.

You must also consider the timing with a self-running presentation. Since there is no way for a viewer to tell the presentation, "Okay, I'm done reading this slide; bring on the next one," you must carefully plan how long each slide will remain onscreen. This kind of timing requires some practice! Chapter 25 deals with these timing issues and also explains how to record voice-over narration.

User-Interactive

A user-interactive presentation is like a self-running one except the viewer has some input. Rather than standing by passively as the slides advance, the viewer can tell PowerPoint when to advance a slide. Depending on the presentation's setup, viewers may also be able to skip around in the presentation (perhaps to skip over topics they're not interested in) and request more information. Chapter 26, "Designing User-Interactive Presentations," explains how to place action buttons on slides that let the viewer control the action.

This kind of presentation is most typically distributed over the Internet or a company intranet. The user copies the presentation to his or her computer and then runs it using either PowerPoint or a free program called PowerPoint Viewer that you can provide for download. You can also translate a PowerPoint presentation to HTML format (the native format for World Wide Web pages), so that anyone with a Web browser can view it. However, presentations lose a lot of their cool features when you do that (such as the sound and video clips), so consider the decision carefully. Chapter 27 contains much more information about this type of presentation.

Step 3: Choosing the Appropriate Template and Design

PowerPoint comes with so many presentation templates and designs that you're sure to find one that's appropriate for your situation. PowerPoint provides three levels of help in this arena, as you learn in Chapter 7. You can use an AutoContent Wizard to work through a series of dialog boxes that help you create a presentation based on a presentation template, you can apply a design template, or you can work from scratch.

PowerPoint includes two kinds of templates: presentation templates and design templates. Presentation templates contain sample text and sample formatting appropriate to certain situations. For example, there are several presentation templates that can help you sell a product or service. The AutoContent Wizard is the best way to choose a presentation template.

If you want to take advantage of the sample text provided by a presentation template, you should make sure you choose one that's appropriate. PowerPoint includes dozens, so you should take some time going through them to understand the full range of options before making your decision. (See "Starting a Presentation Based on a Presentation Template" in Chapter 7.) Remember, once you've started a presentation using one presentation template, you can't change to another and take advantage of its sample text without starting over.

A design template, in contrast, is just a combination of fonts, colors, and graphics, and you can apply a different design to any presentation at any time. Therefore, it's not as crucial to select the correct design up front, because you can play with these elements later. You learn a lot more about these design templates in Chapter 7.

Tip   You aren't stuck with the color scheme that comes with a particular presentation template. If you like the sample text in one presentation template and the color scheme in another, start with the one containing the good sample text. Then *steal* the color scheme from the other one later, as explained in "Changing the Presentation Design" in Chapter 11.

Generally speaking, your choice of design should depend on the audience and the way you plan to present. Here are some suggestions:

✦ To make an audience feel good or relaxed about a topic, use blues and greens. To get an audience excited and happy, use reds and yellows. For slides you plan to project on a slide screen or show on a PC, use dark backgrounds with light lettering. For slides you plan to print and hand out, dark on white is better. See "Changing the Color Scheme" in Chapter 11.

✦ For readability, use serif fonts like Times New Roman. For a casual, modern feel, use sans-serif fonts like Arial. Refer to "Changing the Font" in Chapter 9 for more information.

✦ The farther away from the screen the audience will be, the larger you need to make the lettering.

✦ It's best if all slides use the same design and color scheme, but there may be exceptions when your interests are best served by breaking that rule. For example, you might shake things up midway through a presentation by showing a key slide with a different color background. See "Changing the Background" in Chapter 11.

Note

The previous version of PowerPoint came with two versions of each of its presentation templates: Standard and Online (for Web publishing). In PowerPoint 2000, however, each template has only one version. When you work through the AutoContent Wizard, you can specify if the presentation will be used on the Web. That adds the additional controls that the Online version of the template added in PowerPoint 97.

Step 4: Developing the Content

Only after you have made all the decisions in Steps 1 through 3 can you start developing your content in a real PowerPoint presentation. This is the point at which Chapter 7 picks up, guiding you through creating the file and organizing slides.

Then comes the work of writing the text for each slide, which most people prefer to do in Normal view. (Remember, you learned about Normal view in Chapter 5.) Type the text on the outline, reformat it as needed to make certain bits of it special (for example, setting a key phrase in bold or italics), and you're ready to roll. The slide pane on the right shows how it will look. Figure 6-1 shows an outline developed in Outline view.

Developing your content may include more than just typing text. Your content may include charts (either created in PowerPoint or imported from another program, such as Excel), pictures, and other elements. You learn about graphics in Chapters 12 and 13, and about various kinds of charts in Chapters 14 and 15. Chapter 16 covers importing content from other programs.

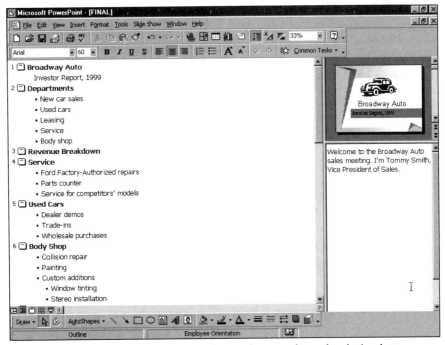

Figure 6-1: Develop your text content first and worry about the design later.

Step 5: Creating the Visual Image

The term *visual image* refers to the overall impression that the audience gets from watching the presentation. You create a polished, professional impression by making small tweaks to your presentation after you have the content down pat.

Visual image can be enhanced by making minor adjustments to the slide's design. For example, you can give a dark slide a warmer feel by using bright yellow instead of white for lettering. Repositioning a company logo and making it larger may make the headings look less lonely (see Figure 6-2 and 6-3). A product picture may be more attractive in a larger size or with a different-colored mat around it. All of these little touches take experimentation and experience.

Figure 6-2: The look of this sparsely populated page can be easily improved.

Figure 6-3: After enlarging and repositioning the logo, this page makes a sharper impact.

Most audiences like consistency. They like things they can rely on, like a repeated company logo on every slide, accurate page numbering on handouts, and the title appearing in exactly the same spot on every slide. You can create a consistent visual image by enforcing such rules in your presentation development. It's easier than you might think, because PowerPoint provides a Slide Master specifically for images and text that should repeat on each slide. You see it in action in Chapter 11.

Step 6: Adding Multimedia Effects

If you're creating a self-running presentation, multimedia effects can be extremely important for developing audience interest. Flashy videos and soundtracks can make even the most boring product fun to hear about. How about a trumpet announcing the arrival of your new product on the market, or a video of your CEO explaining the reasoning behind the recent merger? Chapters 18 and 19 deal with the mechanics of placing sound and video clips into a presentation and controlling when and how they play.

Caution   Even if you are going to be speaking live, you still might want to incorporate some multimedia elements in your show. Be careful, however, not to let them outshine you or appear gratuitous. Be aware of your audience (see Step 1), and remember that older and higher-level managers want less flash and more substance.

All kinds of presentations can benefit from animations and transitions on the slides. *Animations* are simple movements of the objects on a slide. For example, you might make the bullet points on a list fly onto the page one at a time so you can discuss each one on its own. When the next one flies in, the previous ones can turn a different color so the current one stands out. You can also animate charts, making data series appear one at a time, so it looks like the chart is building. You learn about animations in Chapter 20.

Transitions are animated ways of moving from slide to slide. The most basic and boring transition is to simply remove one slide from the screen and replace it with another, but you can use all kinds of alternative effects like zooming the new slide in; sliding it from the top, bottom, left, or right; or creating a *windowshade* transition effect. Transitions are covered in Chapter 20.

Step 7: Creating the Handouts and Notes

This step is applicable only for speaker-led presentations. With a live audience, you may want to provide handouts so they can follow along. The handouts can be verbatim copies of your slides, or they can be abbreviated versions with just the most basic information included as a memory-jogger. Handouts can be either black and white or color.

PowerPoint provides several handout formats. You can print from one to six slides per printout, with or without lines for the audience to write additional notes. Chapter 21 walks you through selecting the appropriate size and format and working with your printer to get the best results.

Note   A continual debate rages in the professional speakers' community over when to give out handouts. Some people feel that if you distribute handouts before the presentation, people will read them and not listen to the presentation. Others feel that if you wait until after the presentation to distribute the handouts, people will frantically try to take their own notes during the presentation or will not follow the ideas as easily. There's no real right or wrong, it seems; so distribute them whenever it makes the most sense for your situation.

As the speaker, you may need your own special set of handouts with your own notes that the audience should not see. PowerPoint calls these Notes Pages. There is even a special view in PowerPoint called Notes Pages view (see Figure 6-4) that you can use to page through your presentation onscreen and view/change your notes. Notes, like handouts, are covered in Chapter 21.

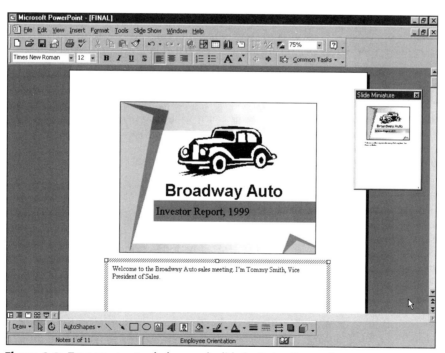

Figure 6-4: Type your notes below each slide in Notes Pages view.

Step 8: Rehearsing the Presentation

No matter which type of presentation you are creating (speaker-led, self-running, or user-interactive), you need to rehearse it. The goals for rehearsing, however, are different for each type.

Rehearsing a Live Presentation

When you rehearse a live presentation, you check the presentation slides to ensure they are complete, accurate, and in the right order. You may need to rearrange them (see Chapter 7) and hide some of them for backup-only use (see Chapter 24).

You should also rehearse using PowerPoint's presentation controls that display each slide on a monitor and let you move from slide to slide, take notes, assign action items, and even draw directly on a slide. Make sure you know how to back up, how to jump to the beginning or end, and how to display one of your backup slides. These skills are covered in Chapter 22.

If you are going to present from a remote location, rehearsal becomes doubly important because you must master the equipment or technology used for the transmission. PowerPoint includes a wonderful utility for presenting over the Internet or over a network or intranet; you learn all about it in Chapter 23.

Rehearsing a Self-Running Presentation

With a speaker-led presentation, the presenter can fix any glitches that pop up or explain away any errors. With a self-running presentation, you don't have that luxury. The presentation itself is your emissary. Therefore, you must go over and over it, checking it many times to make sure it is perfect before distributing it. Nothing is worse than a self-running presentation that doesn't run, or one that contains an embarrassing error.

The most important feature in a self-running presentation is timing. You must make the presentation pause the correct amount of time for the audience to be able to read the text on each slide. The pause must be long enough so that even slow readers can catch it all, but short enough so that fast readers do not get bored. Can you see how difficult this can be to make perfect?

PowerPoint has a Rehearse Timings feature (Figure 6-5) designed to help you with this task. It lets you show the slides and advance them manually after the correct amount of time has passed. The Rehearse Timings feature records how much time you spend on each slide and gives you a report so you can modify the timing if necessary. For example, suppose you are working on a presentation that is supposed to last 10 minutes, but with your timings, it comes out to only 9 minutes. You can add additional time for each slide to stretch it out to fill the full 10 minutes. Chapter 25 covers timing.

Figure 6-5: With PowerPoint, you can rehearse timings so your audience has enough time to read the slides but doesn't get bored waiting for the next one.

You may also want to record voice-over narration for your presentation. You can rehearse this too, to make sure that the voice matches the slide it is supposed to describe (which is absolutely crucial, as you can imagine!). You learn about voice-overs in Chapter 25, too.

Rehearsing a User-Interactive Presentation

In a user-interactive presentation, you provide the readers with onscreen buttons they can click to move through the presentation, so timing is not an issue. The crucial factor with a user-interactive presentation is link accuracy. Each button on each slide is a link. When your reader clicks a button for the next slide, it had better darned well take him to the next slide and not to somewhere else. And if you include a hyperlink to a Web address on the Internet, when the reader clicks it, the Web browser should open and that page should appear. If the hyperlink contains a typo and the reader sees File Not Found instead of the Web page, the error reflects poorly on you. Chapter 26 covers creating and inserting these links.

If you are planning to distribute your presentation via the Internet, you have a big decision to make. You can distribute the presentation in its native PowerPoint format and preserve all its whiz-bang features like animations and videos. However, not everyone on the Internet owns a copy of PowerPoint, obviously, so you limit your audience. PowerPoint supplies a free program called the PowerPoint Viewer that you can post for downloading on your Web page, but not everyone will take the time to download and install that, so you may turn off potential viewers before you start.

The other option is to save the presentation in HTML (Web) format. When you save in HTML format, you convert each of the slides to a Web page, and you add links (if you didn't already have them) that move from slide to slide. You lose your animations, transitions, sounds, videos, any animated graphics, and some other extras, but you retain your text and most static elements of the presentation. The advantage is that everyone with a Web browser can view your presentation with no special downloads or setup.

You learn more about preparing a presentation for the Internet, no matter which method you choose, in Chapter 27.

Step 9: Giving the Presentation

For a user-interactive or self-running presentation, giving the presentation is somewhat anticlimactic. You just make it available and the readers come get it. Yawn.

However, for a speaker-led presentation, giving the speech is the highlight, the pinnacle of the process. If you've done a good job rehearsing, you are already familiar with PowerPoint's presentation controls, described in Chapter 22. Be prepared to back up, to skip ahead, to answer questions by displaying hidden slides, and to pause the whole thing (and black out the screen) so you can hold a tangential discussion. Chapter 22 covers all these situations in case you need to review them.

What remains then? Nothing, except setting up the room and overcoming your stage fright. Chapter 28 provides some hints about using a meeting room most effectively and being a dynamic speaker. Check them out — and then go get 'em, winner!

Summary

Creating effective PowerPoint presentations requires more than just knowing the software. It requires careful planning and step-by-step preparation. In this chapter, you learned about the steps you need to take, from start to finish, to assemble the PowerPoint slides for your next great success:

✦ Step 1: Identify your audience and purpose. No flip answers are acceptable here; spend some time thinking about the right answers.

✦ Step 2: Choose your presentation method. Will you give a live, speaker-led show, distribute it online, or set up a self-running kiosk show?

✦ Step 3: Choose a template and design. PowerPoint comes with dozens of professional-quality templates, some of which include sample text. Choose the one that matches your answers in Steps 1 and 2.

✦ Step 4: Develop the content. Flash is useless without substance. Create the text for your presentation in Outline view in PowerPoint or import an outline from Word.

✦ Step 5: Create the visual image. Polish your presentation design by making sure that the slides are attractive and consistent.

✦ Step 6: Add multimedia effects. Only after the content and overall image are solid should you add extras like sound, video, transition, and animation.

✦ Step 7: Create handouts and notes. If you are giving a live presentation, you may want notes for yourself (speaker notes) and notes for your audience (handouts).

✦ Step 8: Rehearse. Run through your presentation several times to make sure it is free from embarrassing mistakes. If necessary, add timing controls and voice-over narratives.

✦ Step 9: Give the presentation. Take a deep breath and imagine the audience in their underwear! If you're familiar with PowerPoint's presentation controls, you'll do fine.

✦　　✦　　✦

Building Your Presentation

Starting a New Presentation

There are several ways to create a new presentation in PowerPoint, ranging from the full-service (the AutoContent Wizard) to the no-frills (starting with a blank screen). Each method has its benefits and drawbacks.

✦ **AutoContent Wizard**. You work through a series of dialog boxes to select sample content that matches the presentation you want to give.

- *Pros*: It is very easy, and the sample slides can help you figure out how to structure your speech.

- *Cons*: The Wizard chooses the design; you must change the design template later if you don't like it. Also, the sample slides may not fit what you want to say, and the AutoContent Wizard can be time-consuming to go through.

✦ **Presentation template**. You choose a template containing sample content from the same list as the one you see with the AutoContent Wizard, but you do not go through all the AutoContent Wizard dialog boxes.

- *Pros*: It provides sample content more quickly than the AutoContent Wizard.

- *Cons*: Disadvantages are the same as for AutoContent Wizard, except for the time-consuming part.

✦ **Design template**. You choose a template containing a background design, colors, font choices, and other formatting, and then you manually create each slide that goes into the presentation.

- *Pros*: You pick the design yourself to match your message; it is quicker and easier than starting with a blank screen.

- *Cons*: There is no sample content guidance, and it takes some time to create the slides needed.

✦ **Blank presentation**. You start a new presentation that contains no slides and no formatting, and you add it all yourself from the ground up.

- *Pros*: This method provides maximum flexibility; you do not have to clean up any formatting or content that you didn't want in the first place.

- *Cons*: It can be very time-consuming to build an entire presentation completely from scratch, and it requires a greater knowledge of PowerPoint's features than you would otherwise need.

For your first few presentations, I suggest using the AutoContent Wizard. Then, graduate to using either a presentation template or a design template, depending on the situation. You will rarely find a need to start with a blank template, but I include coverage of it in this chapter just in case.

Note The steps in this chapter suppose that you have *not* just started PowerPoint, and therefore the PowerPoint dialog box is *not* displayed. If you do see the PowerPoint dialog box onscreen, you can use it as an alternative to the methods shown in the following sections to start a new presentation using the AutoContent Wizard, a design template, or a blank template.

Creating a Presentation with the AutoContent Wizard

As I mentioned earlier, the AutoContent Wizard provides the highest level of automation in creating a new presentation. Beginners find it very useful, as it saves lots of time and forestalls the need to learn about PowerPoint's many formatting features to create a decent-looking show.

Tip You won't be stuck with the choices that the AutoContent Wizard makes when it creates your presentation, by the way. If it assigns a design that you don't like, you can change it. If it creates slides that you don't need, you can delete them and/or add others. You have a full range of customization options at your disposal, as always.

To use the AutoContent Wizard, follow these steps:

1. Choose File ➪ New. The New Presentation dialog box opens.
2. Click the General tab.
3. Double-click the AutoContent Wizard. The Wizard starts.
4. Click Next to bypass the introductory screen.
5. Select the category of presentation you want to give. You can use the category buttons to narrow the list (General, Corporate, Projects, and so on), or click All to see all the presentation templates. See Figure 7-1.

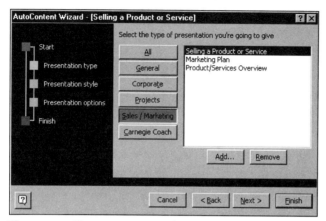

Figure 7-1: Choose a presentation category, and then select an individual presentation template to use.

Note One of the categories, Carnegie Coach, contains presentation templates with sample content from the Dale Carnegie Institute, a noted public speaking organization. These presentation templates are especially helpful for beginning speakers.

6. Select the template you want to use from the list displayed. Then, click Next.

7. When asked the type of output you need, choose the medium you plan to use to give your show: Onscreen presentation, Web presentation, Black and white overheads, Color overheads, or 35mm slides. Then, click Next.

Note The Wizard wants to know the medium in Step 7 so it can format the slides correctly. For example, 35mm slides need to be a different size and shape than slides shown on a computer screen, and Web presentations need navigation buttons on each slide.

8. When prompted for a presentation title, enter it in the Presentation title text box.

9. In the Items to include on each slide section (see Figure 7-2), enter a footer for the presentation if you want one. This text will repeat at the bottom of each slide. You might use your company name, for example, or CONFIDENTIAL.

If you want a date and/or slide number on each slide, leave those checkboxes marked (see Figure 7-2). Otherwise deselect them. The elements you select from this section of the dialog box are added to the Slide Master, which you learn about in Chapter 11.

10. Click Finish. The Wizard creates the presentation. See Figure 7-3.

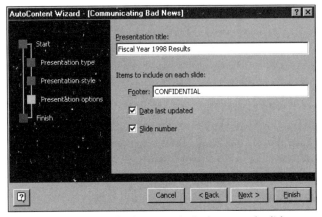

Figure 7-2: Choose the items to include on each slide.

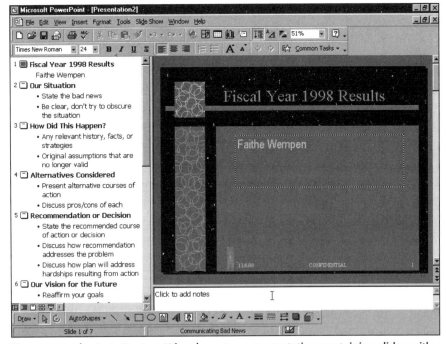

Figure 7-3: The AutoContent Wizard creates a presentation containing slides with sample text and consistent presentation-wide formatting.

Tip   The one bad thing about using a presentation template is that you don't get to choose the design. However, you can change the design as much as you want after creating the presentation. To change the design template applied to the presentation, choose Format ➪ Apply Design Template. See Chapter 11 for details.

Starting a Presentation Based on a Presentation Template

If you want to take advantage of PowerPoint's sample content but you don't want to go through the AutoContent Wizard (which takes some time, doesn't it?), you can create a presentation based on one of the presentation templates. These are the same templates that the AutoContent Wizard draws from; the only difference is that with the following method, they aren't broken down nicely into categories, so you have to know which one you want.

To select an available presentation, follow these steps:

1. Choose File ➪ New to open the New Presentation dialog box.

2. Click the Presentations tab. A list of the available presentations appears as shown in Figure 7-4.

3. Click the presentation you want. Don't worry about the formatting and colors; you can change those elements later. Just pick the one that sounds the most like the content you want.

4. Click OK to create a new presentation. Placeholders appear where you must put information, as shown in Figure 7-5. (This information would have been inserted by the AutoContent Wizard if you had used it.)

5. Replace the bracketed text placeholders with the correct information. See Chapters 8 and 9 for more information about editing text.

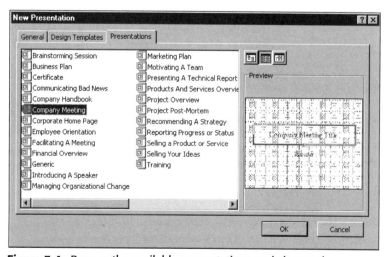

Figure 7-4: Browse the available presentations and choose the one you want.

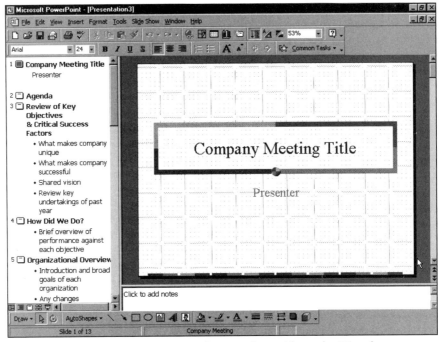

Figure 7-5: When you use a presentation template without the Wizard, some placeholders appear for information that the Wizard would have provided.

Starting a Presentation Based on a Design Template

When you start with a design template, you start with all the same formatting advantages as with a presentation template: a predesigned background, a prechosen color scheme, prechosen fonts and sizes assigned to predeveloped styles, and so on. This can save you boatloads of time if you need a professionally formatted presentation right away.

The one thing you don't get with a design template is sample slides. Not only do you not get any sample content, you don't get any slides at all! After you start a presentation based on a design template, the New Slide dialog box opens so you can create your first slide manually. And then you go from there.

To create a new presentation based on a design template, follow these steps:

1. Choose File ➪ New to open the New Presentation dialog box.

2. Click the Design Templates tab.

3. Click one of the designs to see a sample of it in the Preview area (see Figure 7-6).

Note   If you see a message in the preview area instead of a sample, that template is not installed. To install it, select it and click OK. You will need your Microsoft Office 2000 CD.

4. Click OK to create the presentation. The New Slide dialog box appears.

5. Click a layout (the default one, Title Slide, is a good choice for the first slide). Then click OK.

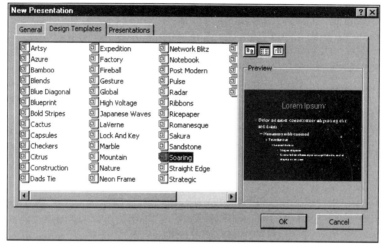

Figure 7-6: Browse the design templates by clicking one and looking at its preview.

Starting a Presentation from Scratch

The from-scratch method is for people who know enough about PowerPoint to know exactly what they want — formatting, content, the whole works — and who aren't finding it in any of the presentation templates and design templates. When you create a blank presentation, it's just that — a completely white background on the slides, plain Arial font, no special *anything*.

To create a blank presentation, follow these steps:

1. Choose File ➪ New to open the New Presentation dialog box.

2. Click the General tab.

3. Double-click Blank Presentation. The New Slide dialog box appears.

4. Select the layout for your first slide (the default Title Slide is fine) and click OK.

Ten Great Presentation Templates

Not sure which presentation template to use? Try some of these.

1. **Facilitating a Meeting.** This template's sample content guides you step by step through facilitating a group discussion. You learn about opening a meeting with an anecdote that stimulates interest, encouraging participation, and creating solutions. Copious notes in the notes pane supplement each slide.

2. **Project Post-Mortem.** *Post mortem* means after death, and you can use this template to run a meeting that discusses a project after it has been completed. You can help the audience remember the original goals and discuss how well they were achieved.

3. **Company Handbook.** This template helps you create a comprehensive picture of your company's personnel policies, including training, performance reviews, recruiting, termination, and compensation.

4. **Corporate Home Page.** If you are interested in setting up a company presence on the Internet, this template can help you get started by creating a series of attractive Web pages that are linked together in a cohesive Web site.

5. **Motivating A Team.** This is one of the Dale Carnegie Training presentations that comes with PowerPoint. These presentation templates all use the same design (which you can easily change). This one provides not only sample content for a presentation, but also valuable business advice. The other templates in the Dale Carnegie series are Facilitating A Meeting, Introducing A Speaker, Managing Organizational Change, Presenting A Technical Report, and Selling Your Ideas.

6. **Selling a Product or Service.** Sales pitches are the most common type of presentations, and this template teaches you how to structure your sales message — first by explaining the customer requirements, and then by explaining how the product meets them.

7. **Business Plan.** Every company needs a business plan, but it can sometimes be difficult to know how to start one. You can create a business plan easily by filling in the information requested on the sample slides here. Start with your mission statement; explain your team and its challenges and strengths; and then proceed through your goals and objectives to your plan for meeting them.

8. **Certificate.** This is not a real presentation that you will show onscreen; instead, it is a template for creating certificates to give to others as motivational aids.

9. **Training.** This template can help you structure a training session for employees or customers. It helps you outline what needs to be taught, the vocabulary needed for understanding, and the salient points of each topic to address.

10. **Generic.** If your presentation needs don't fit with any of the presentation templates that come with PowerPoint, consider the Generic template. It provides some general pointers for presenting any kind of information.

Adding Slides

Now that you have a new presentation, and at least one slide, you are ready to start creating your message. If you already have slides from a presentation template in place, your first task can be to edit the text to convey your own words. See Chapters 8 and 9 for text editing details. You may even want to delete some of the slides; see the "Deleting Slides" section later in this chapter.

However, if you created a presentation based on a design template, or a blank presentation, you need to create some more slides. You can do this in any of these ways:

✦ To create plain slides consisting of a heading and a single bulleted list, type the text in the outline pane. To make a line of text into a slide title, promote it (Alt+Tab). To make a line of text into a bullet underneath a slide title, demote it (Tab). See Chapter 8 for more information.

✦ To create a slide using any of the AutoLayouts, click the New Slide button to open the New Slide dialog box. See Figure 7-7. Click the layout you want, then click OK.

✦ To make a duplicate of a slide you already have, select it (see the following section) and choose Edit ➪ Duplicate (Ctrl+D). Or, select the slide, choose Edit ➪ Copy (Ctrl+C), and then choose Edit ➪ Paste (Ctrl+V).

Note   Why might you want to duplicate an existing slide? Perhaps it contains several elements that you want to place on several slides in a row. (If you want the same element on all slides, however, you should place it on the Slide Master, described in Chapter 11.) Or perhaps you want to repeat a certain important slide periodically throughout a presentation to reinforce its message.

Of all the methods of adding new slides, the most important and flexible method is to use the New Slide dialog box (Figure 7-7). That's because this dialog box offers dozens of predesigned slide layouts, called *AutoLayouts*. These slides contain placeholders for not only text, but graphics, charts, tables, and other useful elements. (You saw some of these in Chapter 1.) In Chapter 10, you learn how to change a slide's AutoLayout after its initial creation. After you create a new slide that contains placeholders, you can click a placeholder to open whatever controls are needed to insert that type of object. For example, if you click a placeholder for clip art, the Clip Gallery opens. You learn more about the various kinds of slide objects and how to place them on your slides in later chapters.

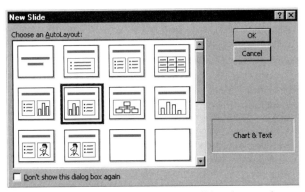

Figure 7-7: When you create a new slide, choose the appropriate AutoLayout for it from the New Slide dialog box.

Selecting Slides

PowerPoint has three broad types of commands: those that operate on a single slide, those that operate on a selected group of slides, and those that operate on the entire presentation file.

Most of the single-slide commands, such as a command that inserts an object, are executed from Normal or Notes Page views, in which you see only a single slide, so selecting the slide per se is not an issue. The selected slide is simply the one that is displayed.

Most of the group-of-slides commands, such as deleting, moving, or applying a transition effect, are best performed in Slide Sorter view. Since you see multiple slides at a time in that view, you must select the slides you want to affect. Here are options for selecting slides in Slide Sorter view:

   ✦ To select a single slide, click it.
   ✦ To select multiple slides, hold down the Shift key as you click each one. Figure 7-8 shows several slides selected.
   ✦ To select a contiguous group of slides (for example, slides 1, 2, and 3), click the first one, then hold down the Shift key as you click the last one.

To cancel the selection of multiple slides, click anywhere away from the selected slides.

Selected slides

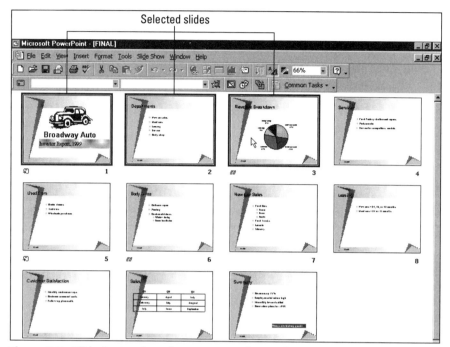

Figure 7-8: Slide Sorter view allows you to select and act on multiple slides at once.

Deleting Slides

Especially if you created your presentation using the AutoContent Wizard or a template, you may want to get rid of some of the slides. Perhaps the sample presentation is longer than your actual one needs to be, or perhaps you have inserted your own slides instead.

One way to delete a single slide is to display it in Normal view (or one of the other single-slide views), or select it in Slide Sorter view, and then choose Edit ➪ Delete Slide.

In Slide Sorter view, you can delete multiple slides at once. Select the slides to be deleted, then either choose Edit ➪ Delete Slide or simply press the Delete key on the keyboard.

If you make a mistake with deleting, you can use the Undo command (Edit ➪ Undo or the Undo button on the Standard toolbar) to undo the deletion. See the following section for more information.

Undoing Mistakes

Here's a skill that can help you in almost all of the other chapters in this book: undoing. The Undo command allows you to reverse past multiple actions. You can use it, for example, to reverse all the deletions made to your presentation in the preceding section.

The easiest way to undo a single action is to click the Undo button on the Standard toolbar. You can click it as many times as you like; each time, it undoes one action. (If you don't like using the toolbar button, you can use its equivalent menu command: Edit ➪ Undo.) Ctrl+Z is the keyboard shortcut for this command; you might find that more convenient still.

You can undo multiple actions all at once by opening the Undo button's drop-down list, as shown in Figure 7-9. Just drag the mouse across the actions to undo (you don't need to hold down the mouse button). Then click when the desired actions are selected, and presto, they are all reversed. You can select multiple actions to undo, but you can't skip around. To undo the fourth item, for example, you must undo the first, second, and third ones, too.

Redo is the opposite of Undo. If you make a mistake with the Undo button, you can fix the problem by clicking the Redo button. Like the Undo button, it has a drop-down list, so you can redo multiple actions at once. If you haven't used the Undo feature, the Redo button is not available.

Rearranging Slides

The best way to rearrange slides is to do so in Slide Sorter view. In this view, the slides in your presentation appear in thumbnail view and you can move them around on the screen to different positions, just like you would manually rearrange pasted-up artwork on a table.

Undo button   Redo button

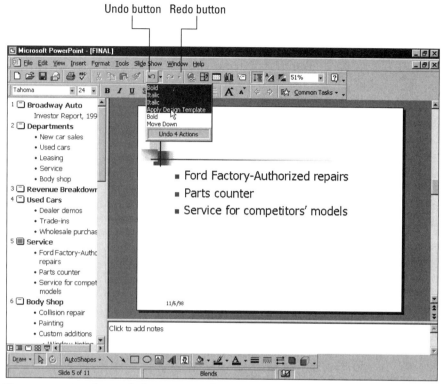

Figure 7-9: Use the Undo button to undo your mistakes.

To rearrange slides, use the following steps:

1. Switch to Slide Sorter view.

2. Select the slide you want to move. You can move multiple slides at once if you like.

3. Drag the selected slide to the new location. The mouse pointer changes to show a little rectangle next to the pointer arrow as you drag. You also see a vertical line that shows where the slide will go if you release the mouse button at that point. See Figure 7-10.

4. Release the mouse button. The slide moves to the new location.

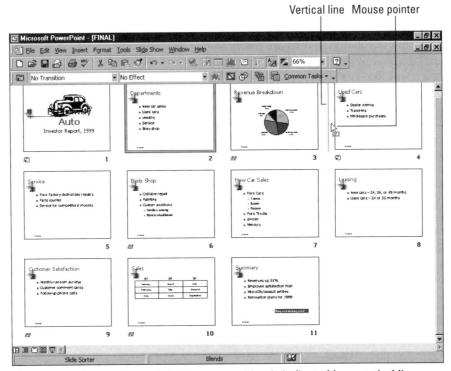

Figure 7-10: As you drag a slide, its new position is indicated by a vertical line.

You can also rearrange slides in any view that includes the outline pane. This is not quite as easy as Slide Sorter view, but it's more versatile. You can not only drag entire slides from place to place, but you can also move individual bullets from one slide to another.

Tip   You might want to display the Outlining toolbar for this task. To do so, right-click one of the other toolbars and choose Outlining.

1. Switch to a view that includes the outline pane (Normal or Outline).

2. Position the mouse pointer over the slide's icon. The mouse pointer changes to a four-headed arrow.

3. Click. The entire text of that slide becomes selected.

4. Drag the slide's icon to a new position in the outline. As you drag, you see a horizontal line showing where the slide will go. See Figure 7-11.

5. Release the mouse button when the horizontal line is in the right place. All the slide's text moves with it to its new location.

Mouse pointer

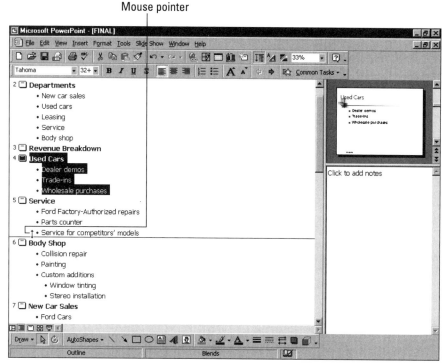

Figure 7-11: You can drag the slide's icon to move it or use the Outlining toolbar buttons.

If you prefer, instead of Step 4, you can move the slide using the Move Up and Move Down buttons on the Outlining toolbar. Just follow Steps 1 through 3 and then click one of those buttons to move the slide up or down one slide in the outline. Some people prefer to use the toolbar buttons to move a slide if the destination is out of view onscreen. That way, you don't have to try to scroll and drag at the same time to reach the slide's destination.

There are also keyboard shortcuts for moving a slide up or down on the outline. You might find that these are faster than clicking the toolbar buttons. The shortcuts are Alt+Shift+up arrow key to move up and Alt+Shift+down arrow key to move down.

All of these movement methods work equally well with single bullets from a slide. Just click to the left of a single line to select it, instead of clicking the Slide icon in Step 3.

Don't Forget to Save

At this point, you should probably save your work. You don't want anything to happen to it! Choose File ➪ Save to save it, as you learned in Chapter 4.

Summary

In this chapter, you got off to a great start with your new presentation. You learned the four ways of creating a new presentation, and, presumably, used one of them to start your own new project. You also learned about adding, rearranging, and removing slides from your presentation.

The next two chapters give you the full scoop on text editing in PowerPoint. By the time you finish them, you'll understand all about text boxes, text formatting, tables, and all the other ways to put your words on a slide.

✦   ✦   ✦

Conveying Your Message with Text

In most presentations, text is the most important element. Without your textual message, it's all just pretty pictures and flash. That's why the first thing you learn to do here, now that you've created your presentation shell, is to enter the text. Then, in later chapters, you learn how to enhance that text with graphic objects and formatting.

Creating New Slides: A Review

Take a moment to review what you learned in Chapter 7 about creating new slides. You can create a slide in either of these ways:

- ✦ On the outline, promote a line of text to the highest outline level by pressing Shift+Tab or by clicking the Promote button on the Outlining toolbar.

- ✦ Open the New Slide dialog box (Insert ⇨ New Slide or Ctrl+M) and select one of the AutoLayouts for a new slide.

You can also create new slides by importing content from other programs or other presentations, as you learn later in this chapter.

How Text Appears on Slides

Text appears on a slide in text boxes. When you create a slide from the outline, the slide has a title text box containing whatever text was in the line you promoted. The slide may also have a Body text box, containing whatever lines of text are subordinate to the title text on the outline. See Figure 8-1.

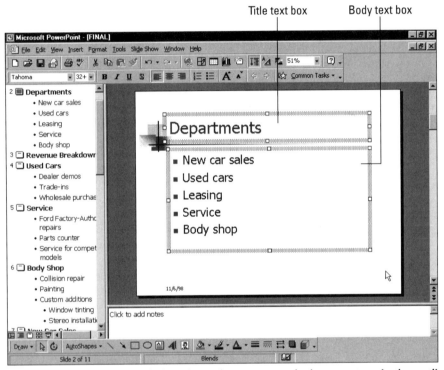

Figure 8-1: Most slides, including those that are created when you type in the outline pane, contain two text boxes.

When you create a slide from the outline, you enter your content at the same time you create the slide. However, when you create a slide with the New Slide dialog box, the content is not yet there. Placeholders mark where you should put the content. The placeholders depend on the AutoLayout you chose. Most of the AutoLayouts contain at least a Title text box, and either a Body text box placeholder or a placeholder for some other kind of object. Figure 8-2 shows the placeholders for text for a slide created with the Bulleted List AutoLayout.

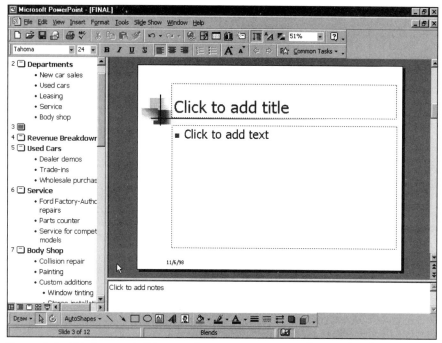

Figure 8-2: This inserted slide contains no content yet, only text placeholders.

There are two classes of text boxes. Figure 8-3 shows one of each:

✦ **Automatic text boxes.** These are the normal text boxes, the ones that correspond to text on your outline. These text boxes can be moved and resized, but not deleted. Even if you delete all the text from one of them, it is still there as a placeholder. The initial positioning and formatting of these text boxes are controlled by the Slide Master (see Chapter 11) and by the AutoLayout that you choose for the slide.

✦ **Manual text boxes**. These are special text boxes created with the Text Box button on the Drawing toolbar. The text in these boxes is not part of your outline because PowerPoint does not see the box and its contents as text—it sees a drawn object that happens to contain some letters. These text boxes can be moved, resized, and deleted.

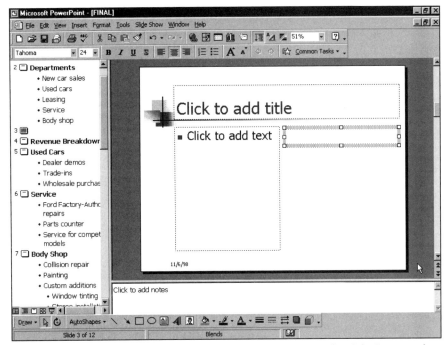

Figure 8-3: The text box on the left is automatic; the one on the right is manual.

The difference between the two may not seem significant right now, but you learn the significance later when you begin changing the formatting and layout of your slides.

Replacing Text Placeholders

If you have inserted a slide containing a text box using the New Slide dialog box, placeholders appear in text boxes on the slide, as shown in Figure 8-2. Click a placeholder to move the insertion point there, then type your text. Press Enter to start a new line, or click outside the text box to quit.

If you need to place text in a spot where there is no placeholder, change the slide's layout (Format ➪ Slide Layout), as explained in Chapter 11, so that different placeholders appear. Or see the "Adding Text Boxes" section later in this chapter to add a manual text box.

Note   Here's an interesting puzzler for you: If you type text to replace a placeholder (for example, on a Bulleted List AutoLayout slide), and then you change the slide's layout (Format ➪ Slide Layout) so that the slide no longer has a placeholder for text, what happens to the text?

Here's the answer: The text remains on the slide, but it becomes an *orphan*. If you delete the text box, it's simply gone; a placeholder for a text box does not reappear. It does not, however, become a manual text box, because its content still appears on the outline, and a manual text box's content would not.

Replacing Sample Text

If there is sample text on your slides (if you start with a presentation template or the AutoContent Wizard, for example), you must delete it and then type your own text in its place. To delete the sample text, highlight it and press Delete, or highlight it and simply begin typing; the new typing replaces it. You can do this either on the outline or the slide.

Resizing or Moving a Text Box

You can resize a text box to change how much space it takes up on your slide. You might want to do this, for example, to make room to place another object on your slide, such as a graphic. To resize a text box, drag one of its corner selection handles (white squares) with your mouse, as shown in Figure 8-4. A dotted outline shows where the box is going.

What happens to the text in a resized box? Nothing, usually. If you make a text box larger than its original size, you simply create more white space. The letters do not get bigger. (To change the size of the letters, see the "Formatting Text" section in Chapter 9.) Similarly, if you make the text box smaller, but all of the text still fits in it, that text will not change size either. However, if you make a text box so small that the text in it no longer fits, PowerPoint resizes the text so that it is all still visible. But PowerPoint remembers the original size of the text, and when you make the text box larger again, it regrows the text size to its original state.

To move a text box (without changing its size), simply drag it by any part of its border except a selection handle. Position the mouse pointer over a border so the pointer turns into a four-headed arrow. Then drag the text box to a new position.

Adding Manual Text Boxes

If there is room on the slide (or if you can make room by resizing or moving another object), you might want to add your own text box to the slide. For example, suppose you have a bulleted list on the slide, but you want to place a comment next to it in a separate column. You might add a text box to the slide to do this.

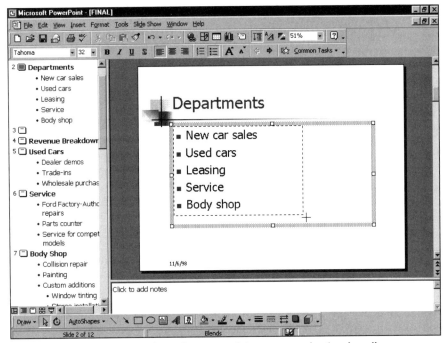

Figure 8-4: To resize a text box, drag one of the corner selection handles.

Caution

As I mentioned earlier, any text that you type in a manually placed text box does not appear on your outline. It is considered a graphic and is not displayed, even though it is only text. If you need to have two columns of text and want them both to show up on the outline, use the AutoLayout that contains two side-by-side bulleted lists.

To place a text box on a slide manually, follow these steps:

1. Click the Text Box button on the Drawing toolbar. The mouse pointer turns into a vertical line.

2. Drag the mouse pointer across the slide to draw a box where you want the text box to be (see Figure 8-5), then release the mouse button.

3. Type the text that will appear in the text box.

4. Move or resize the text box as needed.

Mouse pointer

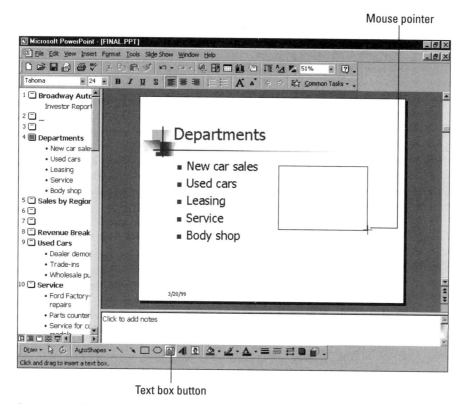

Text box button

Figure 8-5: Click the Text Box button and then draw the text box where you want it to be.

Finding and Replacing Text

Like all Microsoft applications, PowerPoint has a good built-in Find tool. It enables you to search for (and, optionally, replace) a string of text anywhere in your presentation. The feature works the same way in all views (except Slide Show, in which it isn't applicable).

Tip

PowerPoint can find and replace text in both kinds of text boxes: automatic and manual. However, it searches the outline first, so automatic text boxes get first priority. After it has finished searching the outline, it displays a message asking whether you want to search the remaining text on slides and notes. If you click OK, it looks at the manual text boxes and the notes pages.

Take a look at the Find function first because it's simpler than Find and Replace. Say Bob Smith has just gotten fired this morning. (Poor Bob.) Now you need to go through your presentation and see whether Bob's name is mentioned so you can take out any lines that refer to him. Follow these steps to find a text string (such as Bob Smith):

1. Choose Edit ➪ Find or press Ctrl+F. The Find dialog box appears.

2. Type what you want to find in the Find what text box, as shown in Figure 8-6.

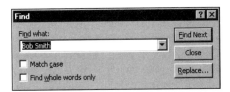

Figure 8-6: Type what you want to find, and then click the Find Next button.

Tip   If you want to find a text string that you have searched for before, open the Find what drop-down list and select it. That's faster than retyping it.

3. If you want to find only whole words or want to match the case, mark the appropriate checkbox.

4. Click Find Next. The display jumps to the first instance of the text in your presentation, starting from wherever your insertion point was positioned, working downward through the presentation, then looping back to the top.

5. If the found instance was not the one you were looking for, or if you want to see if there are other instances, click the Find Next button again until you've seen all the instances. (You get a message — The search text was not found — when that happens, and you must click OK to clear the message.)

6. Click Close when you are finished finding.

You can also do a replace, which is like a Find *plus*. The action finds the specified text and then replaces it with other text that you specify. Suppose, for example, that you are preparing a presentation for the Acme Corporation's sales staff. Two days before the presentation, you find out that Acme has just been purchased by Primo Corporation. So you need to go through the entire presentation and change every instance of Acme to Primo.

Tip   While you are using the Find feature, as explained in the preceding steps, you can switch to the Replace dialog box by clicking the Replace button. When you do so, your Find string transfers over, so you don't have to retype it.

To find and replace a text string, follow these steps:

1. Choose Edit ➪ Replace or press Ctrl+H. The Replace dialog box appears.

2. Type the text you want to find in the Find what text box. If you have previously used Find or Replace, the most recent text you found appears in the text box already.

3. Type the new text in the Replace with text box. For example, if you were replacing *layoffs* with *downsizing*, it would look like Figure 8-7.

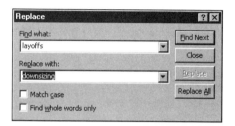

Figure 8-7: Enter what you want to find and what you want to replace it with.

4. If you want whole words only or a case-sensitive search, select the appropriate checkbox.

5. Click Find Next to find the first instance.

6. If you want to replace that instance, click the Replace button. The next instance appears automatically. Otherwise, click Find Next to go on.

7. Repeat Step 6 to check and selectively replace each instance, or click the Replace All button to change all instances at once.

8. When you are finished, click Close. (You may have to click OK first to clear a dialog box telling you that the specified text was not found.)

Importing Text from Other Pprograms

PowerPoint accepts text from a variety of other programs, so you don't have to start from scratch when building your presentation if you already have notes in another format.

The text import works best if the text is in an outline format in a word processing program such as Word or Excel. Microsoft Word has a special Outline view that you can use to create outlines much like the ones you create in PowerPoint; it is a simple matter to import such an outline into PowerPoint. Many other popular word processing programs have outline modes, too. If yours doesn't, simply format the various heading levels as different heading styles (heading 1, heading 2, and so on), or wait to assign outline levels until you have brought the text into PowerPoint. Outlines typed in columns in a spreadsheet such as Microsoft Excel are easy to import as well.

To import text from an outline, follow these steps:

1. Click the outline pane in PowerPoint in the spot where you want the new slides to be inserted.
2. Choose Insert ➪ Slides from Outline. The Insert Outline dialog box opens. See Figure 8-8.
3. Locate the file containing the outline you want to use and select it.
4. Click Insert. The text is imported into your PowerPoint presentation.

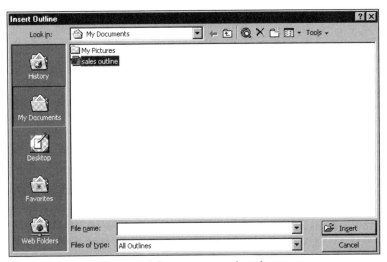

Figure 8-8: Choose a Word document or other document or spreadsheet from which to import your outline.

Importing Slides from Existing Presentations

You can also copy slides from other PowerPoint presentations into the one you are working on. If you frequently give presentations, for example, you may have a certain number of slides you use to always open a presentation. These slides might include your company name and a summary of your major products. You can set up these boilerplate slides in a generic presentation and then import them as needed into each new presentation.

1. Display the slide that will immediately precede the ones you're adding.
2. Choose Insert ➪ Slides from Files. The Slide Finder dialog box appears.
3. Click the Browse button. The Browse dialog box appears.
4. Navigate to the PowerPoint file that contains the slides you want to copy and double-click it.

5. In the Slide Finder dialog box, click the Display button. The slides in the selected presentation appear, as shown in Figure 8-9.

6. In the Select slides area, click each slide you want to copy. Use the horizontal scroll bar under the slide images as needed to see more slides.

7. Click the Insert button to insert the selected slides into the current presentation.

8. Click the Close button to close the Slide Finder dialog box. The chosen slides appear in the new presentation. The new slides take on the design of the new presentation, so they blend in with the existing slides.

Figure 8-9: Select the slides you want to import by clicking them.

Working with a Table

A table is a great way to organize little bits of data into a meaningful picture. For example, you might use a table to show sales results for several salespeople or to contain a multicolumn list of team member names.

Inserting a Table

The best way to insert a table on a slide is to start with an AutoLayout that includes a table placeholder. Follow these steps to create a new slide that uses a table:

1. Choose Insert ➪ New Slide or click the New Slide button on the Standard toolbar. The New Slide dialog box appears.

2. Click the Table AutoLayout (rightmost one in the top row) and click OK.

3. Click in the Title text box and type a title for the slide.

4. Double-click the icon above the words Double-click to add table. The Insert Table dialog box appears. See Figure 8-10.

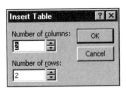

Figure 8-10: Choose the number of columns and rows you want in your table.

5. Enter the number of columns and number of rows, and click OK. A table grid appears on the slide, and the Tables and Borders floating toolbar appears, too. See Figure 8-11.

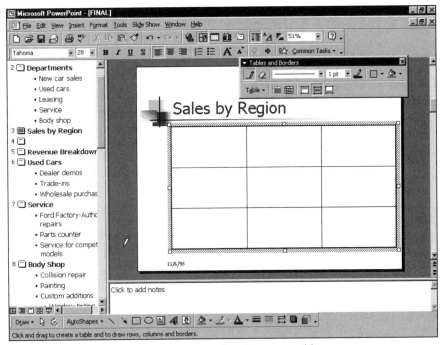

Figure 8-11: Now you are ready to type data into your table.

6. Type in the first cell of the table, and press Tab to move to the next cell. (A *cell* is a block at the intersection of a row and a column.)

7. Continue entering text in the cells, pressing Tab to move to the next one. To move to the previous cell, press Shift+Tab. You can also use the arrow keys on the keyboard to move between cells.

8. When you are finished entering text in the table, click anywhere away from it to deselect it.

The Tables and Borders toolbar appears whenever your table is selected. It contains lots of tools you can use to change your table. You look at some of them in the following sections.

Changing the Number of Rows and Columns

The most significant item on the Tables and Borders toolbar is the Table menu. Click Table to open it, as shown in Figure 8-12. If you accidentally close it, choose View ➪ Toolbars ➪ Tables and Borders to make it reappear.

The Table menu contains the following important commands that help you insert and remove rows and columns:

✦ **Insert Columns to the Left.** Adds a new column to the left of the column containing the insertion point.

✦ **Insert Columns to the Right.** Same as above, except inserts to the right.

✦ **Insert Rows Above.** Adds a new row above the one containing the insertion point.

✦ **Insert Rows Below.** Same as above, except it inserts the row below the current one.

✦ **Delete Columns.** Deletes the column containing the insertion point.

✦ **Delete Rows.** Deletes the row containing the insertion point.

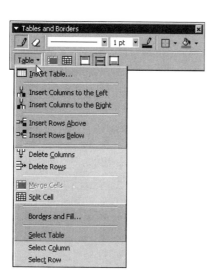

Figure 8-12: The Table menu provides commands that insert and delete rows and columns in the table.

You can select a row or column in the table by positioning the mouse pointer at the very top or left edge of the row or column—so that the mouse pointer turns into a thick black arrow—and then clicking. Figure 8-13 shows a column selected. You can also select a column by moving the insertion point into any cell in the row or column and then choosing Select Row or Select Column from the toolbar's Table menu.

To select a single cell, move the insertion point into it. To select multiple cells, drag the mouse pointer across them while holding down the left mouse button.

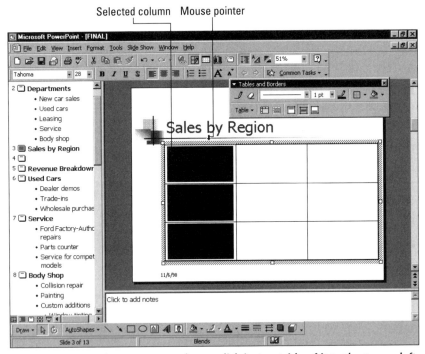

Figure 8-13: To select a row or column, click just outside of it to the top or left.

You can use any of the insert or delete commands from the Table menu on more than one row or column at a time. Simply select more than one before issuing the command. To select multiple rows or columns, select one, and then hold down the Shift key while you select another. When you have more than one row or column selected and you issue an insert command, PowerPoint inserts the same number of items as you had selected. For example, if you select two columns and then choose Table ⇨ Insert Columns to the Right, it inserts two columns to the right of the selected ones.

If you need more rows or columns in some spots than in others, try the Split Cell and Merge Cells commands, available both as buttons on the Tables and Border toolbar and as commands on the Table menu. Split Cell splits the currently selected cell into two cells, each half the size of the original. (This command is available only when a single cell is selected.) Merge Cells merges the selected cells into a single cell. (This command is available only when multiple cells are selected.)

Formatting Text in Cells

Formatting text in cells is the same as formatting any other text in PowerPoint. Turn to the "Formatting Text" section in Chapter 9 for the full scoop. (Here's a preview hint: Use the buttons and drop-down lists at the left end of the Formatting toolbar.)

Aligning Text in Cells

You can set the alignment of the text in cells both vertically and horizontally. Your vertical choices are Top, Center, and Bottom; your horizontal ones are Right, Center, and Left. Figure 8-14 shows each of the available combinations in a table. I've zoomed in on it a bit so you can see it more clearly. (Of course, it's not much of a look that way, is it? You'd be smarter to stick to a single alignment in your own table.) To set the alignment for a cell, select it (you can select more than one at a time) and then click one of the alignment buttons.

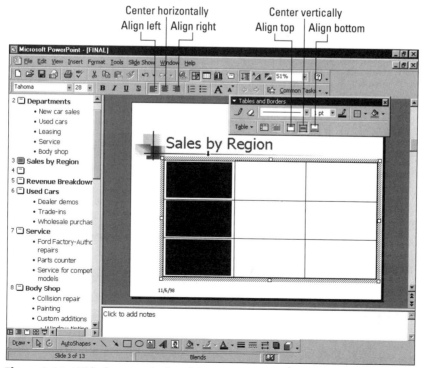

Figure 8-14: With three vertical and three horizontal alignment choices, you have nine potential combinations.

Formatting Cell Borders

The border lines around each cell are very important because they separate the data in each cell. By default, there is a 1-point (that's ¹/₇₂ of an inch) border around each side of each cell, but you may want to make some or all borders fatter, a different line style (dashed, for example), a different color, or gone altogether to create your own effects. Here are some examples:

✦ To make a list of names appear to be floating in multiple columns on the slide (that is, to make it look as if they are not really in a table at all, but just lined up extremely well), remove all table borders. In Figure 8-15, the borders on the top row have been removed, and the column headings appear to be floating above the grid.

✦ To create a header row at the top, make the border beneath the first row of cells darker or thicker than the others. In Figure 8-15, the bottom of the first row/top of the second has been assigned a 6-point line.

✦ To make it look as if certain items have been crossed off of a list, format those cells with diagonal borders. This creates the effect of an X running through each cell. (These diagonal lines are not really borders in the sense that they don't go around the edge of the cell, but they're treated as borders in PowerPoint.) In Figure 8-15, January has both diagonal borders applied.

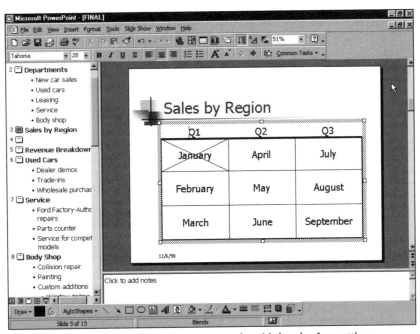

Figure 8-15: Here are some things you can do with border formatting.

To format a cell's border, follow these steps:

1. Select the cell(s) that you want to format.

Caution   When you apply top, bottom, left, or right cell borders, they apply to the entire selected block of cells if you have more than one cell selected. For example, suppose you select two adjacent cells in a row and apply a left border. The border applies only to the leftmost of the two cells. If you want the same border applied to the line in between the cells, you must apply an Inside Vertical border.

2. Select a border style from the Border Style drop-down list. The default is solid, but you can choose a variety of dotted or dashed lines.

3. Select a border thickness from the Border Width drop-down list. The default is 1 point.

4. Click the Border Color button and choose a different color for the border if desired. The colors that appear on the palette that opens are the colors from the current color scheme for the presentation. (Learn more about that in Chapter 11.) You can choose a color not shown there by clicking More Border Colors.

Note   Remember, everything on a slide, including a table, is an *object*. In Chapter 10, when you learn how to format objects, you will see a lot more about color selection tools like Border Color and Fill Color that you see in passing in this chapter. There you learn how to select custom colors, use fill effects, and more.

5. Click the down arrow next to the Border Sides button to open its drop-down list of borders. See Figure 8-16. Then click the button for the border positioning you want to apply. For example, to place the border on all sides of all selected cells, click the All Borders button, which is the one that looks like a windowpane.

6. If you need to apply the border to any other sides, repeat Step 5. If you need to turn the border off for any side that currently has a border, click the button for that side to toggle it off.

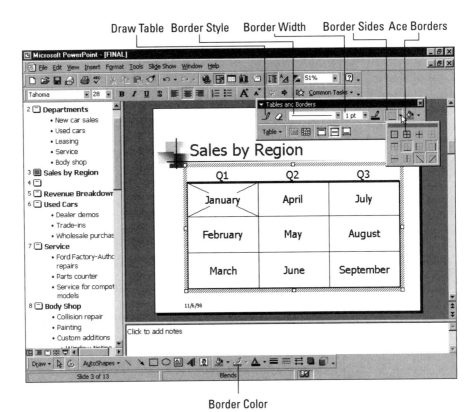

Figure 8-16: Use the controls on the Tables and Borders toolbar to format the border of each cell.

Tip

Notice the Draw Table button on the Tables and Borders toolbar. You can click it to turn the feature on, and then draw borders wherever you want them in the table. Use the Border Style, Border Width, and Border Color buttons to select the drawing color. When you are finished, click the Draw Table button again to turn the feature off.

Changing Row Height and Column Width

You may have noticed in Figures 8-15 and 8-16 that the top row, the one with Q1, Q2, and Q3, was a lot thinner than the others. That's because I resized it. To resize a row or column, follow these steps:

1. Position the mouse pointer on the border below the row or to the right of the column that you want to resize. The mouse pointer turns into a line with arrows on each side of it.

2. Holding down the mouse button, drag the row or column to a new height or width. A dotted line appears as shown in Figure 8-17, showing where it will go.

3. Release the mouse button.

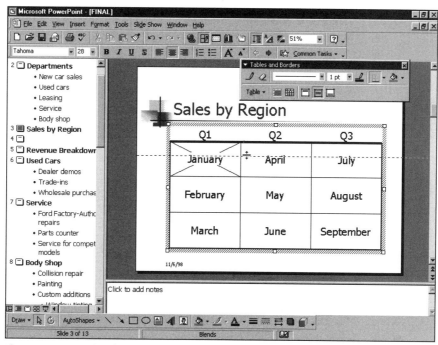

Figure 8-17: Resize the rows or columns of your table as needed to eliminate wasted space or make more room for longer text strings.

Caution Resizing a row or column changes the size of the table. If you make several rows taller or several columns wider, your table could start running off of the slide. PowerPoint does not warn you when your table exceeds the slide's area; you have to watch for that yourself.

Changing Cell Color

By default, table cells have a transparent background so that the color of the slide beneath shows through. Most of the time, this looks very nice, and you should not need to change it. Sometimes, however, you might want a different color background for some or all of the cells in the table.

To change the color of the cells, follow these steps:

1. Select the cell(s) to affect.

2. Click the down arrow next to the Fill Color button on the Tables and Borders toolbar. A palette of colors opens. See Figure 8-18.

3. Select the color you want. The colors shown are from the palette of colors used in the current color scheme for the presentation. Most of the time, you will want to stick with these colors.

Fill color button

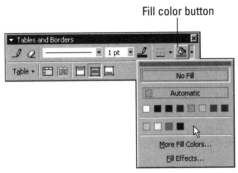

Figure 8-18: Choose a background color for the selected cell(s).

To remove the background color, repeat the steps but choose No Fill instead of a color.

There is a lot more you can do with fill color. You can choose More Fill Colors to choose a different color, or choose Fill Effects to choose gradients, patterns, or other special effects. But you can find that discussion in Chapter 10, where I explain how to do this, once and for all, for all object types generically. (It's the same, after all, for most of them.)

Summary

In this chapter, you learned how to enter and edit text in a presentation, and how to create and work with a table. These are important skills, as the average presentation is more than 75 percent text. Graphics, sounds, and other objects usually make up a very small part of a presentation. However, those objects are important attention-getters, and I cover them later in this book in detail.

The next chapter builds on this one by helping you format the text you've just entered. You learn how to change the text's color and attributes, how to modify text box backgrounds and indents, and lots more.

✦   ✦   ✦

Formatting Text and Text Boxes

When you apply a design template to a presentation (as you learn in Chapter 11), it assigns fonts to various elements (headings, body text, and so on) that work harmoniously together. Therefore, you don't want to start changing text formatting willy-nilly, or you'll end up with an inconsistent-looking mess. If you want to make a global change to the presentation (for example, format all the slide titles differently), make your change on the Slide Master. See Chapter 11 for details.

But assuming you have a good reason to make changes to your text, what can you do with it? Lots of things. You can dress it up, dress it down, move it, recolor it — the possibilities are endless.

Changing the Font

Office 2000 comes with lots of different fonts, and you may have acquired some additional fonts by installing other programs, too. Windows fonts are generic — that is, they work with any program. So a font that came with WordPerfect, for example, works with Word and PowerPoint.

A *font* is a typeface, a style of lettering. For example, compare the lettering of this book's headings to the lettering in this line of text you are reading now. Those are two different fonts.

Appearance-wise there are two basic kinds of fonts: serif (those with little *tails* on each letter, like the little horizontal lines on the bottoms of the letters *I* and *t*, for example) and sans-serif (those without the tails). The headings in this book are sans-serif and the regular paragraph text is serif.

Tip

Experts say that serif fonts are easier for people to read in long stretches because the tails make letter recognition easier. Sans-serif fonts are better for headings because they're eye-catching and clean-looking. The fonts chosen for this book were no accident! Some fonts of each kind you may have on your system include the following:

Courier (serif)

Arial (sans-serif)

Times New Roman (serif)

In your presentations, try to use sans-serif fonts for short lines of information or big headings. Use serif fonts when you're presenting a whole paragraph of text. But remember, be consistent with their usage! If the bullet text on one slide is in a sans-serif font, the bullet text on the next slide should be too.

Almost all of the fonts that you have on your system are probably TrueType fonts, so you can resize them to any size you want, from as small as 6 or 8 points to over 72 points. A point is $1/72$ of an inch; it's a measurement of how tall the tallest letter in the character set is.

To change the font or size of some text, follow these steps:

1. Select the text.
2. Open the Font drop-down list on the Formatting toolbar and choose a different font.
3. Open the Font Size drop-down list and choose a different size.

Tip

To quickly increase or decrease the selected text's font size, click the increase Font or Decrease Font button on the Formatting toolbar. These look like large and small capital *A*'s, respectively, and they bump the point size on selected text up or down by one place on the size list. This change is not always one point. If you open the Font Size drop-down list, you see that sometimes there is a larger jump between listed sizes.

Ten Great Fonts That Come with Office 2000

You get lots of cool fonts with Office 2000, but here are some that are especially good for presentations:

For headings:	For body text:
Arial Black	Arial
COPPERPLATE GOTHIC BOLD	Arial Narrow
Dom Casual	Times New Roman
Impact	Comic Sans MS
Rockwell	*Lucida Handwriting*

Changing Text Attributes

You can also change the attributes of the text. Attributes are special modifiers such as bold, italic, underlined, and shadowed. These attributes are separate from your font and size choices, because any attribute can be applied to any font at any size. Figure 9-1 shows samples of PowerPoint's available text attributes.

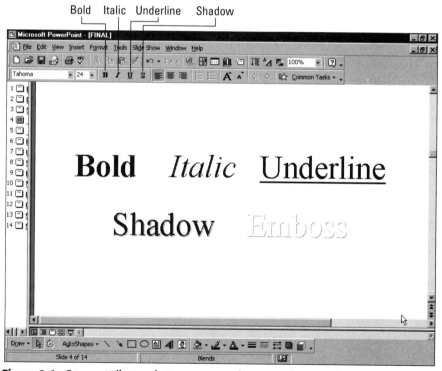

Figure 9-1: Some attributes that you can apply to your PowerPoint text.

To apply bold, italic, underline, or shadow, simply select the text and then click the appropriate button on the Formatting toolbar. See Figure 9-1. To apply embossing, you must open the Font dialog box (Format ⇨ Font) and mark the Emboss checkbox there.

Note   Also in the Font dialog box are controls for setting superscript and subscript. Superscript characters appear above the regular text, like X^2. Subscript characters appear below the regular text, like H_2O.

Here are some ideas for using text attributes:

✦ Apply the shadow attribute to make the text look richer and more 3D.

✦ Apply the italic attribute to new vocabulary words that the audience may not be familiar with; then define those terms in your speech.

✦ Make certain words bold for more emphasis.

✦ Try underlining your slide titles to separate them from the body of the slide.

✦ Avoid using underlining to emphasize a word in a paragraph; the effect looks too much like typewriter text.

Changing Text Alignment

You saw earlier how to control text alignment in a table cell; it works the same way with regular text too, except there is no vertical alignment. To align a paragraph to the left, center, or right of its text box, click one of the alignment buttons on the Formatting toolbar, as shown in Figure 9-2.

Note   Alignment refers to the text's position in its text box, not on the slide. If you want a text box centered on the slide but the text left-aligned within the box, simply move the text box where you want it.

There is a fourth alignment option, Justify, that does not come up very often in PowerPoint. If a paragraph has more than one line, this alignment option aligns all lines except the last one with both the right and left edges of the text box. It ignores the last line of the paragraph, so if the paragraph has only one line, it is essentially the same as Left alignment. Justify looks good for large paragraphs, but is of limited usefulness for the brief bullet points that are the hallmark of most slides. To use Justify, select Format ⇨ Alignment ⇨ Justify. (You can also set the other alignments from this menu, but you seldom will want to because the toolbar buttons are faster and easier.)

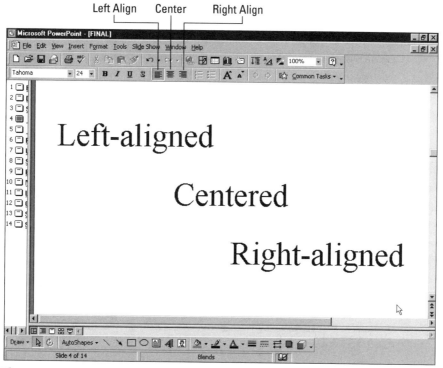

Figure 9-2: You may occasionally need to change the alignment of some paragraphs within a text box.

Changing The Text Color

Color really makes your text stand out! When you apply different design templates, the text color changes, but you can also manually change the color of any text by following these steps:

1. Select the text.

2. Open the Font Color pop-up list (on the Drawing toolbar) by clicking the arrow next to the button.

3. Choose a different color for your text, as shown in Figure 9-3. The colors shown are the colors in the color scheme currently in use in your presentation.

4. Click away from the text to deselect it and see your results.

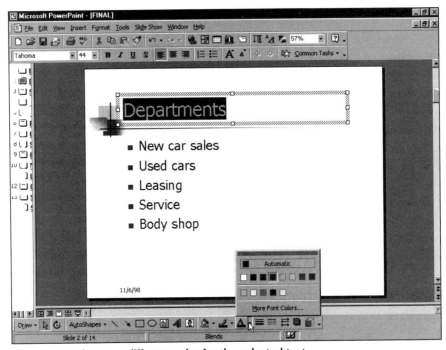

Figure 9-3: Choose a different color for the selected text.

If you don't see the color you want, click the More Font Colors option in Step 3 and choose a color from the Colors dialog box. Then, click OK. You learn more about choosing colors for text and other objects in Chapter 10.

Color is more than just decoration—you can also use it to help convey your message. Here are some ideas:

✦ Different colors connote different emotions. Choose the colors that make your audience feel the way you want. For example, choose red lettering to indicate urgency, or green to say "all is well."

✦ If you are using a dark background, try yellow lettering instead of the usual white. Yellow is a much warmer color that will make the audience feel more positive.

✦ If you are *building* from one slide to another—for example, if you're showing a list that builds from one slide to the next—make all the bullets on the list that you are not discussing at the moment a neutral color, perhaps a darker or lighter shade of your background color. Then make the one line that you are referring to at the moment a bright, contrasting color.

Text Formatting Shortcuts

Now that you know the basics for formatting text, it's time to take a look at some text formatting shortcuts that can save you some time.

Changing the Type Case

If you change your mind about the capitalization in your presentation, you can quickly change the text with the Change Case command in PowerPoint. For example, perhaps you started out thinking that you wanted all the headings to be in all capitals, but you later decided that Title Case is more appropriate (where just the first letters of all the words are capped). To make a change without having to retype, follow these steps:

1. Select the text.

2. Choose Format ➪ Change Case. The Change Case dialog box appears.

3. Click the case you want to use:

    • **Sentence case.** This is like a normal sentence, capped at the beginning and with a period at the end.

    • **lowercase** This is all lowercase letters.

    • **UPPERCASE** This is all uppercase letters.

    • **Title Case** This capitalizes the first letter of each word.

    • **tOGGLE cASE** This reverses the current capitalization and is extremely handy if you accidentally type a few paragraphs with the Caps Lock on and need to correct your error.

4. Click OK.

Changing Fonts Globally with Replace Fonts

Say your coworker created a 40-slide presentation in which he used the Carnival font. But now you need to work with the presentation on your own computer, and you don't have that font! You need to change all instances of the Carnival font to a font you have.

Another reason you might want to replace a certain font is simply because you've changed your mind. It seemed like a good idea initially to use a script font for your headings, but now that you see the entire presentation, you realize that plain old Arial would have been a better choice. In both cases, the easy way out of the situation is to use the Replace Fonts feature to replace all instances of one font with another instantly.

1. Choose Format ➪ Replace Fonts. The Replace Font dialog box opens.

2. Open the Replace drop-down list and choose the font to be replaced. Only the fonts currently in use in the presentation appear on this list.

3. Open the With drop-down list and choose the font to substitute for it. This list contains every font installed on your system.

4. Click the Replace button. Every instance is replaced.

5. Click Close to close the dialog box.

Copying Text Formatting with Format Painter

Once you get some text formatted just the way you like it, it's an easy affair to copy that formatting to some other text. This is such a great timesaver! Assume that it takes you six steps to format a particular paragraph the way you want it, with a special font, size, color, and so on. You can then use the Format Painter to transfer that formatting to another paragraph without having to go through those six steps again.

To use Format Painter, follow these steps:

1. Select the paragraph that is already formatted the way you want.

2. Click the Format Painter button on the Standard toolbar.

3. Select the text you want to change by dragging across it with the mouse.

Formatting Text Boxes

Lines and colors (sometimes called *borders and shading*) can really dress up your text boxes. They provide sort of a pseudographic effect without the hassle of creating a separate rectangle. You can place a line around a text box to make it stand out on its own. Colors (background shading) are useful within text boxes to further make the text stand out. Figure 9-4 shows an example.

There are two ways of adding lines and background colors to your text box. One is to use the buttons on the Drawing toolbar to control the fill color and the line style and color around the box. These controls are pointed out in Figure 9-4; since Chapter 10 goes into them in detail, I won't belabor them now.

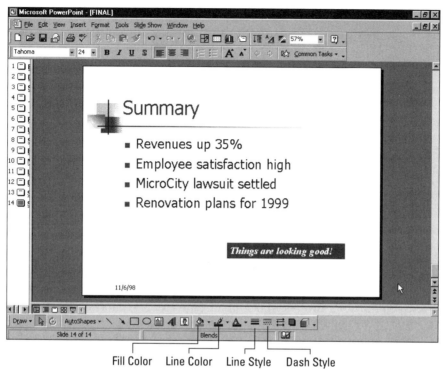

Figure 9-4: Apply borders and shading (color) to a text box to make it stand out.

The other method is to use the Format Text Box dialog box. This method has the advantage of letting you apply both a border color and an inside color at once, while if you use the toolbar tools you must apply them separately. Follow these steps to see the dialog box method at work:

1. Select the text box, so that selection handles appear around it.

2. Right-click its border and choose Format Text Box (or Format Placeholder) from the shortcut menu. The command name varies depending on whether it is an automatic or manual text box. Either way, the Format Text Box dialog box opens.

3. Click the Colors and Lines tab if it is not already displayed.

4. Open the Color drop-down list in the Fill area and choose a color. See Figure 9-5. For information about Fill Effects and the other special options listed, see Chapter 10.

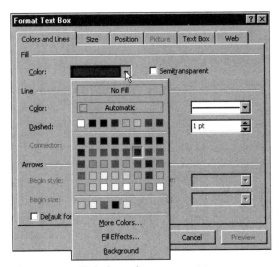

Figure 9-5: Click the color you want to use.

5. Open the Color drop-down list in the Line area and choose a line color for the border around the outside of the text box.

6. Open the Style drop-down list and choose a line style.

7. Open the Dashed drop-down list and choose a dash style, if you don't want a solid border.

8. Open the Weight drop-down list and choose a line weight, if you are not satisfied with the line weight shown in the Style box.

9. Click OK.

Adjusting Line Spacing

You might have noticed as you were typing text into a text box that when you press Enter, you start a new paragraph. By default, PowerPoint leaves a blank line between paragraphs and single-spaces all paragraphs. You can change this if you want. Here are some examples:

✦ Within a bullet list, you might want to eliminate the extra line between paragraphs so your bullet items appear closer together.

✦ If you want to make a large paragraph easier to read, you might add extra space between the lines.

✦ If you need more space between paragraphs, you could add it with the line spacing controls rather than using Enter to insert extra returns between paragraphs.

To adjust line spacing, follow these steps:

1. Select the paragraph(s) to format.

2. Choose Format ⇨ Line Spacing. The Line Spacing dialog box appears. See Figure 9-6.

Figure 9-6: Use the Line Spacing dialog box to change the space between lines and paragraphs.

3. To change the spacing between lines, change the number in the Line spacing text box. (The default is 1.) Leave the drop-down list next to it set to Lines.

Tip   For more precise measurement, open the drop-down lists that show Lines in the text box and change the settings to Points. Then you can enter the measurements by points (remember, one point is 1/72 of an inch).

4. To change the spacing between paragraphs, change the number in the Before paragraph or After paragraph text box.

5. Click OK to close the dialog box.

The line spacing is calculated as a percentage of the tallest font used in that paragraph. For example, if the largest font in the paragraph is 16 point, and you have Line spacing set to 1.5, the actual line spacing you get is 24 points: 16 × 1.5.

There is both a Before and After control, as you saw in Step 4; that's so you can specify the extra space between paragraphs as being either before or after each paragraph. In general, you should use one or the other, but not both. If you enter both a Before and After value, you may get more space than you intended. For example, if you set both Before paragraph and After paragraph to 1 line, you get one line of space before paragraph number 1, but two lines of space between subsequent paragraphs — one line after the initial paragraph and one line above the paragraph that follows it.

Setting Tabs

If you have worked with a typewriter or word processor, you are probably familiar with tabs. You set them, and then press the Tab key to move the insertion point to them quickly. Each text box has its own tab settings in PowerPoint, and you set them (as you do in Microsoft Word) with the Ruler.

Note   Unlike in Word, tab settings apply to the text box as a whole in PowerPoint, not to individual paragraphs.

To set tab stops, follow these steps:

1. View the slide containing the text box in Normal or Slide view.

2. If the Ruler does not appear, choose View ➪ Ruler.

3. Click inside the text box you want to set tabs for.

4. Click the Ruler where you want to set the tab. A little *L* appears, showing that you've just placed a left tab stop.

You can also have centered, right-aligned, or decimal-aligned tab stops. To set one of these, click the Tab Type button at the far left of the ruler. Each time you click this button, it cycles through the available tab stop types:

L	Left
⊥	Center
⅃	Right
⅃.	Decimal

Setting Indents

You may have noticed the little gray triangles at the left end of the ruler. These are indent markers; they show how far from the edge of the text box the actual text starts. They're askew in Figure 9-7 because I've got a bullet list, and the first line in a bullet paragraph is indented less than subsequent lines (to account for the bullet). In text boxes without bullets or numbered lists, the triangles align with one another by default.

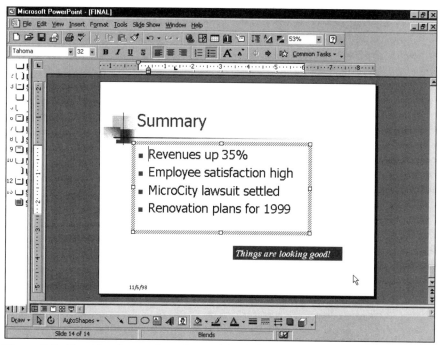

Figure 9-7: The triangles on the ruler and the little rectangle beneath them control paragraph indentation.

You can drag these triangles to change the indentation:

✦ Drag the top triangle to change the first line indent.

✦ Drag the bottom triangle to change the subsequent line indent.

✦ Drag the rectangle beneath the bottom triangle to change both triangles at once.

The paragraph indents, like the tabs, apply to the entire text box. You can't have two paragraphs with two different indent settings in the same text box. If you want this effect, you have to create a new text box to hold the second bit of text separately.

The exception to this is multilevel bullet lists. These are allowed in a single text box, as you see in the next section.

Formatting Bulleted and Numbered Lists

You have already seen how easy it is to create a bulleted list in PowerPoint. When you create a slide based on an AutoLayout that includes a bullet list, or when you type a new slide in the outline pane, you get bullets automatically.

You can turn off the bullets for any paragraph(s) by selecting them and clicking the Bullets button on the Formatting toolbar to toggle the bullet(s) off. In that same way, you can apply bullets to paragraphs that don't currently have them.

You can also format any paragraph(s) as a numbered list. This is just like bullets except numbers replace the bullets. To do so, select the paragraphs and click the Numbering button on the Formatting toolbar.

PowerPoint also lets you have lists embedded within lists, as shown in Figure 9-8. To create one bulleted list within another, go to the outline pane and select the lines that should be made subordinate. Then, press Tab to demote them in outline level.

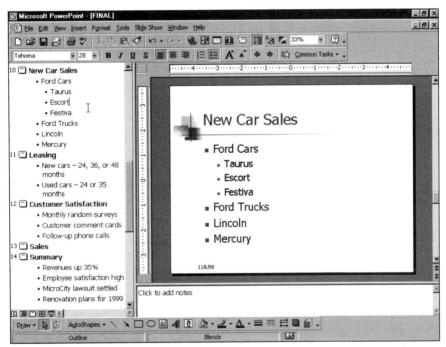

Figure 9-8: To create a multilevel outline, demote the paragraphs in the outline pane.

You may have noticed in Figure 9-8 that the bullet character is di...
outline levels. For the first level, it's a large blue square; for the seco...
red one. PowerPoint does that automatically to help keep you from get...
confused. But you can also choose the bullet character yourself for each i...

You can choose from a wide variety of bullet characters, from simple dots and
blocks to checkmarks, happy faces, and more. You can change the bullet for an
individual paragraph, for all paragraphs on the slide, or for the entire presentation.
It's all in what you select:

- ✦ To change a single paragraph, click in that paragraph before you make the
  change.

- ✦ To change all the bullets on the slide, select all of the text before you make the
  change.

- ✦ To change all the bullets in the entire presentation at that outline level, make
  the change on the Slide Master.

To change the bullet character, follow these steps:

1. Select the text as appropriate. (See the above guidelines.)

2. Choose Format ➪ Bullets and Numbering. The Bullets and Numbering dialog
   box opens. See Figure 9-9.

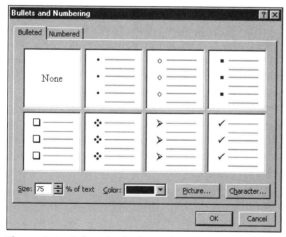

Figure 9-9: Select the bullet style you want.

s displayed. If it isn't, click it.

styles shown.

other bullet modifications:

the bullet in relation to the text, change the
x.

or for the bullet, choose a color from the Color

bullet, click the Picture button and select a graphic
et dialog box that appears. Then, click OK.

om a font (such as a symbol from the Wingdings
acter button and choose a character from the Bullet
dialog box. Then click OK.

6. Click OK to apply your bullet change.

Summary

In this chapter, you learned how to format both text boxes and the text within
them. Combined with what you learned in the preceding chapter, you now have all
the skills you need to create text-based presentations in PowerPoint.

Throughout this chapter, I've been promising that you'll learn more about objects.
The next chapter explains what objects are (basically, they're everything on a slide)
and what they all have in common. Armed with that knowledge, you'll be able to
work with almost any of the special object types, such as sounds, movies, graphics,
and so on, that you encounter later in the book.

✦   ✦   ✦

Working with Slide Objects

Everything on a slide is an *object*. That means that everything on a slide sits in its own box, and each box can be moved, sized, and formatted independently. In the last two chapters, you saw that text and tables sit in their own boxes. Here's a fairly exhaustive list of elements that can be objects on slides, and the chapters in which you can find them:

+ Text boxes (Chapters 8 and 9)

+ Imported objects from other programs (this chapter and Chapter 16)

+ Clip art (Chapter 12)

+ Imported pictures (Chapter 12)

+ WordArt (Chapter 13)

+ Lines and shapes you draw with the Drawing toolbar (Chapter 13)

+ Charts that plot data graphically (Chapter 14)

+ Organization charts (Chapter 15)

+ Sound files (Chapter 18)

+ CD audio tracks (Chapter 18)

+ Video clips (Chapter 19)

+ Action buttons (Chapter 26)

+ Hyperlinks (Chapter 26)

Most of the manipulation you can do on an object is the same, regardless of the object type. So in this chapter, I teach you those basic object-handling skills so you don't have to go over the process separately for the object types that you look at in individual chapters later.

Inserting an Object

As I have pointed out earlier, there are two ways to place an object on a slide. One is to choose an AutoLayout that contains a placeholder for that object type, and the other is to place the object manually. A brief review of both of these methods follows. More information about each object type is in the chapter later in the book that pertains to it.

Note   Most of the example figures in this chapter use simple shapes drawn with PowerPoint's shape tools on the Drawing toolbar. You might want to draw some shapes yourself on a blank slide (that is, one formatted with the Blank AutoLayout) if you want something to practice on. See Chapter 13 if you need help drawing these shapes.

Placing an Object with a Placeholder

When you choose an AutoLayout that contains a placeholder, an icon appears in the spot where the object goes, along with a message to double-click it. When you do so, a dialog box or wizard appears to guide you through the process of inserting the object. (See the appropriate chapter later in the book for the specific object type you are interested in.)

Placing an Object Manually

When you place an object on a slide manually, you don't have a placeholder to call up the appropriate dialog box for you. Instead, you click a toolbar button or choose an object type from the Insert menu (see Figure 10-1) to start the ball rolling. Then, a dialog box appears (the same one that you get with a placeholder, in most cases) and you make your object selection.

Selecting Objects

No matter what type of object you are dealing with, you select it in the same way: Click it with the mouse. Handles appear around it (white squares), as shown in Figure 10-2.

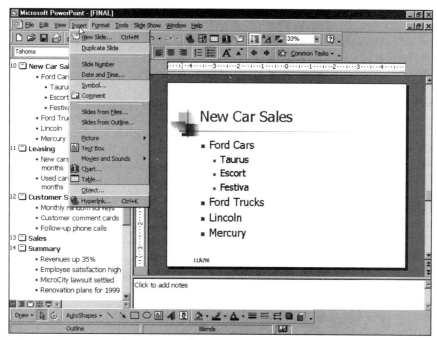

Figure 10-1: You can insert most object types from the Insert menu.

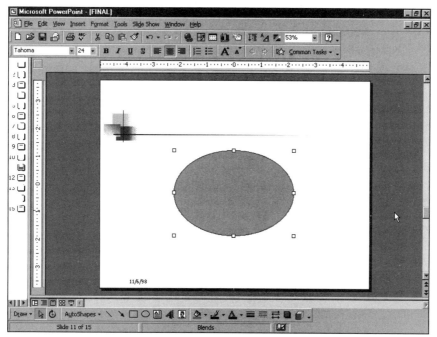

Figure 10-2: Selection handles (handles, for short) appear around a selected object.

You have learned about selecting single objects already in earlier chapters, but now it's time to go one step further and select multiple objects. For example, suppose you have drawn several shapes (see Chapter 13) and you want to select them as a group so you can move them. Or, suppose you want to move two text boxes together.

To select more than one object, click the first one to select it, then hold down the Ctrl key as you click the other one. They both become selected.

If you can't easily click each object (perhaps because they are overlapping one another), an easy way to select a whole group is to drag a box around them. For example, suppose you wanted to select all the shapes in Figure 10-3. You would drag a box around them, as shown in Figure 10-3, to select them all, as shown in Figure 10-4. To do so, click and hold down the mouse button above and to the left of the objects, and drag down and to the right until you create a box around them. Then, release the mouse button.

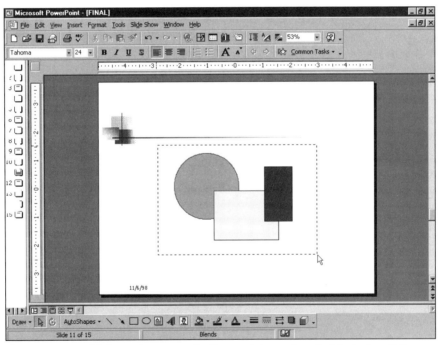

Figure 10-3: Hold down the mouse button and drag a box that includes all the shapes you want to select.

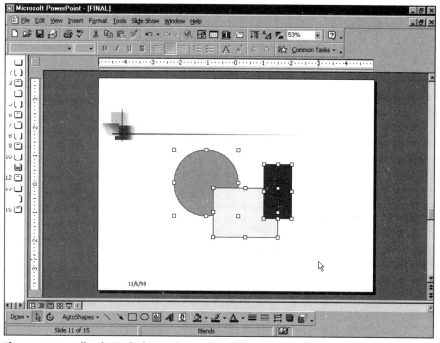

Figure 10-4: All selected objects have their own selection handles.

Moving and Copying Objects

You can move or copy objects anywhere you like: within a single slide, from one slide to another, or from one presentation to another. You can even copy or move an object to a completely different program, like Microsoft Word or Excel.

Within a Slide

To move an object on a slide, drag it with the mouse. Just position the mouse pointer over any part of the object except a handle, so that the mouse pointer changes to a four-headed arrow, then drag the object to a new location. A dotted outline shows where the object is going. See Figure 10-5.

Moving and Copying Objects

You can move or copy objects anywhere you like: within a single slide, from one slide to another, or from one presentation to another. You can even copy or move an object to a completely different program, like Microsoft Word or Excel.

Within a Slide

To move an object on a slide, drag it with the mouse. Just position the mouse pointer over any part of the object except a handle, so that the mouse pointer changes to a four-headed arrow, then drag the object to a new location. A dotted outline shows where the object is going. See Figure 10-5.

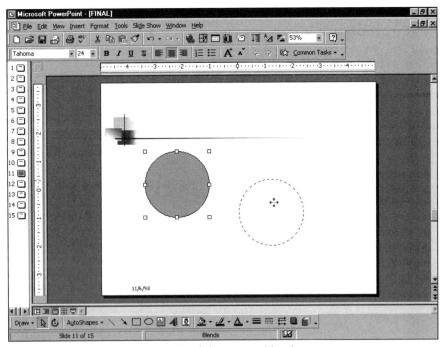

Figure 10-5: Drag an object on the slide to reposition it.

To copy an object on a slide, use the Copy command. Select the object and press Ctrl+C to copy (or choose Edit ⇨ Copy). Then, press Ctrl+V to paste it (or choose Edit ⇨ Paste). Then you can drag the copy wherever you want it on the slide.

Tip   Whenever you need to cut, copy, or paste, you have a variety of methods to choose from. There are the Cut, Copy, and Paste toolbar buttons, the Copy, Cut, and Paste commands on the Edit menu, and the shortcut key combinations Copy (Ctrl+C), Cut (Ctrl+X), and Paste (Ctrl+V).

From One Slide to Another

To move an object to a different slide, cut and paste works best. Select the object and press Ctrl+X (or choose Edit ⇨ Cut). Then display the slide where you want it and press Ctrl+V (or choose Edit ⇨ Paste).

To copy to a different slide, do the same thing except use Copy (Ctrl+C or Edit ⇨ Copy) instead of Cut.

Tip   Don't forget, if you want an object to appear in the same spot on every slide in the presentation, add the object to the Slide Master rather than trying to copy it onto every slide. See Chapter 11.

From One Presentation to Another

The best way to move or copy from one presentation to another is also with the Cut, Copy, and Paste commands. Select the object, cut or copy it, and then display the destination slide in the other presentation. Then paste.

Another way to move or copy between presentations is with drag and drop. You learned in Chapter 5 how to display multiple presentations at once by opening multiple files, using the Window ⇨ Arrange All command, and changing the Zoom in both windows to Fit, so you can see both slides in their entirety. Then you can drag the object from one window to the other to move or copy it. To move, simply drag. To copy, hold down the Ctrl key as you drag. See Figure 10-6.

Shape being copied

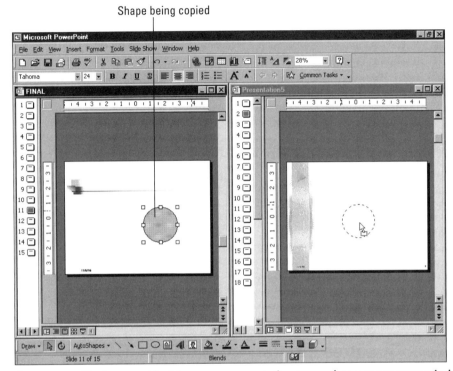

Figure 10-6: To drag an object from one presentation to another, arrange your windows so that both are visible.

Caution

An object moved or copied to a different presentation might change its color. Why? If you chose a color for the object from the initial color choices that pop up, you probably chose a color placeholder for the template rather than a particular color. For example, suppose the design template you are using comes with its own color scheme that uses 10 colors. Assume that color #3 of those is gray. If your object is formatted as color #3 (gray), and you copy it to a different presentation in which color #3 is blue, the object changes to blue when it gets there. You learn more about this in the "Changing an Object's Coloring" section later in this chapter.

To Another Program

You can also move and copy objects from PowerPoint into other programs. Suppose, for example, you have created a table on a slide (See Chapter 8) and you want to include it in a report in Word. You could move or copy it there with either cut and paste or drag and drop—your choice.

The cut-and-paste method, of course, involves the Cut, Copy, and Paste commands that you saw in the preceding sections. Select the object, cut or copy it, and paste it. For drag and drop, resize the PowerPoint window so that you can also see the destination window and then drag the object there.

Repositioning Objects

It's somewhat of an artificial word distinction, but I'm using the terms *move* and *reposition* in this chapter to mean two different things. In the preceding section, you learned how to move objects in large ways—to a totally different spot on a slide, to a different slide, or even to a different program. In this section, I show you how to move—reposition—an object just a tiny bit with the Snap, Nudge, and Align or Distribute commands. These ways of making little movements can make a big difference in your work.

For example, suppose you have three objects on a slide and you want them to all be at the exact same spot horizontally. It would be very difficult to eyeball the alignment perfectly, but you can easily use the Snap feature to snap the objects to an invisible grid, or use the Align command to align them all neatly.

Snapping

There is an invisible grid on every slide to which all objects *snap*. In other words, if you move an object and position it so that it doesn't quite align with the gridlines, when you release the object, it moves slightly to snap into alignment with the nearest gridlines. This feature is on by default. To turn it off, click the Draw button on the Drawing toolbar, and then choose Snap ⇨ To Grid. See Figure 10-7. (You may have to pause a moment after opening the Draw menu to wait for the Snap command to appear.) Repeat the same steps to toggle it back on.

Figure 10-7: Toggle the grid on and off here.

Tip   You don't have to turn the Snap To Grid feature off every time you want to temporarily override it. Just hold down the Alt key as you drag or draw an object to suspend it.

You can also turn on/off a feature called Snap To Shape (also shown in Figure 10-7). This one is off by default. It helps you precisely align shapes (for example, to draw complex pictures where one line must exactly meet another) by snapping shapes into position in relation to one another. You will not want to use this feature all the time because it makes it harder to position objects precisely in those instances where you do *not* need one shape to align with another.

Nudging

If you are one of those people who have a hard time positioning objects precisely by dragging them, you'll appreciate the Nudge command. It moves an object slightly in the chosen dimension without altering its other dimension. For example, suppose you have positioned a text box in exactly the right spot vertically but it is a little bit too far to the right. If you drag it manually, you might accidentally change the vertical position. Instead you can use Nudge Left (Draw ➪ Nudge ➪ Left), as shown in Figure 10-8.

Figure 10-8: The Nudge command lets you move an object slightly in one direction.

Aligning or Distributing

You can align or distribute objects either in relation to the slide itself or in relation to other objects. Here are some examples:

✦ You can align an object to the top, bottom, left, right, or center of a slide.

✦ You can align two objects in relation to one another so they are at the same vertical or horizontal position.

✦ You can distribute three or more objects so that the spacing between them is even.

Note   The commands on the Align or Distribute menu are not always available. They are available if you have selected Relative To from that menu (that is, if that command has a checkmark next to it), or if you have selected two or more objects (for aligning) or three or more objects (for distributing).

Aligning an Object in Relation to the Slide

To align a single object in relation to the slide, follow these steps:

1. Choose Draw ➪ Align or Distribute. If you do not see a checkmark next to the Relative to Slide command, click it to place one there.

2. Reopen the menu (Draw ➪ Align or Distribute), if needed, and choose one of the horizontal align commands: Align Left, Align Center, or Align Right. See Figure 10-9.

3. Reopen the menu again (Draw ➪ Align or Distribute), and choose one of the vertical align commands: Align Top, Align Middle, or Align Bottom.

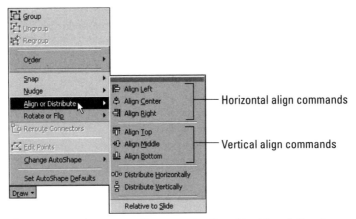

Figure 10-9: Choose an alignment for the object in relation to the slide.

Aligning Two or More Objects with One Another

You can also align two objects in relation to one another. This works by assigning the same setting to both objects. For example, in the first illustration Figure 10-10, the objects are in their starting positions. The second illustration, Figure 10-11, shows what happened when I used the Draw ➪ Align or Distribute ➪ Align Top command to move the lower object to the same vertical position as the higher one. If I had used Align Bottom, the higher object would have been moved to match the lower one. If I had used Align Center, both objects would have moved to split the difference between their two positions.

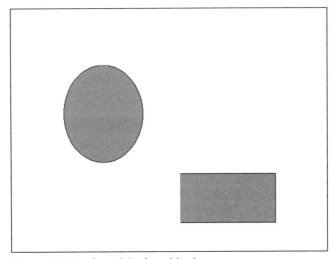

Figure 10-10: The original positioning.

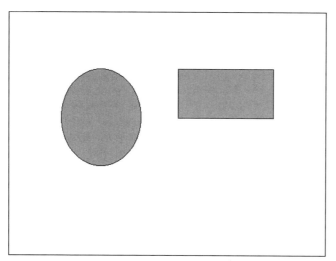

Figure 10-11: The positioning after applying the Align Top command.

To align two or more objects with one another, follow these steps:

1. Choose Draw ➪ Align or Distribute. If the Relative to Slide command has a checkmark next to it, click it to turn it off.

2. Select both objects. (To select multiple objects, hold down the Shift key as you click each one.)

3. Choose Draw ➪ Align or Distribute and then the alignment command desired.

Distributing Objects

Distribution works only in relation to the slide or with three or more objects selected. When you distribute objects, you spread them evenly over a given space. For example, suppose you have just aligned four boxes vertically, as shown in Figure 10-12, and now you want to even out the space between each box. You can apply the Distribute Horizontally command to create the uniform spacing shown in Figure 10-13.

To distribute objects, follow these steps:

1. Select the objects. To do so, hold down the Shift key while you click each one or drag an outline that encircles all the objects.

2. Choose Draw ➪ Align or Distribute and then either Distribute Vertically or Distribute Horizontally.

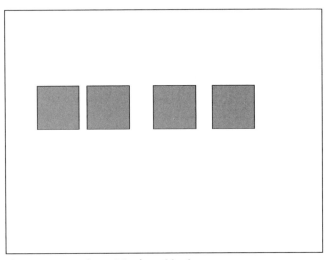

Figure 10-12: The original positioning.

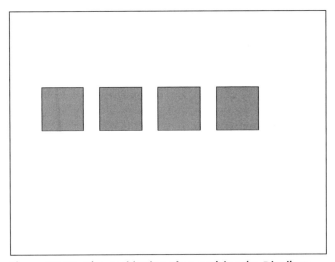

Figure 10-13: The positioning after applying the Distribute Horizontally command.

Resizing Objects

In Chapter 8, you learned how to resize a text box. All objects can be resized in this same way. Simply drag a corner selection handle to change the object's size and shape. The mouse pointer changes to a double-headed arrow when it is over a selection handle, as you may recall from resizing text boxes in Chapter 8. And a dotted outline shows where the resized object will be, as shown in Figure 10-14.

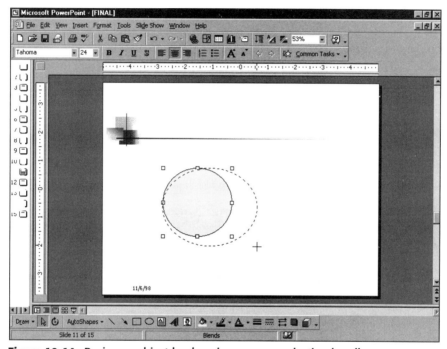

Figure 10-14: Resize an object by dragging a corner selection handle.

When you resize an object's box, the object inside usually changes its size and shape, too. For example, if the object is a graphic, the graphic gets smaller so the whole thing can continue to be seen. If you do not want this (for example, perhaps you want to crop off some of the white space around the picture), you can use the Cropping tool, which is explained in Chapter 12.

Deleting Objects

To delete an object, just select it and press the Delete key on the keyboard. That's the easiest way; other alternatives include choosing Edit ➪ Clear and right-clicking the object and choosing Cut. (Actually, cutting the object is not the same as deleting it; Cut moves it to the Clipboard, so you can use Paste to place it somewhere else. However, if you cut something, and then never paste it, it's effectively the same as deleting it.)

To delete more than one object at once, select multiple objects before pressing the Delete key.

Layering Objects

You can stack objects on top of each other to create special effects. For example, you might create a logo by stacking a text box on top of an oval or a rectangle, as in Figure 10-15. (See Chapter 8 to learn how to create a text box; see Chapter 13 to learn how to draw an oval.)

 Tip   You can also type text directly into a drawn shape without bothering with layering; simply right-click the shape and choose Add Text. You learn more about this in the discussion of AutoShapes in Chapter 13.

Drawn shape   Text box

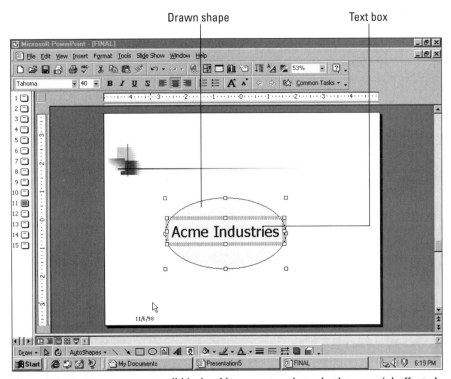

Figure 10-15: You can create all kinds of logos, artwork, and other special effects by layering objects.

Note

If you stack one object on another, the top object covers up the one underneath unless the top object's background is set to None. Text box backgrounds are set to None by default, but if you stack other objects, you may need to know how to do this. Just select the object, right-click it, and choose Format from the menu that appears. (The actual name of the format command varies with the type of object; it might be Format AutoShape if you are working with a drawn shape, for example.) Then, on the Colors and Lines tab, open the Color drop-down list in the Fill area and chose No Fill.

By default, objects stack in the order that you create them. For example, in Figure 10-15, the text box appears over the shape because the shape was created first, so it's on the bottom of the stack. You could move the shape, but it would continue to be under the text box.

If you need to reorder the objects in a stack, follow these steps:

1. Click the top object in the stack.
2. Click the Draw button on the Drawing toolbar. A menu appears.
3. Point to Order. A submenu appears. See Figure 10-16.
4. Choose the command that reflects what you want to do with the object. Send to Back makes that object the bottom one in the pile; Send Backward sends it back one position (assuming there are more than two objects in the stack).
5. Now a different object is the top one. Repeat the steps to change its position, too, if necessary. Repeat until all objects are in the order you want them in the stack.

Figure 10-16: Choose a different position in the stack for the top object.

Working with Object Groups

You have already learned how to select multiple objects and work with them as a single unit. For example, you might select several shapes together that collectively form a picture you have drawn.

If these objects are always going to be considered a single unit, you can save yourself some time by grouping them. When you group two or more objects, those objects become a single object for the purposes of moving and resizing. You can always ungroup them later if you need to work with the objects separately.

Note   Most of the clip art pieces that come with PowerPoint consist of a series of shapes grouped together to form a picture. You can ungroup a clip art picture to break it down into its pieces, and then move or delete certain pieces. You might have fun doing that as an exercise. See Chapter 12 for more information about clip art.

To group two or more objects together follow these steps:

1. Select all the objects to be grouped.
2. Click the Draw button on the Drawing toolbar. Pause for a moment until the full menu opens.
3. Click the Group command. The objects now form a group.

To ungroup, select the grouped object and choose Ungroup from that same Draw button menu.

Formatting an Object's Border

You may want to place a border or frame around an object to accentuate it. Some objects have a border by default; others don't, and you must add one if you want it.

Many beginners make the mistake of placing a drawn rectangle around an object when they want a border around it. This works, but it is inefficient. Because the rectangle and the object it frames are two separate objects, they move separately, so when you resize or move the object, the rectangle has to be moved and resized separately. (You could group the objects, but that would be another step.) A much easier way to put a frame around an object is to simply turn on the object's line.

Every object has the potential to have a line (that is, a border) around it. All you have to do is turn it on. For drawn shapes, the line clings to the shape itself and looks like someone has taken a pencil and outlined the shape. For text and graphic boxes, the line runs around the outer edge of the object frame, in the same area that the selection handles appear. Figure 10-17 shows some examples of lines around various types of objects.

Text box   Drawn shape borders cling to the shape   Chart

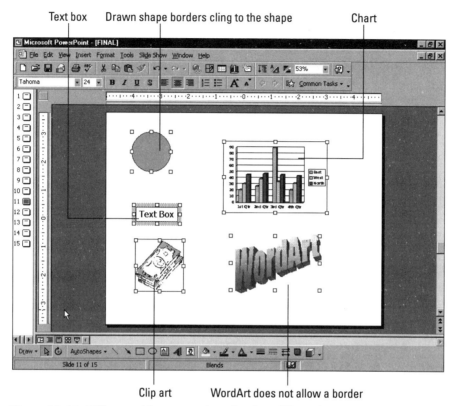

Clip art   WordArt does not allow a border

Figure 10-17: Different object types show borders differently.

The easiest way to control the border on an object is to use the buttons on the Drawing toolbar. Each of these buttons opens a pop-up list of choices.

Icon	Action
	Choose whether or not there will be a border and what color it will be.
	Choose how thick the line will be, and whether it will be a single, double, or triple line.
	Choose whether the line will be solid, dashed, or dotted.

When you click the Line Color button, as shown in Figure 10-18, the colored squares that appear are the default colors for the design template that is currently applied. If you choose one of these colors and then change the design template, the colors of the line changes, too. If you want a color that will stay put no matter what the template says, click More Line Colors to open a Colors dialog box and choose the color from there. (You see this dialog box in use in the following section.)

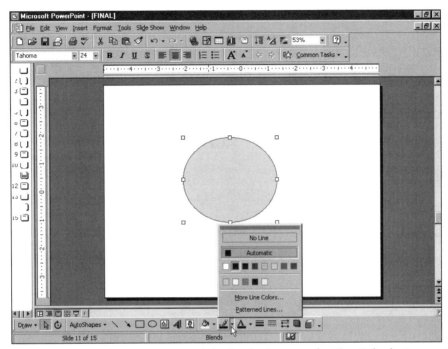

Figure 10-18: An easy way to control the border is to use the Line Color button on the Drawing toolbar.

On the Line Color button's menu, you can also choose Patterned Lines to open a Patterned Lines dialog box from which you can choose a pattern. However, unless your line is very thick, your audience won't be able to discern the pattern, and the line just looks broken.

You can also change the line color from the object's Format dialog box. (Its exact name varies depending on the object; for a text box, for example, it's Format Text Box.) Right-click the object and select its Format command to open the dialog box, then click the Colors and Lines tab, as shown in Figure 10-19. Then, choose a line color, style, weight (thickness), and dashed style from the drop-down lists there.

Changing an Object's Coloring

Almost all objects let you choose a coloring for both their fill (their inside, or background) and their line (their border). I just told you about the line controls; now it's time to look at the fill ones.

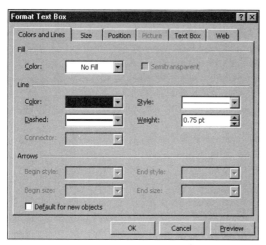

Figure 10-19: You can control an object's border with the controls in the Line section on the Colors and Lines tab of its Format dialog box.

To choose a color for an object, you can use the Color drop-down list in the Format dialog box (see Figure 10-19), but it's easier to access the same list from the Fill Color button on the Drawing toolbar, as shown in Figure 10-20.

From here, you can make several choices:

✦ Select Automatic to set the object's formatting to the default for that type of object for the design template in use.

✦ Click one of the colored squares on the first row to choose a color that goes with the chosen design template. That way, your object will not clash with the rest of the presentation. If you change templates, the object color changes, too.

✦ Click one of the colored squares on the second row to choose a color that you have previously used for an object in this presentation. Any colors you choose for an object are added here, so you can use them again.

✦ Click More Fill Colors to open the Colors dialog box and choose a color from there. (Find more on this topic in the following paragraphs.)

✦ Click Fill Effects to open the Fill Effects dialog box and choose a special effect. (Find more on this topic in the section called "Using Special Effect Fills" later in this chapter.)

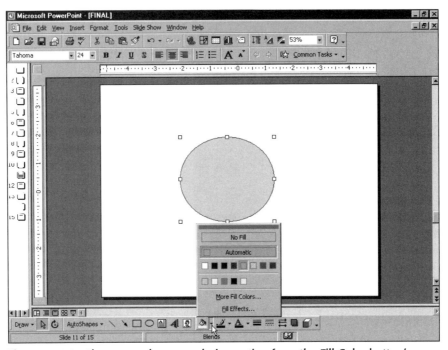

Figure 10-20: Choose a color or a coloring option from the Fill Color button's menu.

If you choose More Fill Colors from the Fill Color menu, the Colors dialog box appears, shown in Figure 10-21. You can use this dialog box to choose a color for the object that will not change even if you change the design template in use.

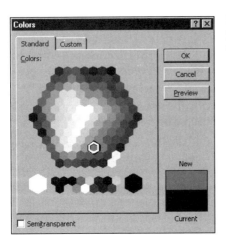

Figure 10-21: Select a color from the Standard palette or use the Custom tab to create your own color.

Most people can find the color they want on the Standard tab in the Colors dialog box. It shows a wide variety of colors. Just click the one you want and click OK.

If you need a specific color, however, you may need to use the Custom tab, shown in Figure 10-22. On this tab, you can enter the precise numbers for a color, to match, for example, the exact color for a company logo.

Colors can be defined numerically using three numbers: hue, saturation, and luminosity. You can type the numbers into the Hue, Sat, and Lum fields on the Custom tab. The hue is the tint (that is, green versus blue versus red). A low number is a color at the red end of the rainbow; a high number is a color at the violet end. Saturation refers to the vividness of the color, and luminosity is the lightness/darkness. A high luminosity mixes the color with white; a low luminosity mixes the color with black.

An alternate way to define colors is by specifying numbers for red, green, and blue. Using this measurement, a 0, 0, 0 is pure black and a 255, 255, 255 is pure white. All other colors are some combination of the three colors. For example, pure blue is 0, 0, 255. A very pale blue would be 200, 200, 255. You can play around with the numbers in fields on the Custom tab if you like. The new color appears in the New area near the bottom of the dialog box. Then, click OK to accept your choice.

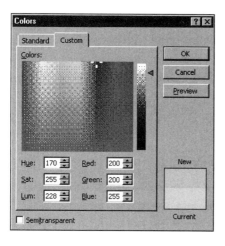

Figure 10-22: You can define a custom color for an object if you need a precise, numerically defined color.

Tip

You can create an interesting see-through effect with the color by marking the Semitransparent checkbox.

Using Special Effect Fills

If you choose Fill Effects for the object's color, a Fill Effects dialog box appears with four tabs: Gradient, Texture, Pattern, and Picture. These are the four kinds of effects you can assign to an object. They are a kind of coloring, but they do not produce solid colors; instead, they produce multicolored or multishaded patterns and textures that can create stunning visual effects!

These same special effects can be applied to slide backgrounds, as well as objects. You learn about changing a slide background in Chapter 11. To save time, I go over all the effects in detail here, and you can refer back here as needed when you get to Chapter 11.

For each of the special effects, you need to open the Fill Effects dialog box. As a reminder, here's how to do it:

1. Select the object.
2. Open the Fill Color menu from the Fill Color button on the Drawing toolbar, then choose Fill Effects.

Working with Gradients

If you've ever watched a sunset (and who hasn't?), you know how the red of the sun slowly fades into the blue/black of the evening sky. You may not have thought of it quite this way before, but that's a *gradient*. Whenever one color turns gradually into another one, it's a gradient. Gradients are often used on large shapes on logos and on backgrounds. Figure 10-23 shows an oval with a gradient fill.

On the Gradient tab in the Fill Effects dialog box, you can choose three kinds of gradients:

✦ **One color:** This gradient uses one color plus either black or white.

✦ **Two color:** This gradient uses two colors that you choose.

✦ **Preset:** This gradient option lets you select one of the preset color combinations that come with PowerPoint.

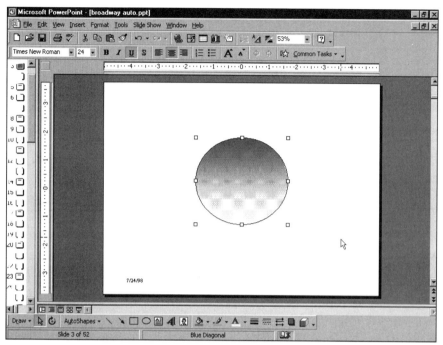

Figure 10-23: This oval has a gradient that fades from orange at the top to white at the bottom.

Setting a One-Color Gradient

If you click the One color option button on the Gradient tab, the single-color controls appear. You can use this when you want a single color to gradually fade to either white or black. See Figure 10-24

Open the Color 1 drop-down list and choose the color you want. (As with other color selections, you can choose one of the colors that comes with the template from the initial list, or you can click More Colors to access the Colors dialog box that you saw in Figures 10-21 and 10-22.)

After choosing the color, drag the slider below it to change the darkness or lightness. At the midpoint, there is no gradient at all — both colors are the chosen one. As you slide the slider toward Dark, a second color (black) begins to be used for the gradient in the Sample area. If you slide it toward Light, the second color used becomes white.

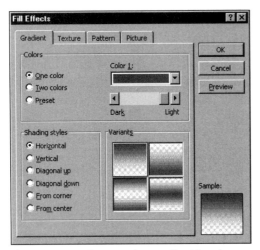

Figure 10-24: A one-color gradient involves one color plus a certain amount of either black or white.

After setting up your one-color gradient, you need to choose a shading style from the Shading styles area of the dialog box. See "Choosing a Shading Style" later in this section for details.

Setting a Two-Color Gradient

When you select the Two colors option button, the Light/Dark slider goes away and is replaced by a Color 2 drop-down list. Choose the second color you want from here. Then choose a shading style, as explained in "Choosing a Shading Style."

Using a Preset Gradient

Preset gradients are nice timesavers. When you click the Preset option button, a Preset colors drop-down list appears. You can select from a variety of preset two-color gradients with picturesque names like Daybreak and Horizon. Try each of them out, and check the Sample area to see if any fit your needs. Then choose your shading style, explained below.

Choosing a Shading Style

The Shading style determines which way the colors *run*. In a Horizontal shading style, for example, the colors run in bands from left to right, like a sunset. You can also choose Vertical, Diagonal up, or a variety of others, as shown in Figure 10-24.

Each shading style has variants. When you click a Shading style button, the variants appear in the Variants area, and you can click one of the variant examples to select it.

When you are finished, click OK to accept your choice and apply the formatting to the object.

Applying a Texture

On the Texture tab of the Fill Effects dialog box, you can choose from a variety of simulations of textured surfaces, such as marble, straw, sandpaper, and so on. Scroll through the list and find the one you want (see Figure 10-25), click it, and then click OK.

Caution   Textures can look very impressive in an onscreen presentation! You might make the background for a slide look like an oak panel or a slab of marble, for example. However, textures do not show up very well on overhead transparencies and other low-tech presentation media.

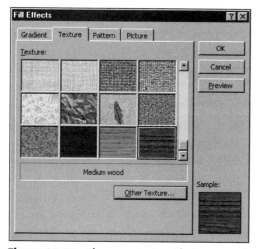

Figure 10-25: Choose a texture that you want to use to fill the object.

Applying a Pattern

Patterns are not as flashy as gradients or textures, but they have their uses. A pattern, simply stated, is an arrangement of lines or shapes of one color over the background of another color. For example, a pinstripe suit has a pattern of gray or white lines over a black, blue, or gray background. You get the idea.

To apply a pattern, click the Pattern tab in the Fill Effects dialog box and then click a pattern that you want to use. See Figure 10-26. You can choose the foreground and background colors from drop-down lists at the bottom of the dialog box.

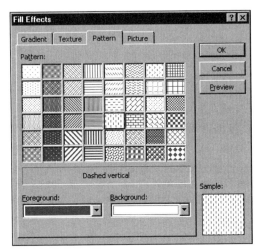

Figure 10-26: Choose the pattern you want, and select a foreground and background color.

Filling an Object with a Picture

In rare cases, you might want to fill an object with a picture. It makes for a very interesting effect, but can quickly become overdone if used too often. One good application of this is to place an AutoShape, such as a star (see Chapter 13), and fill it with a picture of a person. This makes the shape into a picture frame for the picture, as shown in Figure 10-27.

Caution It's seldom a good idea to use a picture for a slide background. It can make the text hard to read, and people may get tired of seeing the same picture over and over on every slide.

Here's how to fill with a picture:

1. Click the Picture tab in the Fill Effects dialog box. There won't be any pictures there at first; don't worry.

2. Click the Select Picture button to open the Select Picture dialog box, then browse your hard disk or network to find the picture you want to use.

Tip You can turn on a preview pane, as shown in Figure 10-28, by opening the View drop-down list in the dialog box and choosing Preview.

3. When you locate the picture you want, double-click it to return to the Fill Effects dialog box.

4. Click OK to place the picture in the object.

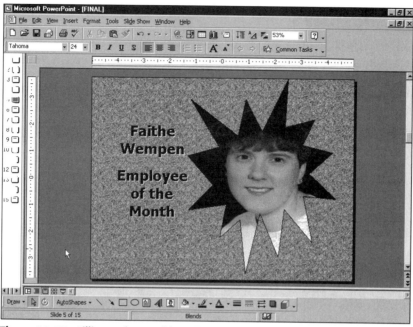

Figure 10-27: Filling a shape with a picture can make the shape into a picture frame. You may think of other reasons to fill objects with pictures, too.

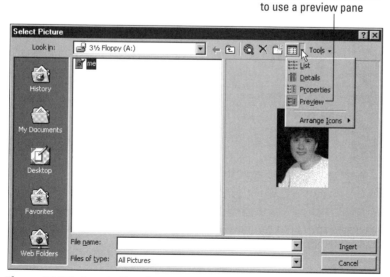

Figure 10-28: Locate the picture you want to use to fill the object.

Adding Shadows

In Chapter 9, you learned about applying the Shadow attribute to your text. But you can also apply a shadow to any object: a text box, a picture, a chart, a drawn shape, and so on. Further, the shadows you apply to these objects are much more versatile than the shadows that you apply to text. You can control the positioning of the shadow, control how far it appears to be away from the text, and more.

As you can see in Figure 10-29, different object types use shadows differently. WordArt and AutoShapes apply the shadow directly to the object. The shadow clings to the actual object. Other objects apply the shadow both to the frame itself and to whatever is in the frame if the background fill is set to No Fill. (Check out the text boxes in Figure 10-29. The top text box has a background fill set to white, while the bottom one has the background fill set to No Fill.) If an object has a background fill (even if it is the same as the color of the slide), the shadow applies only to the outer frame of the object. You can see this in the photo and the drawn shape in Figure 10-29.

Figure 10-29: Almost any object can have a shadow, but different object types apply the shadow differently.

To apply a shadow to an object, follow these steps:

1. Click the object.

2. Click the Shadow button on the Drawing toolbar. A pop-up menu appears. See Figure 10-30.

3. Click the button for the type of shadow you want. Or, to turn off a shadow, choose No Shadow.

Besides the simple buttons on the Shadow shortcut menu, there are several more sophisticated shadow controls. To see them, choose Shadow Settings from the pop-up menu. A Shadow Settings toolbar appears, shown in Figure 10-30, containing controls that help you fine-tune the shadow. See Table 10-1 for an explanation of them.

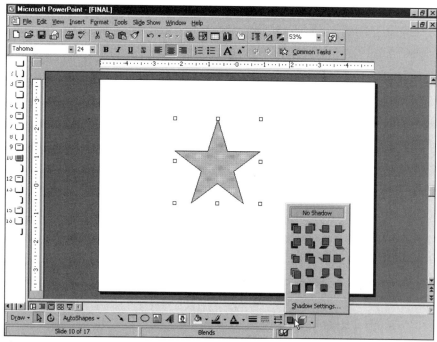

Figure 10-30: The buttons on the Shadow Settings toolbar control the shadow.

Table 10-1
Shadow Settings Toolbar Buttons

Button	Name	Purpose
	Shadow On/Off	Toggles the shadow on/off
	Nudge Shadow Up	Moves the shadow up slightly
	Nudge Shadow Down	Moves the shadow down slightly
	Nudge Shadow Left	Moves the shadow to the left slightly
	Nudge Shadow Right	Moves the shadow to the right slightly
	Shadow Color	Opens a drop-down list of colors for the shadow

Once you apply a basic shadow to an object, the Nudge buttons can help you increase or decrease the height and width of the shadow. For example, you might want to make a shadow more prominent, to make it more obvious that the shadow is there. The larger the shadow, the greater the effect of the object floating on the slide.

 Caution   If you change the shadow color, make sure you stick with a color that is darker than the object. Lighter-colored shadows do not look realistic.

Adding 3D Effects

Although similar to shadows, 3D effects make an object look like it has sides, like it's ready to jump off the slide. You can use 3D effects, for example, to make a circle look like a pillar, or a rectangle look like a box.

You can use either a shadow or a 3D effect on an object, but not both. When you apply one, it cancels the other.

To apply a 3D effect, follow these steps:

1. Select the object.

2. Click the 3-D button on the Drawing toolbar. A pop-up menu of effects appears. See Figure 10-29.

3. Click the button for the type of 3D effect you want. Or, to turn the 3D effect off, choose No 3-D.

Click here for the toolbar   Pop-up menu

Figure 10-31: Choose a 3D effect from the menu to apply to your object.

There is also a special toolbar for 3D effects, which you can display by choosing 3-D

Table 10-2
3D Settings Toolbar Buttons

Button	Name	Purpose
%a	3-D On/Off	Toggles the 3D effect on/off
⬆	Tilt Down	Rotates the shape down slightly
⬆	Tilt Up	Rotates the shape up slightly
<▷	Tilt Left	Rotates the shape left slightly
<▷	Tilt Right	Rotates the shape right slightly
🖐	Depth	Opens a list on which you can select the depth of the 3D effect

Continued

		Table 10-2	

Button	Name	Purpose
	Direction	Opens a list on which you can select the direction of the 3D effect
	Lighting	Opens a list on which you can select where the "light" is coming from for the object shading
	Surface	Opens a list of surface types for the object
	3-D Color	Opens a list of colors for the 3D sides of the object

Summary

This chapter taught you how to format objects. These skills will come in very handy in the upcoming chapters, as you learn to place specific types of objects on your slides, because you will know right away how to change their appearance once you get them onto the slide. Whether it's a chart, a piece of clip art, or a drawn shape, you'll know just what to do with it.

In the next chapter, expect to shift gears a bit and learn about changing the appearance of entire slides and entire presentations. You learn how to apply different slide AutoFormats and design templates, and how to change the color scheme and the background design used on a slide.

✦   ✦   ✦

Improving the Visual Impact

Changing the Presentation's Look

Changing an Individual Slide's Layout

Now that you have a basic presentation started, let's make it better. In this chapter you'll learn how to apply different formatting to change your presentation's appearance.

Most of the slide formatting you learn about in this chapter affects the entire presentation. But before getting into that, take a moment to review the process for changing a slide's layout.

Recall from earlier chapters that AutoLayouts control what placeholders appear on a slide. When you insert a new slide into your presentation, you choose which AutoLayout to use. There are over a dozen AutoLayouts, each suited for a particular combination of slide elements.

Note If you created a presentation with sample content, or if you created slides from the outline pane, those slides use the Bullet List AutoLayout, the default layout.

When you change a slide's AutoLayout, any content that you inserted using a placeholder remains, but new placeholders appear for the new AutoLayout. So, for example, suppose you create a slide with the Bullet List AutoLayout, and then you change to an AutoLayout for an organization chart. The bullet list remains on the slide, but the placeholder box for the organization chart runs over the top of it. The two elements can coexist on the slide, but you must resize the boxes so they don't overlap.

To change the AutoLayout in use for a slide, follow these steps:

1. Select the slide.

2. Choose Format ⇨ Slide Layout. The Slide Layout dialog box opens. It looks just like the New Slide dialog box you saw back in Chapter 7.

3. Click the new layout you want for the slide. See Figure 11-1.

4. Click Apply to apply the new layout.

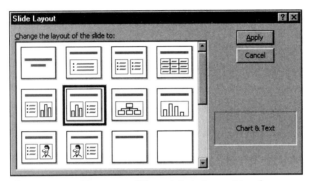

Figure 11-1: Choose a different AutoLayout to change the placeholders that appear on the slide.

Tip   Sometimes it can make more sense to switch to a Blank AutoLayout and then add the objects to the slide manually. If you don't see an AutoLayout that reflects the slide objects you want to include, consider building your own with a blank slide.

Using a Different Slide Size and Shape

One of the questions on the AutoContent Wizard is what format you plan to use for the presentation. This is an important question because the presentation format determines the appropriate size and shape for the slides. Slides designed for an onscreen display are sized to fit the dimensions of a computer screen; slides destined for a 35mm slide projector are a different size.

If you used the AutoContent Wizard to create your presentation, your slides are probably already the right size and shape. If you created the presentation in another way, however, you might want to check the size and shape to make sure it is what you want. You should do this before getting too far into your final presentation polishing, because changing the size of the slides may throw manually placed content off a little bit. (Perhaps a graphic you have placed is no longer in exactly the same spot, for example.)

Here are the slide sizes and shapes you can choose from:

✦ **Onscreen show:** 10 × 7.5 inches, resized on the fly as needed to fill the monitor in use. (This is the default size.)

✦ **Letter paper:** 10 × 7.5 inches, which is an 8.5 × 11 sheet of paper with a one-half-inch margin on each side.

✦ **A4 paper:** 10.83 × 7.5 inches, which is an alternate paper size (210 × 297mm) popular in European countries.

✦ **35mm slides:** 11.25 × 7.5 inches, which is wider than computer screens.

✦ **Overhead:** 10 × 7.5 inches, because overhead projection screens are often slightly more square than 35mm slides.

✦ **Banner:** 8 × 1, which is a specialty format good for banner graphics on Web pages.

✦ **Custom:** Enter your own dimensions.

You can also control the orientation of the slides. The default is Landscape, which is wider than it is tall. The alternative is Portrait, which is taller than it is wide. Almost all presentation formats use Landscape; you will rarely find a projector or presentation medium that requires Portrait.

To check and change (if needed) the slide dimensions and orientation, do the following:

1. Choose File ➯ Page Setup. The Page Setup dialog box appears, showing the current settings. See Figure 11-2.

2. Open the Slides sized for drop-down list and choose the format for the presentation.

3. If you choose Custom in Step 2, enter the exact width and height needed.

4. If you want the slide numbering to start at a number other than 1, enter it in the Number slides from box. (You might want this, for example, if a show is a continuation of another show.)

5. In the Slides area, choose Portrait or Landscape. The default is Landscape.

6. In the Notes, handouts & outline area, click Portrait or Landscape. The default is Portrait, because the printed pages are usually printed on regular paper.

7. Click OK.

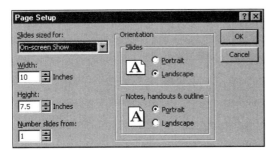

Figure 11-2: Change the file size and orientation in the Page Setup dialog box.

Changing the Color Scheme

Each design template comes with at least two color schemes. Besides the default colors, you can choose from at least one alternative coloring without abandoning your chosen design. For example, if the default coloring for a template is a dark background, an alternative color scheme might provide a light or white background. There may also be a grayscale color scheme for creating presentations in black and white.

You can change the color scheme for an individual slide or for the entire presentation. Most experts agree that you should not vary the color scheme from slide to slide; it should remain consistent. Therefore, if you are going to change the coloring for a single slide, make sure you have a compelling reason. For example, you might want to start a presentation out with a black-and-white color scheme, and then at the height of the drama — the point where you introduce your new product or your most important message — you switch to full color.

To change the color scheme, follow these steps:

1. If you want the change to affect certain individual slides, select them in Slide Sorter view.

2. Choose Format ➪ Slide Color Scheme. The Color Scheme dialog box opens.

3. Click one of the color schemes shown. Depending on the template you used, there may be two, three, four, or even more of them to choose from. See Figure 11-3.

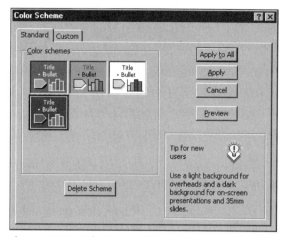

Figure 11-3: Select one of the alternative slide color schemes.

4. (Optional) To change some of the colors in the chosen scheme, click the Custom tab. See Figure 11-4.

5. Click the colored square next to the element you want to change (for example, Background).

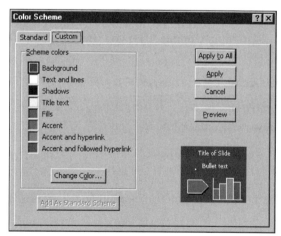

Figure 11-4: You can change any of the individual colors in the scheme from the Custom tab.

6. Click the Change Color button. The Background Color dialog box appears.

Note   Remember, you worked with a Colors dialog box in Chapter 10, and I said you would see it again often? Well here it is again in Step 6. Select a Standard or Custom color just as you learned to do there.

7. Select the color you want from either the Standard or Custom tab and then click OK.

8. Repeat Steps 5 through 7 for each color you want to change.

9. (Optional) To save the new colors as a scheme (so it will appear on the Standard tab), click the Add As Standard Scheme button.

10. Click the Apply to All button to apply the new colors to all slides in the presentation, or click Apply to apply it only to the selected slides.

Tip   You can see how your changes are shaping up without closing the dialog box. Just click Preview and then drag the title bar of the dialog box to move it off to the side so you can see the slide underneath.

Changing the Background

One way to change the slide background, as you just saw, is to change its color in the color scheme. Another way is to apply a different design template, which you see later in this chapter.

But there is also a very direct method of changing the slide background: the Background command. You can use this command whenever the other colors are fine and you don't need a new template applied, yet you want a different background behind your slides.

A background can be a plain color, but it can also be a gradient pattern, a graphic image, or a texture. Backgrounds can be all kinds of interesting things! Remember learning about applying special fill effects to objects in Chapter 10? Well, those same special fills work really well for backgrounds, too.

To change the background, follow these steps:

1. If you want to change the background only for certain slides, select them in Slide Sorter view. (It's best to keep the background consistent for all slides, though.)

2. Choose Format ➪ Background. The Background dialog box appears.

3. Open the drop-down list (see Figure 11-5) and choose one of the following:

   • A colored square from the first row, to select one of the colors from the template.

   • A colored square from the second row, to select a color that you have previously used in this presentation.

- More Colors, to open the Colors dialog box to choose a color.

- Fill Effects, to open the Fill Effects dialog box to choose a pattern, texture, gradient, or picture.

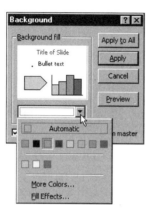

Figure 11-5: Choose a background color or effect.

4. If you chose More Colors or Fill Effects, use the dialog box that appears to make your selection. See Chapter 10 for details.

5. In the Background dialog box, click Apply to All to apply the change throughout the presentation, or click Apply to apply it only to the selected slides.

Tip

Some templates include background graphics that run over the top of the selected background color or pattern. To omit these from your slide(s), select the Omit background graphics from master checkbox in the Background dialog box, or remove them manually from the Slide Master, which you learn about later in this chapter.

Ten Great Background Ideas

Not sure what background might be appropriate for your show? Here are some ideas and suggestions.

1. If you're presenting a speech about wildlife or nature, use scanned pictures of nature scenes as the backgrounds for your slides. Use a different one for each slide, so the audience doesn't get bored. Choose them from the Picture tab of the Fill Effects dialog box.

2. For a subtle look that is more interesting than a plain background, try using a patterned background where the foreground and background colors are very similar (perhaps a dark blue and an even darker blue).

3. Use the Green Marble texture for a cool, expensive feel.

4. Use one of the wood textures (Walnut, Oak, or Medium Wood) for a warm, rich feel.

5. Try a one-color gradient behind your title slide with the From Title shading style to make it look like a subtle burst of color is centering on the title.

6. Then, use a different gradient shading style with the same coloring for the other slides in the presentation.

7. If your company has a particular color associated with it (for example, IBM has a certain shade of blue), find out the exact numeric specification for it, and build it using the Custom tab in the Colors dialog box.

8. If you are not sure what design template you will be using for the final presentation, choose one of the colors on the top row of the drop-down list in the Background dialog box. Then, if the design template changes, and with it the colors used, the background will also change so it won't clash.

9. For a dramatic build in a presentation, start with a drab background on the first slide, such as gray or pale tan, and gradually, with each slide, change the background color to a brilliant white or yellow.

10. To return to the default background color or shading for the template in use, choose Automatic as the background color.

Changing the Presentation Design

By now, you are probably quite familiar with design templates and how they work. (If not, refer to Chapter 7.) Design templates give your presentation its backbone of appearance choices: colors, fonts, backgrounds, and so on. You can choose a design template when you create the presentation or you can apply one later.

When you apply a design template to your presentation, all the colors and formatting change, but you do not get any sample content that the template might contain. You get sample content only if you start a new presentation based on that template. (Remember, not all templates even *have* sample content; only the ones designated presentation templates do. All templates, however, have formatting you can borrow.)

To change the design, follow these steps:

1. Choose Format ⇨ Apply Design Template. The Apply Design Template dialog box opens.

2. If you do not see a preview pane, as shown in Figure 11-6, open the Views drop-down list and choose Preview.

Up one level button   View button

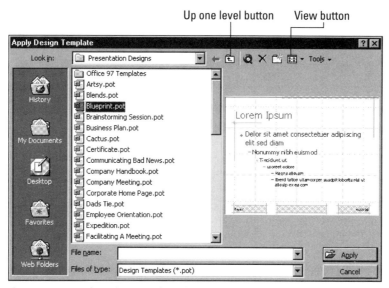

Figure 11-6: Select the template that contains the formatting you want to borrow.

3. (Optional) If you want to browse the presentation templates that contain sample content, click the Up One Level button, then double-click the Presentations folder.

4. When you find the template that looks like it has the formatting you want, click Apply.

 Tip   You can create your own templates containing the formatting that you like to use, and then apply that template's design to all the presentations you create. Just save your work as a template. See Chapter 4 for information about saving.

Ensuring Consistency with the Slide Master

As I mentioned earlier in the book, the Slide Master is a template that affects each slide in the presentation. When you apply a design to a presentation, you are really applying it to the Slide Master, and thereby affecting every slide in the presentation. The Slide Master is shown in Figure 11-7.

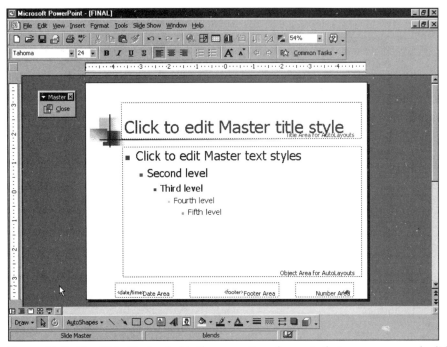

Figure 11-7: The Slide Master holds the repeating elements that appear on each slide.

To open the Slide Master, choose View ➪ Master ➪ Slide Master. You do not have to have the Slide Master open in order to apply a different template, but you might want to open the Slide Master in order to manually add, edit, and delete objects on it. You can move things around, change colors and patterns, and a lot more. Anything that you can do to a regular slide, you can do to the Slide Master, and thereby affect all the slides in the presentation at once.

Caution

Take a moment to think about what you want to do, and why you think it's best done to the Slide Master. Not all changes are appropriate to make to the Slide Master; some are better made to individual slides. You wouldn't want the same chart to appear on every single slide, for example! However, other additions — such as a company logo — do need to appear on each slide. It is this latter kind of object that you can add to your Slide Master to save yourself the time and trouble of adding it individually to every slide.

For example, with the Slide Master you can make several types of changes:

✦ Change the positioning of the title and the text box on each slide by moving these boxes on the Slide Master.

✦ Change the bullet characters used by default for various bullet list levels by selecting a level in the Slide Master's text box and changing its character.

- ✦ Remove the placeholders at the bottom of the Slide Master for the current date and/or the page number.

- ✦ Change the font used, the text alignment or color, or any other text formatting.

- ✦ Place the slide number and/or date and time in some other spot on the slide by clicking where you want it and choosing Insert ➪ Page Number or Insert ➪ Date and Time.

When you are finished working with the Slide Master, click the floating Close button to go back to your normal slides.

In addition to the Slide Master, PowerPoint includes three other masters: Title Master, Handout Master, and Notes Master. Title Master is just like Slide Master except it is for the slides that use the Title AutoLayout. The Title Master exists because the title slide often needs to be different in font size and text placement, and may have other differences, too. The Handout Master controls the elements that go on the handouts you print, and the Notes Master controls how the notes pages you print will appear. To open one of these masters, choose View ➪ Master and then the one you want. You learn more about the Notes Master and Handout Master in Chapter 21.

Summary

In this chapter, you learned how to change the background, color scheme, and overall design of the slides in your presentation. Now you can modify not only the objects that you place, but the background on which they appear. You also learned how to modify the global settings for the presentation by displaying and working with the Slide Master.

In the next chapter, you can have some fun with the Clip Gallery, and learn to insert clip art, scanned images, and other pictures. I also teach you how to modify any image in PowerPoint, to crop it, change its properties, and so on.

✦   ✦   ✦

Adding Clip Art and Other Images

◆ ◆ ◆ ◆

In This Chapter

Working with the
Clip Gallery

Finding clips

Downloading more
clips from the Internet

Inserting scanned
images

Editing graphics

◆ ◆ ◆ ◆

The Clip Gallery is PowerPoint's organizer for clip art and images, sounds, and videos. In this chapter, you tackle it from the perspective of clip art and images, and then in later chapters you revisit it for sounds and videos.

Note   If you are upgrading from PowerPoint 97, you'll notice that the Clip Gallery has been completely revamped. It's much easier to use now, but the new controls take some getting used to.

Clip art is predrawn art that comes with PowerPoint. There are hundreds of common images that you can use royalty-free in your work, without having to draw your own. For example, suppose you are creating a presentation about snow skiing equipment. Rather than going to the expense of hiring an artist to draw a picture of a skier, you can use one of PowerPoint's stock drawings of skiers and save yourself a bundle. And the audience will be none the wiser if you choose the clip art thoughtfully.

Inserting Clip Art into PowerPoint

To open the Clip Gallery and choose a drawing, follow these steps:

1. Display the slide on which you want to place the clip art.

2. If it's handy, insert the PowerPoint (or Office) CD in your CD-ROM drive. If you do this, the Clip Gallery's picture listing includes all the extra artwork on the CD. If you don't, the Clip Gallery includes a much smaller list of artwork.

3. If the slide has a clip art placeholder (i.e. "Double-click to add clip art"), double-click it.

Or, to place clip art manually, choose Insert ➪ Picture ➪ Clip Art, or click the Clip Art button on the Drawing toolbar.

Either way, the Clip Gallery appears. (If you are inserting the clip manually, it's called Insert Clip Art, but it's the same box otherwise.) See Figure 12-1.

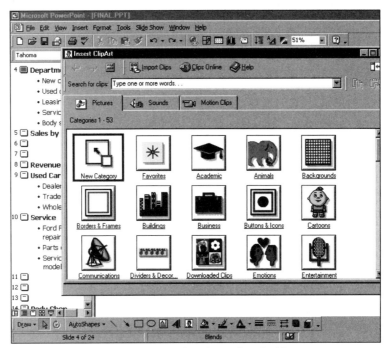

Figure 12-1: The Pictures tab in the Clip Gallery holds the clip art that PowerPoint provides.

4. Scroll through the list of categories and click the category you want to see.

5. If you find a clip you want to use, click it. A pop-up menu of icons appears, as shown in Figure 12-2.

6. Click the top button, which is Insert Clip.

7. Click the Close (X) button to close the Insert ClipArt dialog box.

Click All Categories to go back to the list of categories   Click here to insert the clip

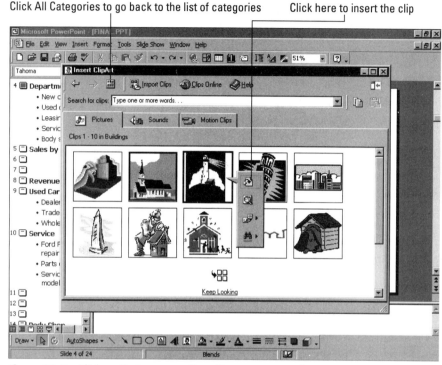

Figure 12-2: Click a clip to open a list of icons representing things you can do to it.

Tip

The All Categories button takes you back to the list of categories. There is also a Back button (the left-pointing arrow button) that takes you back to the preceding screen. In the case of the steps above, that would be the list of categories, but as you work more with the Clip Gallery, the preceding screen may not always be that one.

The second button in Figure 12-2 is Preview. If you click that one, a Preview window pops up showing the clip in a larger size, as in Figure 12-3. When you are finished looking at a preview, click the Close (X) button in its corner or click the Preview button again to close it and return to the Clip Gallery.

Tip

You can keep the list of categories open and open a new Clip Gallery window containing a category's clips. Just right-click the category and choose Open in New Window.

Click here to preview

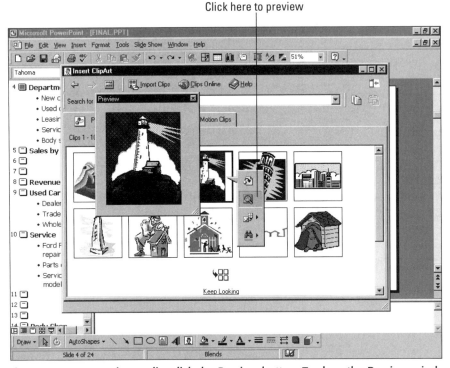

Figure 12-3: To preview a clip, click the Preview button. To close the Preview window, click its Close (X) button or click the Preview button again.

Choosing Appropriate Art

Don't just slap down any old image in your presentation! You must never use clip art simply because you can; it must be a strategically calculated decision. Here are some reasons for using art, and ways to make it look good:

✦ If your message is very serious, or you are conveying bad news, don't use clip art at all. It looks frivolous in such situations.

✦ Use cartoonish images only if you specifically want to impart a lighthearted, fun feel to your presentation.

✦ PowerPoint's Clip Gallery comes with several styles of drawings, ranging from simple black-and-white shapes to very complex shaded color drawings. Try to stick with one type of image rather than bouncing among several drawing styles.

✦ Use only one piece of clip art per slide. Don't use clip art on every single slide, or it gets overpowering.

✦ Don't repeat the same clip art on more than one slide in the presentation unless you have a specific reason to want to do so.

✦ If you can't find a clip that's exactly right for the slide, don't use a clip at all. It is better to have none than to have an inappropriate image.

✦ If clip art is important, buy more. Don't try to struggle along with the clips that come with PowerPoint; impressive clip art collections are available at reasonable prices at your local computer store.

Working with Clip Categories

In the preceding steps, you narrowed down the type of clip you were searching for by picking a category. Besides using these categories, you can create your own categories, and you can add clips to a special category called Favorites, where you can store the clips that you use often for easy access.

Clips are not exclusive to one category or another. The same clip can appear in several different categories. If you add a clip to the Favorites category, for example, it also continues to appear in its original category, too. So don't worry about messing up the original organization scheme.

Creating a Category

To create your own category, follow these steps:

1. In the Clip Gallery's list of categories, click New Category. The New Category dialog box opens.
2. Type the name for your new category. See Figure 12-4.
3. Click OK. The new category is created.

Figure 12-4: Create new categories as needed to help you manage your clips.

Adding Clips to a Category

Next, you need to add some clips to your new category. One way to do this is to locate a clip you want to place there and then copy it into your category. Follow these steps:

1. In the Clip Gallery, locate the clip that you want to copy into another category.
2. Click the clip. The menu of four buttons appears, as you saw earlier.
3. Click the third button, Add Clip to Category. A text box pops open, as shown in Figure 12-5.
4. Open the drop-down list and choose the category to add the clip to.
5. Click Add.

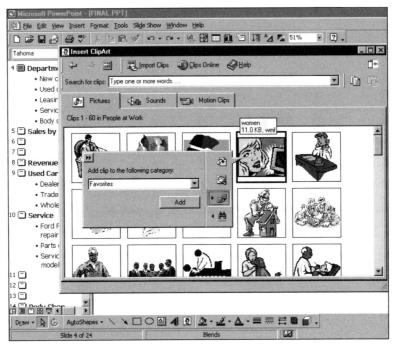

Figure 12-5: Add the chosen clip to Favorites, to the category you just created, or to any other category.

Notice in Figure 12-5 that the default category to add to is Favorites. You can add any clip to any category, but Favorites is the easiest to work with, since it always exists and it is usually at the top of every category list.

Searching by Clip Keywords

Another way to work with clip art is with keywords. In addition to belonging to one or more categories, each clip has one or more keywords that help identify its subject. You can search for clips on certain subjects by typing one or more keywords in the Search for clips text box.

To search for a clip by a keyword, follow these steps:

1. In the Clip Gallery, click the All Categories button to display the list of categories, if it does not already appear.

2. In the Search for clips text box, type a search word (for example, women or computer).

3. Press Enter. The clips that have that keyword assigned to them appear.

4. Work with the clips as you normally would.

Managing a Clip's Properties

Each clip has a Properties dialog box. It contains the clip's description, a list of the categories to which it belongs, and the list of keywords assigned to it. All of these things you can change.

Follow these steps to view (and change, if needed) a clip's properties:

1. In the Clip Gallery, right-click a clip and choose Clip Properties from the shortcut menu. The Clip Properties dialog box appears.

2. On the Description tab, confirm the clip's description. See Figure 12-6. This is the name that appears when the clip is selected. (It is not the clip's filename; the filenames for clips are usually quite cryptic, like bd06790_, as shown in Figure 12-6.) You should not need to change the description, but you can if necessary.

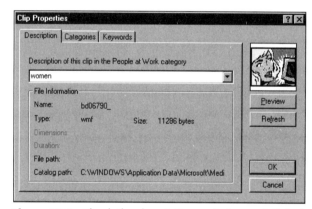

Figure 12-6: Check the description and change it if desired.

3. On the Categories tab, a list of all the categories appears. A checkmark appears in the checkbox next to each category to which the clip is assigned. Select or deselect checkboxes to add the clip to a category or remove it from one. (You can also create new categories from here by clicking the New Category button.) See Figure 12-7.

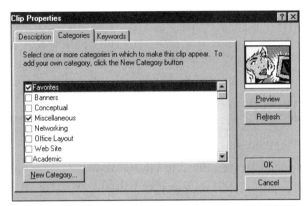

Figure 12-7: Choose which categories the selected clip should appear in.

4. On the Keywords tab, a list of the clip's current keywords appears. To remove a keyword, click it and click Remove Keyword.

5. If you want to add a keyword to the clip, click the New Keyword button. A New Keyword dialog box appears. Type the new keyword, and click OK.

6. When you are finished modifying the clip's properties, click OK.

Linking Your Own Art to the Clip Gallery

Besides the clips that come with PowerPoint, you can also include your own artwork in the Clip Gallery. This can be very handy, because then you don't have to browse for the file each time you want to use it. (See the "Importing a Graphic from a File" section later in this chapter for details about that.)

You can include images of all image formats in the Clip Gallery, not just the default .WMF format that PowerPoint's clip art comes in. (The abbreviation .*WMF* stands for Windows Meta File, by the way.) The image formats that PowerPoint supports include .EMF, .WMF, .JPG, .PNG, .BMP, .PCX, .DIB, .RLE, .EPS, .DXF, .PCT, .CGM, .CDR, .DRW, .TIF, .TGA, .PCD, .GIF, .WPG, .FPX, and .MIX.

Note

The three-letter codes listed above are not really image formats, per se; they are *file extensions*, letter combinations that come after the period in a file's name that tell Windows and your applications what file format to expect when reading the file. For example, the Zsoft PC Paintbrush format uses the extension .PCX, so when you see a file with a .PCX extension, you can be 98 percent sure that the file is in .PCX format. (It's not a 100 percent reliable system because a file can be renamed to have a different extension.)

To import art into the Clip Gallery, follow these steps:

1. In the Clip Gallery, click the Import Clips button on the toolbar. The Add clip to Clip Gallery dialog box opens. See Figure 12-8.

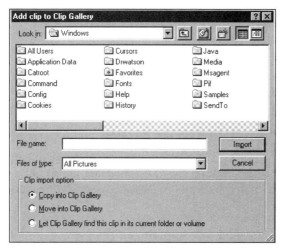

Figure 12-8: Select a graphic file to be included in your Clip Gallery.

2. Navigate to the drive/folder containing the clip you want. (Refer to Chapter 4 if you need help with that.)

3. Click the clip you want to select.

4. In the Clip import option section, choose the option button that describes how you want the clip to be included:

   • **Copy into Clip Gallery:** This option makes a copy of the file and places it into the same folder as the Microsoft clip art on your hard disk. This option offers fastest performance when pulling up clip art images.

   • **Move into Clip Gallery:** This option moves the file from its current location into the Microsoft clip art folder on your hard disk. This option is suitable if you will not be using this clip for anything except placement in Microsoft Office applications.

   • **Let Clip Gallery find this clip in its current folder or volume:** This option creates a shortcut to the clip in the Clip Gallery, but leaves the original where it is. This option is best if you are running out of hard disk space.

5. Click Import to import the clip. The Clip Properties dialog box opens.

6. Type a description for the new clip in the Description of this clip text box.

7. Click the Categories tab and select the categories to which this clip should belong.

8. Click the Keywords tab and enter keywords for this clip.

9. Click OK.

Note   In Microsoft Office 97, the Clip Gallery maintained a distinction between clip art and other images, and kept them on separate tabs; there is no such distinction in the version of the Clip Gallery that comes with PowerPoint 2000.

Getting More Clips from the Internet

Microsoft has much more clip art than will fit on your PowerPoint or Office 2000 installation CD, so they put some of it on the CD and make the rest of it available for download online.

There are hundreds (maybe thousands) more clip art images available to you from the Microsoft Web site. All you need is your copy of PowerPoint and an Internet connection. These are .WMF-format clip art images, the same as the ones you get with your original Clip Gallery, and they import seamlessly into your Clip Gallery when you download them. These images come with their own category assignments, and they are also automatically assigned to the Downloaded Clips category, so you can browse all your downloaded clips at once.

You can also acquire sound clips and video clips online for use with the Sound from Gallery and Movie from Gallery commands that you learn about in Chapters 18 and 19.

Note   If you don't have an Internet connection, use Windows 98's Connection Wizard to create one. You can use a service provider that you choose, or the Connection Wizard can recommend a list of service providers.

To connect to Microsoft's online Clip Gallery, follow these steps:

1. From the Clip Gallery, click the Clips Online button on the toolbar.

2. A message box appears explaining what is going to happen. Click OK to go on.

3. Internet Explorer opens, and if you are not currently connected to the Internet, a Dial-Up Connection box appears, so you can connect. Enter or confirm your User name and Password, then click Connect.

4. Wait for your Internet connection to take place and the Clip Gallery Live page to appear.

5. If this is the first time you have connected to the Clip Gallery Live, an End User License Agreement appears. Read it and click Accept.

6. In the Clip Gallery Live, type keywords for clips you want in the Search Clips by Keyword box and then click Go. See Figure 12-9.

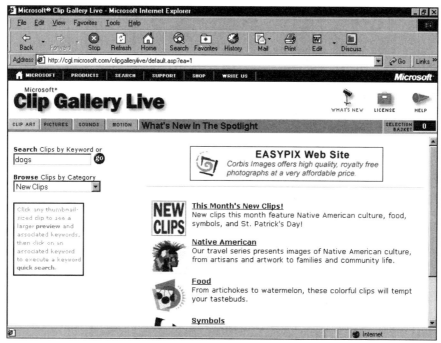

Figure 12-9: Type a keyword that you want to search with, or browse by category.

7. Clips appear that match your keyword(s). Identify a clip that you want and click the checkbox beneath it to select it. Do this for each clip that you want. See Figure 12-10.

8. When you are finished selecting clips, click the SELECTION BASKET link to jump to the Selection Basket. All the clips you chose appear.

9. Click the Download link to begin the download process. A Download Web page appears.

10. Click the Download Now! link. After a short pause for downloading, the Clip Gallery window appears showing your downloaded clips.

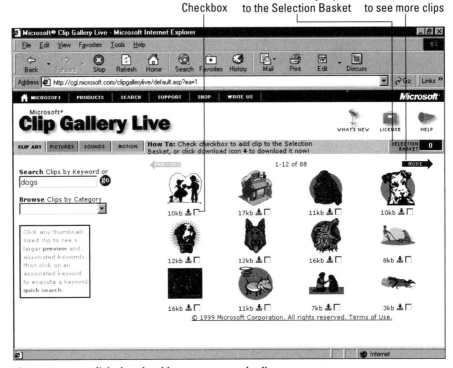

Figure 12-10: Click the checkbox next to each clip you want.

Note   If a File Download box appears asking what you want to do with the download, click Open this file from its current location and then click OK. (This dialog box might not appear.)

Rename and recategorize the new clips as needed, as you learned earlier in this chapter.

Inserting a Scanned Image

If you have a scanner attached to your PC, you can scan a picture directly into PowerPoint. (You can also scan it separately, and then import the saved picture, as explained in the "Importing a Graphics from a File" section later in this chapter.) Scanning directly into PowerPoint saves time because you do not have to run the scanning software and assign a separate filename to the image.

The following steps are useful only if you do not want to modify the image after you scan it. They place the image directly onto your slide, and do not offer the opportunity to resize, crop, or rotate the image. If you need to alter the image after scanning, scan using your normal scanning program, and import into PowerPoint only after you are satisfied with the image.

To place an image directly onto your slide, follow these steps:

1. Place the image to be scanned in your scanner, and verify that the scanner is turned on and hooked up correctly.

2. Choose Insert ➪ Picture ➪ From Scanner or Camera. The Insert Picture from Scanner or Camera dialog box opens.

3. Open the Device drop-down list and choose your scanner. See Figure 12-11.

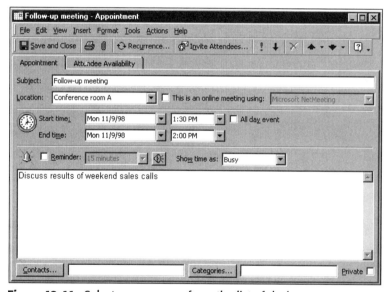

Figure 12-11: Select your scanner from the list of devices.

4. Choose Web Quality or Print Quality. Print quality is a higher quality; Web quality is good enough if you are scanning the image to be displayed onscreen rather than printed.

5. Click Insert to scan the image directly into PowerPoint using the default settings, or click Custom Insert to open your scanner's controls to scan the image. (If you do the latter, go ahead and use the controls to acquire the image as you normally do.)

Importing a Graphic from a File

If you have an image you have already scanned and saved or an image you have acquired from some other source, you can place it into PowerPoint with the Insert ➪ Picture ➪ From File command. This command lets you insert all kinds of images, not just clip art.

As you learned earlier in this chapter, you can place any kind of image in the Clip Gallery and insert it from there, too. However, that can be time-consuming, and if you are going to use a particular image just one time, you may not want to bother with that. Inserting the picture from a file is quick and easy, and does not require you to access the Clip Gallery.

To place a picture from a file, follow these steps:

1. Display the slide on which you want to place the image.
2. Choose Insert ➪ Picture ➪ From File. The Insert Picture dialog box appears.
3. If you do not see a preview pane, as shown in Figure 12-12, click the View button until one appears, or open the View button's drop-down list and choose Preview.

Figure 12-12: Choose the file that you want to use in your PowerPoint presentation.

4. Click the Insert button. The image is inserted onto your slide.
5. Edit the image (resize, move, and so on), as explained in the following section.

Editing Graphics

When you initially place a picture on a slide, it probably doesn't look exactly the way you want it to. That's because it probably needs to be cropped, resized, recolored, reshaped, or some combination of those alterations.

Working with the Picture Toolbar

The Picture toolbar is available whenever a picture is selected. If you don't see it, right-click the picture and choose Show Picture Toolbar.

Almost everything you can do to an image can be done in two ways: using the Format Picture dialog box or using the Picture toolbar. In most cases, the Picture toolbar is the easier method, so that's the method I teach you in the following sections. I mention the tools as I go along, but you might want to preview them in Table 12-1 before getting started.

Table 12-1
Buttons on the Picture Toolbar

Button	Name	Purpose
	Insert Picture	Opens the Insert Picture from File dialog box again so you can add another picture
	Image Control	Switches between grayscale, black and white, color, and watermark image modes
	More Contrast	Increases the difference between the lights and darks
	Less Contrast	Decreases the difference between the lights and darks
	More Brightness	Makes colors in the picture brighter
	Less Brightness	Makes colors in the picture darker
	Crop	Changes the mouse pointer to a cropping tool that you can use to exclude parts of the image
	Line Style	Changes the thickness/style of the border surrounding the clip
	Recolor Picture	Opens the Recolor Picture dialog box
	Format Picture	Opens the Format Picture dialog box
	Set Transparent Color	Enables you to set one color of the image as *see-through* (not available for all images)
	Reset Picture	Restores the original settings that the picture had when you first imported it

Moving and Resizing

You learned all about moving and resizing objects in Chapter 10, and images are no different from other objects.

To move, point at the center of the image (any area except the handles) and drag the image where you want it. To resize an image in one dimension, drag one of the side handles. To resize an image in both dimensions, drag one of the corner handles.

Changing the Image Mode

Most images can be displayed in any of four modes:

✦ **Automatic:** This is usually color if it is a color image. It's the image default appearance and is best for color presentations.

✦ **Grayscale:** This is a gray-shaded version of the original image, with shades of gray substituted for each color. This works well for presentations that must be given in one color, such as a presentation given with transparencies printed on a black-and-white printer.

✦ **Black and white:** The entire image consists of black and white. There is no shading. Any colors are rounded to either black or white, whichever they are closest to. This results in a loss of image quality in an image that had any shading.

✦ **Watermark:** This is a light background image of the original, suitable for placement behind text. Its effect is subtle.

Figure 12-13 shows an image in each of the four modes. (You can't tell much difference between Automatic and Grayscale since this is not a color book, but you could immediately see the difference on your own screen.)

Changing the Colors

To subtly change an image's appearance, you can use the Contrast and Brightness controls on the Picture toolbar. (Refer to Table 12-1 to see them.) Turn up or down the brightness or contrast as needed, just like you would set the controls on your TV or your computer monitor.

You can also change the coloring more dramatically with the Recolor Picture dialog box. It enables you to choose one or more colors used in the image and change them to some other color(s). Follow these steps to change a picture in that way:

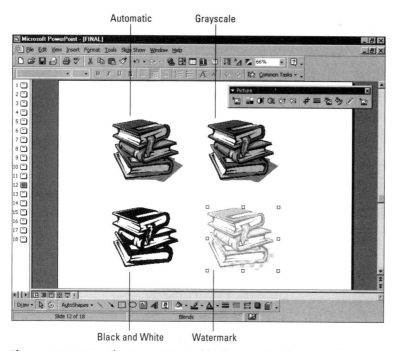

Figure 12-13: Use the Image Control button on the Picture toolbar to switch between image modes.

You cannot recolor a bitmap image (such as a scan) in PowerPoint. You must use a separate image editing program for that, such as Microsoft Image Editor (an extra program that comes on the Office 2000 CD).

1. Select the image that you want to recolor.

2. On the Picture Toolbar, click the Recolor Picture button. The Recolor Picture dialog box appears showing all the colors used in the image. See Figure 12-14.

3. Choose Colors or Fills at the bottom of the dialog box. Colors, the default, shows all the colors in the image, both the lines and the fills. Fills, on the other hand, shows only the fill colors.

Figure 12-14: Choose the colors you want to change, and choose the colors you want to change them to.

Note   What's the difference between a line and a fill in Step 3? A *line* is an outside border that circumscribes the edge of the shape. A *fill* is the color (if any) on the inside of that shape.

4. Click the checkbox next to one of the Original colors. Then open the New drop-down list next to it and select a color to change it to.

5. Click the Preview button to preview the change. Drag the dialog box out of the way as needed so you can see the change in the image.

6. Repeat Steps 4 through 6 for each of the colors you want to change.

7. Click OK.

Setting a Transparent Color

The Transparent Color feature can be really neat, but not all pictures support it. It's available for bitmap images (including scans) that do not already have a transparency setting, and for some, but not all, clip art. For example, suppose you have a scanned photo of your CEO and you want to make the background transparent so it looks like his head is sitting right on the slide. This feature could help you out with that.

Note   Some clip art already has its background set to transparent, which is why it won't work with this Set Transparent Color feature.

Click the picture you want to work with. If the Set Transparent Color button is not grayed out on the Picture toolbar, then you can set a transparent color by following these steps:

1. Make sure the picture is selected.

2. Click the Set Transparent Color button.

3. On the picture, click the mouse on the color that you want to make transparent.

If the results are not what you want, click the Undo button on the Standard toolbar or press Ctrl+Z to undo.

Adding a Background to the Image

You learned in the preceding chapter how to add a background to a slide. You use the same procedure to add a background to an image. Some images (especially clip art) have a transparent background (that is, No Fill), but you can set any background you want for the image by following these steps:

1. Click the image to select it.

2. Open the Fill Color menu from the Fill Color button on the Drawing toolbar. See Figure 12-15.

Fill Color affects the space behind the image

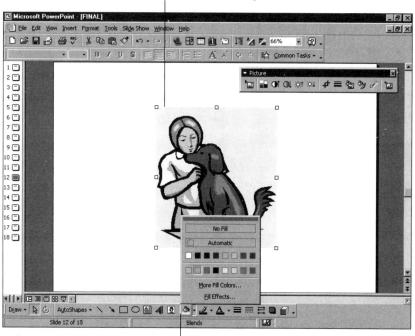

Fill Color button

Figure 12-15: Set a fill color for an image by selecting the image and then choosing from the Fill Color button's menu.

3. Choose a color, or choose More Fill Colors or Fill Effects, as you learned in Chapters 10 and 11.

 Tip   If you want to apply the color that is already selected (that is, the color of the strip on the Fill Color button), just click the Fill Color button. You don't have to open its menu.

Bordering an Image

To apply a border to an image, you use the same technique you learned in Chapter 10 for objects. Select the image and then choose a border color, style, and dash style from the Drawing toolbar. You've been over these controls twice now — once in Chapter 10 and again in Chapter 11 — so I won't belabor them again here.

Cropping an Image

Cropping is for those times when you want only a part of an image and not the whole thing. For example, you might have a great photo of a person or animal, but there is extraneous detail around it, as in Figure 12-16. You can crop out the important object in the image with the cropping tool.

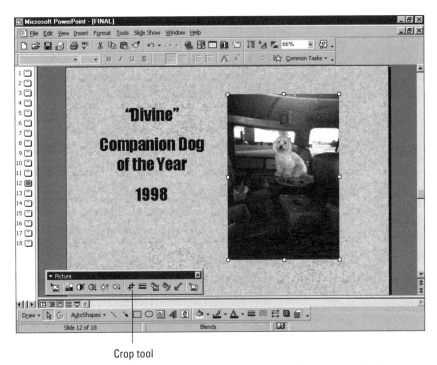

Crop tool

Figure 12-16: Use the cropping tool for an image like this, where the important object is overshadowed by extraneous material.

To use the cropping tool, follow these steps:

1. Select the image.

2. Click the Crop tool on the Picture toolbar. Your mouse pointer changes to a cropping tool.

3. Position the pointer over a side handle on the image frame, on a side where you want to cut some of the image off.

4. Drag the handle inward toward the center of the image until only the part of the image on that side that you want to keep is in the dotted line.

5. Repeat Steps 3 and 4 for each side.

6. After cropping, move or resize the image as needed. Figure 12-17 shows the result of cropping the image from Figure 12-16.

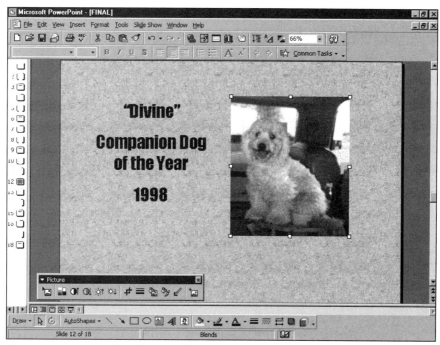

Figure 12-17: Cropping this image has made a great difference in its appearance.

Working with the Format Picture Dialog Box

So far in this section, you have done your work from the Picture toolbar. But you can also modify your image from its Format Picture dialog box. To do so, right-click the image and choose Format Picture, or click the Format Picture button on the Picture toolbar.

In the Format Picture dialog box (Figure 12-18) are the same tabs that you saw when you worked with objects in Chapter 10:

✦ **Colors and Lines tab:** Provides an alternate way of changing the fill color and line color, style, and weight.

✦ **Size tab:** Provides an alternate way of resizing a picture.

✦ **Position tab:** Provides an alternate way of moving the image.

✦ **Picture tab:** Provides an alternate way of cropping the image, controlling its brightness and contrast, and changing its image type.

✦ **Web:** Enables you to enter alternative text to appear in case the image cannot be displayed. (This is used for presentations designed for Web showing only.)

You may never have occasion to use the Format Picture dialog box, since all the controls you need are available from the Picture toolbar.

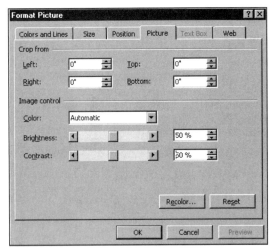

Figure 12-18: Use the Format Picture dialog box to control the picture's placement and appearance.

Summary

In this chapter, you learned how to place images on your slides. You should now be familiar with the Clip Gallery, and know how to acquire more clip art images online and add your own images to the gallery. You also learned how to place an image from a file, bypassing the Clip Gallery, and how to edit an image once you've placed it on your slide.

In the next chapter, you continue working with graphics, but of a different kind. In Chapter 13, you learn how to draw your own lines and shapes with the Drawing toolbar, and how to create and manipulate WordArt.

✦   ✦   ✦

Using the Drawing Tools

All the Microsoft Office 2000 applications use a common Drawing toolbar, on which you find tools for creating lines and shapes and modifying all kinds of objects. You have already seen in earlier chapters how the Fill Color, Line Color, Line Style, and so on can be controlled with these buttons. In this chapter, I introduce you to the buttons at the *other* end of the Drawing toolbar, the ones that create lines and shapes.

You can draw two basic shapes with the Drawing toolbar: rectangles and ovals. There are many other shapes you can use, but they are all AutoShapes. AutoShapes are predrawn shapes, usually more complex than the simple ovals and rectangles. There are dozens of them, including all kinds of arrows, sunbursts, brackets, and symbols. You can also draw a variety of lines. Simple lines, with or without arrows on the end, can be created with the Line tool, but if you want a more complex line, use one of the AutoShape lines.

Drawing Lines and Shapes

You can create and place the most basic lines and shapes with the drawing tools shown in the following table.

Icon	Description
╲	Line
↘	Arrow
▢	Rectangle
◯	Oval

You might, for example, draw a line to separate two elements on the slide, or draw a line with an arrow to point to an important part of a chart. The rectangles and ovals can be used to draw boxes or frames around important slide objects. Figure 13-1 shows a chart with an oval and a line with an arrow enhancing its main point.

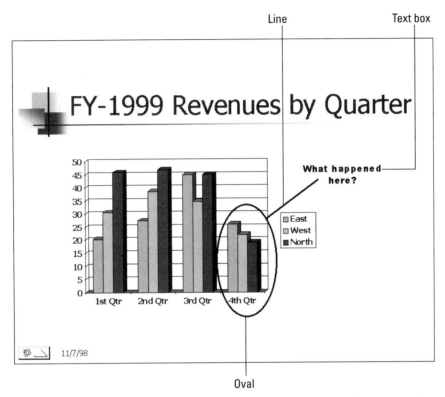

Figure 13-1: You can use simple lines and shapes to accentuate the main point of a slide.

The procedure is the same for each of these tools, although it may take a bit of practice to master them:

1. Display the slide you want to draw on.
2. Click the drawing tool button that you want.
3. Point the mouse pointer where you want the line or shape to begin.
4. Hold down the mouse button and drag to where you want the line or shape to end.
5. Release the mouse button.

If you double-click instead of click in Step 2, you can repeat the procedure from Step 3 to draw more of the same shape. Otherwise, you must go back to Step 2 for each additional shape you want to draw.

You can draw complex objects using these tools, one shape at a time. After drawing a series of shapes, select them all and then use the Group command, which you learned about in Chapter 10, to make them a single object.

Placing an AutoShape

AutoShapes are predrawn shapes that function just like the lines and shapes that you draw with the regular drawing tools. The only difference is their complexity. They're great for people who want shapes like box-style arrows and starbursts but aren't coordinated enough to draw them (or simply don't have the time to waste).

There are several categories of AutoShapes, including Lines, Connectors, Basic Shapes, and so on. Table 13-1 shows each category's menu and explains a bit about how each might be useful.

Table 13.1
PowerPoint AutoShapes

Menu	Name	Description
	Lines	Free-form shapes or lines, or straight lines, with or without arrows. Use these to draw freehand or to call attention to certain objects.
	Connectors	Flow charting connectors that help create relationship lines between other objects.
	Basic Shapes	A variety of geometric shapes and simple symbols.
	Block Arrows	Arrows that are thicker than just lines, useful for flow charting or to call attention to another object.
	Flowchart	Standard flowchart symbols.

Continued

Table 13.1 *(continued)*

Menu	Name	Description
	Stars and Banners	Lively starbursts and swoops for calling attention. Place text inside them for extra impact.
	Callouts	Thought and speech bubbles for cartoons and explanatory boxes.
	Action Buttons	Buttons useful for moving from slide to slide in a user-interactive presentation.

To place an AutoShape, follow these steps:

1. Display the slide you want to place the AutoShape on.
2. Click the AutoShape button on the Drawing toolbar. A menu of AutoShapes appears.
3. Point to a category that you want to look at (for example, Block Arrows). A menu of shapes appears. See Figure 13-2.
4. Click the shape you want. Your mouse pointer turns into a crosshair.
5. Drag on the slide to draw a box where you want the shape to appear. You see the shape as you drag. When you are satisfied with it, release the mouse button.

If you choose the wrong shape, it's easier just to delete the shape and start over if you have not applied any special formatting to it. If you have formatted the shape already (see the following section), you may find it easier to change the shape rather than re-create it. To do so, open the Draw menu (from the Draw button on the Drawing toolbar), choose Change AutoShape, and then select a new shape from the submenu, just as you chose the original AutoShape.

Formatting Drawn Objects

You learned in Chapter 10 how to format an object, and a drawn object is just another object. You can change its line color, fill color, size and shape, and add shadows or 3D effects to it. The sky's the limit! Here's a quick review, so you don't have to turn back to Chapter 10:

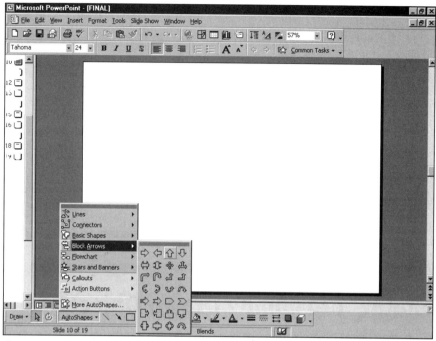

Figure 13-2: Choose an AutoShape from the AutoShapes menu.

Icon	Name	Description
	Fill color	Choose an inside color for the shape or choose No Fill for a clear one. This button is not applicable for lines.
	Line color	Choose an outside color for the shape or a color for the line. If you choose No Line, the shape is borderless. If you choose No Line for a line, the line disappears.
	Line style	Choose a thickness for the border of the shape or for the line.
	Dash style	Choose a dash style for the border of the shape or for the line.
	Arrow style	Choose arrows for one or both ends of the line. This button is not applicable for shapes.

You can also change the order and grouping:

✦ **Order:** Open the Draw menu and choose Order to change the stacking order of multiple objects.

✦ **Grouping:** Open the Draw menu and choose Group to group multiple objects together as a single object.

You can also format a shape by right-clicking it and choosing Format AutoShape to open the Format AutoShape dialog box. For editing purposes, PowerPoint considers all shapes AutoShapes, even if they are simple lines or rectangles drawn with the regular drawing tools.

Tip   If you have formatted a certain line or shape the way you want all future shapes to be, you can set the AutoShape defaults to match it. For example, suppose you want all shapes to have a thick green border and be colored yellow. You could format one shape that way and then set that as the default. To set the default, click the Draw button on the Drawing toolbar and choose Set AutoShape Defaults.

Rotating or Flipping Drawn Objects

You can only rotate and flip drawn objects (lines and shapes) in PowerPoint, not clip art or other imported graphics. Rotating turns the line or shape on an axis, while flipping reverses it either vertically or horizontally.

To rotate a shape 90 degrees to the left or right, choose Draw ➪ Rotate or Flip and then Rotate Left or Rotate Right. To flip a shape vertically or horizontally, choose Draw ➪ Rotate or Flip and then Flip Horizontal or Flip Vertical. Figure 13-3 shows an AutoShape arrow (in the top left) and how it looks with various rotations and flips applied to it. You can apply these modifications one after the other, so, for example, you could rotate a shape 180 degrees (90 plus 90) and then flip it.

Original   Rotate Left   Rotate Right

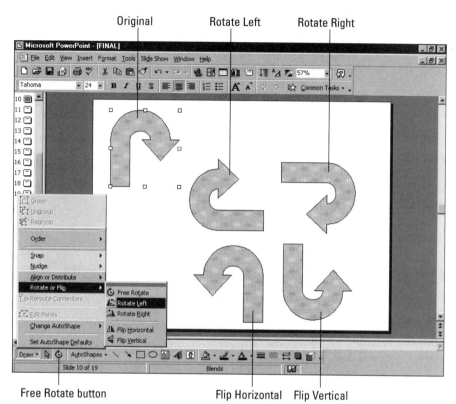

Free Rotate button   Flip Horizontal   Flip Vertical

Figure 13-3: Rotate or flip a shape or line with the commands on the Draw menu.

You can also free-rotate a shape if you need a rotation other than 90 degrees or a multiple of 90 degrees. To free-rotate a shape, follow these steps:

1. Click the Free Rotate button on the Drawing toolbar. Green circles appear around the shape in place of selection handles, and the mouse pointer shows a curved arrow.

2. Move the mouse pointer over one of those green circles.

3. Hold down the mouse button and drag to rotate the shape. A dotted outline shows where the shape is going. See Figure 13-4.

4. Release the mouse button. The shape is rotated.

5. Click the mouse again. Rotation mode is turned off, and the shape's regular selection handles reappear.

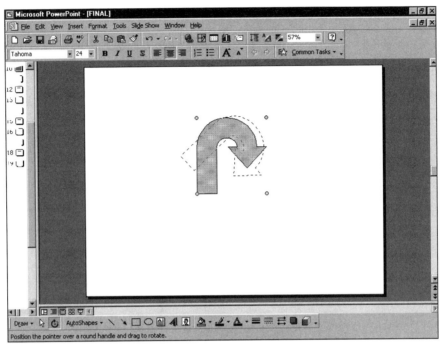

Figure 13-4: Drag a green circle to rotate a shape.

Stretching an AutoShape

Most AutoShapes can be twisted, stretched, and otherwise manipulated to meet any special needs you might have for them. Figure 13-5 shows some examples of what you can do to a curved arrow, for instance. The original AutoShape is in the top-left corner.

The key is in the adjustment handles on the shape. Most shapes have at least one of these yellow diamonds on it. You can drag the yellow diamond to modify the shape. For example, in Figure 13-6, the arrow has a yellow diamond near the top. When you drag the diamond, you modify the thickness and size of the shape.

Some shapes have only one adjustment handle; others have two. It depends on the type of shape and in what ways it can be modified. The shape in Figure 13-6 has only one modification dimension, but the shapes in Figure 13-5 each have two — the thickness and the amount of twist.

Original

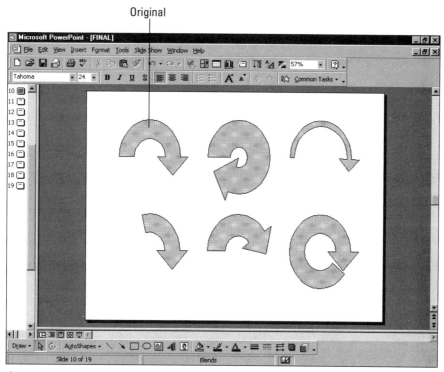

Figure 13-5: You can bend and stretch any AutoShape as needed.

Ten Ideas for Using Drawn Objects

Need a little inspiration to get you started with AutoShapes? Try these ideas:

1. Create a flow chart using the Flowchart AutoShapes. Connect the shapes with Connectors AutoShapes.

2. Use the Freeform shape (one of the Lines AutoShapes) to draw your own shape.

3. Create your own complex math formulas by typing numbers in small text boxes and placing bracket AutoShapes (found on the Basic Shapes submenu) around the parts that should be bracketed.

4. Create a "No" sign (no smoking, no pets, no fear, or whatever) by typing text in a text box and then placing the AutoShape that shows a circle with a line through it (one of the Basic Shapes). Then group the text box and the AutoShape so they form a single object. See Figure 13-7.

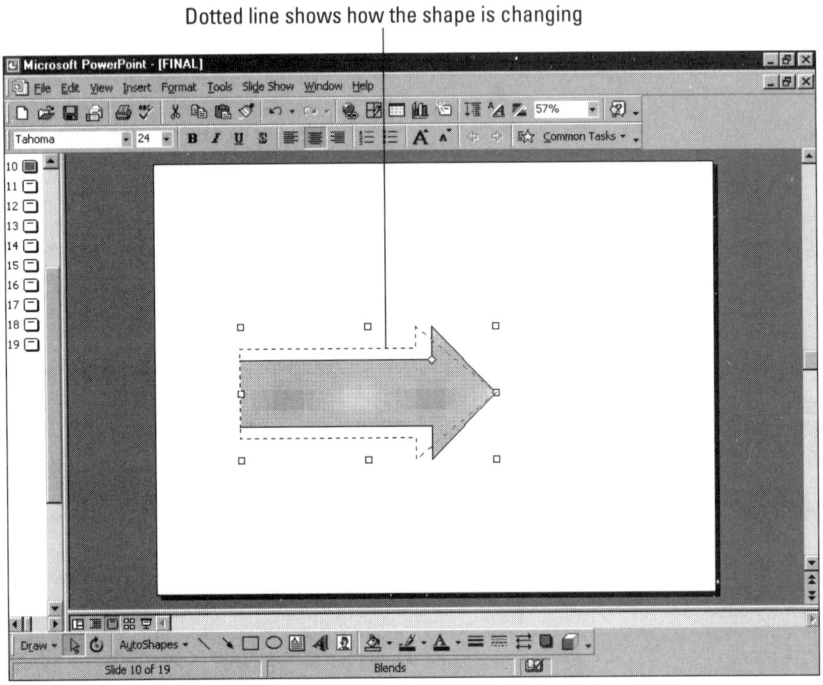

Dotted line shows how the shape is changing

Figure 13-6: Drag the adjustment handle, the yellow diamond, to stretch the shape.

Figure 13-7: You can place an AutoShape on top of a text box like this.

5. Fill an AutoShape with a photo so the shape becomes a picture frame, as you saw in Chapter 10. (Use the Fill Effects command on the Fill Color button's menu.)

6. Place Up or Down block arrows beside bullet points to indicate which are good news and which are bad news.

7. Use the Callouts AutoShapes to place thought or speech bubbles over cartoon characters or to label technical drawings.

8. Place Action Buttons (yes, they're a type of AutoShape) on the Slide Master of a user-interactive presentation. See Chapter 27 for details.)

9. Draw your own objects using multiple shapes, then select all the shapes and group them into a single object with the Draw ⇨ Group command.

10. Place any of the additional AutoShapes that come with PowerPoint 2000 by choosing More AutoShapes from the AutoShapes menu. When you do so, a special version of the Clip Gallery appears listing them, as shown in Figure 13-8. Choose a category, and then insert the one you want, just as you learned to do with clip art in Chapter 12.

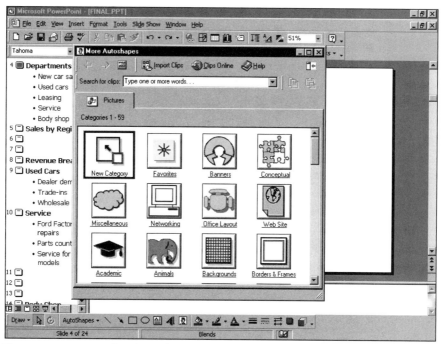

Figure 13-8: Some clips from the Clip Gallery are actually AutoShapes.

Placing WordArt

All of the Office 2000 applications have access to a program called WordArt that helps you create stylized, interesting-looking text. You can take a standard bit of text, such as your company name, and bend, squeeze, and tilt it into an unusual form that will catch the audience's attention. Figure 13-9 shows some WordArt samples.

Caution   Use WordArt sparingly. It can add interest to your text in small quantities, but if you use it too frequently it can be annoying and distracting.

You can create a piece of WordArt easily using some standard settings and then refine it to be exactly what you want. Follow these steps to create some WordArt:

1. Display the slide you want to place the WordArt on.

2. Click the WordArt button on the Drawing toolbar. The WordArt Gallery dialog box appears. See Figure 13-10.

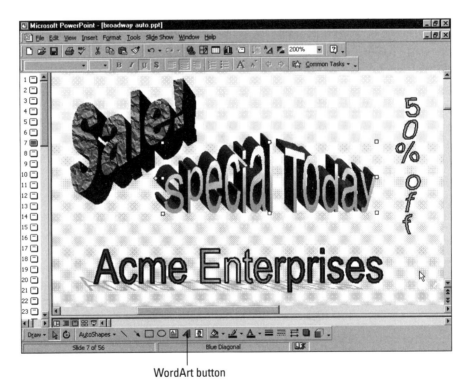

WordArt button

Figure 13-9: Here are some examples of what you can do with WordArt.

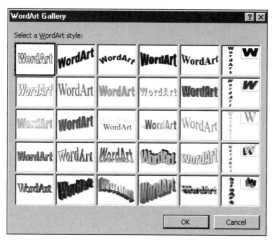

Figure 13-10: Choose an initial design from the WordArt Gallery.

3. Click one of the gallery designs. If there isn't one that matches exactly what you want, pick something similar; you can modify it later.

4. Click OK. The Edit WordArt Text dialog box appears. See Figure 13-11.

Figure 13-11: Type the text you want to use in your WordArt.

5. Type the text you want in the text box.

6. Choose a different Font and Size if needed.

7. If you want the text to be bold or italic, click the Bold and/or Italic button.

Tip   WordArt works best with a simple font like Arial or Times New Roman. It creates its own special effect, so you do not need to start with a fancy font.

8. Click OK when you're done. The finished WordArt appears on the slide. See Figure 13-12.

Modifying WordArt

Once you have placed the WordArt, you can perform almost any modification on it that you can imagine. You can change the wording, change the shape, change the color, size, texture, and so on. You have seen many of these modifications before when you've worked with other objects; others are brand new.

WordArt tool bar

Figure 13-12: The finished WordArt object appears on the slide.

First, review some of the modifications you already know how to do:

✦ Use the Fill Color button to change the front surface of the WordArt. Remember, you can also use the Fill Effects.

✦ Click the 3D button and choose a 3D effect. You can also choose 3-D Settings to open the 3D toolbar (which you learned about in Chapter 10), and from there you can change the color of the sides of the letters.

✦ Click the Shadow button and choose a Shadow effect. You can also click the Shadow Settings button to open the Shadow Settings toolbar. (Again, see Chapter 10 for details.)

✦ Use the Line Color button to choose an outline color for the letters. Use the Line Style and Dash Style buttons, too, if you need to fine-tune the outline.

The WordArt toolbar appears whenever you select a piece of WordArt, and it contains extra buttons for other modifications you can perform. The following table lists the different options and what they do.

Icon	Name	Description
	Insert WordArt	Opens the WordArt Gallery dialog box so you can create an additional WordArt object.
Edit Text...	WordArt Edit Text	Reopens the Edit WordArt Text dialog box for the current WordArt object.
	WordArt Gallery	Reopens the WordArt Gallery dialog box for the current WordArt object.
	Format WordArt	Opens the Format WordArt dialog box.
	WordArt Shape	Opens a pop-up array of shapes you can choose for your WordArt.
	Free Rotate	Enables you to rotate the WordArt. (This button works just like the Free Rotate tool on the Drawing toolbar.)
	WordArt Same Letter Heights	Makes all the letters the same height.
	WordArt Vertical Text	Toggles between vertical and horizontal text orientation.
	WordArt Alignment	Opens a shortcut menu of alignments (centered, right-aligned, and so on).
	WordArt Character Spacing	Changes the spacing between letters (normal, loose, tight, and so on).

If you want to try an exercise that walks you through using some of the WordArt tools, follow these steps:

1. Click the WordArt button on the Drawing toolbar.

2. Click the second WordArt style in the second row of the WordArt Gallery. Then, click OK.

3. In the Edit WordArt Text box, type **On Sale Now**. Then, click OK.

4. Click the WordArt Shape button on the WordArt toolbar. A pop-up list of shapes appears. See Figure 13-13.

Figure 13-13: Choose a different shape for the WordArt.

5. Click the fourth shape in the fourth row.

6. Click the Edit Text button. The Edit WordArt Text box reappears.

7. Change the font to Arial Black. Then, click OK.

8. Drag a corner selection handle of the WordArt to make it taller and narrower.

9. Click the WordArt Character Spacing button and choose Tight from the drop-down list.

10. Open the Fill Color button's list (on the Draw toolbar) and choose Fill Effects.

11. Click the Texture tab. Then, click the Purple Mesh texture and click OK.

12. Click the 3D button on the Drawing toolbar, and click the first 3D box in the top row to apply a 3D effect to the text.

13. Click the 3D button again and choose 3-D Settings to open the 3D Settings toolbar.

14. Click the 3D Color button (on the 3D Settings toolbar) and choose a pale pink for the 3D color. Then close the 3D Settings toolbar (click its X).

15. Drag the WordArt's adjustment handle (the yellow diamond) up slightly, increasing the arc on the WordArt.

Okay, you're done! My result appears in Figure 13-14; how close did you come to that?

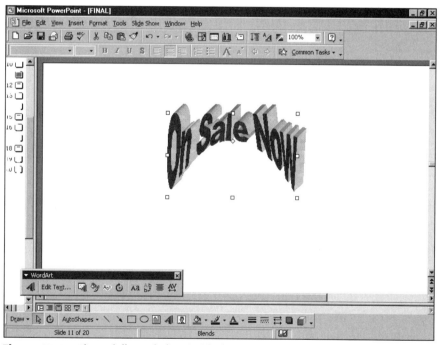

Figure 13-14: If you followed along with the example in the preceding steps, your WordArt should look something like this.

Summary

In this chapter, you expanded your graphics knowledge by learning how to draw your own lines and shapes and how to place AutoShapes. You also learned how to design your own WordArt, and you went through an exercise to help you polish your WordArt formatting skills.

Graphics can be a lot of fun in PowerPoint, but don't get so carried away with them that you forget the main point of your presentation — to communicate information. In the next chapter, you look at graphs, a type of graphic that communicates numerical data very well.

✦   ✦   ✦

Working with Graphs and Charts

PowerPoint doesn't do its own chart creation; it farms out the task to a program called Microsoft Graph. You may have worked with Microsoft Graph in other Office 2000 applications; it works the same in all programs. Microsoft Graph helps you create good-looking charts.

> **Note**
>
> What's the difference between a chart and a graph? Some purists will tell you that a chart is either a plain table (like the ones you learned to create in Chapter 8) or a pie chart, while a graph is a chart that plots data points on two axes (for example, a bar chart). However, Microsoft Graph does not make this distinction, and neither do I in this book. I use the terms *chart* and *graph* interchangeably, just as Microsoft Graph does.

Starting Microsoft Graph

You can place a chart on a slide in two ways: you can use a chart placeholder from an AutoLayout or you can place one manually.

If you are using a placeholder, just double-click it to start Microsoft Graph. If you are placing a chart manually, follow these steps:

1. Display the slide where you want to manually place a chart.

2. Click the Insert Chart button on the Standard toolbar, or select Insert ➪ Chart.

When you do so, Microsoft Graph opens within PowerPoint. You continue to see your PowerPoint slide, but the Standard toolbar's buttons change, and a sample chart and datasheet appear. See Figure 14-1.

Tip   When you first start Microsoft Graph, it may move the Formatting toolbar up to the same line as the Standard one, even if you have set them to be on separate lines in PowerPoint. As I mentioned earlier, this is not the optimal arrangement because you can't see all the tools. To move the Formatting toolbar back below the Standard one, just drag it down there, as shown in Figure 14-1. (See Chapter 2 if you need a reminder about working with toolbars.)

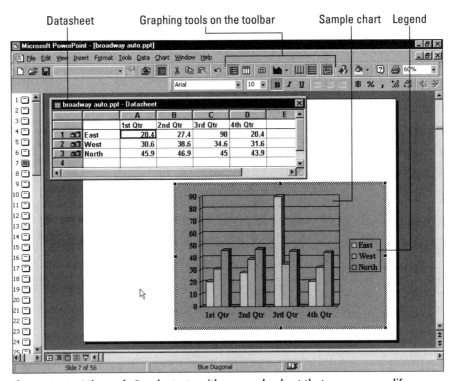

Figure 14-1: Microsoft Graph starts with a sample chart that you can modify.

The *datasheet* contains the data that comprises the chart. There are three *data series* — East, West, and North. Each of them has a separate color code, which is shown in the *legend*. Each series' results are shown over time. The column headings are the times (1st Qtr, 2nd Qtr, and so on). You use this same format when you enter your own data in the following section.

The first time you create a chart, you may want to make up some dummy data, just for practice, or you may want to stick with the sample data provided until you become comfortable. That way, you can experiment with it without fear of messing up your real work. There is a lot to learn about creating and modifying charts in Microsoft Graph!

Tip   At any point, you can return to your PowerPoint presentation by clicking anywhere outside of the chart on the slide. Your PowerPoint controls reappear. To edit the chart again, double-click it to reopen the Microsoft Graph controls.

Creating a Chart

To create your first chart, just change the data on the datasheet to match what you want to display on your chart. You can make up some sample data, as I've done in Figure 14-2, or you can use data for an actual chart you need in your presentation. Don't forget to change the row and column headings, too. You can add rows or columns as needed by simply typing into new cells, or delete rows or columns by clicking on a cell and then pressing Delete to clear it. You can also resize the Datasheet window if you need to, so you can see all your data at once.

Tip   When Microsoft Graph is running, the datasheet is usually displayed. If you need to modify the datasheet later but don't see it, click the View Datasheet button on the Standard toolbar.

Tip   You don't have to reinvent the wheel if you have a perfectly good wheel sitting in your garage already. If you have a chart already created in Microsoft Excel, it's a simple matter to add it to a PowerPoint slide. See Chapter 16 for details.

Changing the Chart Type

The default chart is a column chart, shown in Figures 14-1 and 14-2. There are lots of alternative chart types to choose from, however. Not all of them will be appropriate for your data, of course, but you may be surprised at the different spin on the message that a different chart type presents.

Many chart types come in both 2D and 3D models. You choose which look is most appropriate for your presentation. Try to be consistent, however. It looks nicer to stick with all 2D or all 3D charts rather than mixing the types in a presentation.

Here are some of the types available:

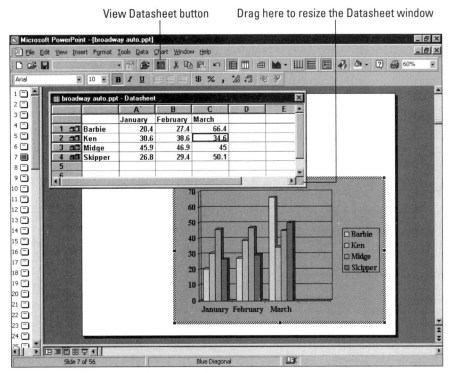

Figure 14-2: Change the data in the datasheet to your own data that you want to plot on a chart.

✦ **Bar and column.** A column chart, shown in Figures 14-1 and 14-2, plots data with vertical bars. A bar chart is the same thing except the bars are horizontal.

✦ **Area and surface.** These charts convey the same information as column charts, but the area between the bars is filled in.

✦ **Line.** Line charts convey the same information as column charts, but instead of the bars, a line or ribbon runs where the tops of the bars would be.

✦ **3D cones, cylinders, and pyramids.** These charts are just like columns except the bars have different, more interesting shapes.

✦ **Pie and doughnut.** These charts show how various parts relate to a whole, rather than showcasing individual number values.

✦ **Bubble and scatter.** These charts show each bit of data as a point (or a bubble) on a grid and are useful for spotting trends among lots of data points.

✦ **Radar.** This is a special-purpose chart that plots points on axes radiating from a center point. Most business presenters never use this type of chart.

Figures 14-3 through 14-5 show some examples of various chart types.

Caution

A pie chart supports only one data series. That means if you have a multiseries block of data in your datasheet and you convert the chart to a pie, only one of those series will appear in the pie. The other data series will be ignored. If you need to keep all the data, but you like the pie's message, use a doughnut chart instead.

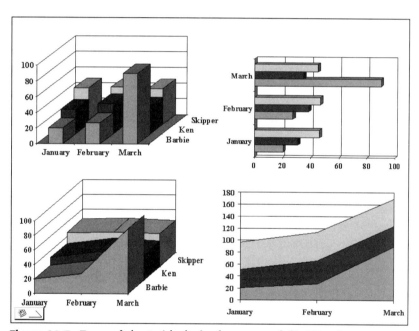

Figure 14-3: Types of charts (clockwise from upper left): 3D column, 3D clustered bar, 2D area, and 3D area.

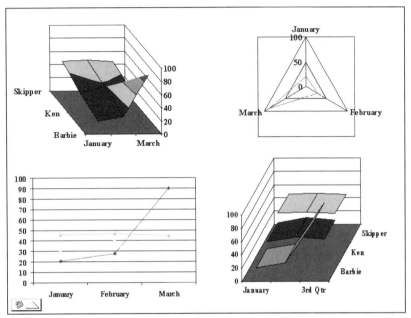

Figure 14-4: Types of charts (clockwise from upper left): surface, radar, 3D line, and 2D line.

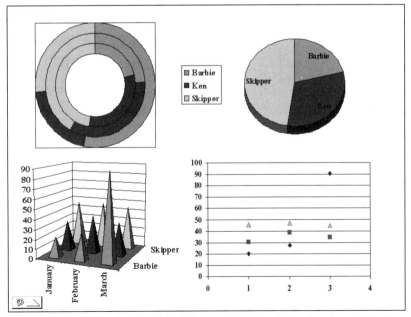

Figure 14-5: Types of charts (clockwise from upper left): doughnut, 3D pie, scatter, and pyramid.

Using the Drop-Down List

There are several ways to change the chart type. The easiest method is to use the drop-down Chart Type list on the Standard toolbar. Unfortunately, it does not provide access to all of the types, but it can be useful if you happen to want one of the types it provides.

1. Double-click the chart to reenter Microsoft Graph, if needed.

2. Click the down-arrow next to the Chart Type button to open its drop-down list. See Figure 14-6.

3. Click the chart type you want to change to.

Figure 14-6: You can change to one of the most common chart types with the toolbar button's list of types.

Using the Chart Type Dialog Box

The more powerful way to change the chart type is with the Chart Type dialog box.

1. Choose Chart ➪ Chart Type. This opens the Chart Type dialog box, shown in Figure 14-7. (You can also right-click the chart and choose Chart Type.)

2. In the Chart Type dialog box, click one of the chart types on the Chart Type list. The available subtypes appear in the pane to the right. For example, if you choose Pie, as shown in Figure 14-7, you can choose from six different subtypes.

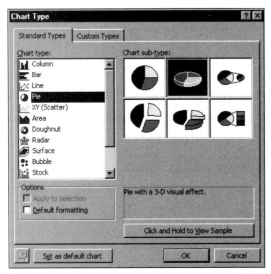

Figure 14-7: You can choose from every available chart type and subtype through this dialog box.

3. Click the subtype you want.

4. If you want to see how your data will look with that type and subtype, click and hold the Click and Hold to View Sample button.

5. When you are satisfied with the chart type you've selected, click OK.

Tip   The default chart type, as you have seen, is Column. If you prefer a different chart type to be the default, make your selection in the Chart Types dialog box and then click the Set as default chart button before you click OK in Step 5. This can save you time because you won't have to change each chart's type that you create.

You may have noticed that there is a second tab in the Chart Type dialog box: Custom Types. When you click that tab (see Figure 14-8), a list of predesigned chart formats/types appears. You can select one of these custom types as a shortcut for choosing a particular chart type and formatting it in a certain way. For example, Figure 14-8 shows Floating Bars selected, and you can see an example of it in the Sample area. You could re-create this custom chart type manually with a combination of chart type and chart formatting commands, but it is much easier simply to apply the custom type from this list.

Making a selection on the Custom Types tab overrides any selection you have made on the Standard Types tab, and vice versa. Microsoft Graph goes with whatever you have most recently selected when you click OK.

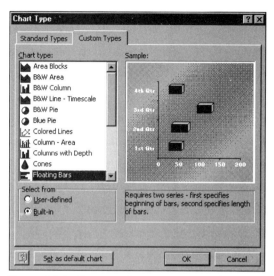

Figure 14-8: You can choose a custom chart type from the Custom Types tab.

Changing the Chart Orientation

By default, the rows of the datasheet form the data series. But if you want, you can switch that around so that the columns form the series. Figures 14-9 and 14-10 show the same chart plotted both ways so you can see the difference.

To switch back and forth between plotting by rows and by columns, click the By Row or By Column buttons on the Standard toolbar.

Note   What does the term *data series* mean? Take a look at Figures 14-9 and 14-10. Notice that there is a legend next to each chart that shows what each color (or shade of gray) represents. Each of those colors, and the label associated with it, is a series. The other variable (the one that is not the series) is plotted on the chart's horizontal (*X*) axis.

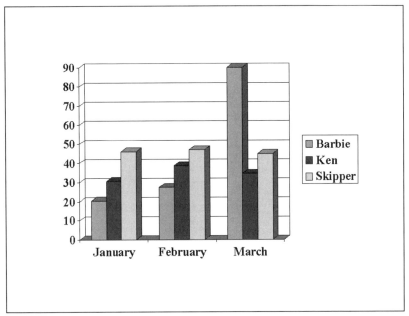

Figure 14-9: The data series are the people's names.

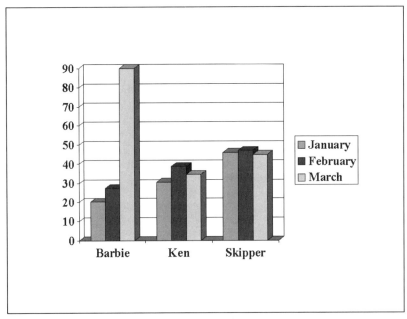

Figure 14-10: The data series are the months.

You should make sure you are using the right data for the data series because a chart carries a very different message when arranged by rows versus by columns. For example, in Figure 14-9, the chart compares the performance of the people against one another for each month. The message here is competition—which person did the best? Contrast this to Figure 14-10, where the series are the months. Here, you're invited to compare one month to another for each person. The overriding message here is time—which was each person's personal best month? It's easy to see how the same data can convey very different messages; make sure that you pick the arrangement that tells the story you want to tell in your presentation.

Adding and Removing Data Series

You may decide after you have created your chart that you need to use more or less data. Perhaps you want to exclude one of the months or add another salesperson. To add or remove a data series, simply edit the datasheet. To do so, follow these steps:

1. Double-click the chart in PowerPoint to open Microsoft Graph if it is not already active.

2. If the datasheet does not appear, click the View Datasheet button on the Standard toolbar.

3. On the datasheet, add information in another row and/or another column. Don't forget to include labels in the first cell of the row or column. See Figure 14-11.

4. If you need to delete a row or column, select it by clicking its row number or column letter and then press the Delete key on your keyboard.

5. When you are finished editing the datasheet, click the slide (outside of the chart area) to return to PowerPoint.

Click a row number to select an entire row

Click a column letter to select an entire column

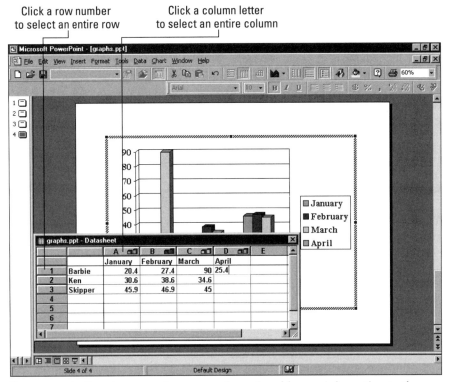

Figure 14-11: Type in an empty row or column to add more information to the chart.

Displaying or Hiding the Legend

The legend, as I mentioned before, is the little box that sits to the side of the chart (or above or below it sometimes) that provides the *key* to what the different colors or patterns mean. Depending on the chart type and the labels in use, you may or may not find the legend useful. If it is not useful for the chart you are working on, you can turn it off by clicking the Legend button on the Standard toolbar. Turning off the legend makes more room for the chart itself, and it grows to fill the available space. See Figure 14-12. Click the Legend button again to turn it back on, if needed.

Hiding the legend is not a good idea if you have more than one series in your chart, because the legend is instrumental in helping people decipher which series is which. However, if you have only one series, as in Figure 14-12, a legend would not be useful.

Legend button

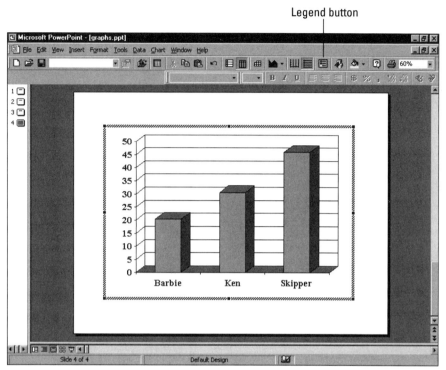

Figure 14-12: Hide the chart's legend if it doesn't provided needed information, and allow more room for your chart.

Adding a Data Table

Sometimes the chart tells the full story that you want to tell, but other times the audience may benefit from seeing the actual numbers on which the chart is built. In those cases, it's a good idea to include the data table with the chart. (A data table contains the same information that appears on the datasheet.)

To display the data table with a chart, click the Data Table button on the Standard toolbar, as shown in Figure 14-13. (If you don't see the Data Table button, make sure you have double-clicked the chart to enter Microsoft Graph.) To turn it off again, click the Data Table button again.

Tip

Sometimes Microsoft Graph doesn't do a very good job of sizing the fonts in the data table appropriately. If the data table's lettering looks too big, you can adjust it. Just right-click the data table and choose Format Data Table. Then, on the Fonts tab of the dialog box that appears, choose a different font size.

Data Table button

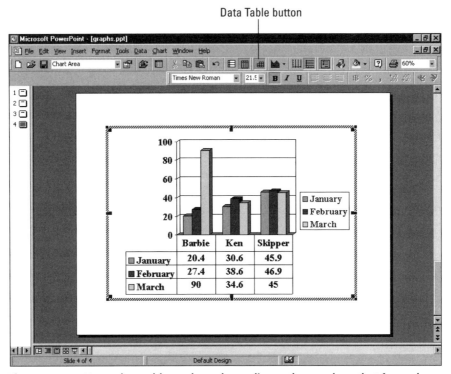

Figure 14-13: Use a data table to show the audience the numbers that formed the chart.

Formatting the Chart

In the following sections, I tell you about chart formatting. There is so much you can do to a chart that the subject could easily take up its own chapter! You can resize a chart, just like any other object, and you can also change fonts; change the colors and shading of bars, lines, or pie slices; use different background colors; change the 3D angle; and much more.

Understanding Chart Elements

Before you can learn how to format the parts of a chart, you need to know what those parts are. So far in this chapter, the parts haven't been a big deal—the chart pretty much hung together as a whole. But if you need to change, for example, the *Y* axis, you had better find out exactly where that is.

Figure 14-14 shows the parts of a typical chart. Most are fairly self-explanatory, but a few require a bit of extra explanation:

✦ The walls are the areas behind the chart. They may or may not include gridlines. On a 3D chart, there may be a side wall as well as a back one. You can color the walls or make them transparent.

✦ The plot area is the inner frame of the whole chart picture. It contains the chart itself.

✦ The chart area is the outer frame. It contains the plot area as well as the legend and data table if either of these elements is used.

✦ The category axis is usually the horizontal, or *X*, axis. It lists the categories that the series are plotted against.

✦ The value axis is usually the vertical, or *Y*, axis. It shows the numbers that the bars (or whatever) reach up to.

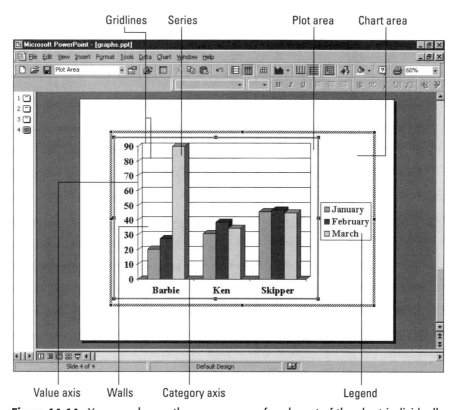

Figure 14-14: You can change the appearance of each part of the chart individually.

Adding Titles and Axis Labels

Most of the time, when you place a chart on a slide, that slide has its own title, so the chart itself does not need a separate title. However, if you have more on the slide than just the chart, it might be useful to have some text over the top of the chart indicating why it's there.

Besides an overall title for the chart, you can also add labels to each axis to describe the unit of measurement it shows (for example, Thousands or Salespeople). Figure 14-15 shows a chart with a title added, plus axis labels for both the vertical and horizontal axes.

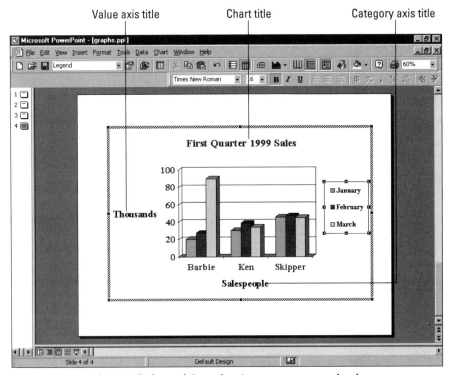

Figure 14-15: Titles can help explain a chart's message more clearly.

To work with titles, follow these steps:

1. With the chart selected in Microsoft Graph, select Chart ➪ Chart Options. Or, you can right-click the Chart area and choose Chart Options from the shortcut menu. The Chart Options dialog box appears.

2. Click the Titles tab if it is not already displayed.

3. Enter a title for the chart in the Chart title text box. See Figure 14-16.

4. Enter a title for the horizontal axis in the Category (*X*) axis field.

5. Enter a title for the vertical axis in the Value (*Z*) axis field. (For an explanation of why it's *Z* rather than *Y*, see the note at the end of these steps.)

6. Click OK.

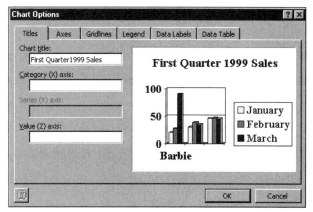

Figure 14-16: Enter the titles and labels you want to use.

Note   If you have taken geometry, you are probably used to calling the horizontal axis of a chart *X* and the vertical axis *Y*. That's the terminology I use in this book, too. However, on some 3D charts in Microsoft Graph, the vertical axis is called *Z* in some dialog boxes, and the axis that runs back to front is called *Y*. In most charts, there is nothing plotted on the back-to-front axis, so you only deal with vertical and horizontal axes. Don't let the fact that the vertical one is called *Z* in some dialog boxes confuse you; it's really your old familiar vertical (*Y*) axis.

Don't worry if the sample area in the dialog box gets all scrunched up and unreadable when you add titles in Steps 3 through 5. Sometimes the sample area does not accurately reflect what your results will look like. Go ahead and click OK to apply the labels, and chances are good that your chart will look fine.

When you add titles, you take away from the available space for the plot area in the chart frame. The chart in the plot area appears smaller after you add titles because Microsoft Graph shrinks it so that it and the added titles and labels all fit in the chart frame.

One way to minimize the space taken up by axis labels is to set them in a smaller font or, in the case of the Y-axis label, to rotate the text so it runs parallel to the axis. To learn how to format titles and labels, see the following section.

Formatting Titles and Labels

Once you have a title or label on your chart, you can change its size, orientation, and font. Just right-click the title you want to format and choose Format Chart Title (or whatever kind of title it is; an axis's label is called Axis Title, for example). The Format Axis Title (or Format Chart Title) dialog box appears.

There are three tabs in this dialog box: Patterns, Font, and Alignment. If you see only one tab (Font) in the dialog box, you have right-clicked the text itself rather than the text box. Close the dialog box and then click beside the text, rather than right on it, to select the text box. Then right-click the text box's frame. If you see three tabs in the dialog box, you know you've gotten it right.

On the Patterns tab, shown in Figure 14-17, you can set a background color for the area behind the text. (Remember, all text sits in a text box on a slide, and each text box can have background formatting.) To place a border around the text box that contains the label, click the Custom option button and then choose a line style, color, and weight. To use a background fill behind the text, click one of the colored squares in the Area part of the dialog box, or click the Fill Effects button to use fill effects, as you learned in Chapter 10.

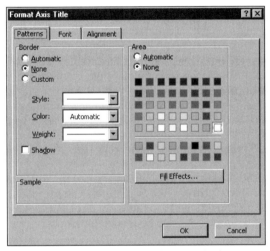

Figure 14-17: The Patterns tab controls the text box in which the title or label sits.

On the Font tab, you can choose all the usual text effects that you learned about in Chapter 8: font, size, font style, underline, color, and so on. See Figure 14-18. You can also choose a background setting for your text in this box. If you set it to Transparent, the text color will pick up from the background on which the text box sits. If you choose Opaque, it won't, but will use its own color instead. The default (Automatic) is Opaque.

Tip　The Auto scale checkbox in Figure 14-18 turns on/off the feature that resizes the text when you resize the text box. It is on by default, so if you make the text box that holds a chart's label or title smaller, the label or title gets smaller to fit.

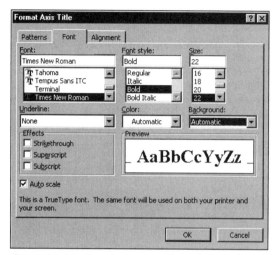

Figure 14-18: Use the Fonts tab to choose the typeface and its attributes.

Finally, the Alignment tab controls the way the text is aligned in its text box. You can set both vertical and horizontal alignment, just like you did in table cells in Chapter 8.

Note　Vertical and horizontal alignments are usually a nonissue in a label or title text box. The text box is usually exactly the right size to hold the text, so there is no way for the text to be aligned other than the way it is. Therefore, no matter what vertical and horizontal alignment you choose, the text looks pretty much the same.

But the coolest feature on the Alignment tab, shown in Figure 14-19, is the Orientation control. With it, you can rotate the text to any angle. For example, you can rotate the label for the vertical axis to run parallel to that axis.

By default, all text starts out formatted horizontally, at 0 degrees of tilt. But it doesn't have to stay that way; you can rotate it to any number of degrees, from 1 to 359. (360 is a full circle, so 360 is the same as 0.) To rotate the text, drag the red diamond up or down. The word Text rotates as you drag it. In Figure 14-19, it is dragged all the way to the top, resulting in text that runs straight up. You can also type an angle measurement (for example, 90) in the Degrees text box instead of dragging the red diamond, if you prefer.

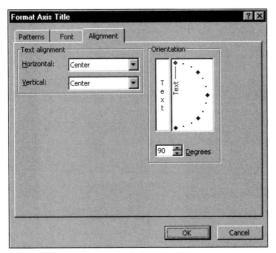

Figure 14-19: Change the text alignment and orientation on the Alignment tab.

Formatting the Chart Area

Your next task is to format the big picture: the chart area. The chart area is the big frame that contains the chart and all its accouterments: the legend, the data series, the titles, and so on.

The chart area controls two important elements: the background of the chart frame and the default font in the chart frame. To change them, follow these steps:

1. Point the mouse pointer at the area outside of the legend (if you have one), or slightly inside the chart frame. A screen tip should pop up reading Chart area. If you see something different, move the mouse elsewhere until you see that.

2. Right-click and choose Format Chart Area from the shortcut menu that appears. The Format Chart Area dialog box appears.

3. Click the Patterns tab if it's not already displayed. Its controls look just like the ones you saw for a text box in Figure 14-17.

4. Change the chart area's border and/or background if desired.

5. Click the Font tab. These controls set the default font for the entire chart. (The controls look just like the ones you saw in Figure 14-18.) If you do not specify otherwise, all text in the chart will have the font you choose here.

6. Make your font selection.

7. Click OK.

Adjusting the Axes

No, axes are not the tools that chop down trees. Axes is the plural of axis, and an axis is the side of the chart containing the measurements that your data is plotted against. For example, in Figure 14-20, the category axis (*X*, horizontal) contains the names of salespeople, and the value (*Y*) axis contains dollar amounts (0 through 100).

There are a number of things you can do to an axis. The option with the biggest potential impact on the chart is changing the scale. For example, take a look at the chart in Figure 14-20. The bars are so close to one another in value that it is difficult to see the difference between them. Compare that to the same data shown in Figure 14-21, but with an adjusted scale. Since the scale is smaller, the differences appear more dramatic.

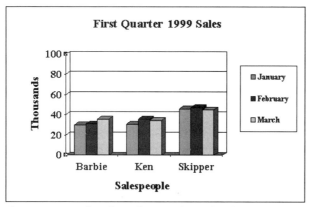

Figure 14-20: This chart doesn't show the differences between the values very well.

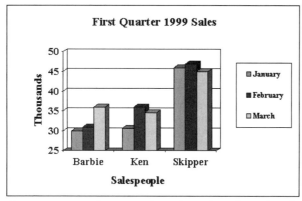

Figure 14-21: A change to the value axis scale makes the differences easier to see.

You will probably never run into a case as dramatic as the difference between Figures 14-20 and 14-21 because Microsoft Graph has an auto setting for the scale that's turned on by default. However, you may sometimes want to override it for a special effect.

To set the scale for an axis, follow these steps:

1. Point your mouse at the axis to be scaled (probably the vertical axis) and wait for a screen tip to pop up telling you you're pointing at the axis. If you don't see it, move the mouse until you do.

2. Right-click and choose Format Axis from the shortcut menu.

3. In the Format Axis dialog box, click the Scale tab. See Figure 14-22.

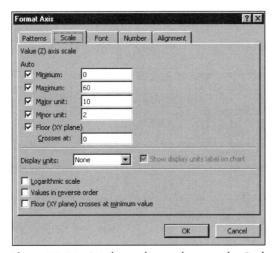

Figure 14-22: Set the scale numbers on the Scale tab.

4. (Optional) If you want any of these special features, select their checkboxes. Each of these checkboxes recalculates the numbers in the Minimum, Maximum, Major Units, and Minor Units text boxes. Don't select any of these after you have entered specific values if you want to keep your entered values.

   • **Logarithmic scale.** Rarely used by ordinary folks, this checkbox recalculates the Minimum, Maximum, Major Units, and Minor Units according to a power of 10 for the value axis based on the range of data. (If that explanation doesn't make any sense to you, you're not the target audience for this feature.)

   • **Values in reverse order.** This checkbox turns the scale backwards so the greater values are at the bottom or left.

• **Floor (*XY* plane) crosses at minimum value.** This checkbox sets the value of the text box labeled Crosses at to the smallest value represented on the chart. For example, if the shortest bar on the chart were $5,001, the minimum value on the scale would be $5,001, and that bar would have no height.

5. If you do not want the automatic value for one of the measurements, deselect the Auto checkbox for it and enter a number manually in its text box.

   • **Minimum is the starting number.** The usual setting is 0 (as in Figure 14-20), but in Figure 14-21 it starts at 25.

   • **Maximum is the top number.** This is 100 in Figure 14-20, and 50 in Figure 14-21.

   • **Major unit is the unit by which gridlines stretch out across the back wall of the chart.** In Figure 14-20, gridlines appear by twenties; in Figure 14-21, by fives.

   • **Minor unit is the interval of smaller gridlines between the major ones.** Most charts look better without minor units. They can make a chart look cluttered. Leave this set to Auto.

6. If you want a specific number at the floor other than the number you entered under Minimum, enter it in the Crosses at text box. (This is rarely done; usually the floor shows the minimum value.)

7. Click OK and then take a look at the results on your chart.

You may have noticed that the Format Axis dialog box has several other tabs besides Scale. These tabs contain settings you can change for your axis. Many of these controls are like ones you have seen earlier:

✦ **Patterns.** You can set text and background colors and patterns the same as for other parts of the chart.

✦ **Font.** Changing the font used to display the axis labels is the same as changing any other font.

✦ **Number.** You can change how the numbers on your axis appear, such as making them appear as percentages, currency, or another format.

✦ **Alignment.** You can align the axis text just as you can align the titles and labels on the chart.

Formatting the Legend

With a multiseries chart, the value of the legend is obvious — it tells you what colors represent which series. Without it, your audience won't know what the various bars or lines mean.

You can do all the same formatting for a legend that you can for other chart elements you've seen so far. Just right-click the legend, choose Format Legend from the shortcut menu, and then use the tabs in the Format Legend dialog box to make any of these modifications:

✦ **Change the background.** Use the Area controls on the Patterns tab.

✦ **Change the border around the legend.** Use the Border controls on the Patterns tab.

✦ **Change the font, font size, and attributes.** Use the controls on the Font tab or use the drop-down lists and buttons on the Formatting toolbar.

✦ **Change the placement of the legend in relation to the chart.** These controls are on the Placement tab. (You can also drag the legend's frame around the chart area to manually place it where you want it.)

Note   The controls on the Placement tab refer to the legend's position in relation to the chart, not to the legend text position within the legend box.

Adding Data Labels

Data labels aren't appropriate for every chart. In fact, so far I haven't used any of them at all in the sample charts I've displayed! Data labels announce the value, percentage, series, and so on for a bar, slice, or other value marker. The best place to use them is on a pie chart, since there's a fairly large expanse of area for each slide. Series and percentage data labels are shown in Figure 14-23. Notice that this figure doesn't contain a legend. It doesn't need one because the data labels convey the legend information.

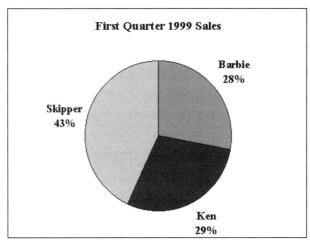

Figure 14-23: For some types of charts, data labels can help make the meaning clearer.

To add data labels, follow these steps:

1. Right-click the chart area and choose Chart Options from the shortcut menu.
2. Click the Data Labels tab. See Figure 14-24.

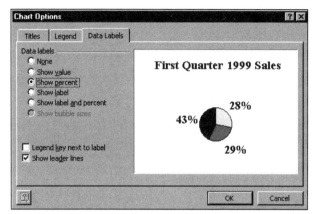

Figure 14-24: Choose the type of labels you want to appear on your chart.

3. Click the option button for the kind of labels you want:

   • **None.** No labels (the default).

   • **Show value.** Shows the actual value from the cell on the datasheet.

   • **Show percent**. Shows what percentage of the whole each slice represents.

   • **Show label**. Shows the label from the legend.

   • **Show label and percent**. A combination of Show percent and Show label. (This is what appears in Figure 14-23.)

Note   If the sample area in the dialog box shows the labels, percentages, or values too large, don't worry about it. Your chart will probably look fine.

4. If you are using Show label or Show label and percent, deselect the Legend key next to label checkbox.
5. Click OK. Your labels appear on your chart.

Formatting Gridlines and Walls

Gridlines help the readers' eyes follow across the chart. Gridlines are related to the axes, which you learned about earlier in the chapter. You have both vertical and horizontal gridlines available for your use, but most people use only horizontal ones. Walls are nothing more than the space between the gridlines, formatted in a different color than the plot area. Set the Walls area to None, and good-bye walls. (Don't you wish tearing down walls were always that easy?)

In most cases, the default gridlines that Microsoft Graph adds work well. However, sometimes you might want to make the lines thicker or a different color, or turn them off altogether.

To change which gridlines are displayed, just click the Category Axis Gridlines or Value Axis Gridlines buttons on the toolbar. These buttons toggle the gridlines on and off. See Figure 14-25. Or, you can follow these steps to set gridlines more precisely:

1. Right-click the chart area and choose Chart Options.

2. In the Chart Options dialog box, click the Gridlines tab. If you don't have a Gridlines tab, you are not using a chart type that supports them. (For example, pie charts do not.)

3. Select or deselect the Major Gridlines and Minor Gridlines checkboxes for each of the axes. If you're using a 2D chart, it has two dimensions (X and Y); 3D charts have three (X, Y, and Z, but Y is probably dimmed and unavailable). See Figure 14-25.

4. If you are using a 3D chart type, a 2D walls and gridlines checkbox appears on the Gridlines tab. If you want to make the walls and gridlines 2D, select it.

5. Click OK.

You can format gridlines the same way you format other objects on a chart. Just right-click a gridline and choose Format Gridline. Any changes you make affect all the gridlines of that type (for example, all horizontal Major ones).

When you open the Format Gridlines dialog box, you see two tabs. One is for Scale, which is the same as the Scale settings for the axis that gridline touches. Any changes made in one place are reflected in the other. The other is Patterns, and the controls there are the same as the controls you saw earlier for changing the other chart parts. The only difference is that the None option is grayed out. That's because you can't turn gridlines off from here. You must use the procedure outlined in the preceding steps or use the toolbar toggle buttons.

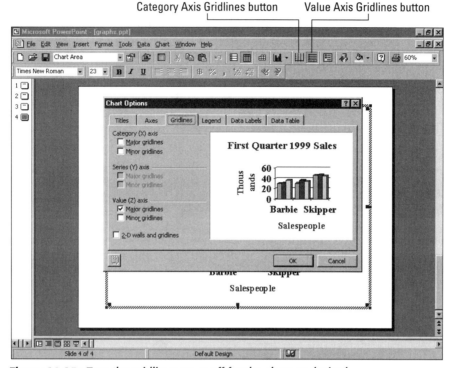

Figure 14-25: Turn the gridlines on or off for the chart as desired.

Formatting the Data Series

Now comes the fun part. You get to change the colors of the bars, lines, or slices, move them around, and otherwise tinker.

To format a data series, just right-click the bar, slice, or whatever, and choose Format Data Series from the shortcut menu. Then, depending on what type of chart you've got, you see different tabs that you can use to modify the series appearance.

You can format either the data series (all bars, lines, or whatever in the series) or the individual data point. When you right-click the data point, if you see and select Format Data Series, the changes you make affect the entire series. If you want to format the individual data point instead (for example, one individual bar), double-click the data point and then try right-clicking it again. The menu option should then read Format Data Point. Most of what you learn in the upcoming sections applies equally to either data series or data points.

Controlling Series Patterns and Ccolors

The first stop in the Format Data Series dialog box is the Patterns tab. This operates the same way as the Patterns tab you worked with for backgrounds. There is only one small addition: an Invert If Negative checkbox. This swaps the foreground and background colors if the number represented by the data point is negative. It applies to pies, bars, columns, and areas.

The colors you choose on this tab apply only to the particular series you right-clicked if there is more than one series in your chart. That's because you will want to select the color for each series separately rather than having them all appear in the same color.

Controlling the Bar or Column Shape

On the Shape tab (see Figure 14-26), you can choose what shape you want the bars or columns to be. Why settle for an ordinary bar? Have some fun with these. Don't forget, however, that you don't want to do anything to distract from your message. Don't make each series in the chart a different bar shape, for example.

One of the coolest shapes is the sawed-off pyramid (number 3 in Figure 14-26). The highest data point is a full pyramid, but the shorter ones look like their tops have been sawed off. Number 6 is the same effect, but with a cone.

Controlling the Data Series Labels

The Data Labels tab in the Format Data Series dialog box contains the same controls as the Data Labels tab you worked with in the Chart Options dialog box, except that these controls apply only to the one selected series. You could use these, for example, to add data labels only for the series that you wanted to spotlight.

Controlling Other Series Options

The Options tab is different for different chart types. It contains options specific to that type. For example, Figure 14-27 shows the options for a column chart. You can set the gap between bars and the overall chart depth.

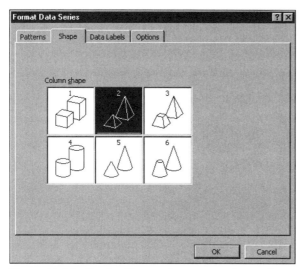

Figure 14-26: On the Shape tab, you can choose from among several bar and column shapes.

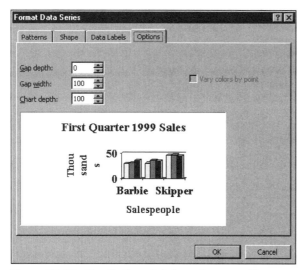

Figure 14-27: The Options tab for column and bar charts enables you to set the gaps between bars.

Figure 14-28 shows the Options tab for a pie chart. Here, you can set the angle of the first slice, effectively rotating the slices so that any slice is at any position you want. This can be very handy if the data labels are all bunched up on a pie chart. By modifying the position of the first slice, you can rotate the pie so that the large slices are at the top or bottom, where there is less room for data labels, and the smaller slices are on the sides, where there is more room.

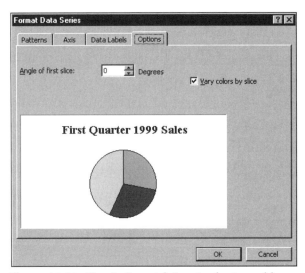

Figure 14-28: The Options tab for pie charts enables you to specify the angle of the first slice.

There is also a Vary colors by slice checkbox on the Options tab for pie charts. Leave this checked. If you deselect it, all the slices will be the same color, and you won't be able to tell them apart without data labels.

Changing the 3D Effects

This feature is a little bit advanced, but can be a real lifesaver when you have a 3D chart that needs some tweaking.

Not all of Microsoft Graph's charts turn out perfectly right away. The application can't anticipate how your data is going to look in a chart, so sometimes in a 3D chart some of the data bars or lines are obscured by other, taller ones in front of them. For example, in Figure 14-29, the back row's values are not visible because the middle row is too tall. Modifying the 3D settings makes the chart appear at a different angle and brings the obscured data points into view.

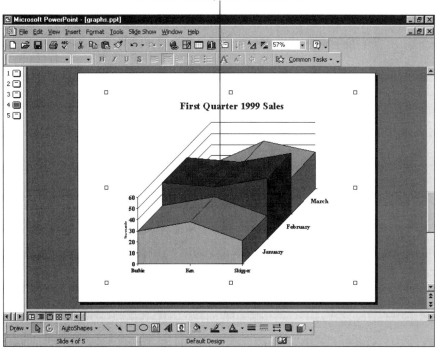

Figure 14-29: This chart could benefit from some 3D setting changes to make the back row more readable.

A quick way to tilt a chart differently is to drag a corner of the floor. To do this, point the mouse pointer at a corner of the floor so that a pop-up reads Corner. Then, click and hold down the mouse button. The display turns to a wireframe view of the chart. Drag, continuing to hold down the mouse button, to change the angle (see Figure 14-30). Then release the mouse button to redisplay the chart.

You can also change the 3D view with a dialog box, as shown in these steps:

1. Right-click the chart area and choose 3-D View.

2. In the 3-D View dialog box, shown in Figure 14-31, click the buttons to change the view, then click Apply to try out the settings. (Drag the title bar of the dialog box to move it out of the way as necessary.)

   • Use the Elevation buttons to tilt the chart up and down.

   • Use the Rotation buttons to rotate the chart. When you rotate a chart so much that the walls are in the way, the walls move to the opposite side.

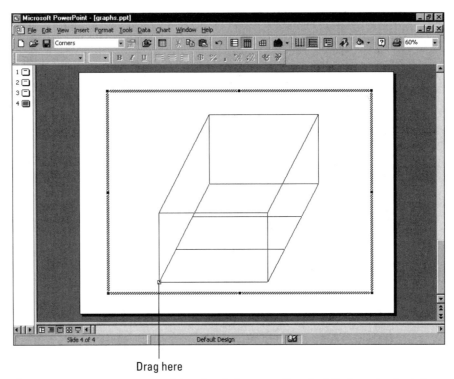

Drag here

Figure 14-30: Drag a corner of the chart's floor to adjust its 3D tilt and orientation.

Elevation buttons

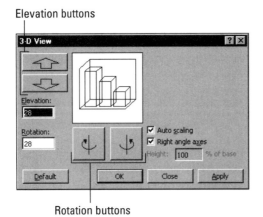

Rotation buttons

Figure 14-31: Use these 3D tools to adjust the view of the chart.

3. (Optional) In the Height text box, enter a percentage of the base width to represent the height of the chart. The default is 100; a setting of less than 100 makes a short, squat chart, while a setting of more than 100 makes a taller, thinner chart.

4. When you are satisfied with your settings and have tested them by clicking Apply, click OK. Figure 14-32 shows the chart from Figure 14-29 adjusted so that all data points are visible.

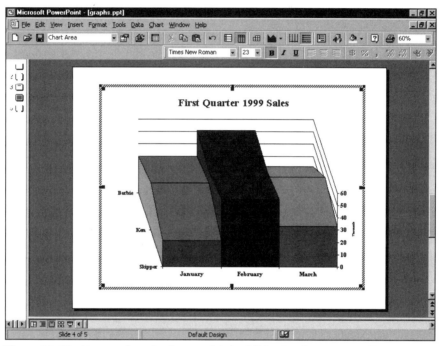

Figure 14-32: Now each series is completely visible, thanks to some 3D adjustments.

Summary

In this chapter, you learned how to create and format charts using Microsoft Graph. You covered a lot of ground here, learning not only how to create and modify charts, but how to format them. In the next chapter, you move on to another kind of object that has its own special program within PowerPoint for creating it: organization charts.

✦   ✦   ✦

Working with Organization Charts

Just as charts and graphs can enliven a boring table of numbers, as you saw in the preceding chapter, an organization chart can enliven a personnel discussion. An organization chart helps the audience understand the hierarchy of a company or a team in a visual way, so they don't have to juggle names and titles mentally as you speak. You can also use an organization chart to create a simple flow chart to illustrate a process, or to show a flow or progression over time (for example, of various versions of a product).

If you have tried to create an organization chart using the shapes and lines on PowerPoint's Drawing toolbar, you have my sympathy. It's nearly impossible to get all the lines and shapes lined up just so, and even harder to center text neatly within each shape. Luckily, PowerPoint comes with a special program exactly for this purpose: Microsoft Organization Chart.

Tip Microsoft Organization Chart is not installed with the default Office or PowerPoint setup routine. If you try to use Microsoft Organization Chart and find that it is not installed, you need to rerun the PowerPoint or Office installation program. See Appendix A for details.

Should you include your organization's structure in your presentation? That's a question that depends on your main message. If your speech is *about* the organization, then of course, yes. If not, show the organization structure only if it serves a purpose to advance your speech.

Many presenters have found that an organization chart makes an excellent backup slide. You can prepare it and have it ready in case a question arises about the organization. Another useful strategy is to include a printed organization chart as part of the handouts you distribute to the audience, without including the slide in your main presentation.

Starting Microsoft Organization Chart

There is an AutoLayout designed specifically for an organization chart; using it is one of the easiest ways to create an organization chart slide. Create a new slide using that AutoLayout (Insert ➪ New Slide) or switch a slide's layout to it (Format ➪ Slide Layout), and then double-click the placeholder. (See Chapter 10.)

You can also place an organization chart manually on a slide. To do so, choose Insert ➪ Picture ➪ Organization Chart.

Either way, the Microsoft Organization Chart window appears, as shown in Figure 15-1. (By default, it appears nonmaximized, but I have maximized it in the figures in this chapter so you can see it better.) A default organization chart appears, consisting of one Manager box and two Subordinate boxes.

Entering Names and Titles

Start out by filling in the names and titles for the boxes that appear. (You learn to add, remove, and move boxes in the "Changing the Chart Structure" section later in this chapter.) As shown in Figure 15-1, the Manager box (the top box) is selected already when you start Microsoft Organization Chart, and the words Type name here are highlighted.

1. Type the name of the top person in your organization and press Enter. The Type title here line become highlighted.

2. Type the person's title and press Enter. The <Comment 1> line becomes highlighted.

3. (Optional) Type a comment if desired. If you have more than one comment, press Enter again and type in the <Comment 2> line.

4. When you are finished with that person, press Esc.

5. Click inside the next box you want to enter data in (for example, the box for one of the subordinates) and repeat the steps.

Title bar reports the linked PowerPoint file

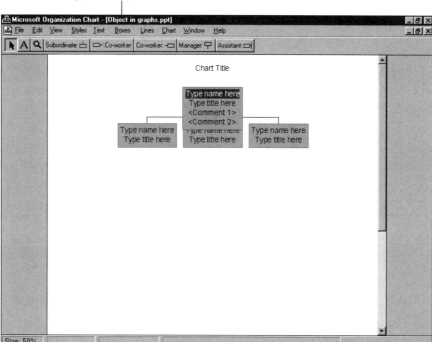

Figure 15-1: The Microsoft Organization Chart program opens in its own window on top of PowerPoint.

Figure 15-2 shows a completed chart that uses the four default boxes. Notice that one of the subordinate boxes contains a comment, making that box three lines long. The other two subordinate boxes have also grown in size to match, so that there is no inconsistency in the formatting on a given level.

Changing the Chart Structure

Unless you happen to have exactly one manager and three subordinates in your organization, you probably need to change the chart structure. This can include adding boxes, removing boxes, making people report to different submanagers, and so on.

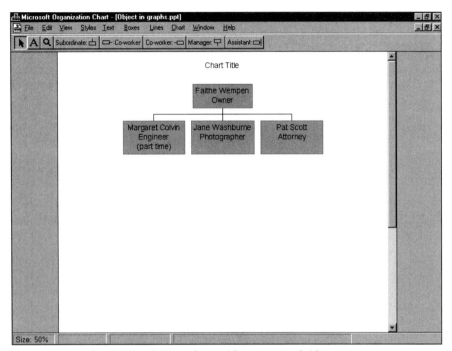

Figure 15-2: A basic organization chart with names and titles.

Adding Boxes

Before you start adding boxes to the chart, you should understand a little bit about the box types that are available. When you add a box to the chart, you add it in relation to an existing box. You can't add any boxes as independent entities, unconnected to the rest. (No box is an island!) With that in mind, a new box can have one of four relationships to an existing box:

✦ **Subordinate:** The new box reports to the existing box.

✦ **Manager:** The existing box reports to the new box.

✦ **Assistant:** The new box is an assistant to the existing box. (Some organizations differentiate between an assistant and a subordinate; others classify assistants as subordinates.)

To add a box to your default organization chart, follow these steps:

1. Click one of the buttons on the toolbar to represent the new box's relationship to an existing one. The mouse pointer changes to a box shape.

2. Click the existing box that the new one should relate to. A blank box appears in the appropriate position. For example, if you are adding a subordinate to a manager, a blank box appears beneath it. See Figure 15-3.

3. Click in the new box and type the name, title, and comments, as you learned in the preceding section.

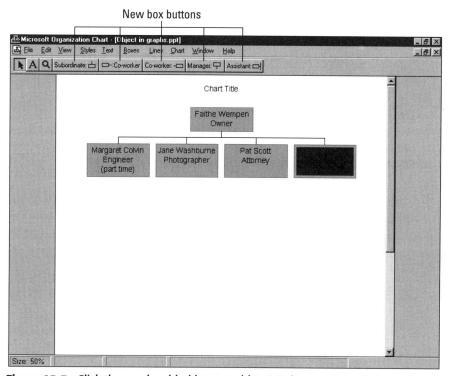

Figure 15-3: Click the newly added box to add text to it.

Moving and Deleting Boxes

When you move boxes around on an organization chart, relationships are everything. You may have worked with programs in the past where you could click a box and drag it wherever you wanted, but Microsoft Organization Chart does not work quite like that. You can do a certain amount of dragging boxes, but it's always in relation to another.

Using Cut and Paste

Suppose a subordinate now reports to a different manager. To move that person in the chart with cut and paste, follow these steps:

1. Select the box that needs to move.

2. Press Ctrl+X or choose Edit ⇨ Cut.

3. Select the box for the person to whom he or she should now report.

4. Press Ctrl+V or choose Edit ⇨ Paste.

One way to delete a box is to cut it (Ctrl+X) and then never paste it anywhere. An even more straightforward way is to select it and press Delete on the keyboard.

Dragging

You can also drag a box to a new position, but this can be hard because if your mouse pointer isn't pointing exactly at the right place, you end up activating the text in the box rather that moving the box. Here's what to do:

1. Click the box you want to move.

2. Position the mouse pointer just outside the box, so that the mouse pointer is an arrow (not an insertion point.)

3. Hold down the left mouse button and move the mouse pointer over the box that it should be related to. If you see an outline of the box, you know you are successfully dragging. If the placeholders in the box open for editing, you know you've done it incorrectly; click outside the box to cancel and then try again.

4. Drag the box over the top of a box that you want it to be subordinate to or a coworker of. Notice that a little symbol appears that looks either like a subordinate box or a right- or left-pointing arrow. The symbol changes as you move your mouse pointer over different parts of the destination box. Figure 15-4 shows a box being moved and the Subordinate symbol appearing.

5. When the destination box is highlighted and you see the appropriate symbol (arrow or subordinate box) for the correct relationship, release the mouse button to drop the box into place. If you make a mistake, press Ctrl+Z to undo and try again.

The above procedure is very frustrating for me—it takes me several tries to move a box this way! That's why I prefer the cut and paste method.

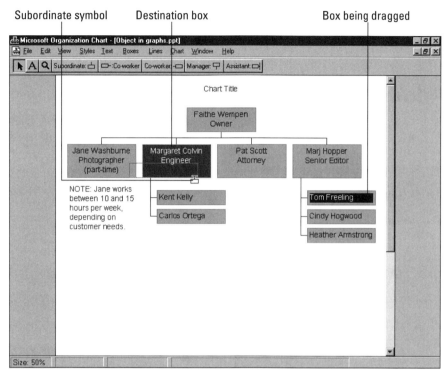

Figure 15-4: When you drag a box, you can make it a subordinate or a peer (coworker) of another box by watching for a symbol as you drag.

Working with Several Boxes at Once

If you have a lot of moving, formatting, or whatever to do, you may want to select multiple boxes before performing the action. This can certainly save you some time if, for example, seven subordinates all need to move to report to the same new manager.

There are several ways to select multiple boxes, depending on what your goal is:

✦ To select more than one box manually, click the first box, and then hold down the Shift key while you click the other boxes.

✦ To select all of a certain type of box (for example, all managers, which would be everyone who has at least one person reporting to him or her), choose Edit ➪ Select and then a category (such as All Managers).

✦ To select certain levels of the chart (a level being a *row*), choose Edit ⇨ Select Levels. In the dialog box that appears, indicate which levels you want to select and click OK.Ω

Adding Titles and Notes

So far, you have ignored that placeholder at the top of the chart: Chart Title. Now it's time to fill it in. To do so, click those words to move the insertion point there, then drag across the entire phrase to select it. Type your new title.

You can also add some text boxes that aren't connected to the rest of the chart for subtitles or explanations. To do so, follow these steps:

1. Click the Enter Text button on the toolbar (the capital *A*).

2. Click anywhere in the work area to position the insertion point.

3. Type your text. You can press Enter to start another line as needed.

4. When you are finished, click anywhere away from the text. The text appears to float on the chart, as shown in Figure 15-5.

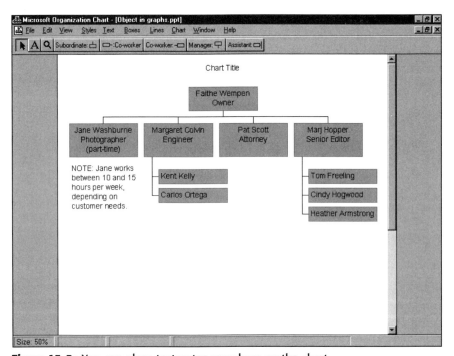

Figure 15-5: You can place text notes anywhere on the chart.

When you add text this way, it becomes an object on the chart. When you click it, selection handles appear around it. You can drag it around on the chart the same way you drag objects around in PowerPoint. The chart title, however, is fixed in place; you can't drag it around.

Formatting the Chart

Now look at some of the things you can do to make your chart more appealing and eye-catching. These formatting options don't affect the content or meaning of the chart, but as you have probably learned from experience, sometimes content is not the only thing that affects people's understanding — formatting can make a big difference, too.

Changing the Grouping Style

There are lots of ways to arrange the boxes on an organization chart, and so far you've seen just one of them.

Open the Styles menu and check out all the little pictures of organization styles. Figure 15-6 shows the styles you can choose. Whenever there is a group of boxes under a manager, you can format that group in any of the ways shown.

1. Select the boxes that you want to change the grouping style for. Typically, these should be boxes of the same level, reporting to the same manager.

2. Open the Styles menu and click the button representing the style you want.

Figure 15-7 shows a sample chart that uses two of the alternative styles — one for the first-level subordinates and one for the second level.

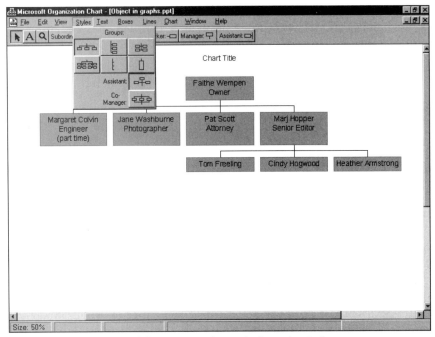

Figure 15-6: Choose a different grouping style from the Styles menu.

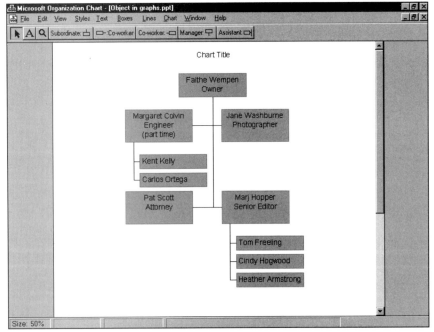

Figure 15-7: Here are a couple of alternative grouping styles in use.

Drawing Extra Lines and Rectangles

Besides the lines and boxes that contain your content, you might also want to add some extra lines and rectangles. These can be purely for decoration, or they can show additional fine points in the organizational structure, such as *dotted-line reporting* (where a person reports primarily to one manager but is also responsible to a limited degree for the projects of some other manager).

 Caution   Be careful that any decorative lines and shapes you include do not detract from the main parts of the chart. It is all too easy to draw the audience's eye away from the important point with some extraneous decoration.

Just like PowerPoint, Microsoft Organization Chart has its own drawing tools. They are not displayed by default, but you can easily display them by choosing View ➪ Show Draw Tools or pressing Ctrl+D.

Here are the tools and what each one does.

Icon	Description
＋	Draws a horizontal or vertical line. This line is not tied to any particular box, so you can put it anywhere.
╱	Draws a straight line at any angle or direction.
⠿	Draws a reporting line between two boxes. You must start at the edge of one box and end it at the edge of another; otherwise, an error message appears.
▭	Draws a decorative rectangle. You might use this, for example, to group several boxes together as a department.

You can format these lines and shapes in the same way that you format other objects on the organization chart. You learn about these later in the chapter, but here's a shortcut. For a line, select the line and use the commands on the Lines menu. For a rectangle, use the commands on the Boxes menu.

Formatting Text

Just like in PowerPoint, you can format the text to use a different font, size, color, attribute, and so on. For example, you might want to make the text smaller so you can create a more complex organization chart.

Note   When you change the size of the font in a box, the font changes only for the selected box (or boxes). However, because all boxes of the same level must be the same size, if the box has to expand to accommodate larger text, all the boxes of that level in the chart get larger too, even though their text size does not change.

To format some text, follow these steps:

1. Select all of the boxes and other text notes containing the text you want to format.

2. Choose Text ➪ Font. The Font dialog box opens. See Figure 15-8.

3. Choose a font from the Font list.

4. Choose a size from the Size list.

5. Choose any special formatting attributes, like bold or italic.

6. Click OK. The selected text changes.

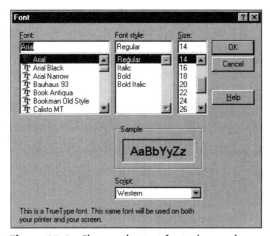

Figure 15-8: Change the text font, size, and attributes, just like in PowerPoint.

You can also change the text alignment in boxes. By default, text is centered in a box and left-aligned in a text note. Just choose Left, Right, or Center from the Text menu to change the alignment of a selected box or note.

Text color is controlled by the Text ➪ Color command. When you issue this command, a Color dialog box appears, which is nothing more than a palette of colored squares. Click the color that you want and then click OK.

Formatting Boxes

The boxes pick up their default colors from the presentation's color scheme. That way, if you change the color scheme, the organization chart can adjust itself automatically. However, you can assign any colors you want, or even make the boxes transparent. For example, you might want to change the boxes of certain employees (such as part-timers) to a different color to differentiate them from the others. You can also change the border thickness and style that surrounds each box.

1. Select all the boxes that you want to reformat.

2. Choose Boxes ➪ Color. A Color dialog box appears, showing an assortment of colored squares.

3. Click the color you want for the selected boxes. (The gray raised button in the bottom-right corner sets the color to Transparent.)

4. Click OK.

5. Choose Boxes ➪ Shadow. A submenu of shadow types appears. See Figure 15-9.

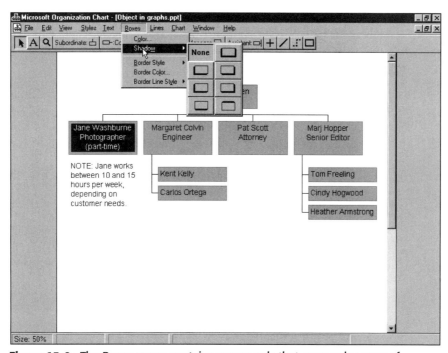

Figure 15-9: The Boxes menu contains commands that open submenus of formatting choices.

6. Click the shadow type you want for the boxes.

7. Choose Boxes ➪ Border Style. A submenu of border styles appears.

8. Click the border style you want.

9. Choose Boxes ➪ Border Color. A Color dialog box appears.

10. Click the color you want. If you want no border, choose the same color as the inside color for the box.

11. Click OK.

Formatting Lines

The lines that you control with the Lines menu are the lines that connect one box to another. These are drawn automatically for you, but you can change their thickness, color, and style (solid, dashed, or dotted).

Note   Dotted lines are traditionally used in organization charts to indicate shared or tangential responsibility. For example, an employee might report mainly to one manager but have dotted-line reporting to another. Perhaps although the second manager does not have responsibility for the employee, he or she may sometimes assign work or provide guidance.

You might want to make certain lines thicker to emphasize them. For example, you could make the lines that denote the main organization bolder than those that show a satellite office.

To select a line, click it. To select more than one line, hold down the Shift key while you click multiple lines. It is hard to tell when a line is selected; it looks somewhat fuzzy or dotted when selected, but you may have to squint to see it.

After selecting the line, open the Lines menu and choose a command:

✦ The Thickness command provides a selection of line thicknesses, including None.

✦ The Style command lets you choose solid, dotted, or dashed.

✦ The Color command opens a palette of colors, just as you saw for text and for boxes.

Tip   If you need to create two separate charts within a single chart, you could set the line that joins the two parts to None, effectively removing it so the parts appear separate.

Changing the Chart Background

Like all objects, an organization chart can have a colored background. Your choices of color are more limited for an organization chart than for most objects in that you can't use textures or patterns. However, you have a variety of solid colors to choose from.

To set the chart background, choose Chart ➪ Background Color. In the Color dialog box, click the color you want and click OK.

Saving the Chart

After creating your organization chart, you can return to PowerPoint. To do so, choose File ➪ Exit and Return to {*filename*}. A dialog box appears with the message that the object has been changed and asks whether you want to update it. Click Yes. There you have it! Your organization chart now appears on a slide in PowerPoint. You can move it, resize it, and otherwise adjust it as you can any other object. (See Chapter 10.)

Other Programs You Can Use

Microsoft Organization Chart is a rather limited program. If you find that your organization charting needs exceed what the program can provide, you might want to turn elsewhere for a different program.

One excellent program for flow charts in particular is RFFlow, which is included in demo form on the CD that accompanies this book. You may also want to experiment with Visio, a commercial product that creates all kinds of organization, flow, and process diagrams.

Summary

In this chapter, you learned how to create and modify organization charts with Microsoft Organization chart, an accessory program that comes with PowerPoint (or Microsoft Office). You can now create a chart, add or remove levels of reporting, and format the chart's boxes and lines.

In the next chapter, I tell you how to incorporate data from other programs, including third-party programs that have nothing to do with PowerPoint. After you learn this skill, you will be able to include almost any kind of content in any PowerPoint presentation—the sky's the limit.

✦   ✦   ✦

Incorporating Data from Other Programs

All objects are basically alike in PowerPoint once you get them into the presentation. But how you place an object in your presentation can depend on what kind of object it is.

As you have already seen, PowerPoint contains an assortment of miniprograms that place various types of objects: WordArt, Microsoft Graph, Microsoft Organization Chart, the Clip Gallery, and so on. These are easy; you just choose the desired object type from the Insert menu in PowerPoint and away you go. Graphics are similarly easy, no matter what program they come from.

However, there are a lot of other objects that don't fall into any of these categories, and that might be useful occasionally in a presentation. Examples include text from a word processing document, a slide from a different presentation program, a chart from a spreadsheet, or any of many other objects. With these objects, you need to be a little bit sneaky when you bring them in to PowerPoint.

There are two ways to bring *foreign objects* into your presentation. The method you choose depends on how you want the object to behave. If you want the object to be a full citizen of your presentation — that is, to leave its home application behind and never look back — you can do a simple cut or copy and paste. However, if you want the object to maintain a link with its native land, you should use the Object Linking and Embedding (OLE) methods described later in this chapter instead.

Caution   If you do not have a strong reason for using OLE, use the simpler cut-and-paste method instead. It is far less strain on your computer's brain, and your presentation will load and save much more quickly.

Copying Content from Other Programs

You have two choices for copying content to a PowerPoint slide: using copy and paste or dragging.

Using Copy and Paste

The easiest way to put something into PowerPoint is to use the Windows Clipboard. Because almost all Windows-based programs employ the Clipboard, you can move data from any program to almost any other with a minimum of fuss. Follow these steps:

1. Create the object in its native program or open the file that contains it.

2. Select the object you want, and choose Edit ➪ Copy.

3. Switch to PowerPoint, and display the slide on which you want to place the object.

4. Choose Edit ➪ Paste. The object appears on the slide.

5. Move or resize the new object as necessary on the slide.

Don't forget that there are many alternative methods for using the Copy and Paste commands. The shortcut keys are among the fastest: Ctrl+C for copy and Ctrl+V for paste.

Dragging

In some cases, you can also use drag and drop to move an object from some other application to PowerPoint. This works only in programs that support it. (Not all Windows programs do.) If you're not sure whether a program supports it, try it and see.

Here's how to drag and drop:

1. Create the object in its native program or open the file that contains it.

2. Open PowerPoint and display the slide on which you want to place the object.

3. Resize both applications' windows so that both the object and its destination are visible onscreen.

4. Select the object in its native program.

5. If you want to copy, rather than move, hold down the Ctrl key.

6. Drag the object to the PowerPoint slide. See Figure 16-1. An outline appears on the PowerPoint slide showing where the new object will go.

7. Release the mouse button. The new object is moved or copied.

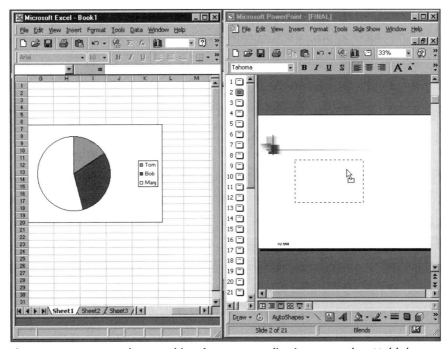

Figure 16-1: You can drag an object from one application to another. Hold down the Ctrl key to copy rather than move.

Introducing OLE

The abbreviation OLE stands for *Object Linking and Embedding*. It enables Windows-based applications that support it to share information dynamically. That means that the object remembers where it came from and has special abilities based on that memory. Even though the name OLE is a little scary (it ranks right up there with SQL in my book!), the concept is very elementary, and anyone can understand and use it.

You already understand the term *object* in the PowerPoint sense, and the term is very similar to that in the case of OLE. An object is any bit of data (or a whole file) that you want to use in another program.

Two actions are involved in OLE: linking and embedding. Here are quick definitions of each:

✦ *Linking* creates a link between the original file and the copy in your presentation so that the copy is always updated.

✦ *Embedding* creates a new object in your presentation or edits an existing one in its native application without leaving PowerPoint.

Embedding by itself doesn't maintain a link to any data file. It just inserts a copy into your document, like the regular Copy command. However, it does maintain a link to the application that created it, so you can double-click the embedded object to open that program. Conversely, linking by itself doesn't embed.

Some objects can be both linked and embedded; others only one or the other. Linked objects must already exist independently of the PowerPoint presentation because they are referred to by name in the link. The instructions to the computer might be, "Go out and find Sales.xls and bring me the most recent version of what's in cells A1 through C8." Embedded objects can be created on the fly right in PowerPoint. Don't worry if you don't fully understand this yet; it will become clearer.

Caution   OLE links can slow down your presentation's loading and editing performance. Therefore, you should create OLE links and embedding last, after you have finished adding content and polishing the formatting.

OLE isn't suitable for every task. If you want to use an object (like an Excel chart or a picture from a graphics program) that will not change, it's best to copy it there normally. Reserve OLE for objects that will change and that you will always need the most recent version of.

Here are some ideas of when OLE might be useful:

✦ If you have to give the same presentation every month that shows the monthly sales statistics, link to your Excel worksheet where you track them during the month. Your presentation will always contain the most current data.

✦ If you want to draw a picture in Paint (a program that comes with Windows) or some other graphics program, embed the picture in PowerPoint. That way, you don't have to open Paint (or the other program) separately every time you want to work on the picture while you're fine-tuning your presentation. You can just double-click the picture in PowerPoint.

✦ If you know that a coworker is still finalizing a chart or drawing, link to his or her working file on the network. Then whenever changes are made to it, your copy will also be updated. (Beware, however, that once you take your presentation away from the computer that has network access, you will no longer be able to update the item.)

Linking and/or Embedding a Part of a File

As I mentioned earlier, you can link or embed either a part of an existing file or the whole thing. If you need only a part of an existing file, you use the following procedure:

1. In its native application, create or open the file containing the data you want to copy.

2. If you have just created the file, save it. The file must have a name before you go any further.

3. Select the data you want.

4. Choose Edit ⇨ Copy.

5. Switch to PowerPoint and display the slide on which you want to paste the data.

6. Choose Edit ⇨ Paste Special. The Paste Special dialog box opens. See Figure 16-2.

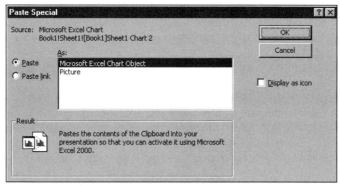

Figure 16-2: Use the Paste Special dialog box to link or embed a piece of a data file from another program.

7. If you want to embed only, leave Paste selected. If you want to link (with or without embedding) click Paste Link. If Paste Link is not available, you probably did not save the file back in Step 2.

8. Choose the format from the As list. The formats change depending on the object type and whether you chose Paste or Paste Link in Step 7. Here are some of the types you might see:

   • **Object.** Any type that ends with the word object is an OLE-capable format that enables embedding. Choose this if you want to include embedding.

- **Formatted Text (.RTF).** This data type formats text as it is formatted in the original file. For example, if the text is formatted as underlined, it is pasted as underlined. This format does not support embedding.

- **Unformatted Text.** This is the same as formatted text except it does not retain any formatting.

- **Picture.** The object comes in as a Windows Metafile picture. It is not embedded.

- **Device Independent Bitmap.** The object comes in as a bitmap picture, like a Windows Paint image. It is not embedded.

9. If you want the pasted object to appear as an icon instead of as itself, click the Display as Icon checkbox. This is useful for pasting sounds and video clips, because you can play them later by clicking the icon. This checkbox may be unavailable if the object type you chose in Step 8 does not support it.

10. Click OK. The object is placed in your presentation.

If you linked the object, each time you open your PowerPoint presentation, PowerPoint checks the source file for an updated version.

If you embedded the object, you can double-click it at any time to open it in its native application for editing.

Embedding an Existing File (with or without Linking)

Sometimes you may want to place an entire file on a PowerPoint slide — for example, if the file is small and contains only the object that you want to display. To create this connection, you use the Insert ➪ Object command, which is handier than the procedure you just learned because you do not have to open the other application.

When working with whole, named files, you cannot avoid embedding. You can either embed only, or you can both embed and link:

1. In PowerPoint, display the slide on which you want to place the file.

2. Choose Insert ➪ Object. The Insert Object dialog box opens.

3. Click the Create from file option button. The controls change to those shown in Figure 16-3.

4. Click Browse, and use the Browse dialog box to locate the file you want. Then click OK to accept the filename.

5. If you want the file to be linked, click the Link checkbox.

6. Click OK. The file is inserted on your PowerPoint slide.

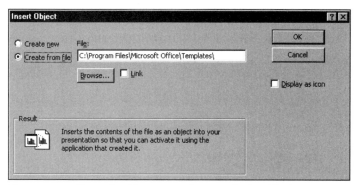

Figure 16-3: Enter the filename or browse for it with the Browse button.

Embedding a new file

If you want to embed a *foreign object* but you haven't created that object yet, a really easy way to do so is to embed it on the fly. When you do this, the controls for the program open within PowerPoint and you can create your object. Then, your work is saved within PowerPoint rather than as a separate file.

1. Open PowerPoint and display the slide on which you want to put the new object.

2. Choose Insert ⇨ Object. The Insert Object dialog box appears.

3. Click Create new. A list of available object types appears. See Figure 16-4.

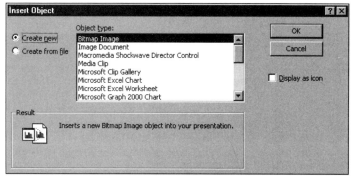

Figure 16-4: Choose the object type you want to create. The object types listed come from the OLE-compliant programs installed on your PC.

4. Click the object type you want and then click OK. The application opens.

5. Create the object using the program's controls. See Figure 16-5.

6. When you are finished, click anywhere on the slide outside of that object's frame. Your PowerPoint controls return to normal, and the object floats on the slide.

7. Resize and move the object as necessary.

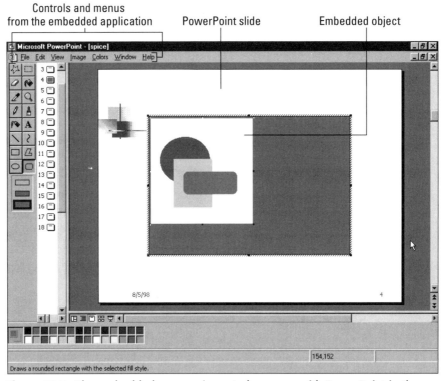

Figure 16-5: The embedded program's controls appear, with PowerPoint in the background.

Because you are creating a file that doesn't have a name or saved location separate from the PowerPoint presentation, you can't link it to anything; embedding is the only option.

Working with Linked and Embedded Objects

Now that you have a linked and/or embedded object, what can you do with it? Lots of things. You can edit an embedded object by double-clicking it, of course. And you can update, change, and even cancel the links associated with a linked object. The following sections provide some details.

Editing an Embedded Object

To edit an embedded object, follow these steps:

1. Display the slide containing the embedded object.

2. Double-click it or choose Edit ➪ Object. The object's program's controls appear. They might be integrated into the PowerPoint window, like the ones for Paint that you saw in Figure 16-5, or they might appear in a separate window.

3. Edit the object as needed.

4. Return to PowerPoint by doing one of these things:

   • If the embedded object is not linked to a saved file, click the slide behind the object to return to PowerPoint.

   • If the embedded object is also linked, choose File ➪ Exit. (Remember, the menu system that appears is for the embedded application, not for PowerPoint.) When asked to save your changes, click Yes.

You can also edit a linked object directly in its original application, independently from PowerPoint. Close your PowerPoint presentation and open the original application. Do your editing, and save your work. Then, reopen your PowerPoint presentation and the object will reflect the changes.

Changing How Links Are Updated

Links are automatically updated each time you open your PowerPoint file. However, updating links slows down the file opening considerably, so if you open and close the file frequently, you may want to set the link updating to Manual. That way, the links are updated only when you issue a command to update them.

To set a link to update manually, follow these steps:

1. Open the PowerPoint presentation that contains the linked object(s).

2. Choose Edit ➪ Links. The Links dialog box appears. See Figure 16-6.

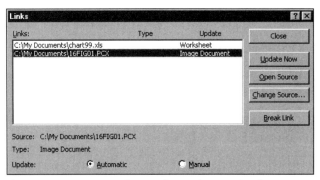

Figure 16-6: You can change the update setting for or break the links in your presentation here.

3. Click the link that you want to change.

4. Click the Manual option button.

5. If you want to change any other links, repeat Steps 3 and 4.

6. If you want to update a link now, select it and click the Update Now button.

7. Click OK.

8. Choose File ➪ Save to save the presentation changes (including the changes to the link settings).

When you set a link to Manual, you have to open the Links dialog box and click Update Now, as in Step 6, each time you want to update it. Or, you can right-click the object and choose Update Link from its shortcut menu.

Breaking a Link

When you break a link, the object remains in the presentation, but it becomes an ordinary object, just like any other picture or other object you might have copied there. You can't double-click it to edit it anymore, and it doesn't update when the source changes. To break a link, reopen the Links dialog box (Figure 16-6), click the link to break, and then click Break Link. If a warning box appears, click OK.

Exporting PowerPoint Objects to Other Programs

You can copy any object in your PowerPoint presentation to another program, either linked or unlinked. For example, perhaps you created a graph using Microsoft Graph for one of your PowerPoint slides, and now you want to use that graph in a Microsoft Word document.

To use a PowerPoint object in another program, you do the same basic things that you've learned in this chapter, but you start with the other program. Here are some examples:

✦ To copy an object from PowerPoint, select it in PowerPoint and choose Edit ⇨ Copy. Then switch to the other program and choose Edit ⇨ Paste.

✦ To embed (and optionally link) an object from a PowerPoint presentation in another program's document, choose it in PowerPoint and choose Edit ⇨ Copy. Then, switch to the other program and choose Edit ⇨ Paste Special.

✦ To embed or link an entire PowerPoint presentation in another program's document, use the Insert ⇨ Object command in that other program, and choose your PowerPoint file as the source.

Summary

In this chapter, you learned the mysteries of OLE, a term you have probably heard bandied about but were never quite sure what it meant. You can now use objects freely between PowerPoint and other programs, and include links and embedding for them whenever appropriate.

In the next chapter, you take a final look at your presentation to make sure there aren't any embarrassing errors like spelling mistakes or formatting inconsistencies, and you learn about numbering slides and using the Style Checker.

✦   ✦   ✦

Pre-Show Presentation Polishing

17

Before you hit the road with your show, take an hour or
so to check your work and polish its appearance. This
chapter will help you make your show sparkle.

Using Headers and Footers

To keep your work organized and cohesive, you can include
repeated or sequential information on each slide, handout,
and/or notes page. For example, you can number your
handout pages sequentially, or you can repeat the company's
name at the bottom of each slide. When such repeated
information appears at the top of the slide or page, it's a
header; when it appears at the bottom, it's a footer.

Turning Slide Footer Information On or Off

There are three repeated elements you can include (or not) on
each slide: the date (and/or time), the slide number, and the
footer text (which can contain any text you specify).

You can make the date update automatically each time you
open the presentation, or you can specify a fixed date. A fixed
date is useful if you want the slides to show the date on which
you plan to give a one-time presentation; an automatically
updated date works well for a presentation you give more
than once.

To turn these elements on or off, follow these steps:

1. If you don't want the same settings for all slides in the presentation (except title slides), select the slides you want to affect in Slide Sorter view or in the outline pane of Normal view.

2. Choose View ➪ Header and Footer. The Header and Footer dialog box opens.

3. Click the Slide tab if it is not already displayed.

4. If you want the date on the slide, make sure the Date and time checkbox is marked. See Figure 17-1.

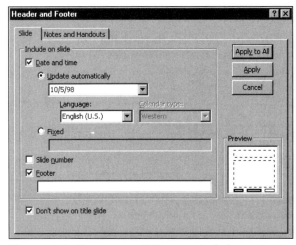

Figure 17-1: Turn on or off the repeated elements at the bottom of each slide.

5. Choose Update automatically or Fixed, depending on the date type you want.

   If you chose Update automatically, open the drop-down list and choose a date format. If you use a different language or calendar than English, choose them from the Language and Calendar type drop-down lists.

   If you chose Fixed, type the date, in the exact format that you want it to appear, in the Fixed text box.

6. If you want the slide number to appear on the slide, make sure the Slide number checkbox is marked.

7. If you want to include footer text on the slide, make sure the Footer checkbox is marked and then type the text for it in the Footer text box.

8. If you don't want these elements to appear on the title slide, mark the Don't show on title slide checkbox. This suppresses the date, slide number, and footer text on all slides formatted with the Title AutoLayout.

9. Click Apply to All to apply the change to all slides in the presentation (recommended) or Apply to apply the change only to the selected slide(s).

Tip   Slide numbering starts with 1 by default. If you want to start the slide numbering with a number other than 1, choose File ➪ Page Setup and change the number in the Number Slides From text box, as explained in Chapter 11.

Formatting Slide Footer Information

In the preceding steps, you chose whether or not to use repeated footer elements on your slides. Now you can indicate how the elements should be formatted when they appear.

In working with the Slide Master (see Chapter 11), you may have noticed the Date Area, Footer Area, and Number Area. See Figure 17-2. These placeholders show where these elements will appear on each slide — *if* you have set them up to appear at all. If you have any of these elements turned off, moving or formatting their text boxes on the master has no effect on the presentation's appearance.

You can drag these Date, Footer, and Number text boxes around on the Slide Master to control the positioning. You can even drag them to the top of the slide, effectively making the Footer Area box into a header!

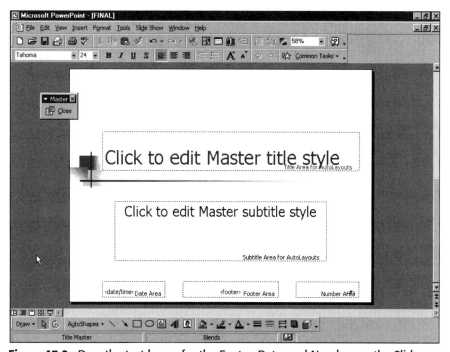

Figure 17-2: Drag the text boxes for the Footer, Date, and Number on the Slide Master to reposition them if needed.

You can also format the dummy text in these text boxes to choose the font, size, and attributes of the text to appear in them. Follow these steps to format the date, slide number, or footer text:

1. Click in the box for the area you want to format (Date Area, Footer Area, or Number Area).

2. Double-click the bracketed placeholder to select it (for example, <date/time>).

3. Change the font, size, attributes, alignment, or any other formatting for the placeholder. Refer back to Chapter 8 as needed.

4. Click away from the box to deselect the placeholder.

5. Format other placeholders if needed; then click the Close button to exit the Slide Master.

Correcting Your Spelling

If you think that a spelling check can't improve the look of your presentation, just think for a moment how ugly a blatant spelling error would look in huge type on a five-foot projection screen. Frightening, isn't it? If that image makes you nervous, it should. Spelling mistakes can creep past even literate people, and pop up where you least expect them, often at embarrassing moments.

Fortunately, like other Microsoft Office programs, PowerPoint comes with a powerful spelling program that can check your work for you at any time, minimizing the number of embarrassing spelling mistakes. The Office programs all use the same spelling checker, so if you are familiar with it in another Office application, you should be able to breeze through a spell check in PowerPoint with no problem.

Caution   When PowerPoint marks a word as misspelled, it really just means that the word is not in its dictionary. Many words, especially proper names, are perfectly okay to use and yet not in PowerPoint's dictionary, so don't believe PowerPoint against your own good judgment.

Checking an Individual Word

As you work, PowerPoint underlines words that aren't in its dictionary with a red wavy line. Whenever you see a red-underlined word, you can right-click it to see a list of spelling suggestions, as shown in Figure 17-3. Click the correction you want or click one of the other commands:

✦ **Ignore All:** Ignores this and all other instances of the word in this PowerPoint session. If you exit and restart PowerPoint, the list is wiped out.

✦ **Add:** Adds this word to PowerPoint's custom dictionary. (You learn more about this later in the chapter.)

✦ **Spelling:** Opens the full-blown spelling checker, described below.

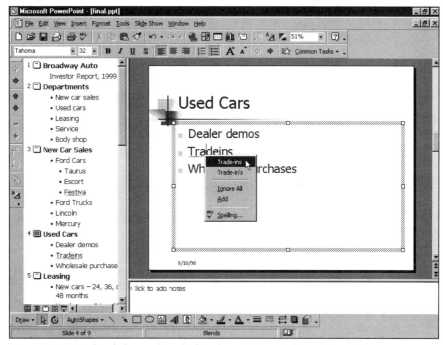

Figure 17-3: Right-click a red-underlined word for quick spelling advice.

Note

If you don't want to see the wavy red underlines onscreen, you can turn off that feature of the spelling checker. To do so, select Tools ➪ Options and click the Spelling and Style tab. From there, select Hide Spelling Errors in This Document. Then click OK.

Checking the Entire Presentation

If your document is long, it can get tiresome to individually right-click each wavy-underlined word or phrase. In such cases, it's easier to use the full-blown spell-check feature in PowerPoint to check all the words in the entire presentation.

To begin the spelling check, click the Spelling toolbar button, select Tools ➪ Spelling and Grammar, or press F7. If there are no misspelled words in your presentation, PowerPoint presents a dialog box telling you that your spell check is complete. Click OK to close that dialog box.

If, on the other hand, PowerPoint finds a misspelled word, you can choose from several dialog box control options (as shown in Figure 17-4):

Figure 17-4: When PowerPoint finds a misspelled word with the spelling checker, you can respond to it using these controls.

✦ **Not in dictionary:** Shows the misspelled word.

✦ **Change to:** Shows what the spelling will be changed to if you click the Change or Change All button. You can choose a word from the Suggestions list or type your own correction here.

✦ **Suggestions:** Lists words close to the spelling of the word you actually typed. Choose the correct one, moving it to the Change to box, by clicking it.

✦ **Ignore:** Skips over this occurrence of the word.

✦ **Ignore All:** Skips over all occurrences of the word in this PowerPoint session only.

✦ **Change:** Changes the word in the presentation to the word in the Change to text box.

✦ **Change All:** Changes all occurrences of the word in the entire presentation to the word in the Change to text box.

✦ **Add:** Adds the word to PowerPoint's custom dictionary so that it will recognize it in the future.

✦ **Suggest:** Displays the suggestions in the Suggestions box if you have set the spell checker's options so that suggestions do not automatically appear.

✦ **AutoCorrect:** Adds the word to the AutoCorrect list so that if you misspell it the same way in the future, PowerPoint automatically corrects it as you type. See the "Using AutoCorrect to Fix Common Problems" section later in this chapter.

✦ **Close:** Closes the Spelling checker dialog box.

When PowerPoint can't find any more misspelled words, it displays a dialog box (or message from the Office Assistant) to that effect; click OK.

Tip If you have more than one language dictionary available (for example, if you are using PowerPoint in a multilingual office and have purchased multiple language packs from Microsoft), you can specify which language's dictionary to use for which text. To do so, select the text that's in a different language than the rest of the presentation, and then choose Tools ➪ Language. Select the language from the list and click OK.

Checking Style and Punctuation

As you create your presentation, you are probably focusing on the meaning of the words, not the formatting. Even later, as you begin to apply text formatting, some picky little errors may slip by you. Perhaps you ended each bullet point with a period on one slide but not another, or maybe you capitalized every word in some headings but only the first word of others.

PowerPoint can help with this by applying style and punctuation rules that you specify. It's not pushy about the rules, and it won't make changes automatically without your consent. Instead, it merely suggests ways to make the presentation more consistent and attractive.

Note You can accept the default style and punctuation rules, or you can make some changes. (Most people accept the defaults.)To change the style and punctuation rules, see the following section.

Style and punctuation checking happens automatically. Whenever PowerPoint sees a problem, a little light bulb appears on the slide. Click it, and you see the Office Assistant appear with a suggestion, as shown in Figure 17-5. Click one of the available options to make the change or ignore the style rule.

Setting Spelling and Style Options

You can control how PowerPoint decides what spelling and style suggestions to make. For example, suppose you want PowerPoint to ignore words in uppercase (which are probably acronyms that won't make sense as regular words anyway) or to let you know about inconsistent punctuation in titles but not in body text. You can set up PowerPoint to work the way you want.

To view the spelling and style options, follow these steps:

1. Select Tools ➪ Options. The Options dialog box opens.
2. Click the Spelling and Style tab. See Figure 17-6.
3. Turn on/off the checkboxes for any of the listed options:

Figure 17-5: I clicked a light bulb (no longer visible here, but it was next to the mouse pointer) to find out what suggestion the Office Assistant had to offer.

Figure 17-6: Change the spelling options on this tab or click the Style Options button to set style options.

- **Checking spelling as you type:** Turns on/off the automatic spell check.

- **Hide spelling errors in this document:** Turns on/off the wavy underlines in the presentation that indicate spelling errors.

- **Always suggest corrections:** If you deselect this option, no choices appear in the Suggestions area of the Spelling check dialog box. This might help the spell-check speed on an extremely old and slow computer.

- **Ignore words in UPPERCASE:** If you select this option, the spelling check does not flag words that appear in all caps.

- **Ignore words with numbers:** If you select this option, the spelling check does not flag letters that are grouped together with numbers, such as license plate numbers like BRQR123.

4. If you want to use style checking, make sure the Check style checkbox is marked.

5. Click the Style Options button to open the Style Options dialog box. See Figure 17-7.

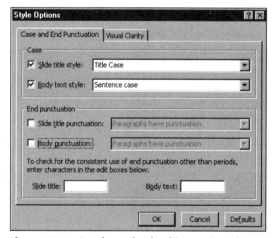

Figure 17-7: Set the style-checking options here.

6. If you want to check the case of slide titles and/or body text, make sure to mark the Slide title style and/or Body text style checkboxes.

7. For each, choose a style from the drop-down list:

- **Sentence case:** Checks that the first letter of the first word and nothing else is capitalized, just like in a sentence.

- **lowercase:** Checks that all letters of all words are in lowercase.

- **UPPERCASE:** Checks that all letters of all words are in uppercase.

- **Title Case:** Checks that the first letter of each word begins with a capital letter, just like in a title.

8. If you want to check end punctuation in the style check, make sure to mark the Slide title punctuation and/or Body punctuation checkboxes. (They are not marked by default.)

9. For each, choose either Paragraphs have punctuation or Paragraphs do not have punctuation from the drop-down list.

10. If you are using different punctuation than a period at the end of paragraphs, enter the different characters in the Slide title and/or Body text boxes.

11. Click the Visual Clarity tab. See Figure 17-8.

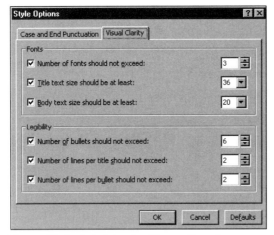

Figure 17-8: Set style-checking options for formatting and legibility.

12. In the Fonts section, choose settings for each of the rules you want to apply, or deselect a rule's checkbox to disable checking for it:

- **Number of fonts should not exceed:** Warns you if you use more than the specified number of different fonts. In general, presentations look nicest when they do not use too many different fonts.

- **Title text size should be at least:** Warns you if the title text on a slide is not at least the specified number of points in size. (Remember, a point is 1/72 of an inch.) If a title is too small, it can get lost on the slide.

- **Body text size should be at least:** Warns you if the body text on a slide is not at least the specified number of points in size. If body text is too small, it may be unreadable to the audience members at the back of the room.

13. In the Legibility section, choose settings for each of the rules you want to apply, or deselect a rule's checkbox to disable checking for it:

   - **Number of bullets should not exceed:** Warns you if you have more than a certain number of bullets on a slide. Too many bullets can make a confusing slide.

   - **Number of lines per title should not exceed:** Warns you if a slide's title is longer than two lines. In general, short titles (one line) are best; more than two lines can be confusing.

   - **Number of lines per bullet should not exceed:** Warns you if a bulleted paragraph wraps to more than a certain number of lines. Generally, bullet points should be short so the audience can read them quickly.

14. Click OK to save your style settings.

15. Click OK to save your spelling and style options.

Using AutoCorrect to Fix Common Problems

With AutoCorrect, PowerPoint can automatically correct certain common misspellings and formatting errors as you type. One way to put a word on the AutoCorrect list, as you saw earlier, is to click the AutoCorrect button during a spelling check. Another way is to directly access the AutoCorrect options.

To access AutoCorrect, select Tools ➪ AutoCorrect. The AutoCorrect dialog box appears, as shown in Figure 17-9. At the top of the dialog box is a series of checkboxes that help you fine-tune some other corrections that AutoCorrect makes besides spelling corrections:

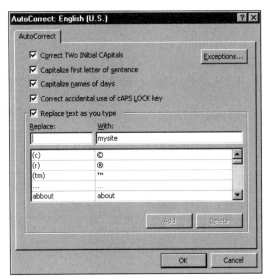

Figure 17-9: Set up the AutoCorrections that you want PowerPoint to handle as you type.

✦ **Correct TWo INitial CApitals:** If you accidentally hold down the Shift key too long and get two capital letters in a row (such as MIcrosoft), PowerPoint corrects this error if you leave this checkbox marked.

✦ **Capitalize first letter of sentence:** Leave this checkbox marked to have PowerPoint capitalize the first letter of the first word after a sentence-ending punctuation mark, such as a period, or to capitalize the first letter of the word that occurs at the beginning of a paragraph.

Tip   Click the Exceptions button to open an AutoCorrect Exceptions dialog box. Here, you can enter a list of capitalization exceptions, such as abbreviations that use periods but aren't at the end of a sentence (like approx. and Ave.). You can also set up a list of Two Initial Capitals exceptions.

✦ **Capitalize names of days:** Leave this checkbox marked to make sure the names of days, like Sunday, Monday, and so on, are capitalized.

✦ **Correct accidental use of cAPS LOCK key:** If you leave the Caps Lock on, PowerPoint can sometimes detect it and fix the problem. For example, if you typed the sentence "hE WAS GLAD TO SEE US," PowerPoint could conclude that the Caps Lock was inappropriately on and would turn it off for you and fix the sentence.

✦ **Replace text as you type:** This checkbox enables the main portion of AutoCorrect: the word list. You must leave this checkbox on if you want AutoCorrect to correct spelling.

On the list in the dialog box, you see a number of word pairs. To the left is the common misspelling, and to the right is the word that PowerPoint substitutes in its place. Scroll through this list to get a feel for the corrections PowerPoint makes.

To add a word pair to the list, type the misspelling in the Replace box and the replacement in the With box. Then click the Add button. You can also add corrections through the Spelling dialog box.

If PowerPoint insists on making a correction that you do not want, you can delete that correction from the list. Simply select it from the list and click Delete. For example, one of my clients likes me to code certain headings with (C) in front of them, so the first thing I do in any Office program is remove the AutoCorrect entry that specifies that (C) must be converted to a copyright symbol (©).

When you are finished, click OK to close the AutoCorrect dialog box.

Caution Don't use AutoCorrect for misspellings that you may sometimes want to change to some other word or you may introduce embarrassing mistakes into your document. For example, if you often type "pian" instead of "pain," but sometimes you accidentally type "pian" instead of "piano," don't tell PowerPoint to always AutoCorrect to "pain," or you may find that PowerPoint has corrected your attempt at typing *piano* and made it a *pain*!

Summary

In this chapter, you put some finishing touches on the text and formatting of your presentation. By now it's starting to look pretty good, eh? You learned how to spell-check and how to set the spelling check options. You also learned how to create headers and footers for your slides and handouts and how to check for style consistency.

The next chapter begins a new part of the book: multimedia. In this part, you learn how to add whiz-bang effects to your presentation such as sounds, movies, transitions, and animations. These features are effective only if you plan to present the show using a computer; if you are printing overhead transparencies or using 35mm slides, you should skip ahead to Part V, "Presenting Speaker-Led Presentations."

✦   ✦   ✦

Multimedia

Adding Sounds

Sounds should serve the purpose of the presentation. You should never use them simply because you can. If you add lots of sounds purely for the fun of it, your audience may lose respect for the seriousness of your message.

That said, there are lots of legitimate reasons to use sounds in a presentation. Make sure you are clear on what your reasons are before you start working with them. Here are some ideas:

- ✦ You can assign a recognizable sound, such as a beep or a bell, to each slide, so that when your audience hears the sound, they know to look up and read the new slide.

- ✦ You can record a short voice-over message from a CEO or some other important person who couldn't be there in person.

- ✦ You can punctuate important points with sounds or use sounds to add occasional humorous touches.

However, if you are trying to pack a lot of information into a short presentation, you should avoid sounds, as they take up time playing. You should also avoid sounds and other whimsical touches if you are delivering very serious news. You may also want to avoid sounds if you will be presenting using a very old and slow computer, because any kind of media clip (sound or video) will slow such a system down even more, both in loading the presentation and in presenting it.

There are several ways to include a sound in a presentation:

- ✦ Insert a sound file as an icon. The sound plays during the presentation whenever anyone points to or clicks that icon, depending on the settings you specify.

- ✦ Associate a sound with an object (such as a graphic), so that the sound plays when anyone points to or clicks that object.

✦ ✦ ✦ ✦

In This Chapter

Planning how to use sounds

Selecting a sound

Specifying when a sound will play

Assigning a sound to a slide transition

Assigning a sound to an object

Adding an audio soundtrack

Finding more sounds

✦ ✦ ✦ ✦

✦ Associate a sound with an animation effect (such as a series in a graph appearing), so that the sound plays when the animation effect occurs. See Chapter 20 for more information about animation.

✦ Associate a sound with a slide transition (a move from one slide to the next), so that the sound plays when the next slide appears. See Chapter 20 for details.

Computer sound files come in several formats. The most common is Wave, or WAV. These files take up a lot of space per second of recording, so this format is used mostly for short sounds. Another common format is MIDI, or MID. This type is not recorded audio but, rather, computer-generated music. It takes up much less space per second to store, so MIDI files are often used for longer sound clips. PowerPoint supports a wide variety of audio formats in addition to these, including RMI, AU, AIF, AIFF, and AIFC.

Caution   The sounds that come with Microsoft Office are royalty-free, which means you can use them freely in your presentation without paying an extra fee. If you download sounds from the Internet or acquire them from other sources, however, you must be careful not to violate any copyright laws. Sounds recorded from television, radio, or compact discs are protected by copyright law, and your company might face serious legal action if you use them in a presentation without the permission of the copyright holder.

Inserting a Sound File As an Icon

The most elementary way to use a sound file in a presentation is to place the sound clip directly on a slide as an object. An icon appears for it, and you can click the icon during the presentation to play the sound. This method works well if the presence of an extra icon on your slide doesn't bother you, and if you want to be able to play the sound (or not play it) at exactly the right moment in the presentation.

Note   If you would like precise control over when the sound plays but you find the Sound icon distracting, assign the sound to another object on the slide instead, as explained in the "Assigning a Sound to an Object" section later in this chapter. When you do that, the object to which you attach the sound serves the same function as an icon; you click the object to play the sound.

You can place a sound file on a slide in either of two ways: by selecting a sound from the Clip Gallery, or by selecting a sound from a file on your computer or network.

Choosing a Sound from the Clip Gallery

You learned about the Clip Gallery in Chapter 12. Its primary function is to help you insert clip art (graphics), but it also manages sounds and movie files. The Clip Gallery is a good place to start if you are not sure what sound files are available or what kind of sound you want. It enables you to browse the sounds that come with PowerPoint.

Follow these steps to choose a sound from the Clip Gallery:

1. Choose Insert ➪ Movies and Sounds ➪ Sound from Gallery.

2. Click a category for the type of sound you want. If the category doesn't have any sounds in it, or doesn't have the sound you want, click the Back button to return to the list of categories and try again.

Tip
You might want to create a new category called Sounds to hold sound clips in one convenient location. See Chapter 12 for details about creating categories and assigning them to clips.

3. Click the sound you want to use and then click the Insert Clip button on the pop-out menu that appears. See Figure 18-1. The Sound icon appears on the slide as shown in Figure 18-2.

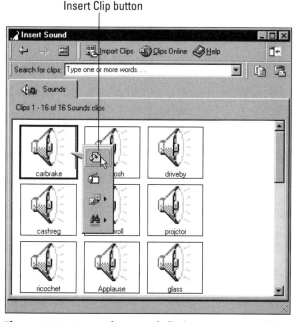

Figure 18-1: Insert the sound clip just as you would insert a piece of clip art.

Sound icon

Figure 18-2: The sound clip appears as a small speaker icon on the slide.

4. If the Office Assistant appears asking whether you want the sound to play automatically, click No.

5. At this point, the Clip Gallery is still open, although it may be hidden behind the PowerPoint window if the Office Assistant butted in to ask you the question in Step 4. If you don't see the Clip Gallery onscreen, click its bar on the Windows taskbar to bring it back into view.

6. If you want to insert another sound clip, repeat Steps 2 through 5. If you are finished with the Clip Gallery for now, close it by clicking its Close (X) button.

Tip

You can add sound clips to the Clip Gallery. There are several sounds on the Office 2000 CD in a folder called `Windows\Media\Office2k`, and there are even more on your hard disk in the `Windows\Media` folder. You can import these into the Clip Gallery just as you did with clip art in Chapter 12. You can also import any other clips that you may have on your system. Make sure you assign at least one category to each of the clips you import so you will be able to locate the clips in the future by clicking the category.

Once the Sound icon is on the slide, you can move and resize it like any other object. See Chapter 10 for details. You can also specify when the sound will play: either when the mouse pointer moves over it or when you click it. See the "Specifying When a Sound Will Play" section later in this chapter to learn how to set that.

Choosing a Sound from a File

If the sound you want is not accessible from the Clip Gallery, you can either add it to the gallery, as you learned to add a clip in Chapter 12, or you can simply import it from a file. The former is better if you plan on using that clip a lot; the latter makes more sense if you are using the clip only once or expect to use it only infrequently.

Tip   There are many sound files in the `Windows\Media` folder on your hard disk if you installed PowerPoint or Office 2000 using the default options.

Follow these steps to insert a sound from a file:

1. Choose Insert ➪ Sounds and Movies ➪ Sound from File. The Insert Sound dialog box opens.

2. Navigate to the drive and folder that contain the sound you want. If you are not sure what location to use, try `Windows\Media` on the hard disk where Windows is installed. See Chapter 4 for a refresher on changing the drive and folder.

3. Click the sound file you want to use, as shown in Figure 18-3, and then click OK. A Speaker icon appears on the slide, as you saw in Figure 18-2.

Figure 18-3: Choose a sound file from your hard disk or other location (such as on your company's network).

Specifying When a Sound Will Play

Now that you have a Sound icon on your slide, you need to decide when it should play. By default, a sound plays when you click its icon during the presentation. To test this now (if you want to), jump to Slide Show view and click the Sound icon. When you're done, press Esc to return to editing the presentation.

You can also set the sound to play when you simply point the mouse at the icon (never mind clicking). If you want to set it to work that way, follow these steps to change the icon's action settings:

1. Click the icon to select it. Selection handles appear around it.

2. Choose Slide Show ➪ Action Settings or right-click the icon and choose Action Settings from the shortcut menu. The Action Settings dialog box appears.

3. Click the Mouse Over tab.

4. Click the Object action option button. See Figure 18-4.

5. Make sure that Play is selected from the Object action drop-down list.

6. Click OK.

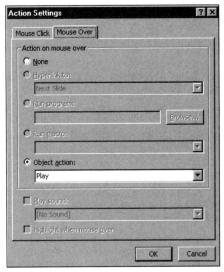

Figure 18-4: To make a sound play when the mouse is over its icon, set it up on the Mouse Over tab.

When you are finished, reenter Slide Show view and try out the Sound icon again. For more information about Slide Show view, see Chapter 22.

Assigning a Sound to an Object

Many presenters find the Sound icons distracting and unprofessional-looking, and they prefer to assign sound files to clip art or other objects placed in the presentation. That way, they still have precise control over when a sound plays (for example, when they click the clip art), but the means by which they control the sound is hidden.

Although you can assign a sound to any object, many people assign their sounds to graphics. For example, you might attach a sound file of a greeting from your CEO to the CEO's picture.

Follow these steps to assign a sound to an object:

1. Insert the object that you want associated with the sound. The object can be any graphic, chart, text box, or other object.

2. Right-click the object and choose Action Settings from the shortcut menu. The Action Settings dialog box appears.

3. Select the Play Sound checkbox.

4. Open the Play sound drop-down list and browse the available sounds. See Figure 18-5.

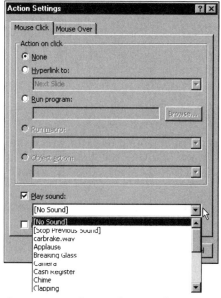

Figure 18-5: Choose the sound to assign to the object.

5. Click the sound you want to use.

   If the sound you want does not appear on the list, scroll to the bottom of the list and choose Other Sound. This opens the Add Sound dialog box. Make your selection from this box (changing the drive and folder as needed) and click OK.

Note   The first time you select a sound from the Play Sound list, you may be prompted to reinsert your Office 2000 CD-ROM so PowerPoint can install the needed sound files. Just follow the prompts that appear.

6. Click OK. The object now has the sound associated with it so that when you click it during the presentation, the sound plays.

Assigning a Sound to an Animation Effect

Animation effects, as you learn in Chapter 20, are movements of objects on a slide. The most common kind of animation effect is a delay in appearance. For example, if you animate the bulleted list on a slide, the bullets appear one at a time, each time you click the mouse or press a key, instead of all at once.

I won't go too deeply into animation effects here, because they're covered in detail in Chapter 20, but here are some quick steps for assigning a sound to an animation:

1. Display the slide that contains the object(s) you want to animate.

2. Choose Slide Show ➪ Custom Animation. The Custom Animation dialog box opens.

3. Make sure there is a checkmark next to the object you want to animate. If there isn't, click to place one there.

4. Make sure the object you want is selected in the Check to animate slide objects area.

5. On the Effects tab, choose an animation sound from the Entry animation and sound area. The default is No Sound, but you can change that or any sound on the list, or choose Other Sound to browse for a different sound. See Figure 18-6.

6. Set any other animation effects desired, as described in Chapter 20.

7. Click OK.

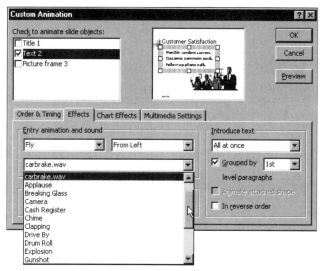

Figure 18-6: Select the object to assign a sound to.

Assigning a Sound to a Slide Transition

A *slide transition* is a movement from one slide to another. The transition can be a simple replacement (No Transition), or it can be some effect like Box In, Blinds Horizontal, or Cover Down. You learn more about transitions in Chapter 20.

You can assign a sound to the transition so that a sound plays when one slide replaces another. For consistency, you probably want to assign the same sound to all slide transitions in your presentation. An exception would be if you want the sounds to provide comic relief; you can select a different silly sound for each one.

To attach a sound to a transition, follow these steps:

1. Choose Slide Show ⇨ Slide Transition. The Slide Transition dialog box opens.

2. Open the Sound drop-down list and choose the sound you want or choose Other Sound to browse for a different sound. See Figure 18-7.

3. If you want the sound to play constantly until another sound is scheduled to play, mark the Loop Until Next Sound checkbox.

4. Click Apply to apply to the selected slide, or Apply to All to apply to all slides.

Figure 18-7: Assign a sound to the transition from the Sound drop-down list.

Ten Sound Ideas for Business

Unsure about what sounds to use? Try these ideas on for size:

1. **Applause or Clapping:** These are two separate, similar sounds. Use them when presenting good news, a success story, or a new product.

2. **Breaking Glass:** Use to indicate you are "breaking the mold," introducing something bold and innovative, or breaking a sales record.

3. **Camera or Slide Projector:** These subtle clicking sounds work great as a sound transition from slide to slide.

4. **Cash Register:** Play this sound when you are talking about racking up more sales or making more profits.

5. **Drum Roll:** This sound is great for building suspense before unveiling a new concept, product, or service.

6. **Explosion:** Use to dramatize how you are "blowing up" the competition, the previous rules, or the old ways of thinking.

7. **Gunshot:** This sound is reminiscent of the starting gun at the beginning of a race—use it to kick off a sales competition.

8. **Screeching Brakes:** Use this sound when you're talking about stopping the frantic pace to analyze what you're doing or "putting the brakes on" bad behavior.

9. **Typewriter:** This sound can be really cool when it is combined with the Letter by Letter introduction of text with an animation effect. It looks like the text is being typed!

10. **Whoosh:** Use this sound with a slide transition that flies or sweeps the next slide onto the screen.

Adding a CD Audio Soundtrack

Lots of great music is available on CD these days, and most computers contain a CD-ROM drive that reads not only computer CDs but also plays audio ones. PowerPoint takes advantage of this fact by letting you play tracks from an audio CD during your presentation.

Adding a CD audio clip to a slide is much like adding a Sound Clip icon. (You learned to do that earlier in this chapter.) You place the clip on the slide and a little CD icon appears that lets you activate the clip. Then, you can set properties for the clip to make it play exactly the way you want.

Caution

The audio track is not stored with the presentation. The audio CD you've selected must be in the CD drive of the computer you're using to present the show. Therefore, you can't use CD audio tracks in presentations that you plan to distribute on disk or over the Internet, because the computers on which it will run will not have access to the CD.

If you need to include audio from a CD in a presentation that will be shown on a PC without access to the original audio CD, you can record a part of the CD track as a .WAV file using Windows Sound Recorder program or some other audio recording utility. Keep in mind, however, that .WAV files can be extremely large, taking up many megabytes for less than a minute of sound.

Placing a CD Track on a Slide

To play a CD track for a slide, you must place an icon for it on the slide. You can actually place a range of tracks, such as tracks 1 through 4 from a CD, using a single icon. Follow these steps:

1. Choose Insert ⇨ Movies and Sounds ⇨ Play CD Audio Track. The Movie and Sound Options dialog box appears.

2. Enter the starting track number in the Track box under Start. See Figure 18-8.

Figure 18-8: Specify a starting and ending track, and optionally, a time within those tracks.

3. Enter the ending track number in the Track box under End. If you want to play only a single track, the Start and End numbers should be the same.

4. If you want to begin the starting track at a particular spot (other than the beginning), enter that spot's time in the At box under Start. For example, to start the track 50 seconds into the song, enter **00:50**.

5. If you want to end the ending track at a particular spot, enter that spot's time in the At box under End. The default setting is the total playing time for all selected tracks. For example, in Figure 18-8, track 1 is both the starting and ending track, and the time for that track is 4:04. If I wanted to end it 10 seconds early, I could change the At setting under End to 3:54.

6. (Optional) If you want the selected track(s) to repeat until stopped, mark the Loop until stopped checkbox. (Usually you would not want to use this option for a CD track.)

7. Click OK. A message appears asking whether you want the sound to play automatically when the slide appears.

8. Click Yes or No.

9. The Sound icon now appears in the center of the slide. Drag it elsewhere if it is in the way of your slide content. You can also resize it if you want, as you would any other object.

The CD track is now an animated object on your slide. By *animated*, I mean that it is an object that has some action associated with it. You learn more about animation in Chapter 20. Depending on your choice in Step 8, the CD track will activate either when the slide appears (Yes) or when you click its icon during the presentation (No).

Controlling When a CD Track Plays

You can set many of the same properties for a CD track on a slide that you can set for a sound file icon. For example, you can use the Action Settings command to specify whether the clip should be activated with a mouse click or simply a mouse point. Refer back to the "Specifying When a Sound Will Play" section earlier in this chapter for details.

You can also animate the CD track icon itself and specify multimedia settings for it. These settings include whether the show pauses or continues while the track plays, and the number of slides it continues to play. Follow these steps to set these options:

1. Select the CD Track icon on the slide.

2. Choose Slide Show ➪ Custom Animation. The Custom Animation dialog box appears.

3. Click the Multimedia Settings tab.

4. If you want the slide show to continue while the track plays, click the Continue slide show option button. See Figure 18-9.

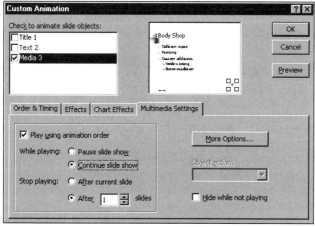

Figure 18-9: You can control when the CD track stops playing and what happens in the show while it plays.

5. If you want the clip to stop playing when you advance to the next slide, choose the After current slide option button. Or, if you want the CD to continue, click the After button and specify a number of slides in the text box.

6. (Optional) If you need to change which track plays and for how long, click the More Options button to reopen the Movie and Sound Options dialog box (Figure 18-8).

7. (Optional) If you want the CD Track icon to disappear while the clip is not playing, click the Hide while not playing checkbox.

Caution   Don't set the hide option for the CD track icon unless you have the track set up to play automatically when the slide appears. If you've set up the presentation so you have to start the track manually, you won't be able to see the hidden icon to click it and activate it during the presentation.

8. Click the Order & Timing tab.

9. In the Start Animation area, confirm your preference — either On mouse click or Automatically. See Figure 18-10.

10. If you choose Automatically, specify a number of seconds after the slide appears or the previous animation finishes that PowerPoint should wait before playing the CD track.

11. Click OK.

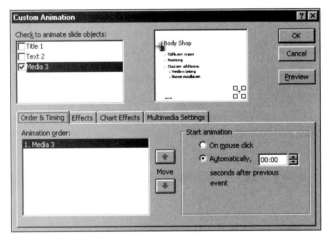

Figure 18-10: Set when the clip will start playing on the Order & Timing tab.

Recording a Sound

Most PCs have a microphone jack on the sound card where you can plug in any of a variety of small microphones. If you have a microphone for your PC, you can record your own sounds to include in the presentation. I'm referring to simple, short sounds right now; to record a voice-over narration, see Chapter 25.

To record a sound, follow these steps:

1. Display the slide on which you want to place the sound clip.

2. Choose Insert ⇨ Movies and Sounds ⇨ Record Sound. The Record Sound dialog box appears. See Figure 18-11.

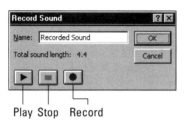

Play Stop Record

Figure 18-11: Record your own sounds using your PC's microphone.

3. Type a name for the sound in the Name box, replacing the default Recorded Sound label that appears there.

4. Click the Record button (the red circle).

5. Record the sound. When you are finished, click the Stop button (the black square).

6. (Optional) To play back the sound to make sure it's okay, click the Play button (the black triangle).

7. Click OK to place the sound on the slide. A Sound icon appears on the slide.

8. Use the controls you learned about earlier in this chapter to set when and how the sound plays.

Getting More Sounds

There are lots more sounds available from the Microsoft Web site. Just use your Clip Gallery to connect there, as you learned in Chapter 12. Here's a review:

1. In the Clip Gallery, click the Clips Online button.

2. A dialog box may appear explaining that Windows is getting ready to connect to the Web. If you see this box, click OK.

3. Your Web browser opens, and if you are not connected to the Internet, a Dial-Up Connection box appears. If it does, enter your username and password and click Connect to establish the connection.

4. Wait to be connected to the Internet and for the Clip Gallery Live page to appear.

5. If this is the first time you have connected to the Clip Gallery Live, an End User License Agreement appears. Read it and click Accept.

6. In the Clip Gallery Live, click the Sounds tab.

7. Choose a category from the Browse Clips by Category list or type a keyword in the Search Clips by Keyword box and click Go.

8. When you see a sound clip that you want, click the checkbox next to it to add it to your selection basket. Change categories as needed, tagging each clip that you want.

9. When you are finished selecting clips, click the Selection Basket link to jump to the Selection Basket. All the clips you chose appear.

10. Click the Download link to begin the download process. A Download Web page appears.

11. Click the Download Now! link. The clips are automatically downloaded into a new copy of the Clip Gallery window.

12. Click the Close button (X) to close this copy of the Clip Gallery.

13. If it does not automatically appear, switch back to the open copy of the Clip Gallery. (Use the Windows taskbar.)

14. If the clips you just downloaded do not appear, display the Downloaded Clips category.

15. (Optional) Recategorize each clip to place it in the appropriate category. You might want to create a new category called Sounds to hold all your sounds, for example. See Chapter 12 for details.

16. Insert one of the clips into your presentation, as described in the preceding set of steps, or close the Clip Gallery.

17. Close your Internet connection, if necessary, and close Internet Explorer.

Summary

In this chapter, you learned about the many ways you can use sound in your presentation. You learned how to place a sound object on a slide, how to associate sounds with transitions and animations, and how to record your own sounds. You even learned how to assign a CD soundtrack to one or more slides. The next chapter continues in this same multimedia vein by looking at how you can place video clips on slides.

✦   ✦   ✦

Adding Videos

Video clips (aka *movies*) are not appropriate for every presentation. If you plan to use one or more of them, you should have a very definite purpose in mind.

There are two kinds of movies: live-action (recorded movies) and cartoons (animated movies). PowerPoint can show both kinds, in a variety of file formats.

You can record live video with a video camera and use it to achieve the following:

+ Present a message from an important person who could not attend the presentation in person

+ Show how a product works

+ Tour a facility through the eyes of a video camera

You can use an animated video clip to achieve the following:

+ Demonstrate how a planned product will be built or how it will work after it is manufactured. (This may require some creation in a separate 3D animation program.)

+ Add a whimsical touch or lighten the mood with some of the simple cartoon movies available with PowerPoint or through the Microsoft Web site.

Note   In this chapter, I use the terms *movie* and *video* interchangeably, just as PowerPoint does.

Placing a Movie on a Slide

Your first step is to place the movie on the slide. After that, you can worry about position, size, and playing options. Just as with audio clips, you can place a clip on a slide with the Clip Gallery or by placing a file directly.

Choosing Movies from the Clip Gallery

Just as with sounds and graphics, you can organize movie files with the Clip Gallery. I don't go into it in detail here, since the Clip Gallery is discussed in detail in Chapter 12 and reviewed in Chapter 18.

Note   By default, your Clip Gallery may not contain any movie clips; you may have to add these yourself using the Import Clip procedure you learned in Chapter 12. You can use the Clips Online button in the Clip Gallery to connect to Microsoft's Web site and download some animated movies that you can use in your presentations. See the "Getting More Movies" section later in this chapter to review the Clips Online feature.

To select a movie from the Clip Gallery, follow these steps:

1. Display the slide that you want to place the movie on.

2. Choose Insert ➪ Movies and Sounds ➪ Movie from Gallery. The Clip Gallery appears.

3. Select a category. If the category you choose has no movies, click the Back button to return to the list of categories and choose another one.

Tip   You may want to categorize your movie clips in a special category you create called Movies to make it easy to browse them all in a single location in the future.

4. Click the clip you want to insert.

5. On the pop-up menu of buttons that appears, click the Insert Clip button. See Figure 19-1.

6. Close the Clip Gallery. The clip appears on the slide, in the middle.

7. Move and resize the clip as needed.

To test the movie, enter Slide Show view and click it to play it. You can control when and how a movie plays; you learn to do that later in this chapter.

Getting More Movies

You may not have much of a selection of movies to choose from in the Clip Gallery initially, but many more movies are available from the Microsoft Web site. I explainin Chapter 12 how to connect to the Microsoft Clip Gallery Live to get more clips of all kinds, but here is a quick review:

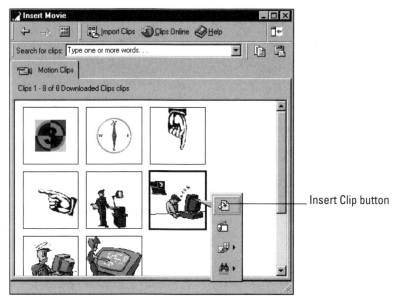

Insert Clip button

Figure 19-1: Click the clip you want and then click the Insert Clip button.

1. In the Clip Gallery, click the Clips Online button.

2. A dialog box may appear explaining that Windows is getting ready to connect to the Web. If you see this box, click OK.

3. Your Web browser opens, and if you are not connected to the Internet, a Dial-Up Connection box appears. If it does, enter your username and password and click Connect to establish the connection.

4. Wait to be connected to the Internet and for the Clip Gallery Live page to appear.

5. If this is the first time you have connected to the Clip Gallery Live, an End User License Agreement appears. Read it and click Accept.

6. In the Clip Gallery Live, click the Motion tab. See Figure 19-2.

7. Choose a category from the Browse Clips by Category list or type a keyword in the Search Clips by Keyword box and click Go.

8. When you see a movie that you want, click the checkbox next to it to add it to your selection basket. Change categories as needed, tagging each clip that you want.

9. When you are finished selecting clips, click the Selection Basket link to jump to the selection basket. All the clips you chose appear.

10. Click the Download link to begin the download process. A Download Web page appears.

Motion tab

Figure 19-2: Click the Motion tab to browse the available movies.

11. Click the Download Now! link. A File Download box appears asking what you want to do with the download.

12. Click Open this file from its current location and then click OK. A new Clip Gallery window appears showing your downloaded clips.

13. Click the Cancel button to close this copy of the Clip Gallery.

14. Switch back to the open copy of the Clip Gallery (use the Windows taskbar).

15. Display the Downloaded Clips category. Your downloaded clips appear.

16. (Optional) Recategorize each clip to place it in the appropriate category. You might want to create a new category called Movies to hold all your movies, for example. See Chapter 12 for details.

17. Insert one of the clips into your presentation, as described in the preceding set of steps, or close the Clip Gallery.

18. Close your Internet connection, if necessary, and close Internet Explorer.

Importing a Movie from a File

If the movie that you want is not in the Clip Gallery (and you don't want to bother with placing it there, as you learned to do in Chapter 12), you can place it directly on the slide, just like any other object. For example, you might have video of your CEO's last speech saved to a disk.

Note Converting video from a video camera or videotape requires some sort of video capture device, such as a Snappy or an Iomega Buz. These devices are sold in most computer stores. Basic models start at around $100.

To insert a video clip from a file, follow these steps:

1. Display the slide on which the movie should appear.

2. Choose Insert ➪ Movies and Sounds ➪ Movie from File.

3. In the Insert Movie dialog box, change the drive and folder as necessary to locate the clip you want. See Figure 19-3.

4. Select the clip and click OK. The movie clip appears on the slide.

5. Move or resize the object as desired.

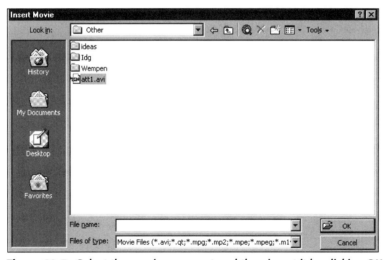

Figure 19-3: Select the movie you want and then insert it by clicking OK.

Setting Movie Options

Video clips are a lot like sounds in terms of what you can do with them. You can specify that they should play when you point at them or click them, or you can make them play automatically at a certain time.

Movies that you download from the Microsoft Web site are actually animated GIFs (a type of graphic). They play in a continuous loop the entire time that they appear on the slide. You can't set them to do otherwise. (You can, however, animate one as an object on your slide so that it doesn't appear immediately when the slide appears. See Chapter 20 for details.) Other movies, such as your own recorded video clips (AVI and MOV format), have more settings you can control.

Specifying When a Movie Will Play

The default setting for a video clip is for the clip to play when you click it with the mouse. To set it to play when you point to it, or not to play at all in response to the mouse, follow these steps:

1. Right-click the clip and choose Action Settings. The Action Settings dialog box opens. See Figure 19-4.

2. On the Mouse Click and Mouse Over tabs, click the None button if you want no action, or click the Object Action button if you want it to play in either case.

3. Click OK.

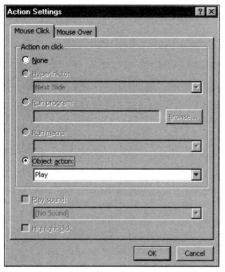

Figure 19-4: Set the Object Action to Play on the Mouse Click and Mouse Over tabs.

Note that the above steps are applicable only for real video clips, not animated GIFs. You can change the setting for an animated GIF, but it does not affect the way the clip plays in the presentation.

Editing the Movie Controls

If you are working with a real video clip (not an animated GIF file), you can also edit the Movie object's controls. These controls enable you to specify whether the video plays in a continuous loop or not, and which frame of the movie remains on the screen when it is finished (the first or the last).

1. Right-click the movie on the slide and choose Edit Movie object. The Movie Options dialog box appears.

2. If you want the movie to play continuously, select the Loop until stopped checkbox. Otherwise, leave it clear to play the movie only once. See Figure 19-5.

3. If you want the first frame of the movie returned to the display after the movie has finished playing, mark the Rewind movie when done playing checkbox. Otherwise, leave it unmarked.

4. Click OK.

Figure 19-5: You can control a few play options from this dialog box for movie files.

Setting Multimedia Options

You can also control multimedia settings for real video clips (not animated GIFs) through the Custom Animation box. These settings enable you to specify whether the video should play automatically when the slide appears, and whether the show should pause while the video plays.

1. Right-click the video clip and choose Custom Animation. The Custom Animation dialog box appears.

2. Click to place a checkmark next to the clip in the Check to animate slide objects area. For example, in Figure 19-6, the selected clip is Media 3.

3. Click the Order & Timing tab if it is not already displayed.

4. In the Start animation area, click Automatically if you want the clip to begin playing automatically when you display the slide, or choose On mouse click if you want it to wait for your signal.

5. If you chose Automatically in Step 4, enter the number of seconds you want it to pause before starting.

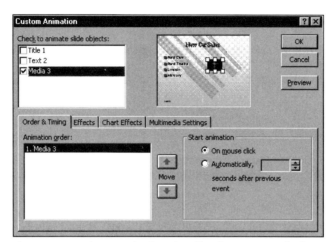

Figure 19-6: Choose whether the clip plays automatically or waits for your mouse click.

6. Click the Multimedia Settings tab.

Note

The More Options button on the Multimedia Settings tab opens the same dialog box that you saw in Figure 19-5 and worked with in the previous set of steps.

7. In the While playing section, choose Pause slide show or Continue slide show to indicate what should happen while the video plays. See Figure 19-7.

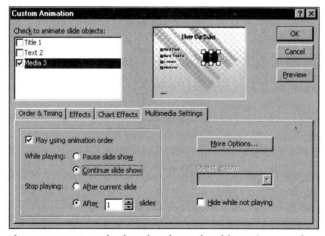

Figure 19-7: Set whether the show should continue as the video plays or not.

8. If you chose Continue slide show in Step 7, the Stop playing controls become available. Choose After current slide to stop the video when you advance to the next slide, or choose After and enter a number of slides to allow the video to continue to play through.

9. If desired, mark the Hide while not playing checkbox, so the video goes away after it plays. Use this option only if the clip is set to play automatically; if you hide a clip that relies on a mouse click to begin playing, you will not be able to activate it.

10. Click OK to confirm your settings.

Choosing the Size of the Video Clip Window

You can resize a video clip's window just like any other object. Simply drag its selection handles. Be careful, however, that you do not distort the image by resizing in only one dimension. Make sure you drag a corner selection handle, not one on a single side of the object.

Be aware also that when you enlarge a video clip's window, the quality of the clip suffers. If you make the clip large and are unhappy with its quality, you can reset it to its original size by following these steps:

1. Right-click the clip and choose Format Picture.

2. On the Size tab, click the Reset button.

3. Click OK.

Balancing Video Impact with File Size and Performance

When you are recording your own video clips with a video camera or other device, it is easy to *overshoot*. Video clips take up a huge amount of disk space, and they can make your PowerPoint presentation file very large.

Depending on the amount of space available on your computer's hard disk, and whether you need to transfer your PowerPoint file to another PC, you may want to keep the number of seconds of recorded video to a minimum to ensure that the file size stays manageable. On the other hand, if you have a powerful computer with plenty of hard disk space and lots of cool video clips to show, go for it!

Be aware, however, that slower, older computers, especially those with less than 32MB of RAM, may not present your video clip to its best advantage. The sound may not match the video, the video may be jerky, and a host of other little annoying performance glitches may occur if your PC is not powerful enough. On such PCs, it is best to limit the live-action video that you use, and rely more on animated GIFs and other simple video clips.

Sources of Movie Clips

Not sure where to find video clips? Here are some places to start:

✦ Your own video camera. For only a few hundred dollars you can buy a simple video eye that attaches to a board in your PC or an adapter that lets you use input from a regular video camera.

✦ Microsoft's Clip Gallery Online Web site. Click the Online Clips button in the Clip Gallery to browse there.

✦ The Internet in general. There are millions of interesting video clips on every imaginable subject. Use the search term *video clips* plus a few keywords that describe the type of clips you are looking for. Yahoo! is a good place to start looking (http://www.yahoo.com).

Caution

Whenever you get a video clip from the Internet, make sure you carefully read any restrictions or usage agreements to avoid copyright violations.

✦ Commercial collections of video clips and animated GIFs. Many of these companies advertise on the Internet and provide free samples for downloading. One such program, Compadre, has included demos on the CD-ROM that accompanies this book. The Compadre Web site is at http://www.threedgraphics.com/compadre/.

Summary

In this chapter, you learned how to place video clips on your slides and how to set them up to play when you want them to.

In the next chapter, you learn about transitions and object animation. With a transition, you can create special effects for the movement from one slide to another. With object animation, you can control the entry and exit of individual objects. You can make them fly in with special effects or build them dramatically one paragraph, bar, or shape at a time.

✦   ✦   ✦

Creating Animation Effects and Transitions

So far in this book, you've been exposed to several kinds of moving objects on a slide. One kind is the animated GIF, which is essentially a graphic that has some special properties that enable it to play a short animation sequence over and over. Another kind is a movie, or video clip, created in an animation program or recorded with a video camera.

But neither of these is what PowerPoint means by *animation*. In PowerPoint, animation is the way that individual objects enter or exit a slide. On a slide with no animation, all of the objects on it simply appear at the same time when you display the slide. (Boring, eh?) But on a slide with some animation applied to it, the bullet points might fly in from the left, one at a time, and the graphic might drop down from the top afterward.

A *transition* is yet another kind of movement. A transition refers to the entry or exit of the slide itself, rather than of an individual object on the slide. You learn about transitions at the end of this chapter.

Here are some ideas for animation:

✦ Animate parts of a Microsoft Graph chart so that the data appears one series at a time. This technique works well if you want to talk about each series separately.

✦ Set up questions and answers on a slide, so that first the question appears, and then, after a mouse click, the answer.

✦ Dim each bullet point when the next one comes into view, so you are, in effect, highlighting the current one.

✦ Make an object appear and then disappear. For example, you might have an image of a lightning bolt that flashes on the slide for one second and then disappears, or a picture of a race car that slides onto the slide from the left and then immediately slides out of sight to the right.

✦ Rearrange the order in which objects make their appearance on the slide. For example, you could make numbered points appear from the bottom up for a Top Ten List.

Using Preset Animation

PowerPoint includes over a dozen preset animation effects that you can apply to text, graphics, and other objects. These effects are easy to use and look very sharp. For example, if you are animating a text box, you can use the Typewriter animation, which types text on the screen one character at a time, or the Reverse Order animation, which makes bullet points appear in bottom-to-top order. When you want to animate a graphic, consider Drive-In, which drives the image in from the right side of the screen, complete with skidding tire sound effect, or Camera, which makes the image appear with the sound and appearance of a camera shutter.

Most of the preset animations include sounds. You learned in Chapter 18 how to assign and remove sounds from animations, and you review the process again later in this chapter.

Caution

As I've said before, be careful not to overuse special effects such as animation. The audience can quickly turn from thinking "what a cool effect!" to thinking "what a silly show-off!" if you use too many different effects or use an effect too frequently.

You can assign preset animation in either Normal view or Slide Sorter view. You must decide which is best for your situation:

✦ **Normal view:** You can animate any object on the slide, and you can choose which object you want to animate. However, you are limited to a list of 14 preset animation effects.

✦ **Slide Sorter view:** You can only animate the main object on the slide, and that main object must have been placed there through an AutoLayout. However, you have a much more extensive list of preset animations to choose from.

If neither of these options sounds appealing, you might consider a Custom Animation instead, which you learn about later in this chapter.

Applying a Preset Animation in Normal View

To assign a preset animation to an object in Normal view (or a variation of it, such as Slide view), follow these steps:

1. Display the slide containing the object you want to animate with preset animation.

2. Select the object. It can be a text box, a graphic, or some other object.

3. Select Slide Show ➪ Preset Animation. A list of effects appears. See Figure 20-1.

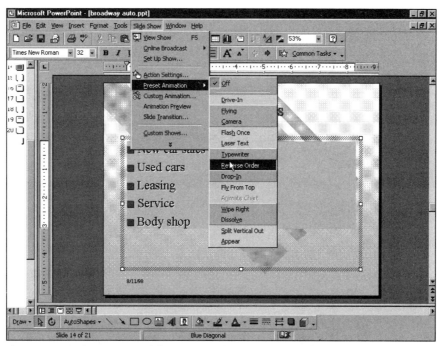

Figure 20-1: Choose one of the preset animation effects. The effects available on the list depend on the type of object you have selected.

4. Select the effect you want. You will probably want to experiment with these to find out what they do.

5. Switch to Slide Show view and test the new animation.

When you test an animation, remember that because you have animated the object, it won't appear immediately on the slide. You must click the mouse or press a key to advance the show and bring the animated object into view. If you want an animated object to appear immediately, without a click or press, you must set it up in Custom Animation, described later in this chapter.

Applying Presets with the Animation Effects Toolbar

Here's a variation on the menu method you just learned. You can display the Animation Effects toolbar and choose from a few of the most common preset animations that way.

Follow these steps to try it out:

1. In Normal or Slide view, click the Animation Effects button on the Formatting toolbar. The Animation Effects floating toolbar appears. See Figure 20-2.

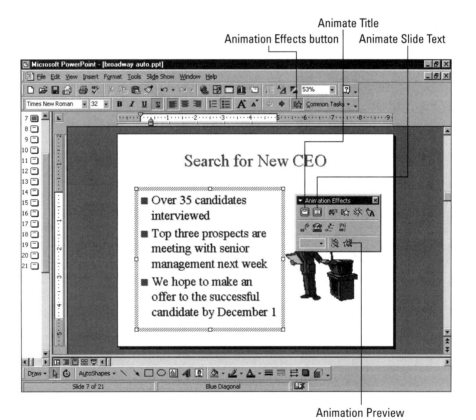

Figure 20-2: You can apply a few of the most common animation effects with the Animation Effects toolbar.

2. Click the object that you want to animate.

3. Click one of the effects buttons to choose your effect. Note that the Text effect buttons are available only if you chose a text box in Step 2.

Icon	Effect
	Drive-In effect
	Flying effect
	Camera effect
	Flash Once
	Laser Text effect
	Typewriter Text effect
	Reverse Order text effect
	Drop-In text effect

If you select the slide's main text box or title in Step 2, and then chose a button in Step 3, the Animate Title or Animate Slide Text button is now depressed, indicating that the title or slide text has been animated. (These buttons are identified in Figure 20-2.) To turn off the animation you have selected, you can click these buttons to toggle them off.

Tip You can preview your animation effects in a small Animation Preview window by clicking the Animation Preview button on the Animation Effects toolbar. This eliminates the need to jump to Slide Show view every time you want to check your work.

You can also use this Animation Effects toolbar, to a limited extent, in Slide Sorter view, which you learn about in the following section. In Slide Sorter view, the Animation Effects button does not appear on the Slide Sorter toolbar, so you can't turn the Animation Effects toolbar on from there in the normal way. Instead, you can right-click one of the other toolbars and choose Animation Effects from the shortcut menu to turn it on.

Applying a Preset Animation in Slide Sorter View

When you apply preset animation in Slide Sorter view, you trade off less flexibility in object selection for more flexibility in the effect applied. In Slide Sorter view, you can't select individual objects on a slide—only the slide itself. So PowerPoint has to guess which object you want to animate. Here are the rules it uses to make the determination:

✦ Only slides that are based on an AutoLayout that contains at least one data block (in addition to a slide title) can be animated this way. That means if you created the slide based on the Blank or Title Only AutoLayout, you cannot animate in Slide Sorter view.

✦ If the slide contains a title and a single data block, the data block is the object animated.

✦ If the slide contains a title, a single data block, and some other object you have placed manually on the slide, the data block is the object animated.

✦ If the slide contains a title and two or more data blocks, one of which is text, the text block is the object animated.

✦ If the slide contains a title and two data blocks, both of which are text, the one on the right or at the bottom is the object animated.

✦ If the slide contains more than two data blocks, and none of them is text, the bottommost, rightmost one is the object animated.

If these rules sound acceptable to you, go ahead and animate your slides using Slide Sorter view. You do get a much nicer assortment of animations here. In addition to the ones on the Slide Show ⇨ Preset Animation list, which is still available here, you can also select from the Preset Animation drop-down list on the Slide Sorter toolbar.

Note   Some of the animations on the Preset Animation drop-down list on the Slide Sorter toolbar are the same as the ones on the Slide Show ⇨ Preset Animation list, but they go by different names. For example, Camera on the Slide Show ⇨ Preset Animation menu is called Box Out on the drop-down list.

To apply a preset animation in Slide Sorter view, follow these steps:

1. Select the slide that you want to apply a preset animation to. You can select multiple slides if you like and apply the same effect to all of them.

2. Open the Preset Animation drop-down list and choose an effect. The list is rather long; scroll through it with its scroll bar. See Figure 20-3.

3. When you've applied a preset animation to a slide, an Animation icon appears beneath it and to the left. To preview the animation, click that icon, or click the Animation Preview button on the Slide Sorter toolbar. See Figure 20-4.

4. If the results of the animation are not what you want, choose a different effect or try a custom animation, described in the following section.

Preset Animation drop-down list

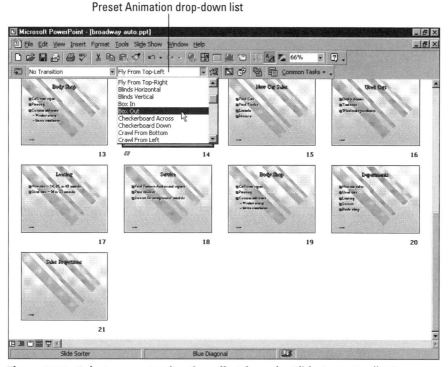

Figure 20-3: Select a preset animation effect from the Slide Sorter toolbar's drop-down list.

Tip   It is possible to mix the two kinds of preset animations on a slide. For example, you can set the main element of the slide to be animated using the Slide Sorter view controls, and then you can switch to Normal view and animate the remaining elements on the slide using the Preset Animation controls with the Slide Show ➪ Preset Animation menu or with the Animation Effects toolbar.

Using Custom Animation

With custom animation, you have full control over the way that the objects on your slide are animated. You can choose not only from the full range of animation effects for each object (including manually placed ones), but you can also specify in what order the objects appear and what sound is associated with their appearance.

Animation icon   Animation Preview button

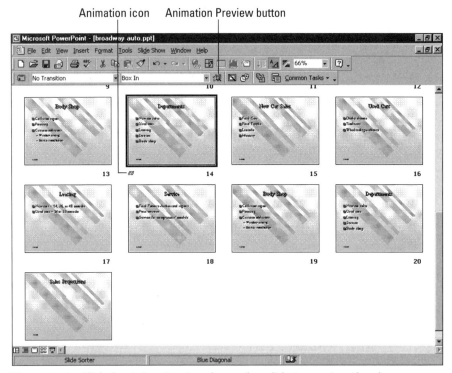

Figure 20-4: Click the Animation icon beneath a slide to preview the chosen animation effect.

Note   You can only set up custom animation from Normal view (or a variation); you can't do it from Slide Sorter view.

To set up custom animation for a slide, follow these steps:

1. Display the slide in Normal or Slide view.

2. Choose Slide Show ➪ Custom Animation or click the Custom Animation button on the Animation Effects toolbar. The Custom Animation dialog box appears.

3. In the Check to animate slide objects list, click to place a checkmark next to each of the objects that you want to animate. The chosen items appear on the Animation order list in the lower portion of the dialog box. See Figure 20-5.

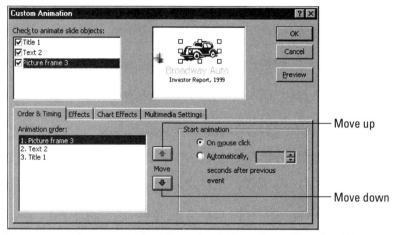

Figure 20-5: Choose which objects should be animated on the slide. All unanimated objects simply appear when the slide appears.

4. On the Animation order list, the objects appear in the order that you mark them in Step 3. To change the order of an object, select it and then click the Move Up or Move Down button to move it on the list.

5. Now it's time to start working with the individual objects. Click the object you want to work with first to select it.

6. In the Start animation area, choose either On mouse click or Automatically to describe how the object should make its appearance.

7. If you chose Automatically in Step 6, enter a number of seconds of delay after the previous event. The default is 0.

Note

If the object you are configuring is the first object animated on the slide, the *previous event* I refer to in Step 7 is the slide's initial appearance (that is, the moment when the slide's background appears). If it is not the first animated object, the previous event is the animation of the object before it.

8. Click the Effects tab. The animation effects controls appear. See Figure 20-6.

9. Set an Entry animation by choosing from the Animation and Direction drop-down lists. For example, Figure 20-6 shows Fly as the animation and From Left as the direction.

10. If desired, choose a sound to associate with the entry animation from the Sound drop-down list. The default is No Sound.

11. If desired, choose an After animation effect. You can leave the object as is (Don't Dim), change it to another color, or hide it altogether, either immediately after animation or upon the next mouse click. See Figure 20-7.

Note As usual, the colors in the top row on the After animation list represent the colors in the chosen color scheme for the presentation, and the colors on the second row are nonscheme colors that you have previously used in the presentation. You can access more colors with the More Colors option, also as usual.

Animation drop-down list   Direction drop-down list

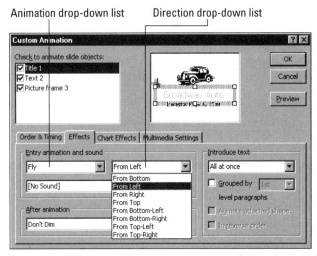

Figure 20-6: Choose an entry animation and direction, and optionally, a sound.

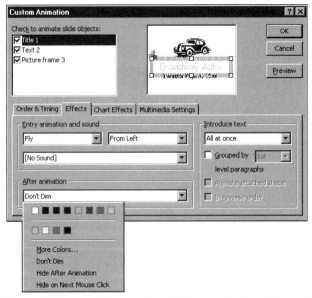

Figure 20-7: Specify what should happen to the object after the animation sequence is complete.

12. If the selected object is text, you can choose how you want to introduce the text:

    - **All at once:** Displays the text all at once, or paragraph by paragraph if you've specified the Grouped by option. (See Step 13.)

    - **By Word:** Displays the text one word at a time, as if the words were being pasted in.

    - **By Letter:** Displays the text one letter at a time, as if it were being typed.

13. If you want each paragraph (or each bullet point) to appear separately, make sure to mark the Grouped by checkbox.

14. Choose the level of grouping. The default is 1st level paragraph, which means that if you have a bulleted list subordinate to another list, the entire first-level bullet with all its subordinates is considered one group.

15. If you want the text to appear in reverse order, mark the In reverse order checkbox. Reverse order builds a list from bottom to top, rather than top to bottom.

16. Click Preview to check your work. If you are happy with it, go on to animate the next object on the slide.

17. When you are finished animating all slides, click OK.

The other two tabs in the Custom Animation dialog box are Chart Effects and Multimedia Settings. Multimedia Settings apply only to sounds and videos; you saw this tab at work in Chapters 18 and 19. The Chart Effects tab is only for Microsoft Graph charts, which you learn about in the next section.

Animating Parts of a Chart

If you have a chart created with Microsoft Graph on a slide, you can introduce the chart all at once or you can set some other custom animation effects for it. You make the chart appear by series (broken down by legend entries), by category (broken down by X-axis points), or by individual element in a series or category. Figures 20-8 and 20-9 show progressions based on series and category so you can see the difference.

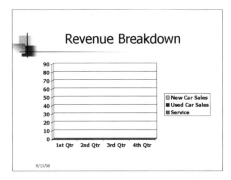

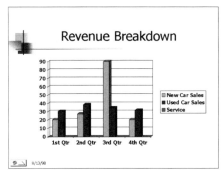
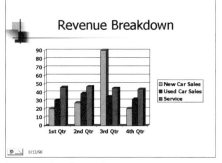

Figure 20-8: In this progression, the chart is appearing by series.

Along with making various parts of the chart appear at different times, you can also make them appear in any of the animated ways you've already learned, such as flying in, dropping in, fading in, and so on. You can also associate sounds with them, and dim them or change them to various colors when the animation is finished.

To animate a chart, follow these steps:

1. Select the chart on the slide.

2. Choose Slide Show ➪ Custom Animation. The Custom Animation dialog box appears with the Chart Effects tab on top.

3. Open the Introduce chart elements drop-down list and choose how the chart should appear. See Figure 20-10.

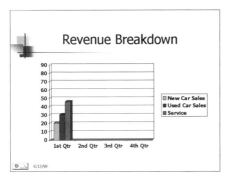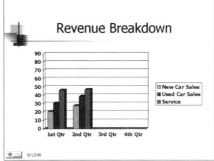
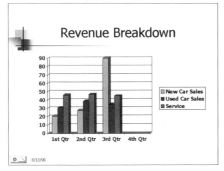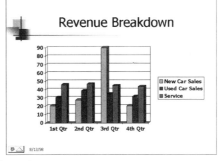

Figure 20-9: Here, the chart is appearing by category.

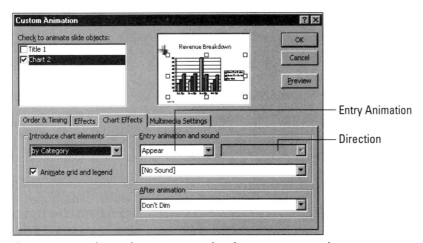

Entry Animation

Direction

Figure 20-10: Choose how you want the chart to appear and what animation and sound should go along with it.

4. If you want the grid and legend to appear with a separate mouse click from the background of the chart (as in the top-left image in Figure 20-8), mark the Animate grid and legend checkbox. If you don't want this effect, deselect the checkbox.

5. If you want the chart to appear on the slide with a special animation effect, such as Fly, choose an effect from the Entry animation drop-down list.

Note   You can choose an effect in Step 5 only if you chose All at Once in Step 3. If you are making different parts of the chart appear at different times, your only choice here is Appear, which means the elements simply appear without any additional special effect.

6. If you choose an effect in Step 5 for which there are directional choices, choose a direction from the Direction drop-down list.

7. (Optional) If you want to play a sound along with the animation, choose the sound you want from the Sound drop-down list. (See Chapter 18 for details.)

8. If you want the elements to do something different after they have been animated, such as disappear or change color, select the effect you want from the After animation drop-down list.

9. Click Preview to preview the effects you have chosen. If it looks right, click OK.

Great Animation Ideas

Here are some ideas for using animation in your own work.

✦ Try to use the same preset animation effect for each slide in a related series of slides. Consistency is important in maintaining a professional image. If you want to differentiate one section of the presentation from another, use a different animation effect for the text in each different section.

✦ If you want to discuss only one bullet point at a time on a slide, set the others to dim or change to a lighter color after animation. Or, to fully purge the spent bullets from the audience's thoughts, hide them altogether by choosing Hide After Animation from the After animation drop-down list in the Custom Animation dialog box.

✦ Animate your chart based on the way you want to lead your audience through the data. For example, if each series on your chart shows the sales for a different division and you want to compare one division to another, animate by series. If you want to talk about the results of that chart over time rather than by division, animate by category instead.

✦ If you want to create your own moving graphic but don't have access to a program that creates animated GIFs, you can build a very simple one on a slide with animation. Simply create the *frames* of the animation — three or more drawings that you want to progress through in quick succession. Then, lay them one on top of another on the slide. In the Custom Animation dialog box, animate all three in the order that they should be played. On the Order & Timing tab, set each one to appear automatically, one second apart. On the Effects tab, set each one to Hide After Animation.

Assigning Transitions to Slides

Transitions are how you get from slide A to slide B. Back in the old slide projector days, there was only one transition: the old slide got pushed out and the new slide plunked into place. But with a computerized presentation, you can choose from all kinds of fun transitions, including wipes, blinds, drives, and much more. These transitions are almost exactly like the animations you saw earlier in the chapter, except they apply to the whole slide (or at least the background — the base part of the slide, if the slide's objects are separately animated).

Note

The transition effect for a slide refers to how the slide enters, not how it exits. So if you want to assign a particular transition to occur while moving from slide 1 to slide 2, you would assign the transition effect to slide 2.

Using the Transition Drop-Down List

The looks of the individual transitions are hard to explain on paper; it's best if you just view them onscreen to understand what each one is. The following steps explain how to assign a transition.

1. Switch to Slide Sorter view.

2. Select the slide(s) for which you want to assign a transition.

3. Open the Transition drop-down list on the Slide Sorter toolbar and choose a transition effect. See Figure 20-11. The effect previews on the selected slide.

4. If you want to preview the effect again, click the Animation Preview button on the toolbar.

Using the Slide Transition Dialog Box

For more control, you can assign a transition using the Slide Transition dialog box instead. If you use the dialog box, you can set extra effects like changing the speed of the transition, choosing whether the slide advances automatically or not, and assigning a sound to the transition.

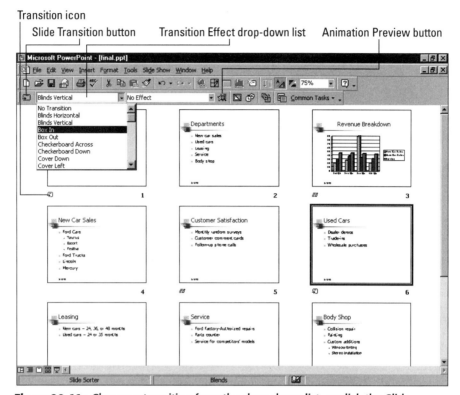

Figure 20-11: Choose a transition from the drop-down list, or click the Slide Transition button to display a dialog box.

Follow these steps:

1. Select the slide(s) for which you want to set a transition. (If you want to set the same transition for all slides in the presentation, you don't have to select them all; you can simply choose Apply to All at the end of the procedure.)

2. Click the Slide Transition button (on the Slide Sorter toolbar) or choose Slide Show ➪ Slide Transition. The Slide Transition dialog box appears. See Figure 20-12.

3. Open the Effect drop-down list and choose the effect you want. To preview the effect, click the picture above the drop-down list.

4. Choose Slow, Medium, or Fast for the effect speed. The default is Fast.

5. In the Advance section, if you want the slide to advance when you click the mouse, leave the On mouse click checkbox marked.

6. If you want the slide to advance automatically after a certain number of seconds, mark the Automatically after checkbox and enter a number (of seconds) in the text box.

Figure 20-12: Use this dialog box to fine-tune the slide transition.

Tip

You can use both On mouse click and Automatically after for a slide. For example, you can set a slide to automatically advance after 30 seconds, but the presenter can also advance it with a mouse click instead of waiting if he or she (and the audience) finishes with the slide sooner.

7. If you want to play a sound with the transition, open the Sound drop-down list and choose a sound, as you learned in Chapter 18.

8. Click Apply to apply the transition effect to the selected slide(s), or click Apply to All to apply it to all slides in the presentation.

Summary

In this chapter, you learned how to animate the objects on your slides to create some great special effects and how to create animated transitions from slide to slide. Use this newfound knowledge for good, not evil! In other words, don't go nuts with applying so many animations that your audience focuses too much on the effects and not enough on your message.

The next chapter starts a new part of the book—the part on speaker-led presentations. If you are planning to give your presentation in a live situation, standing up in front of an audience, this part of the book is for you. If, on the other hand, you are planning to distribute your presentation on disk, in the mail, or over the Internet, you can safely skip the next part.

✦ ✦ ✦

Presenting Speaker-Led Presentations

Creating
Support
Materials

I f you are presenting a live show, the centerpiece of your
presentation is your slides. Whether you show them using
a computer screen, a slide projector, or an overhead projector,
the slides — combined with your own dazzling personality —
make the biggest impact.

But if you rely on your audience to remember everything you
say, you may be disappointed. Even great presentations with
dynamic speakers can go in one ear and out the other without
some sort of reinforcement. Handouts work very well as just
such reinforcement. With handouts, the audience can follow
along with you during the show and even take their own
notes. And then, they usually take the handouts home with
them to review the information again later.

You probably want a different set of support materials for
yourself than you want for the audience. Support materials
designed for the speaker's use are called *speaker notes*. They
contain, in addition to small printouts of the slides, any extra
notes or background information that you think you may need
to jog your memory as you speak. Some people get very
nervous when they speak in front of a crowd; speaker notes
can remind you, if your mind goes blank, of the joke you
wanted to open with or the exact figures behind a particular
pie chart.

The When and How of Handouts

You learned a little bit about handout use in Chapter 6. Presentation professionals are divided as to how and when to use them most effectively. Here are some of the many conflicting viewpoints. I can't say who is right or wrong, but each of these statements brings up issues that you should consider. Each of them, at the bottom line, is an opinion on how much power and credit to give to the audience; your answer may vary depending on the audience you are addressing.

You should give handouts at the beginning of the presentation. The audience can absorb the information better if they can follow along on paper.

This approach makes a lot of sense. Research has proven that people absorb more facts if presented with them in more than one medium. This approach also gives your audience *free will*; they can listen to you, or they can *not* listen and still have the information. It's their choice, and this can be extremely scary for less-confident speakers. It's not just a speaker confidence issue in some cases, however. If you are going to give a lot of extra information in your speech that's not on the handouts, people might miss it because they're reading ahead if you distribute the handouts at the beginning.

You shouldn't give the audience handouts at all because they won't pay as close attention to your speech if they know that the information is already written down for them.

This philosophy falls at the other end of the spectrum. It gives the audience the least power and shows the least confidence in their ability to pay attention to you in the presence of a distraction (handouts). If you truly don't trust your audience to be professional and listen, this approach may be your best option. However, don't let insecurity as a speaker drive you prematurely to this conclusion. The fact is that people won't take away as much knowledge about the topic without handouts as they would if you provide handouts. So, ask yourself if your ultimate goal is to fill the audience with knowledge or to make them pay attention to you?

You should give handouts at the end of the presentation so that people will have the information to take home but not be distracted during the speech.

This approach attempts to solve the dilemma with compromise. The trouble with it, as with all compromises, is that it does an incomplete job from both angles. Because audience members can't follow along on the handouts during the presentation, they miss the opportunity to jot notes on the handouts. And because the audience knows that handouts are coming, they might nod off and miss something important. The other problem is that if you don't clearly tell people that handouts are coming later, some people spend the entire presentation frantically copying down each slide on their own notepaper.

In the end, each speaker must decide for each audience whether and how to use handouts.

Creating Handouts

To create handouts, you simply decide on a layout (a number of slides per page) and then choose that layout from the Print dialog box as you print. No muss, no fuss! If you want to get more involved, you can edit the layout in Handout Master view before printing.

Choosing a Layout

Assuming you have decided that handouts are appropriate for your speech, you must decide on the format for them. You have a choice of two, three, four, six, or nine slides per page.

Note   You can also print out one slide per page, but PowerPoint doesn't consider that a handout per se; rather, it's a printout of the slide. You might use printouts of your slides as handouts if it's important for the audience to have very large copies of each slide.

The two-slide-per-page layout, shown in Figure 21-1, prints two big slides on each page. This layout is good for slides that have a lot of fine print and small details or for situations where you are not confident that the reproduction quality will be good. There is nothing more frustrating for an audience than not being able to read the handouts!

The three-slides-per-page layout shown in Figure 21-2 makes the slides much smaller — less than one-third the size of the ones shown in Figure 21-1. But you get a nice bonus with this layout: lines to the side of each slide for note-taking. This layout works well for presentations where the slides are big and simple, and the speaker is providing a lot of extra information that isn't on the slides. The audience members can write the extra information in the note-taking space provided.

Caution   Here's a true story. I was once at a publishing conference where many of the most important authors and editors in the computer book industry were giving presentations. One man had a great-looking PowerPoint presentation; he had obviously spent a lot of time on it. Unfortunately, the slides had a lot of small print on them. He had chosen a three-slides-per-page layout, as shown in Figure 21-2, which made the type on the slides very tiny. He also had a colored background on the slides, so that further degraded the quality of the handouts. As a result, the handouts were virtually useless. Many of us used the space to the left of each slide to copy down the small print from the slides off the projection screen as quickly as we could. Apparently some people complained, because an announcement was made later in the day that the handouts would be reprinted — in color — and mailed to all attendees within a few weeks. This satisfied the participants, but it was an embarrassing situation for the speaker.

Figure 21-1: The two-slide-per-page layout works well when the slides need to be big.

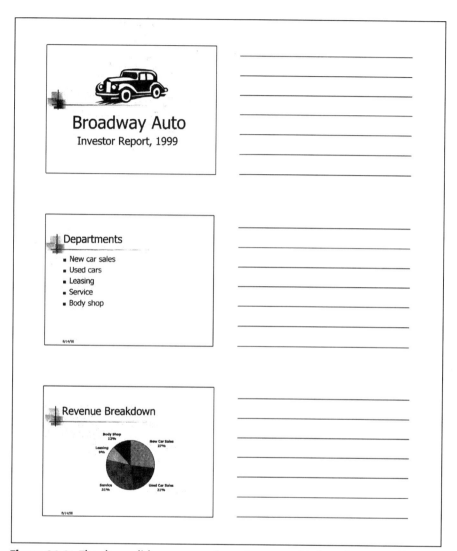

Figure 21-2: The three-slides-per-page format comes with lines for note-taking.

The four-slides-per-page layout uses the same size slides as the three-slide model, but they are spaced out two-by-two without note-taking lines. However, there is still plenty of room above and below each slide, so the audience members still have lots of room to take notes. See Figure 21-3.

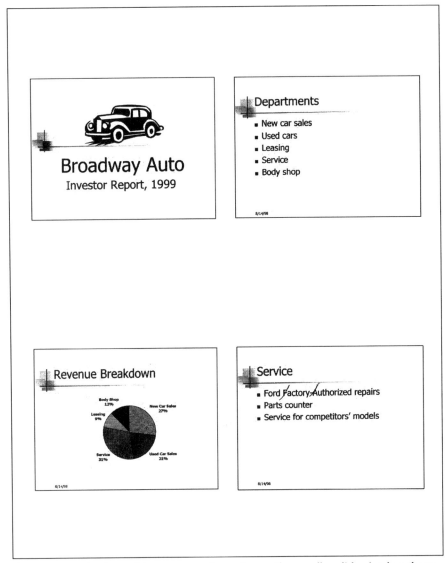

Figure 21-3: The four-slides-per-page format uses the smaller slide size but there are no lines for notes.

The six-slides-per-page layout, shown in Figure 21-4, uses slides the same size as the three-slide and four-slide models, but crams more slides on the page at the expense of note-taking space. This layout is good for presentation with big, simple slides where the audience does not need to take notes. If you are not sure if the audience will benefit at all from handouts being distributed, consider whether this layout would be a good compromise. This format also saves paper, which might be an issue if you need to make hundreds of copies of the handouts.

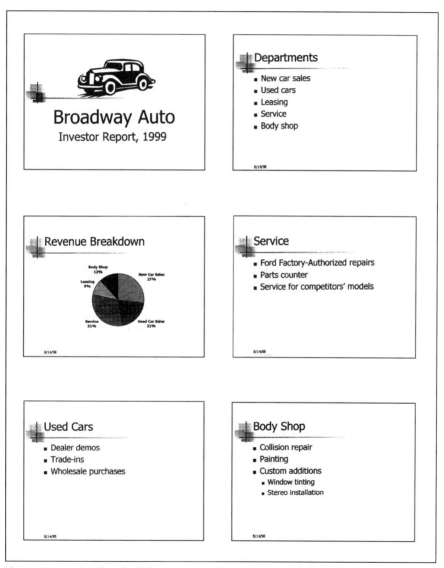

Figure 21-4: Use the six-slides-per-page format to provide handouts on fewer sheets of paper or when the handouts are not critical.

The nine-slides-per-page layout makes the slides very tiny, almost like a Slide Sorter view, so that you can see nine at a time. See Figure 21-5. This layout makes them very hard to read unless the slide text is extremely simple. I don't recommend this layout in most cases, because the audience really won't get much out of such handouts.

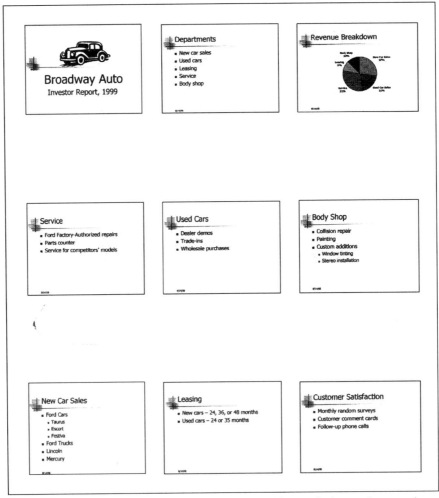

Figure 21-5: The nine-slides-per-page layout is useful as an index or directory, but not as a stand-alone handout in most cases.

However, one very good use for the nine-slides model is as an index or table of contents for a large presentation. You can include a nine-slides-per-page version of the handouts at the beginning of the packet you give to the audience members, and then follow it up with a two-slides-per-page version that they can refer to if they want a closer look at one of the slides.

Changing the Layout of Your Handouts

Just as your slide layout is controlled by the Slide Master, your handout layout is controlled by the Handout Master. To view the Handout Master, choose View ➪ Master ➪ Handout Master.

On the Handout Master, you can set a separate layout for each type of handout (that is, for each number of slides per page). To choose which layout you want to modify, click the appropriate button on the Handout Master toolbar. See Figure 21-6.

Figure 21-6: Choose which handout layout you want to alter.

After choosing the layout to work with, you can do any of the following.

✦ **Use (or not use) headers and footers:** Select View ➪ Header and Footer. This opens the Header and Footer dialog box. On the Notes and Handouts tab, set up which elements should appear as explained later in this chapter.

✦ **Move the header, footer, date, and/or slide number on the handout:** Select the text box for the element to move and drag it to a new spot.

✦ **Change the handout color scheme:** If you have a color printer, right-click the handout area and choose Handout Color Scheme. Then choose a color scheme, just as you did for slides in Chapter 11.

✦ **Change the handout background:** Right-click the handout area, choose Handout Background, and then choose a background. See Chapter 11 for details. Be aware, however, that a patterned or colored background may distract from the slides' message.

Note   If you want to change the size of the slide boxes on the handout or change the margins of the page, consider exporting the handouts to Word and working on them there. See the "Sending Your Presentation to Word" section at the end of this chapter.

Printing Handouts

To print handouts, follow these steps:

1. (Optional) If you want to print only one particular slide, or a group of slides, select the ones you want.

2. Select File ⇨ Print. The Print dialog box appears.

3. Set any options for your printer or choose a different printer. See the "Setting Printer Options" section later in this chapter.

4. In the Print Range area, choose one of the following:

    • **All** to print the entire presentation.

    • **Current slide** to print whatever slide was selected before you issued the Print command.

    • **Selection** to print multiple slides you selected before you issued the Print command.

    • **Custom Show** to print a certain custom show you have set up. (See Chapter 24.)

    • **Slides** to print the slide numbers that you type in the accompanying text box. For example, to print slides 1 through 9, type **1-9**. To print slides, 2, 4, and 6, type **2, 4, 6.**

5. Enter a number of copies in the Number of copies text box. The default is 1. If you want the copies collated (applicable to multipage printouts only), make sure the Collate checkbox is marked.

6. Open the Print what drop-down list and choose Handouts. The Handouts section of the box becomes available. See Figure 21-7.

7. Open the Slides per page drop-down list and choose the number of slides per page you want.

8. If available, choose an Order: Horizontal or Vertical. Not all number-of-slide choices (from Step 6) support an Order choice.

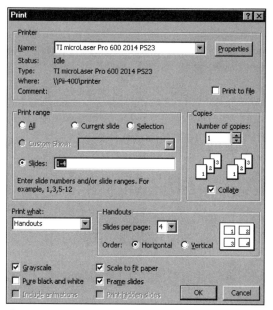

Figure 21-7: Choose Handouts to print and specify what handout layout you want.

Note

Order in Step 7 refers to the order in which the slides are placed on the page. Horizontal places them by rows, Vertical by columns. This ordering has nothing to do with the orientation of the paper (Portrait or Landscape). You set the paper orientation in the Page Setup dialog box (File ⇨ Page Setup), as described in Chapter 11.

9. Select any or all of the checkboxes at the bottom of the dialog box as desired:

- **Grayscale:** Prints in shades of gray (rather than in color). This option is useful if you have a color printer but don't want to print the handouts in color. For example, if you need to duplicate the printout with a black-and-white copy machine, grayscale printouts duplicate better than color printouts.

- **Pure black and white:** Reduces all colors and shading to either black or white. This option is good for creating simple text-based overheads with sharp, crisp blacks, but it ruins nearly all graphics and shading effects.

- **Scale to fit paper:** Enlarges the slides to the maximum size they can be and still fit on the layout. (You learned to control the layout with the Handout Master earlier in this chapter.)

- **Frame slides:** Draws a black border around each slide image.

- **Include animations:** Prints animated objects (as best it can, obviously, since the printout is static). This option is not applicable if your presentation doesn't include animated objects.

- **Print hidden slides:** Includes hidden slides in the printout. This option is not applicable if you don't have any hidden slides in your presentation.

10. Click OK. The handouts print, and you're ready to roll!

Caution   Beware of the cost of printer supplies. If you are planning to distribute copies of the presentation to a lot of people, it may be tempting to print all the copies on your printer. But especially if you have an inkjet printer, the cost per page of printing is fairly high. You will quickly run out of ink in your ink cartridge and have to spend $20 or more for a replacement. Consider whether it might be cheaper to print one original and take it to a copy shop.

Creating Speaker Notes

Speaker notes are like handouts for yourself. Only one printout format is available for them: the Speaker Notes page. It consists of the slide on the top half (the same size as in the two-slides-per-page handout) with the blank space below it for your notes to yourself.

Speaker notes printed in PowerPoint are better than traditional note cards for several reasons. For one thing, you can type your notes right into the computer and print them out on regular paper. There's no need to jam a note card into a typewriter and use messy correction fluid or erasers to make changes. The other benefit is that each note page contains a picture of the slide, so it's not as easy to get lost.

Typing Speaker Notes

You can type your notes for a slide in Normal or Outline view (in the notes pane), or in Notes Page view. The latter shows the page more or less as it will look when you print your notes pages; this can help if you need to gauge how much text will fit on the printed page.

To switch to Notes Page view, choose View ➪ Notes Page. See Figure 21-8. Unlike some of the other views, there is no shortcut button for this view. Once you're in Notes Page view, you can use the scroll bar to scroll down and see more of the notes area. You can scroll further to move from slide to slide, or you can move from slide to slide in the traditional ways (Page Up and Page Down keys on the keyboard or the Next Slide or Previous Slide buttons onscreen).

Tip

Use the Zoom control to zoom in or out until you find the optimal view so that the text you type is large enough to be clear, but small enough so that you can see across the entire width of the note area. I find that 75 percent to 100 percent works well on my screen, but yours may vary.

Just type your notes in the notes area, the same as you would type in any text box in PowerPoint. The lines in the paragraph wrap automatically. Press Enter to start a new paragraph. When you're done, move to the next slide.

Changing the Notes Page Layout

Just as you can edit your handouts layouts, you can also edit your notes page layout. Just switch to its Master and make your changes. Follow these steps:

1. Choose View ➪ Master ➪ Notes Master.

2. Edit the layout, as you have learned to edit other masters (Slide Master in Chapter 11, Handout Master earlier in this chapter). This can include moving, adding, or removing the Header Area, the Date Area, and so on. See Figure 21-9.

3. When you are finished, click the Close button to return to Normal view.

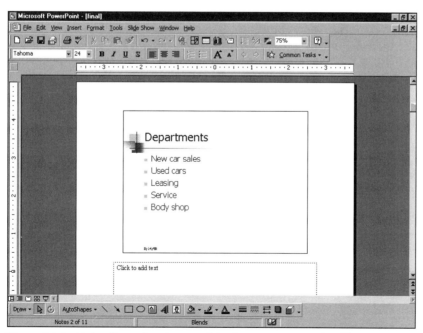

Figure 21-8: Notes Page view is one of the best ways to work with your speaker notes.

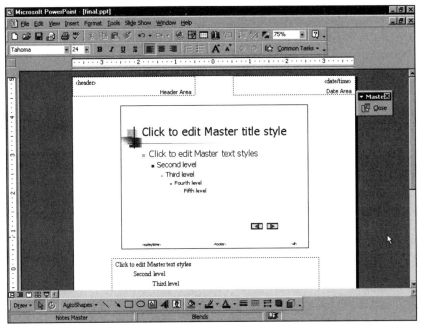

Figure 21-9: You can edit the layout of the notes pages in Notes Master view.

For more information specifically about the headers and footers on the master, see the "Formatting Handout and Notes Page Headers and Footers" section later in this chapter.

Printing Notes Pages

When you're ready to print your notes pages, follow these steps:

1. Choose File ➪ Print. The Print dialog box opens. See Figure 21-10.

2. Open the Print what drop-down list and choose Notes Pages.

3. Set any other options, just as you did when printing handouts earlier in the chapter. (If you need to choose which printer to use or set the options for that printer, see the "Setting Printer Options" section later in this chapter.)

4. Click OK. The notes pages print.

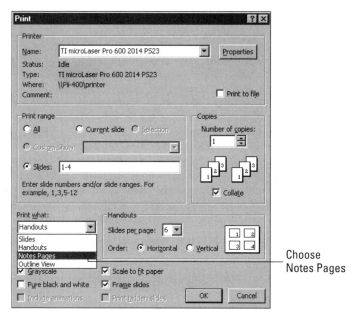

Figure 21-10: To print notes pages, choose Notes Pages as the item to print.

Caution If you print notes pages for hidden slides, you may want to arrange your printouts so that the hidden slides are at the bottom of your pile. That way, you won't get confused when giving the presentation.

Headers and Footers on Handouts and Notes Pages

Headers and footers (repeated text at the top or bottom of each printout) are especially important for audience handouts. For example, you might want to include your company's name in the header of each page or a page number in each footer. You began learning about headers and footers in Chapter 17; here is some more information about them that pertains specifically to notes pages and handout.

Turning Note and Handout Headers/Footers On or Off

You can enable or disable repeated text—date and time, headers, page numbers, and footers—on notes pages and handouts. The process is similar to that for slides that you learned in Chapter 17.

Follow these steps to control what repeated header and footer elements appear on handouts and notes pages:

Note The following steps set up both notes pages and handouts; you can't set them separately. If you need separate settings for each, set the header and footer settings the way you want them for one, then print them, and then set the header and footer settings differently before you print the other.

1. Choose View ➪ Header and Footer. The Header and Footer dialog box opens.

2. Click the Notes and Handouts tab. See Figure 21-11.

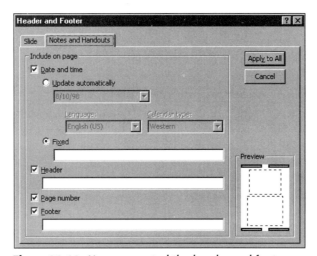

Figure 21-11: You can control the header and footer information for notes pages and handouts here.

3. If you want the date on the printout, make sure the Date and time checkbox is marked.

4. Choose Update automatically or Fixed, depending on the date type you want.

   • If you choose Update automatically, open the drop-down list and choose a date format. If you use a different language or calendar than English, choose it from the Language and Calendar Type drop-down lists.

   • If you choose Fixed, type the date, in the exact format that you want it to appear, in the Fixed text box.

5. If you want header text on the slide, make sure the Header checkbox is marked and then type the text in the Header text box.

6. If you want footer text on the slide, make sure the Footer checkbox is marked and then type the text in the Footer text box.

7. If you want page numbers on the printouts, make sure the Page number checkbox is marked.

8. Click Apply to All.

After choosing the repeating elements you want, you can format their placeholders on the appropriate masters, as described in the next section.

Formatting Handout and Note Page Headers and Footers

As you have learned earlier in this chapter, there are special masters for handouts and notes pages: Handout Master and Notes Master. On these masters, you can format the placeholders for your headers and footers, just like you did with the Slide Master earlier in this chapter.

Choose View ➪ Master and then either Handout Master or Notes Master. On the master layout that appears, select the placeholder you want to format. For example, in Figure 21-12, the header placeholder is selected. Then, change the font, size, attributes, and/or alignment as desired.

Setting Printer Options

In addition to the controls in the Print dialog box in PowerPoint, there are controls you can set that affect the printer you have chosen.

In the Printer section of the Print dialog box (last seen in Figure 21-10), you can open the Name drop-down list and choose the printer you want to use to print the job. Most home users have only one printer, but business users may have more than one to choose from, especially on a network.

Note   The printers that appear on the Name drop-down list come from the list of printers installed in Windows. If you need to install a printer in Windows, choose Start ➪ Settings ➪ Printers and double-click the Add Printer icon.

Placeholder for header text

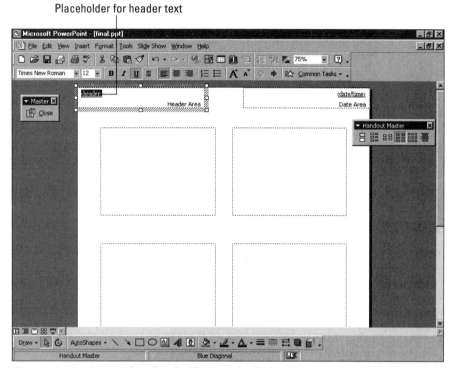

Figure 21-12: Format the placeholders on the Notes Master or Handout Master to control the header and footer formatting.

After choosing a printer, you can click the Properties button to display its Properties dialog box. The properties shown are different for different kinds of printers. Figure 21-13 shows the box for my Texas Instruments MicroLaser Pro 600 printer, a laser printer with PostScript capabilities.

These settings affect how the printer behaves in all Windows-based programs, not just in PowerPoint, so you need to be careful not to change anything that you don't want globally changed. Here are some of the settings you may be able to change for your printer:

- ✦ **Paper size:** The default is Letter, but you can change to Legal, A4, or any of several other sizes.
- ✦ **Orientation:** You can choose between Portrait or Landscape. I don't recommend changing this setting here, though; make such changes in the Page Setup dialog box in PowerPoint instead. Otherwise, you may get the wrong orientation on a printout in other programs.
- ✦ **Paper source:** If your printer has more than one paper tray, you may be able to select Upper or Lower.

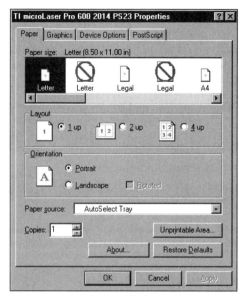

Figure 21-13: Each printer's options are slightly different, but the same types of settings are available for most printers.

✦ **Copies:** This sets the default number of copies that should print. Be careful; this number is a multiplier. If you set two copies here, and then set two copies in the Print dialog box in PowerPoint, you end up with four copies.

✦ **Graphics resolution:** If your printer has a range of resolutions available, you may be able to choose the resolution you want. My printer lets me choose between 300 and 600 dots per inch (dpi); on an inkjet printer, choices are usually 360, 720, and 1,440 dpi. Achieving a resolution of 1,440 on an inkjet printer usually requires special glossy paper.

✦ **Graphic dithering:** On some printers, you can set the type of dithering that makes up images. Dithering is a method of creating shadows (shades of gray) from black ink by using tiny crosshatch patterns. You may be able to choose between Coarse, Fine, and None.

✦ **Image intensity:** On some printers, you can control the image appearance with a light/dark slide bar.

Some printers, notably inkjets, come with their own print management software. If that's the case, you may have to run that print management software separately from outside of PowerPoint for full control over the printer's settings. Such software can usually be accessed from the Windows Start menu.

Printing an Outline

If text is the main part of your presentation, you might prefer to print an outline instead of minislides. You can use the outline for speaker notes, audience handouts, or both. To print the text from Outline view, follow these steps:

1. View the outline in Normal or Outline view and make sure you click in the Outline pane so it is selected.

2. Choose File ➪ Print. The Print dialog box opens.

3. Open the Print what drop-down list and choose Outline View.

4. Set any other print options, as you learned in the section called "Printing Handouts" earlier in this chapter.

5. Click OK.

Be aware, however, that the outline will not contain text that you've typed in manually placed text boxes or any other nontext information, such as tables, charts, and so on.

Sending Your Presentation to Word

You can also create handouts in Microsoft Word, the word processor that comes with Microsoft Office 2000. When you do so, you create handouts or notes pages in Word that are fully formattable. You can change the margins, adjust the placement of individual slides, and so on once you get the materials into Word.

You can send to Word in a variety of formats. Some formats are more appropriate for handouts, others for speaker notes. Here are some suggestions:

For Handouts	For Speaker Notes
Blank lines next to slides	Notes next to slides
Blank lines below slides	Notes below slides
Outline only	Outline only

To send to Word, follow these steps:

1. Choose File ➪ Send To ➪ Microsoft Word. The Write-Up dialog box appears. See Figure 21-14.

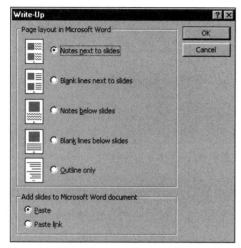

Figure 21-14: Choose a format for sending the presentation to Word.

2. Choose one of the formats shown in Figure 21-14.

3. (Optional) If you want to maintain a link between the PowerPoint file and the Word file, choose Paste link. Otherwise, leave Paste selected. If you maintain a link, changes made to the PowerPoint file will be reflected in the Word file.

4. Click OK. Word opens and the slides appear in the format you chose. See Figure 21-15.

5. Modify the formatting as desired and then print from Word.

6. (Optional) Save your work in Word if you want to be able to print the same pages again later. (You may choose to resend to Word later, after making changes in PowerPoint instead.)

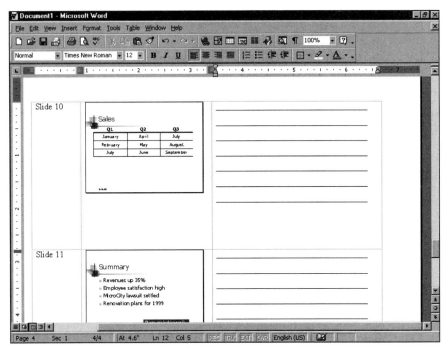

Figure 21-15: With the notes pages or handouts in Word, you can change the margins and other settings.

Tip

The slides appear in Word in a table. You can resize the columns for each element by dragging the column dividers, just like you do in a table in PowerPoint. (Remember, you learned about tables in Chapter 8.)

Summary

In this chapter, you learned how to create hard copy to support your presentation. You can now create a variety of handouts, and write and print out speaker notes for yourself, too. You also learned how to export handouts, notes pages, and outlines to Word, where you can use the full power of Word's formatting tools to create exactly the look you want.

In the next chapter, you take a look at the controls that PowerPoint offers for showing a presentation onscreen. You learn how to move from slide to slide, take notes, "draw" on the slides, and more.

✦　　　✦　　　✦

Controlling a Live Presentation

Copying a Presentation to Another Computer

Often, the PC on which you create a presentation is not the same PC that you will use to show it. For example, you might be doing the bulk of your work on your desktop PC in your office in Los Angeles, but you will need to use your laptop PC to give the presentation in Phoenix.

One way to transfer a presentation to another computer is simply to copy the PowerPoint file (the file with the .ppt extension) using a floppy disk. But this method is imperfect because it assumes that the other PC has all the needed fonts, sounds, and other elements needed for every part of the show. This can be a dangerous assumption. For example, suppose your presentation contains a link to some Excel data. If you don't copy that Excel file too, you won't be able to update the data when you're on the road.

A better way to ensure that you are taking everything you need on the road is to use the Pack and Go feature in PowerPoint. It reads all the linked files and associated objects and makes sure that they are transferred along with the main presentation.

Tip
The best way to transfer a presentation from one computer to another is over a network if both PCs are connected to it. Transfer with a floppy disk (or multiple disks) only if a network connection is not available.

Packing a Presentation with Pack and Go

Follow these steps to transfer your presentation to another PC:

1. Open the presentation that you want to transfer.

2. Choose File ➪ Pack and Go. The Pack and Go Wizard opens.

3. Click Next to begin.

4. When asked which presentation you want to package, leave Active Presentation marked. Then, click Next.

5. When asked what drive it should be copied to, choose A:\ or B:\ for a floppy disk, or to copy over a network, click Choose Destination and then Browse for the location. See Figure 22-1.

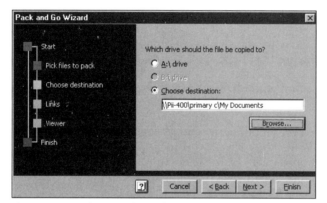

Figure 22-1: Choose where the presentation should be copied.

6. Click Next.

7. If you want the linked files copied (see Chapter 16), make sure the Include Linked Files checkbox is marked.

8. If the destination PC does not have the fonts installed that are used in this presentation, mark the Embed TrueType Fonts checkbox.

9. Click Next.

10. The Wizard asks you whether or not you want to install the PowerPoint Viewer. If the destination PC does not have PowerPoint installed, choose Viewer for Windows 95 or NT.

Caution　If you have room on your laptop (or travel computer), install the full version of PowerPoint, not just the PowerPoint Viewer. That way, if you need to make a small change to the presentation right before you give it (perhaps you found a typo or need to change the date), you can do so. With the PowerPoint Viewer, you cannot do even the smallest bit of editing. The PowerPoint Viewer is more useful when distributing self-serve presentations, such as those described in Chapter 27.

11. Click Next. An explanation appears telling you what choices you have made.

12. Click Finish. The wizard packages, compresses, and transfers the presentation and all its associated files.

13. When you see a message that the packing was successful, click OK.

Unpacking the Presentation in Its New Home

This next part is important: After packing and transferring a presentation, the presentation is in a compressed format. You cannot use it as is; you must run a setup program on the destination computer first. To do this, follow these steps on the destination computer:

1. Choose Start ⇨ Programs ⇨ Windows Explorer.

2. In Windows Explorer, navigate to the drive and folder where you transferred the presentation.

3. Double-click the file `Pngsetup`. A Pack and Go Setup dialog box appears. See Figure 22-2.

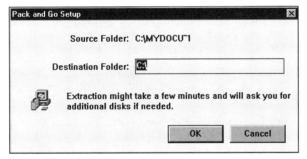

Figure 22-2: You must unpack your presentation using the Pngsetup program.

4. In the Destination Folder text box, enter the drive and folder where the presentation should go. Then click OK.

Note Important: The Pack and Go setup does not support long folder names with spaces in them like My Documents does. So, you must use the abbreviated name for a long folder name on your system, like MYDOCU~1. To convert a long filename into a short one, use the first six letters of the name, omitting spaces. Then add a tilde (~) and then a number. If this is the first folder in this location with that same six first letters, use 1; if it's the second, use 2, and so on.

5. If you see a message that the folder is not empty and that unpacking will overwrite any files of the same name, click OK.

Caution Do not unpack into a folder that contains files of the same name as the incoming ones that you want to keep. For example, if you have a draft version of Final.ppt in your My Documents folder that you want to keep, do not unpack the packed version of Final.ppt there.

6. A message appears that the slide show was successfully unpacked, and you're asked whether you want to run the slide show now. Choose Yes to open the slide show using the PowerPoint Viewer, or choose No.

Working with Audio Visual Equipment

The bulk of this chapter teaches you how to show a presentation, but before you get down to that, you probably want to set up the available equipment. There are many models of projection equipment in conference rooms all across the world, but most of them fall into one of these categories:

✦ **Noncomputerized equipment:** This can include an overhead transparency viewer, a 35mm slide projector, or other older technology. If you have to deal with such equipment, you won't get much out of this chapter. This chapter deals mainly with showing a presentation from a computer.

✦ **Single PC with a single monitor:** On such a system, you can either copy your presentation file to that PC, as explained in the preceding section, or you can shut down that PC and connect its monitor to your laptop.

✦ **Projection system or large monitor without a PC:** You hook your own laptop up to this equipment, as explained in the following section.

✦ **Single PC with a dual-monitor system:** If you want to use this system, you must copy your presentation to that PC. Then, you set up PowerPoint to use the second monitor, as explained later in this chapter. If you don't want to do that, you may be able to shut such a system down and hook up your own laptop to one of the monitors.

In simple presentation situations, you probably will have only one screen available for your show. However, if you are in a setting that has more sophisticated equipment, two screens may be available, or one computer screen and one projection system. The following sections provide some guidance.

Working with a Laptop and a Monitor or ▶

Your laptop computer has a built-in screen, of course; you can view t⌐
as you speak, while your audience sees the slides on a large projection s
external monitor.

Note   You need the full version of PowerPoint on your laptop to do this procedure, n⌐
just the PowerPoint Viewer.

To set this up, follow these steps:

1. Turn off the projector and the PC.

2. Connect the projector to the monitor port on your laptop.

3. Turn both devices back on and start PowerPoint.

4. In PowerPoint, open the presentation you want to show.

5. Choose Slide Show ➪ Set Up Show. The Set Up Show dialog box appears.

6. Click the Projector Wizard button. The Projector Wizard appears. See Figure 22-3.

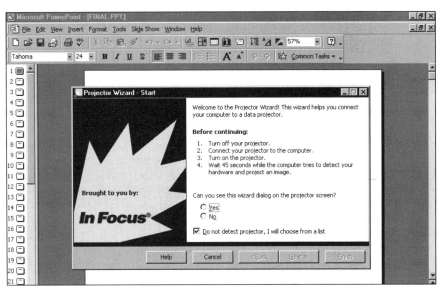

Figure 22-3: The Projector Wizard walks you through the steps of configuring an external monitor or projector.

If you see your PC's desktop image on the projector screen, click Yes. Otherwise, click No. Then, click Next.

8. Follow the instructions onscreen to detect the projector and configure it. The configuration steps may be different from this point on depending on the projector type, but all are fairly self-explanatory.

Working from Two External Monitors

If you are running Windows 98 or Windows NT 5.0 on the presentation PC, you can use two external monitors. One can show you the Normal view of the presentation, complete with your notes and outline, while the audience sees only the slides in Slide Show view on the other one.

Note
To use two monitors, you must have special hardware installed, such as two separate video cards. See the Windows 98 or Windows NT 5.0 Help system for more information.

To choose which monitor to display the show on (in other words, what the audience sees), follow these steps:

1. Choose Slide Show ⇨ Set Up Show. The Set Up Show dialog box appears.

   If you have two monitors successfully configured in Windows, the Show On drop-down list is available. If not, it is grayed out.

2. Open the Show On drop-down list and choose the monitor on which you want to show the presentation. The other monitor displays Normal view in PowerPoint throughout the show.

3. Click OK.

Now you can show the presentation. To do so, simply select the slide in Normal view that you want to display on the second monitor. It appears there in Slide Show view. To move from slide to slide, press Page Down or click the Next Slide button below the vertical scroll bar as you normally would.

Presenting the Slide Show

Now that you have mastered the A/V equipment at your disposal, it's time for the show. (Actually, I hope for your sake that it is not time for the show this very instant, because things will go much more smoothly if you are able to practice using PowerPoint's slide show controls before you have to go live.)

Presenting the show can be as simple or as complex as you make it. At the most basic level, you can start the show, move through it slide by slide with simple mouse clicks or keypresses, and end the show. But to take advantage of PowerPoint's extra show features, such as the Meeting Minder, the drawing tools, and the slide organizer, you must spend a little time studying the following sections.

Starting and Ending a Show

To start a show, do any of the following:

✦ Click the Slide Show View button.

✦ Choose View ➪ Slide Show.

✦ Choose Slide Show ➪ View Show.

✦ Press F5.

These methods are not all exactly alike; if you click the Slide Show View button or choose View ➪ Slide Show, the first slide to appear is the currently selected one in PowerPoint. If you choose Slide Show ➪ View Show or press F5, it starts with the first slide in the presentation, regardless of what slide was selected.

Once the show is underway, you can control the movement from slide to slide as described in "Moving from Slide to Slide," the next section in this chapter.

To end the show, press Esc, or right-click and choose End Show.

Tip
If you want to temporarily pause the show while you have a discussion, you can blank the screen by pressing W for a white screen or B for a black one. To resume the show after doing that, press any key.

Understanding the Onscreen Show Controls

As you display a slide show, the mouse pointer is hidden. To make it appear, move the mouse. When you do so, a button appears in the bottom-left corner of the screen. You can click that button to display a menu of controls. See Figure 22-4. You can get the same menu by right-clicking anywhere on the slide. You learn about these commands throughout the remainder of this chapter.

Note
Because the menu system is identical whether you click the button or right-click anywhere on the slide, I won't mention both methods each time I ask you to choose something from the menu. I ask you to right-click, because it's simpler. But keep in mind that you can also do a regular click on that button as an alternative anytime you like.

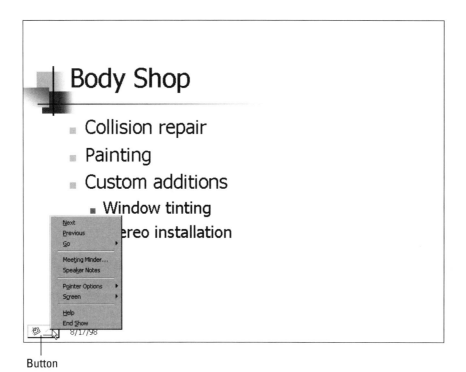

Button

Figure 22-4: Move the mouse during a show to display a button. Click the button to display a menu.

Moving from slide to slide

The simplest way to move through a presentation is to move to the next slide. To do so, any of these methods works:

✦ Press any key on the keyboard except Page Up.

✦ Click the left mouse button.

✦ Right-click and then choose Next.

Caution

If you have animated any elements on a slide, the methods above advance the animation, and do not necessarily move to the next slide. For example, if you have animated your bulleted list so that the bullets appear one at a time, any of the actions on the above list makes the next bullet appear, rather than making the next slide appear. Only after all the objects on the current slide have been displayed does PowerPoint advance to the next one. If you need to immediately advance to the next slide, use the instructions in the next section, "Jumping to Specific Slides."

To back up to the previous slide, use either of these methods:

✦ Press Page Up on the keyboard.

✦ Right-click and then choose Previous.

These forward and back movements imitate a 35mm slide projector, which most presenters are familiar with. But PowerPoint can also jump from one slide to a totally unrelated, nonadjacent one, as shown in the following sections.

Jumping to Specific Slides by Title

There are several ways to jump to a particular slide. One of the easiest is to select the slide you want by its title. To do so, follow these steps:

1. During the slide show, right-click to display the shortcut menu.

2. Point to Go. A submenu appears.

3. Choose By Title. Another submenu appears, listing the titles of all the slides in the presentation. See Figure 22-5.

4. Click the slide title that you want to jump to.

Jumping to Specific Slides with the Slide Navigator

Another way to jump to a particular slide is with the Slide Navigator dialog box. It contains the same list of slides as the submenu you just saw, but they're in a dialog box format. To use this, follow these steps:

1. During the slide show, right-click to display the shortcut menu.

2. Point to Go. A submenu appears.

3. Choose Slide Navigator. The Slide Navigator dialog box opens. See Figure 22-6.

4. Click the slide you want to jump to.

5. Click Go To. The dialog box closes and the chosen slide is displayed.

Viewing Hidden Slides

Slides that you have marked as hidden do not appear in the main flow of the presentation. (To hide a slide, see the "Hiding Slides for Backup Use" section in Chapter 24.) Therefore, the only way to display a hidden slide is to jump to it using either of the methods explained in the preceding section.

There is really no difference between jumping to a hidden slide and jumping to a nonhidden one. You can tell at a glance which slides are hidden because hidden slides have parentheses around their slide numbers. For example, in Figures 22-5 and 22-6, slide 9 is hidden.

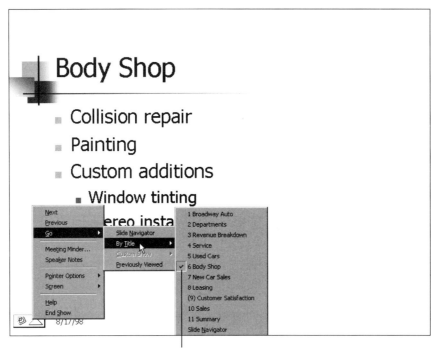

Check mark indicates the current slide

Figure 22-5: Choose the slide you want by title.

Figure 22-6: Select a slide to jump to from a list in the Slide Navigator.

Viewing Your Notes

You have probably printed out any speaker notes that you've created, but Murphy's Law says that when you need your notes, they will be nowhere to be found. Rather than spend long minutes fumbling with your papers, you may want to refer to your notes onscreen.

You can not only view notes during a presentation, but you can take more notes, too. To access your notes pages during a presentation, follow these steps:

1. Display the slide for which you want to view or type notes.

2. Right-click and choose Speaker Notes. A Speaker Notes box appears, showing the current notes for the slide. See Figure 22-7.

3. Read the notes as needed, and add more if appropriate. You might, for example, take notes on audience response to a particular slide.

4. When you are finished with the Speaker Notes box, click Close to close it.

The disadvantage to this, of course, is that if you have a one-screen setup, the audience reads your notes onscreen along with you. But if you have your presentation set up to display on two screens, as described earlier in this chapter, the speaker notes appear only on the presenter's screen.

Drawing Onscreen

Have you ever seen a coach in a locker room, drawing out football plays on a chalkboard? Well, you can do the same thing in PowerPoint. You can have impromptu discussions of concepts illustrated on slides and punctuate the discussion with your own circles and arrows and lines.

All you have to do is turn your mouse pointer into a pen. Right-click and choose Pointer Options ➪ Pen, or press Ctrl+P during the presentation. Then, drag the mouse on the slide to draw. Practice drawing lines, arrows, or whatever; it takes awhile to get good at it.

To erase your lines and try again, press E (for Erase), or right-click and choose Screen ➪ Erase Pen. Drawings are also erased when you advance to the next slide, so if you draw on one slide and then display another, and then return to the drawn-on slide, the drawing won't be there anymore.

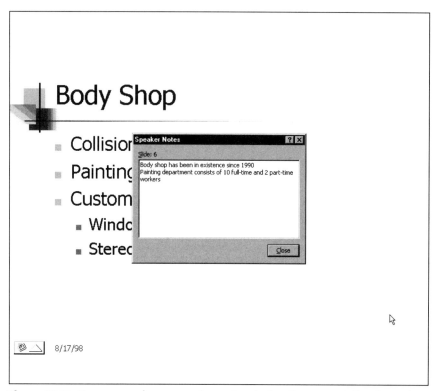

Figure 22-7: You can read your speaker notes during the presentation from the Speaker Notes pane.

Note　There may be times when you want to draw on a totally blank screen instead of on a slide. To blank out the screen for drawing, press the B key for a black screen or W for a white one. The pen color adjusts to be visible (black on white or white on black).

You can change the pen color at any time by right-clicking and choosing Pointer Options ➪ Pen Color and then a color. Nine colors are available: black, white, red, green, blue, cyan, magenta, yellow, and gray.

When might drawing on a slide be useful? Well, perhaps during the discussion portion of your presentation you decide that one point on the slide is not important. You can use the pen to cross it out. Or perhaps a certain point becomes really important during a discussion and you want to emphasize it. You can circle it or underline it with the pen cursor. Figure 22-8 shows how I've punctuated a key point and crossed out another.

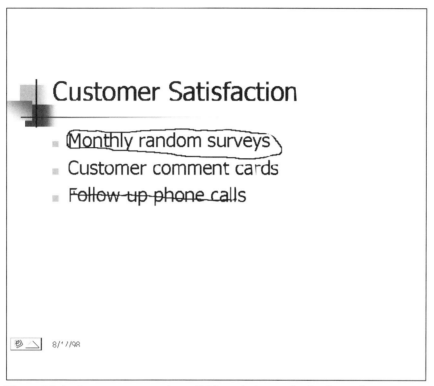

Figure 22-8: An onscreen pen is available to help emphasize key points.

Tip   As you can see from Figure 22-8, the onscreen pen is not all that attractive. If you know in advance that you're going to emphasize certain points, build the emphasis into the presentation by making that point larger, bolder, or a different color.

To change the pen back to a pointer again, right-click and choose Pointer Options ⇨ Arrow, or press Ctrl+A. The pen also changes to a pointer automatically when you switch to a different slide.

Using Meeting Minder

During most meetings, someone takes minutes and distributes them to participants later. The term *minutes* means play-by-play notes about what went on. If you don't have anyone taking care of that, you can tackle it yourself with PowerPoint's Meeting Minder.

Sometimes, action items (things to do) are assigned to various people as well. If nobody else is writing down a record of who volunteered for what assignments, you can keep these records in PowerPoint during your presentation.

Although you can't use this feature for real until the presentation actually starts, you should practice using the Meeting Minder feature ahead of time so you appear confident with it when the time comes.

To display the Meeting Minder, right-click and choose Meeting Minder. The Meeting Minder dialog box appears. See Figure 22-9. It contains two tabs: Meeting Minutes and Action Items.

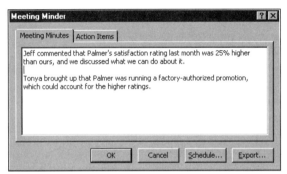

Figure 22-9: Use the Meeting Minder to take minutes and assign action items.

Entering Minutes

The Meeting Minutes tab, shown in Figure 22-9, is pretty straightforward. Just type the minutes into the dialog box as they happen. You must close the Meeting Minder window to advance to the next slide (with the OK button), but you can reopen it whenever you need it. You probably will not need it for every slide.

Caution   Just because PowerPoint provides a means of taking minutes does not mean that you have to use the feature. It is easier to ask someone else to write down the minutes so you can focus your energy on speaking.

Assigning Action Items

On the Action Items tab, you can assign tasks to individuals. If you use Microsoft Outlook, you can transfer the action items to a schedule, too.

First, follow these steps to enter action items into the Meeting Minder:

1. Display the Meeting Minder dialog box if it is not already onscreen (right-click and choose Meeting Minder).

2. Click the Action Items tab. The fields for creating action items appear. See Figure 22-10.

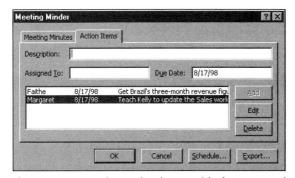

Figure 22-10: Assign action items with these controls.

3. Enter a description in the Description field.

4. In the Assigned To field, enter the name of the person who is to be responsible for the task.

5. Enter a due date in the Due Date field.

6. Click the Add button.

7. Repeat Steps 3 through 6 to add more action items to the list.

Scheduling Outlook Activities from Action Items

If you have Outlook installed on your computer, you can schedule activities (such as meetings) to take care of the action items. This isn't a book about Outlook, of course, so you need to know something about that program to get around in it. But here's a head start:

1. Click the Schedule button in the Meeting Minder. Outlook opens. If you have not used Outlook before, the Outlook Startup Wizard runs; follow its prompts as necessary.

2. An Appointment window opens in Outlook. Schedule the appointment by filling in the fields provided. See Figure 22-11. Then click the Save and Close button.

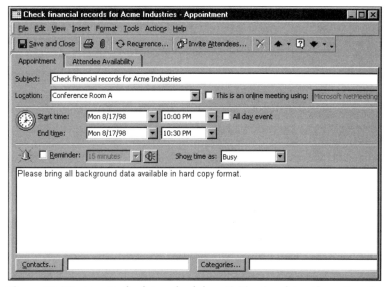

Figure 22-11: Use Outlook to schedule activities involving the action items.

Exporting Minutes and Tasks

You can also export the minutes and the action items to Word and the action items to Outlook. Word is a great tool for cleaning up the hurriedly typed notes that you took during a meeting; from there, you can save and print the minutes, or even e-mail them to others with the File ➪ Send To ➪ E-mail Recipient command.

You do not have to do anything special to Outlook; the Meeting Minder Export sends the action items directly there without your further intervention. The items appear on the Tasks list the next time you open Outlook.

To export minutes and tasks, follow these steps:

1. From the Meeting Minder, click the Export button. The Meeting Minder Export dialog box appears. See Figure 22-12.

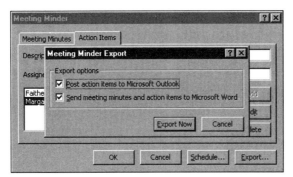

Figure 22-12: Choose which items you want to export.

2. If you want the action items to appear as To-Do items in Outlook, make sure the Post action items to Microsoft Outlook checkbox is marked.

3. If you want to finalize the meeting notes and action items in Word (highly recommended), make sure the Send meeting minutes and action items to Microsoft Word checkbox is marked.

4. Click Export Now. Word opens, and the meeting minutes appear there, with the action items at the bottom. See Figure 22-13.

5. Save and print your work in Word; then close Word.

Note

Outlook is an extremely flexible and capable contact management and scheduling program. For more information about it, check out *Microsoft Outlook For Dummies*, also published by IDG Books Worldwide.

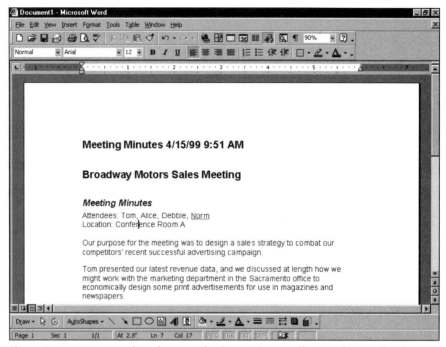

Figure 22-13: Use Word to clean up the formatting, spelling, and so on for the minutes.

Summary

In this chapter, you learned how to prepare for the big presentation. You now know how to pack up a presentation and move it to another PC, how to set up single and multiscreen A/V equipment to work with your laptop, and how to control a presentation onscreen using your computer. You also know now how to jump to different slides, how to take notes during a meeting, and how to assign action items. You're all set! All you need now is a nice starched shirt and a shoeshine.

In the next chapter, you learn about a different kind of live presentation, the kind that involves presenting from a distance. Like an in-person speech, this type of presentation takes place in real time, with the audience listening at the same moment that you are presenting. However, the technological challenges are different because you are trying to bridge a physical distance between you and your listeners. More on that as you turn the page.

✦　　　✦　　　✦

Presenting from a Remote Location

As you've learned throughout this book, there are several ways to present a slide show. One, of course, is via a live, in-person speaker, as you learned in the preceding chapter. Another way is to distribute the presentation file on a disk or to post it on the Internet, where people can download or access it at their leisure.

> **Tip** If you are interested in leaving a presentation on the Internet where people can retrieve and run it at their leisure, see Chapters 26 and 27.

A compromise between these two is remote delivery, or *broadcasting*. With remote delivery, the presenter is presenting in real time, at the same time as the listeners are seeing the slides. The only difference is that the listeners may be several office buildings or several continents away, rather than in chairs a few feet from a podium.

PowerPoint delivers a remote presentation through a Microsoft add-in called NetShow. It works with Internet Explorer, the Web browser, to allow people to see broadcast presentations and other Office documents. This is one of the coolest, most innovative new features in Office 2000! It not only allows you to broadcast a presentation, but also to include video, audio, voice-over narration, and more. You can also save the presentation in HTML format so that it can be replayed for anyone who may have missed the original broadcast (something like setting your VCR to record a TV show).

Note   You can broadcast a presentation, including audio tracks, to up to 15 people at once using the standard NetShow components that come with PowerPoint. If you need to also include video, or if you need to broadcast to more than 15 people, you must employ a NetShow server, which your network administrator may be able to set up for you on your company's Windows NT server. Contact your IT department for details.

You can present a broadcast over a local area network in your company or over the Internet. The setup for both options is the same except for the address at which you store the presentation materials. If you are presenting on a network, you store the presentation on your network server or a shared drive that all participants can access. If you are presenting over the Internet, you store the presentation on your company's Internet server.

System Requirements

To broadcast a presentation, you need PowerPoint (obviously) and Internet Explorer 4.0 or higher. (PowerPoint comes with IE 5.0, so this should not be a problem.) You also need access to a NetShow server if your audience consists of more than 15 people. You need to schedule the broadcast, so you should have Outlook or some other e-mail program installed.

Audience members need a Web browser, preferably Internet Explorer. The audience members should also have e-mail access so they can receive notification of the broadcast. The e-mail that participants receive will contain a hyperlink that they can click when it is time to view the broadcast. If some audience members do not have e-mail access, you can provide the URL to type into their browsers in a hard-copy memo.

Scheduling an Online Broadcast

The first step in preparing for an online broadcast is to schedule it. Scheduling is important because the broadcast will happen at a specified time, and all the participants need to be aware of it well in advance. When you schedule a broadcast, you also choose the basic parameters, such as which presentation will be broadcast, where it will be saved, and so on.

Caution   If your company doesn't have a Windows NT server, with a NetShow server set up, certain broadcast options, such as using video and broadcasting to more than 15 people at a time, will not be available. You can select these options during the setup, but they will result in error messages later when you try to perform the broadcast. I point these out where applicable.

Follow these steps to schedule a broadcast:

1. Open the presentation that you want to broadcast.

2. Choose Slide Show ➪ Online Broadcast ➪ Set Up and Schedule. (You may have to go through a one-time installation process if a dialog box appears prompting you to install the feature.) The Broadcast Schedule dialog box opens. See Figure 23-1.

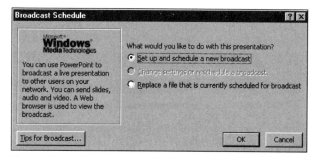

Figure 23-1: Set up or manage your scheduled broadcasts from here.

3. Choose the Set up and schedule a new broadcast checkbox. Then, click OK. The Schedule a New Broadcast dialog box opens.

4. First, fill in the Description tab, shown in Figure 23-2. This information is displayed to the audience members when you broadcast:

   - **Title:** By default, this is the title of the PowerPoint file. Change it, if desired, to a more descriptive or longer name.

   - **Description (optional):** You can enter as much text as you like here to provide the audience members with some background on what the presentation covers and why it is important that they attend.

   - **Speaker:** Put your name here if it does not already appear.

   - **Contact:** Enter an e-mail address where attendees can send their questions about the show.

5. Click the Broadcast Settings tab. See Figure 23-3.

Note

If your company uses online broadcasts regularly, some of the scheduling options on the Broadcast Settings tab may already be set up for you. If there is already an entry in any of the fields discussed in the following steps, you might want to accept that value unless you know for sure that it should be changed.

Figure 23-2: Enter the textual information that you want the audience to read while they are waiting for the show to start.

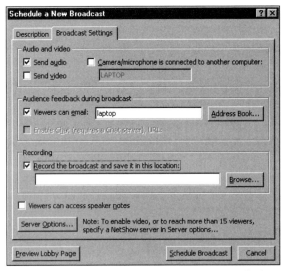

Figure 23-3: Define the broadcast settings with this dialog box.

6. In the Audio and Video section, select or deselect the Send audio and/or Send video checkboxes as desired. Using Send audio sends the sound clips associated with the presentation; Send video sends the video clips and

animations. You can use Send video only if your company has a NetShow server set up.

7. (Optional) If you have a camera or microphone that you want to use during the presentation and it's attached to another computer on your LAN, mark the Camera/microphone is connected to another computer checkbox and enter the computer's network name in the box.

8. In the Audience Feedback during broadcast section, if you want the users to be able to e-mail you, mark the Viewers can email checkbox and enter your e-mail address in the text box. (You can use the Address Book button to browse for addresses, but you probably know your own without looking.)

9. If a chat server is available on your system and you want to use it during the presentation, mark the Enable Chat checkbox, and then enter the URL for the chat server. If this option is grayed out, as in Figure 23-3, a chat server is not available.

10. In the Recording section, if you want to record the broadcast, mark the Record the broadcast and save it in this location checkbox. Then, enter a location in the text box. It can be any location on any drive that you have permission to write to (local or network).

11. If you want your audience to be able to see the speaker notes, mark the Viewers can access speaker notes checkbox.

12. Click the Server Options button. The Server Options dialog box appears. See Figure 23-4.

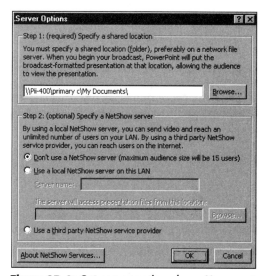

Figure 23-4: Set server options here. You must provide a shared location; the NetShow server use is optional.

13. In Step 1 of the dialog box, enter the path to a drive and folder where the temporary files needed to show the presentation should be stored. Microsoft suggests using a folder on your network server, but if one is not available, you can use a drive and folder on your own hard disk that is set up to be shared. It is important that all participants be able to connect to this location.

If you are presenting the broadcast over the Internet, use a URL that points to your Internet server where you will store the files, such as `http://www.mysite.com/presentation`.

Note   If you are using a drive and folder on your network server, use the network path name in Step 13, not a mapped drive letter. For example, if your laptop computer (named Laptop on the network) has a hard disk (named C Drive) that is mapped as E:\ on your desktop, you would enter a path like this: `\\laptop\C Drive\`, rather than E:\. To set up drive and folder sharing in Windows 95/98, see your network administrator or the Windows Help system.

14. If you are going to have fewer than 16 audience members and you don't plan to include video, mark the Don't Use a NetShow server option button. If you want a larger audience or want to use video, choose Use a local NetShow server on this LAN and then enter the server name in the Server name box.

15. Click OK to return to the Schedule a New Broadcast dialog box.

16. Click the Schedule Broadcast button.

17. If you did not specify a NetShow server in Step 14, a confirmation box appears asking you if this is right. Click Yes.

18. If you use Outlook, an Outlook window appears so you can schedule the broadcast conference. See Figure 23-5. (If you use a different e-mail program, it appears instead.)

Note   If you use a different e-mail program and Outlook is not installed on your PC, the rest of the steps in this procedure are not applicable to you. Instead, an e-mail window appears so you can send an announcement of the scheduled meeting to your recipients. The message they receive will contain a hyperlink to the presentation location.

19. In the Outlook window, enter the invitation recipients in the To box. You can click the To button to select from a list if desired.

20. In the Event Address box, make sure that the address for the stored presentation is correct.

21. Enter the start and end times and dates in the Start time and End time fields.

22. After confirming the rest of the information for the appointment, click the Send button. You return to PowerPoint.

23. A message appears that the broadcast has been successfully scheduled. Click OK.

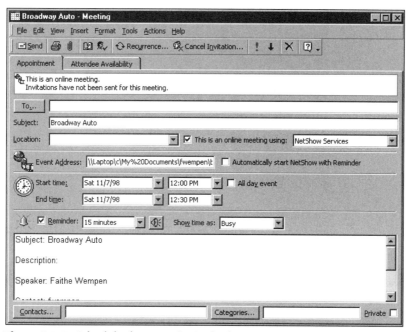

Figure 23-5: Schedule the event in Outlook.

Caution   In Step 23, when you click OK to send the message, PowerPoint places the message in your Outlook outbox. It does not automatically send the contents of your outbox right away unless Outlook is configured to do so. You might have to open Outlook and use the Tools ⇨ Send and Receive command to send the message.

Rescheduling or Changing a Broadcast

Delays and scheduling conflicts are almost the rule rather than the exception these days. If you find that you need to change the date and time of the presentation or make other changes to it, follow these steps:

1. Make sure that the correct presentation is open.

2. Choose Slide Show ⇨ Online Broadcast ⇨ Set Up and Schedule. The Broadcast Schedule dialog box appears. (You saw this back in Figure 23-1.)

3. Click the Change settings or reschedule a broadcast button, and then click OK.

4. If more than one broadcast is scheduled, a list of scheduled broadcasts appears. Click the broadcast you want, if there is more than one, and then click the Change settings button. See Figure 23-6. Otherwise, go on to Step 5.

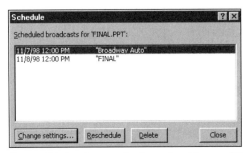

Figure 23-6: Choose the broadcast to modify, if more than one is scheduled.

5. The Change Broadcast Options dialog box appears, which is the same box as the Schedule a New Broadcast dialog box you saw in the preceding section. Make any changes on the Description and/or the Broadcast Settings tab, as you learned in the preceding section. Then click Update.

6. If you see the warning that a maximum of 15 users will be able to see the show, click Yes to continue.

7. When you see the message the information has been updated, click OK.

8. If you need to reschedule the broadcast, click the Reschedule button. Outlook opens the calendar event for the broadcast.

9. Change the date and time shown in the Start time and End time fields, just as you did when you set the date and time originally. Refer back to Figure 23-5.

10. Make any other changes to the event in Outlook.

11. Click the Send Update button. Outlook closes.

Note   Remember, if Outlook is not set to send outbox messages immediately, you need to reopen Outlook manually and send the messages with Tools ➪ Send and Receive.

12. Click Close to close the Schedule dialog box. Your broadcast has been successfully rescheduled and/or changed.

Controlling a Broadcast

You should get ready to broadcast your presentation at least 15 minutes before the scheduled time. That way, if anything goes wrong, you can iron it out before the guests arrive.

To start the ball rolling, follow these steps:

1. Choose Slide Show ⇨ Online Broadcast ⇨ Begin Broadcast. The Broadcast Presentation dialog box opens, and it starts preparing the presentation.

2. When the Microphone Check dialog box appears, follow the instructions in it. This box asks you to read some text into the microphone. Do it and then click OK. See Figure 23-7.

Figure 23-7: Speak into the microphone to check the volume level; then click OK.

3. Make sure that the Status area shows Press Start when ready, as shown in Figure 23-8. If it does not, troubleshoot with your network administrator why the broadcast might not be ready.

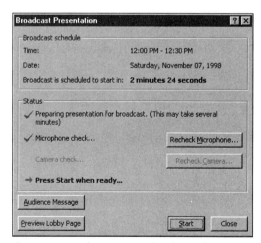

Figure 23-8: The presentation is ready to go whenever you are.

4. (Optional) If you would like to display a message to the audience before the show, such as "There will be a 5-minute delay" or "Thank you for joining us!", click the Audience Message button and type a message. Then, click Update.

5. When it is time for the show to begin, click Start. A dialog box appears to confirm that you want to start the broadcast. Click Yes.

6. Now your first slide appears onscreen, just like in regular Slide Show view. Give your presentation, speaking into the microphone to provide audio if you chose to use audio and/or pointing the video camera at the desired people or objects if you want to include video. The audience sees the slides on their screen, as explained in the next section.

7. When you are finished with the show and you return to PowerPoint, the audience is informed that the show is over.

8. To end the broadcast early, press Esc. A confirmation box appears; click Yes.

Receiving a Broadcast

Each audience member should have received an e-mail listing the presentation's address, or URL. For example, Figure 23-9 shows an e-mail received in Outlook. It is similar in Outlook Express and in other e-mail programs.

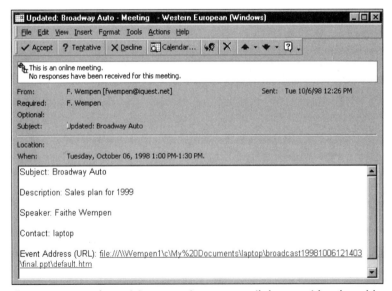

Figure 23-9: Each participant receives an e-mail that provides the address of the presentation.

If you receive such an e-mail in Outlook, you can click the Accept button on the toolbar to indicate that you plan to view the broadcast. When you do so, a dialog box appears, shown in Figure 23-10, asking whether you want to send a response to the person who invited you. Make your selection and click OK. You can then view the event's schedule details at any time by double-clicking it on your Outlook calendar.

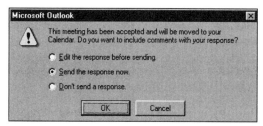

Figure 23-10: When you accept the invitation (Outlook only), you are prompted to send an RSVP to the meeting organizer.

If you use Outlook, and Outlook is running 15 minutes before the presentation (or at whatever reminder time was specified), a Reminder box appears, prompting you to join the broadcast. See Figure 23-11.

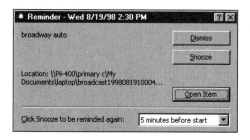

Figure 23-11: Outlook reminds you of the meeting.

Internet Explorer opens the NetShow plug-in and displays the Lobby for the broadcast, shown in Figure 23-12. You wait in the lobby until the presentation starts and then are transferred automatically into the show when it's available.

Countdown to the scheduled start time

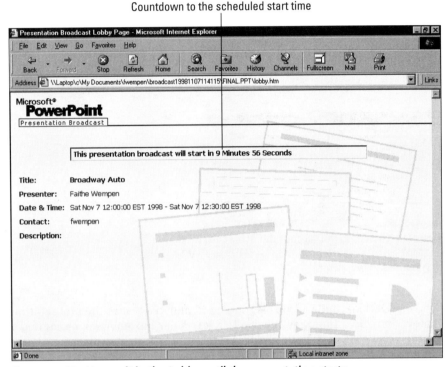

Figure 23-12: You wait in the Lobby until the presentation starts.

Note   If Internet Explorer does not automatically open at that point, click the Open Item button to open the calendar event in Outlook and then click the View NetShow button on Outlook's toolbar.

If you use any other mail program than Outlook, or if you are not running Outlook at reminder time, you can connect manually to the presentation by clicking the hyperlink for the presentation address in the e-mail invitation that you received. If for some reason the hyperlink address in the e-mail is not live—that is, if it's not underlined and clicking it does nothing—you can select it, copy it (Ctrl+C), open your Web browser, and paste it into the Address or URL line (Ctrl+V).

Note   For late-comers: If you connect to the Lobby page and find a message that the broadcast has ended, you also find a Replay Broadcast button. Click it to jump to the folder containing the saved broadcast file (it's in HTML format, so it has an .HTM extension) and double-click it.

When the presentation begins, your browser jumps automatically to the show, and the first slide appears. See Figure 23-13. Just sit back and enjoy the show! If the presenter is using video and your browser supports it, the video clip appears in the Video window to the right of the slide.

Click here to review previous slides   Video feed from camera would appear here

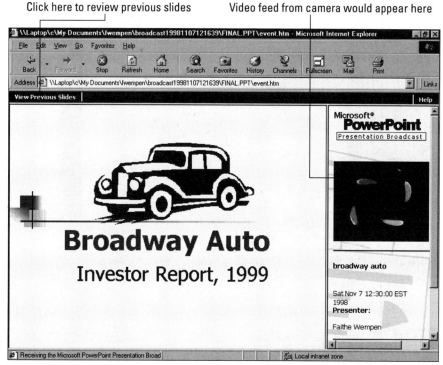

Figure 23-13: View the show in Internet Explorer. The slides advance as controlled by the presenter; there are no controls for you to advance them yourself.

If you miss a slide, you can click the View Previous Slides button at any time to open a separate window where you can see previous slides without interrupting the main presentation.

If you need to leave the presentation, just close your Web browser. If the presenter elected to save a recording of the presentation, you can view it later by redisplaying the Lobby page. If the presentation is over, you see a message to that effect, along with a Replay Broadcast button. Click that button to jump to the folder containing the stored broadcast in HTML format. Double-click the broadcast file to open it in Internet Explorer.

If you are replaying a broadcast but can't get past the first slide, try clicking the View Previous Slides button. A display window opens, as shown in Figure 23-14, with a navigation pane that lets you move freely among all the slides.

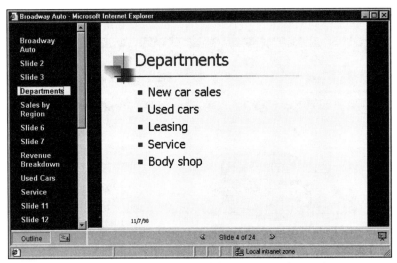

Figure 23-14: Use the View Previous Slides command to review a presentation that has already taken place.

Summary

In this chapter, you learned how to schedule, set up, and present a live presentation over a network or the Internet and how to help your online attendees access your show. Now you can display your great-looking presentation to almost anyone in any location!

In the next chapter, you learn about some of the special considerations involved in preparing long or complex slide shows. When you're presenting in a situation where there are many contingencies and the show may take one of many different turns depending on the questions asked, you'll appreciate PowerPoint's ability to help you prepare for the unknown.

✦   ✦   ✦

Managing Long or Complex Shows

✦ ✦ ✦ ✦

In This Chapter

Hiding slides for backup use

Creating custom shows

Controlling a custom show during a presentation

Merging PowerPoint files to create longer shows

✦ ✦ ✦ ✦

When you work with a presentation that contains many slides (say, 30 or more), it is reasy to get confused. Fortunately, PowerPoint enables you to organize your show into custom shows, and it enables you to hide certain slides for backup use.

Hiding Slides for Backup Use

You may not always want to show every slide that you have prepared. Sometimes it pays to prepare extra data in anticipation of a question that you think someone might ask, or to hold back certain data (for example, data that doesn't make your company or product look particularly good) unless someone specifically requests it.

By hiding a slide, you keep it filed in reserve, without making it a part of the main slide show. Then, at any time during the presentation when (or if) it becomes appropriate, you can call that slide to the forefront to be displayed. *Hiding* refers only to whether or not the slide is a part of the main presentation's flow; it has no effect in any other view.

Tip   If you have only a handful of slides to hide, go ahead and hide them. But if you have a large group of related slides to hide, consider creating a custom show for them, explained later in this chapter.

Hiding and Unhiding Slides

The best way to hide and unhide slides is in Slide Sorter view because a special indicator appears underneath each slide to show whether or not it is hidden. That way, you can tell easily which slides are part of the main presentation.

Follow these steps to hide a slide:

1. Switch to Slide Sorter view (View ➪ Slide Sorter).

2. Select the slides(s) you want to hide. Remember, to select more than one slide, hold down the Ctrl key as you click the ones you want.

3. Click the Hide Slide button on the Slide Sorter toolbar. A gray box and diagonal line appear around the slide number, indicating that it is hidden. See Figure 24-1.

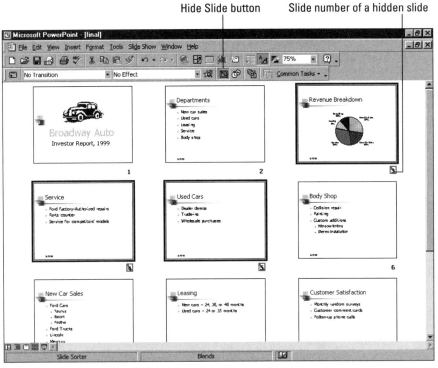

Figure 24-1: The selected slides (3, 4, and 5) are hidden.

To unhide a slide, select the slide and click the Hide Slide button again. The slide's number returns to normal.

Showing a Hidden Slide During a Presentation

When you advance from one slide to the next during a show, hidden slides do not appear. (That's what being hidden is about, after all.) If you need to display one of the hidden slides, follow these steps:

1. In Slide Show view, right-click to display the shortcut menu.
2. Choose Go ⇨ By Title, and then choose the slide you want to jump to. Hidden slides show their slide numbers in parentheses, but you can access them like any other slide. See Figure 24-2.

You can also jump to a hidden slide (or any other slide) using the Go ⇨ Slide Navigator command, as you learned in Chapter 22.

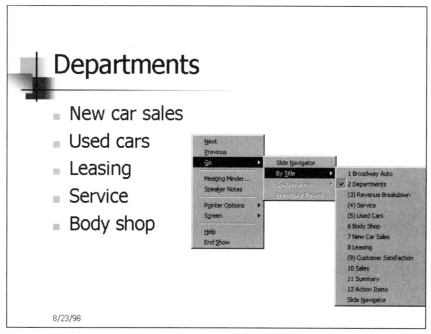

Figure 24-2: Jump to a hidden slide just as you would jump to any other slide.

Caution   When you display a hidden slide, you unhide it only for the moment. If you advance past it, you can't use the Page Up key or the Previous command on the shortcut menu to return to it, the way you would normally return to the preceding slide. You must jump to it again with the Go command.

Using Custom Shows

Many slide shows have a linear flow: First you show slide one, then slide two, and so on, until you have completed the entire presentation. This format is suitable for situations where you are presenting clear-cut information with few variables, such as a presentation about a new insurance plan for a group of employees. However, when the situation becomes more complex, a single-path slide show may not suffice. This is especially true when you are presenting a persuasive message to decision-makers. For example, if you are trying to sell something to a group of executives, you want to anticipate their questions and needs for more information and have many backup slides, or even entire backup slide shows, prepared in case certain questions arise. Figure 24-3 shows a flow chart for such a presentation.

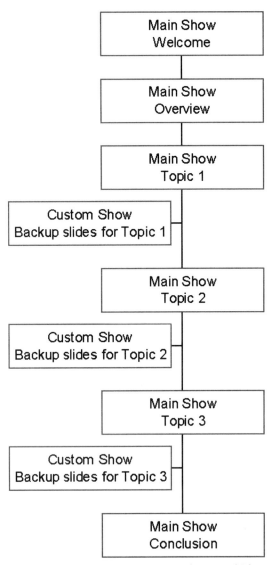

Figure 24-3: You can use custom shows to hide related groups of backup slides.

Tip If you simply want to hide a few slides for backup use, you do not have to go to the trouble of creating a custom show. Instead, just hide the slides.

Another great use for custom shows is to set aside a group of slides for a specific audience. For example, you might need to present essentially the same information to employees at two different sites. You could create custom shows within the main show that include slides that both shows have in common plus slides that are appropriate for only one audience or the other. Figure 24-4 shows a flow chart for a presentation like that.

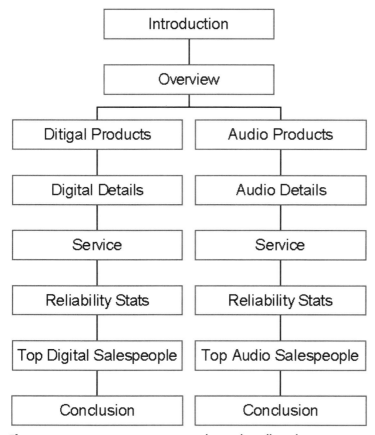

Figure 24-4: You can create custom shows that allow the same presentation to be used for multiple audiences.

Notice in Figure 24-4 that some of the slides in the two custom shows are the same, yet they're repeated in each custom show rather than jumping back to the main presentation. That's because it's much easier to jump to the custom show once and stay there than it is to keep jumping into and out of it.

Slides in a custom show remain a part of the main presentation, too. Placing a slide in a custom show does not exclude it from the regular presentation flow. However, you may decide that you don't want to show the main presentation as is anymore; you may just want to use it as a resource pool from which to select the slides for the various custom shows that you create in it. To learn how to set up PowerPoint so that a custom show starts rather than the main one when you choose Slide Show ➪ View Show, see the "Using a Custom Show as the Main Presentation" section later in this chapter.

Great Uses for Custom Shows

Here are some ideas to get you started thinking about how and why you might want to include some custom shows in your presentation files.

✦ **Avoiding duplication:** If you have several shows that use about 50 percent of the same slides and 50 percent different ones, you can create all of the shows as custom shows within a single presentation file. That way, the presentations can share those 50 percent of the slides that they have in common.

✦ **Managing change:** By following the suggestion above, you make it easy to manage changes. If any changes occur in your company that affect any of the common slides, making the change once in your presentation file makes the change to each of the custom shows immediately.

✦ **Overcoming objections:** You can anticipate client objections to your sales pitch and prepare several custom shows, each of which addresses a particular objection. Then, whatever reason your potential customer gives for not buying your product, you have a counteractive garrison at hand.

✦ **Covering your backside:** If you think you may be asked for specific figures or other information during a speech, you can have that information ready in a custom show (or on a few simple hidden slides, if there is not much of it) to whip out if needed. No more going through the embarrassment of having to say "I'm not sure, but let me get back to you on that."

Creating Custom Shows

To create a custom show, first create all the slides that should go into it. Start with all the slides in the main presentation. Then, follow these steps:

1. Choose Slide Show ➪ Custom Shows. The Custom Shows dialog box opens.

2. Click the New button. The Define Custom Show dialog box appears.

3. Enter a name for your custom show in the Slide show name text box.

4. In the Slides in presentation pane, click the first slide that you want to appear in the custom show.

Tip

You can select multiple slides in Step 4 by holding down the Ctrl key as you click each one you want. However, be aware that if you do this, the slides move to the Slides in custom show pane in the order that they originally appeared. If you want them in a different order, copy each slide over separately, in the order that you want, or rearrange the order as described in Step 7.

5. Click the Add button to copy it to the Slides in custom show pane. See Figure 24-5.

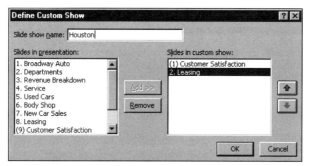

Figure 24-5: Use the Add button to copy slides from the main presentation into the custom show.

6. Repeat Steps 4 and 5 for each slide that you want to include in the custom show.

7. If you need to rearrange the slides in the custom show, click the slide you want to move in the Slides in custom show pane and then click the up or down arrow button to change its position.

8. When you are finished building your custom show, click OK.

9. (Optional) To test your custom show, click the Show button. Otherwise, click Close to close the Custom Shows dialog box.

Editing Custom Shows

You can manage your custom shows from the Custom Shows dialog box, the same place in which you created them. This includes editing a show, deleting one, or making a copy of one.

To change which slides appear in a custom show, and in what order, follow these steps:

1. Choose Slide Show ➪ Custom Shows. The Custom Shows dialog box appears. See Figure 24-6.

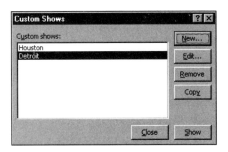

Figure 24-6: Select the custom show to edit, copy, or delete, and then click the appropriate button.

2. Click the custom show you want to edit, if you have more than one.

3. Click the Edit button. The Define Custom Show dialog box reappears. (See Figure 24-5.)

4. Add or remove slides as needed. To add a slide, choose it from the left pane and click Add. To remove a slide, choose it from the right pane and click Remove.

Note   Removing a slide from a custom show does not remove it from the presentation at large.

5. Rearrange slides as needed with the up and down arrow buttons, as you did in the preceding set of steps.

6. (Optional) Change the custom show's name, if needed, in the Slide Show Name text box.

7. Click OK. Your changes are saved.

8. Click Close to close the Custom Shows dialog box.

Copying Custom Shows

A good way to create several similar custom shows is to create the first one and then copy it. Then you can make whatever small changes to the copies are necessary. To copy a custom show, follow these steps:

1. Choose Slide Show ➪ Custom Shows to display the Custom Shows dialog box. See Figure 24-6.

2. Select the show you want to copy if you have more than one custom show.

3. Click the Copy button. A copy of it appears. The filename includes the words Copy of so you can distinguish it.

4. Edit the copy, as explained in the preceding section, to change its name and its content to differentiate it from the original.

5. When you're finished, click Close to close the Custom Shows dialog box.

Deleting Custom Shows

It is not necessary to delete a custom show when you do not want it anymore; it does not do any harm lying idle in your presentation. Since custom shows do not display unless you call for them, you can simply choose not to display it.

However, if you want to make things a bit more orderly than that, you are free to delete a custom show that no longer serves you. Follow these steps:

1. Choose Slide Show ➪ Custom Shows to display the Custom Shows dialog box. See Figure 24-6.

2. Select the show you want to delete.

3. Click the Remove button. It's gone.

4. Click Close to close the Custom Shows dialog box.

Displaying a Custom Show

At any time during your main presentation, you can call up the custom show. There are two ways to do it: you can navigate to the custom show with PowerPoint's regular presentation controls, or you can create a hyperlink to the custom show on your slide. (Hyperlinks are covered in detail in Chapter 26, but I touch on them in this chapter as well.)

You can also set the presentation to display one of the custom shows *instead* of the main presentation. This is useful if you have two complete custom shows, each used for a different audience.

Navigating to a Custom Show

During a presentation, you can jump to any of your custom shows by following these steps:

1. Right-click to display the shortcut menu.

2. Choose Go ➪ Custom Show and then the custom show you want. See Figure 24-7. The custom show starts.

When you start a custom show, you are no longer in the main presentation. To see this for yourself, right-click again, and choose Go ➪ By Title and check out the list of slides. The list shows only the slides from the custom show you're in.

Navigating Back to the Main Show

To jump back to the main show, do this:

1. From the custom show, right-click.

2. Choose Go ➪ Slide Navigator. The Slide Navigator dialog box opens. See Figure 24-8.

3. Open the Show drop-down list and choose All Slides. The entire list of slides appears.

4. Click the slide you want to view, and then click Go To. You are now back to your main presentation.

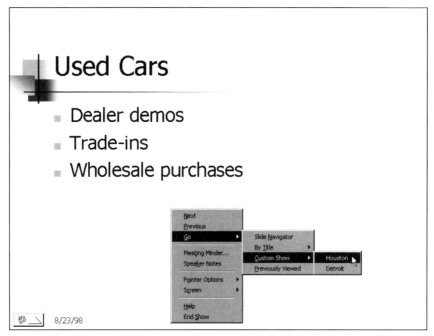

Figure 24-7: Choose the custom show that you want to jump to.

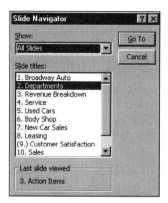

Figure 24-8: Return to the full presentation by choosing All Slides from the Slide Navigator.

Creating a Hyperlink to a Custom Show

You learn a lot about hyperlinks in upcoming chapters, but here's a preview. Hyperlinks are hot links that you place on your slides. When you click a hyperlink, you jump the display to some other location. That's why they're called *hot*. A hyperlink can jump to an Internet location, a different spot in your presentation, an external file (such as a Word document), or just about anywhere else.

One way to give yourself quick access to your custom shows in a presentation is to create hyperlinks for them on certain key jumping-off-point slides.

You can insert a text hyperlink in any text box, and its text is the marker that you click. For example, you can insert a hyperlink for the Houston custom show and the text that appears reads Houston. Or, if you want to get fancier, you can select some existing text or an existing graphic object, and then attach the hyperlink to it. For example, you might type **Click here to see the Houston show** or insert a picture of the Houston skyline, and then use either of those objects as the hyperlink.

Follow these steps:

1. If you are attaching the hyperlink to some other object, select the object.

2. Choose Insert ⇨ Hyperlink. The Insert Hyperlink dialog box appears.

3. Click the Place in This Document icon along the left side of the screen.

4. In the Select a place in this document pane, scroll down to the Custom Shows list.

5. Click the custom show that you want to jump to with this hyperlink. See Figure 24-9.

6. (Optional) If you want to return to the same spot that you left in the main presentation after viewing that custom show, mark the Show and return checkbox.

7. Click OK.

If you're using text for the hyperlink, the text now appears underlined and in a different color. If you are using a graphic, it does not appear different than it did before. However, when you're in Slide Show view, when you move the mouse pointer over the object, the pointer changes into a pointing hand, indicating that the object is a hyperlink. See Chapter 26 for more information about hyperlinks.

Using a Custom Show As the Main Presentation

If you have a complete show contained in one of your custom shows, you may sometimes wish to present it as such. To do so, you must tell PowerPoint that you want to bypass the main presentation and start with the custom show. Follow these steps:

1. Choose Slide Show ⇨ Set Up Show. The Set Up Show dialog box appears.

2. Open the Custom show drop-down list and choose the show you want to use. See Figure 24-10.

3. Click OK. Now when you run the show (with Slide Show ⇨ View Show), the custom show will run. See Chapter 22 for more details about running shows.

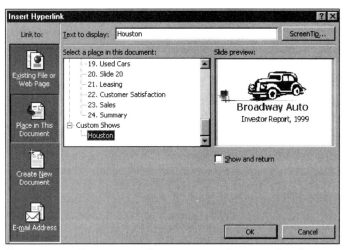

Figure 24-9: Choose one of your custom shows as the place to jump to when the hyperlink is clicked.

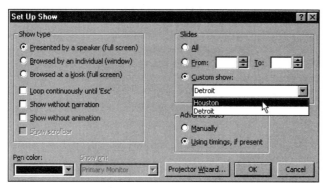

Figure 24-10: Use the Set Up Show dialog box to control which of your custom shows runs when you start the show.

Tip   You do not have to set up a custom show to narrow down the list of slides that appear when you run your presentation. Notice in Figure 24-10 that there are From and To text boxes. To show, for example, slides 5 through 10, you would enter 5 in the From box and 10 in the To box.

Merging PowerPoint Files

Another way to create a longer or more complex show is to merge two or more PowerPoint presentation files into a single, long presentation. For example, suppose you have three presentations, one for each of your sales divisions. You realize that they contain many of the same slides, and you want to be able to update those identical slides only one time, rather than in three places. So you decide to merge the three files. You can continue to have separate shows for each division by creating custom shows within the main show, as you have been learning in this chapter.

When you merge shows, all of the slides take on the formatting of the presentation file into which they are coming. For example, suppose you have a show that uses the Blends design template. If you merge a presentation into it that uses the Marble design template, the incoming slides take on the Blends template's settings upon arrival. This ensures that all the slides in your show have a consistent look. However, if you have applied any special formatting to incoming slides, such as a nonstandard background, font choice, or text box placement, that formatting is retained.

You have already seen this merge process at work in Chapter 8, but you'll review it here. To merge two presentations, follow these steps:

   1. Open the presentation that you want to use for the host.

2. If you want the incoming slides inserted in a certain spot, place your insertion point there in Outline view, or display or select the slide after which the new slides should be placed.

3. Choose Insert ➪ Slides from Files. The Slide Finder dialog box appears.

4. Click the Browse button. The Browse dialog box opens.

5. Select the presentation that you want to merge with the open one. Then, click Open.

6. Click the Display button to display the slides in the incoming presentation.

7. If you want to insert all of the slides, click the Insert All button, and you're done. Otherwise, continue to Step 8.

8. Select the slides you want from the Select Slides area. Use the scroll bar as needed to scroll through the slides. See Figure 24-11.

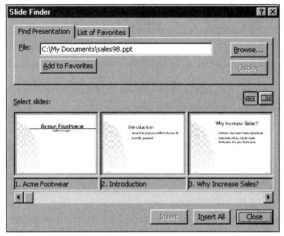

Figure 24-11: Insert slides from another presentation one by one or en masse.

9. Click Insert. The slides are inserted.

10. Click Close to close the dialog box.

11. Clean up the presentation by deleting any unneeded slides and rearranging the remaining ones. Slide Sorter view works well for this.

Summary

In this chapter, you learned how to hide and unhide slides and how to create, manage, and run custom slide shows. These skills can be very handy for making you look like the smooth professional who doesn't have to fumble with the presentation controls to display exactly what you want.

The next chapter starts a new part of the book: one on self-serve presentations. So far, you have learned about ways to run speaker-led shows, but in this busy business world it is sometimes next to impossible to assemble all the key audience members in a room at the same time. With a self-running or interactive presentation, you can create a show that anybody can watch at any time, without you having to be present.

✦　　✦　　✦

Distributing Self-Serve Presentations

◆ ◆ ◆ ◆

In This Part

Designing Self-Running Kiosk Presentations

In the last few chapters, you've been learning how to build and present slide shows that support you as you speak to your audience directly. As discussed in Chapter 6, when you build such presentations, you design each slide to assist you, not duplicate your efforts. Slides designed for a live presentation typically do not contain a lot of detail; they function as pointers and reminders for the much more detailed live discussion or lecture taking place in the foreground.

When you build a self-running presentation, the focus is exactly the opposite. The slides are going out there all alone and must be capable of projecting the entire message all by themselves. Therefore, you want to create slides that contain much more of the details of your message.

Another consideration is audience interest. When you are speaking to your audience live, the primary focus is on you and your words. The slides assist you, but the audience watches and listens primarily to *you*. Therefore, to keep the audience interested, you have to be interesting. If the slides are interesting, that's a nice bonus. With a self-running presentation, on the other hand, each slide must be fascinating. The animations and transitions that you learned about in Chapter 20 come in very handy in creating interest, as do sounds and videos, discussed in Chapters 18 and 19.

In this book, I'm distinguishing between self-running and user-interactive presentations. Both of these show types involve the audience's interaction with a speakerless show; the difference is in the audience's behavior and capability. In a self-running show, the audience is passive; they watch, listen, and wait for the next slide to appear. That's the type of show discussed in this chapter. With a user-interactive show, the audience can control the show's pace and direction through keyboard, mouse, or touch-screen input. You learn about user-interactive shows in Chapter 26.

Note   Another name for a self-running presentation is a kiosk presentation. This name comes from the fact that many self-running informational presentations are located in little buildings, or kiosks, in public areas such as malls and convention centers.

Great Uses for Self-Running Shows

Not sure when you might use a self-running presentation in your daily life? Here are some thought-starters:

✦ **Trade shows:** A self-running presentation outlining your product or service can run continuously in your booth on equipment as simple as a laptop PC and an external monitor. People who might not feel comfortable talking to a salesperson may stop a few moments to watch a colorful, multimedia slide show.

✦ **Conventions:** Trying to inform hundreds of convention-goers of some basic information, like session starting times or cocktail party locations? Set up an information booth in the convention center lobby providing this information. The slide show could loop endlessly through three or four slides that contain meeting room locations, schedules, and other critical data.

✦ **In-store sales:** Retail stores can increase sales by strategically placing PC monitors in areas of the store where customers gather. For example, if there is a line where customers stand waiting for the next available register or clerk, you could show those waiting customers a few slides that describe the benefits of extended warranties or that detail the special sales of the week.

✦ **Waiting areas:** Auto repair shops and other places where customers wait for something to be done provide excellent sales opportunities. The customers don't have anything to do except sit and wait, so they will watch just about anything — including a slide presentation informing them of the other services that your shop provides.

Setting Up a Self-Running Show

The most important aspect of a self-running show is that it loops continuously until you stop it. This is important because there won't be anyone there to restart it each time it ends.

To set up the show to do just that, follow these steps:

1. Choose Slide Show ➪ Set Up Show. The Set Up Show dialog box opens.
2. Click the Browsed at a kiosk (full screen) option button. See Figure 25-1.
3. In the Advance slides area, make sure the Using timings, if present option button is selected.
4. Click OK.

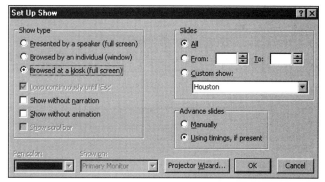

Figure 25-1: Tell PowerPoint that this show will be browsed at a kiosk (in other words, self-running).

You haven't set up the timings referenced in Step 3 yet, but don't worry about that; you learn how to set them up in the following section.

Setting Timings

The duration that each slide appears on the screen is very important in a self-running presentation. If the slide disappears too quickly, the audience is not able to read all that it contains; if the slide lingers too long, the audience gets bored and walks away.

Tip If you are going to record narration for the slides, skip to the "Recording Narration" section later in this chapter. You can set your timings and your narration at the same time, saving a step.

Setting a Single Timing for All Slides

You might choose to let each slide linger the same amount of time onscreen. This gives a consistent feel to the show and works well when all the slides contain approximately the same amount of information. To set this up, use the Slide Transition dialog box, as shown in the following steps:

1. Choose Slide Show ➪ Slide Transition. The Slide Transition dialog box opens.

2. In the Advance area, make sure that the Automatically after checkbox is marked. See Figure 25-2.

3. Enter a number of seconds into the text box. For example, to advance each slide after 10 seconds, enter 00:10. You can use the spin buttons next to the text box to increment the value up or down if you prefer to do that instead of typing the value.

4. Click Apply to All to apply the setting to all the slides in the presentation.

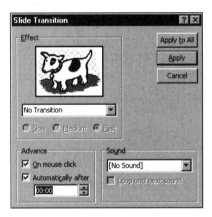

Figure 25-2: To set an automatic transition after a certain number of seconds, enter the number of seconds and then click Apply to All.

As you may have surmised, you can also set the timings for each slide individually through the Slide Transition dialog box, by opening it for each slide and then clicking Apply instead of Apply to All. However, if you want to set different timings for different slides, the Rehearse Timings command provides a much simpler way to do that. It's described in the following section. Then, afterwards, if you need to adjust the timing of a few slides, you can revisit the Slide Transition dialog box for those slides to do so.

Setting Custom Timings for Each Slide

If not all slides should receive an equal amount of screen time, you can set up timings individually for each slide. This helps a lot if some slides contain a lot more text to read or numeric information to digest than others. To set custom timings, you use the Rehearse Timings feature. This feature allows you to practice the show with a timer running that records the amount of time you spend on each slide. It then assigns the timings to the slides so you can run the show using the same timings automatically.

Caution When you set timings with Rehearse Timings, any hidden slide is ignored. If you later unhide that slide, it will not be set to advance automatically. You need to assign it a duration using the Slide Transition dialog box, as explained in the preceding section.

Follow these steps to rehearse timings:

1. Choose Slide Show ➪ Rehearse Timings. The slide show begins, with the Rehearsal box floating on it. See Figure 25-3.

Next button
Pause button   Time for current slide   Repeat button   Total time for the show so far

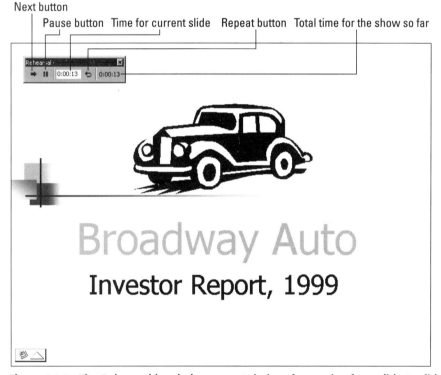

Figure 25-3: The Rehearsal box helps you set timings for moving from slide to slide.

2. Pause until you think it is time for the next slide to appear. Then, click the Next button or press Page Down.

Tip It may help when setting timings to read the text on the slide out loud, rather slowly, to simulate how an audience member who reads slowly would proceed. When you have read all the text on the slide, pause 1 or 2 more seconds and then advance.

3. If you need to pause the rehearsal at any time, click the Pause button. When you are ready to resume, click it again to unpause.

If you make a mistake on the timing for a slide, click the Repeat button to begin timing that slide again from 00:00.

4. When you reach the last slide, a dialog box appears telling you the total time for the show. See Figure 25-4. If you want to preserve the timings you have set, click Yes. Otherwise, click No and return to Step 1 to try again.

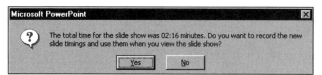

Figure 25-4: Choose Yes to accept your timings or No to reject them.

5. Test your timings by viewing the show (choose Slide Show ➪ View Show or press F5). If any of the timings are off, adjust them with the Slide Transition dialog box, as explained earlier in this chapter.

In Slide Sorter view, the timing for each slide appears beneath it, as shown in Figure 25-5.

Recording Narration

As I mentioned earlier, it's wise to design slides for a self-running presentation to be self-sufficient so that the audience immediately understands them without help. However, sometimes certain slides (or entire shows) can't achieve this for one reason or another. For example, suppose you are creating a self-running show that consists of scanned images of works of art. Almost the entire slide is taken up by each scan, so there is no room for a lengthy text block listing the artist, date, title, and description. In a case like that, recording a voice-over narration might make a lot of sense to relieve the slides from carrying the entire burden of information conveyance.

For a professional-quality show, get the best recording equipment you can afford. Get a high-quality microphone (these are relatively inexpensive at your local computer store),and plug it into a high-quality sound card on the recording PC.

Timing, in seconds

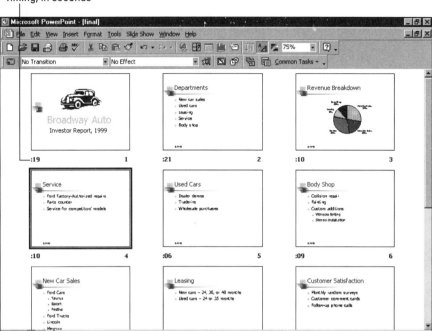

Figure 25-5: The numbers beneath and to the left of each slide represent the custom timings you set with Rehearse Timings.

Then, set the recording quality to the best quality that you can manage without eating up too much hard disk space. Audio recording uses up an obscene amount of disk space; CD-quality (the highest quality) audio consumes about 10 megabytes per minute of recording. That means for a 20-minute show, you would need over 200 megabytes of disk space.

Caution

If you need to transfer the presentation to another PC for the show and you must transfer it using a floppy disk, transfer it first and then record the narration on the show PC (if the show PC has a sound card that you can hook up a microphone to, that is). If you record the narration first, the presentation file will be so large that it won't fit on a floppy disk.

You can store the narration separately from the main presentation, as you learn in Step 11 of the following procedure, but even so, the narration file may be too big to fit on a floppy.

Tip

If you can't avoid recording the presentation narration before transferring it to the show machine and you don't have any means of transfer besides a floppy disk (such as a network, a ZIP drive, or a recordable CD drive), you might try e-mailing the presentation to yourself. Send the e-mail on the machine containing the presentation file, and then receive it using the show machine. (Warning: sending and receiving the e-mail will take a long time, especially with a slow modem.)

Setting Narration Controls

To set up the narration controls, follow these steps:

1. Make sure your microphone is connected and ready.

2. Choose Slide Show ⇨ Record Narration. The Record Narration dialog box appears. See Figure 25-6.

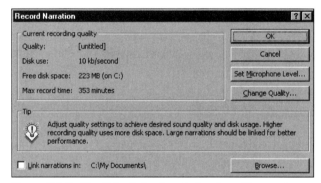

Figure 25-6: Use this dialog box to begin setting up to record narration.

3. Click the Set Microphone Level button. The Microphone Check dialog box appears.

4. Read into the microphone, enabling PowerPoint to set the optimum microphone recording level. See Figure 25-7.

Note

You can also set the recording level by manually dragging the slide bar shown in Figure 25-7, but this is not recommended because you do not know what setting to use without testing the microphone.

5. Click OK to return to the Record Narration dialog box.

6. Click the Change Quality button. The Sound Selection dialog box appears.

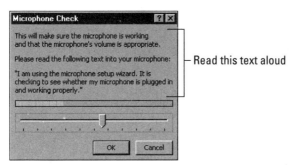

— Read this text aloud

Figure 25-7: Read the text shown on the screen to allow PowerPoint to set the recording level.

7. Open the Name drop-down list and choose a quality. The preset qualities that come with PowerPoint are Telephone Quality (low), Radio Quality (medium), and CD Quality (high). The higher the quality, the more disk space it takes up storing your narration. See Figure 25-8.

Tip

If you can afford the disk space, use CD Quality. This results in the best-sounding recording, which is important in most professional situations.

8. If you want the recording in a certain format or with certain attributes, choose them from the Format and/or Attributes drop-down lists. Beginners should leave these settings alone; adjust them only if you know enough about sound recording to know that you need a particular setting.

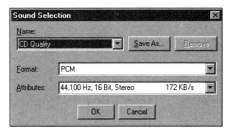

Figure 25-8: Choose a recording quality from the Name box.

9. (Optional) If you made changes in Step 8, you may wish to save your new quality settings. If so, click the Save As button and enter a name for the new setting. Then click OK to accept the name.

10. Click OK to close the Sound Selection dialog box.

11. (Optional) If you want the narration stored in a separate file linked to the presentation, mark the Link narrations in checkbox. If you don't mark this checkbox, the narrations are stored embedded in the presentation file.

12. If you marked the checkbox in Step 11 and you want to change the location of the stored narration file, click the Browse button and choose a different drive or folder. The default is for the narration file to be stored in the same location as the presentation file.

13. Go on to the steps in the next section.

Recording the Narration

Pick up these steps from the preceding ones, or if you are coming here from some other task, choose Slide Show ➪ Record Narration. Then follow these steps:

1. Click OK to close the Record Narration dialog box. If the first slide of the presentation was not selected initially, the Re-record Narration dialog box appears. See Figure 25-9.

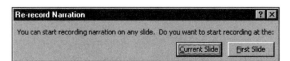

Figure 25-9: Choose where you want to start recording narration.

2. Click First Slide. The slide show begins.

3. Speak into the microphone, recording narration for the first slide. Then, advance to the next slide with the Page Down key.

4. Continue speaking into the microphone and advancing the slides. When you reach the last slide, the screen goes black and a message appears prompting you to press Esc.

5. Press Esc. A dialog box appears reminding you that the narrations have been saved with each slide, and asking whether you want to save the timings also.

6. Click Yes.

7. Test your show by displaying it (press F5) from start to finish and listening to your narration.

Rerecording the Narration for a Slide

Few people get the narration exactly right for the entire presentation the first time they record it. If you want to rerecord the narration for a particular slide, follow these steps:

1. Select the slide that you want to rerecord the narration for.

2. Choose Slide Show ➪ Record Narration.

3. Click OK.

4. The Re-Record Narration dialog box appears (Figure 25-9). This time, click Current Slide.

5. When you are finished recording the narration for that slide, press Esc.

6. A dialog box appears asking whether you want to save the timings as well as the narration. Click Yes.

7. Test the new narration by displaying the slide in Slide Show view.

Tip

Keep in mind that good speakers at the show site are as important as a good microphone at the recording site. Make sure you have external speakers that plug into the show PC's sound card. Don't rely on the tinny little speaker built into a laptop PC!

Deleting the Narration for a Slide

After you add narration to slides, a little Speaker icon appears at the bottom of each slide in all views except Slide Show. See Figure 25-10. You can double-click this icon to preview the narration recording at any time. To remove the narration from a slide, delete this icon.

Figure 25-10: A Speaker icon on each slide holds the narration. Delete it to remove the narration.

Setting Up a Security System

Security is a definite concern in self-running presentations. Any time you leave a computer unattended with the public, you run the risk of tampering and theft. At the very least, some guru geek will come along and experiment with your PC to see what you've got and whether he or she can do anything clever with it. At the worst, your entire computer setup could disappear entirely.

There are two levels of security involved in unattended presentation situations:

✦ The security of the physical hardware

✦ The security that the presentation will continue to run

Securing Your Hardware

For the most foolproof hardware security, get it out of sight. Hide everything except the monitor in a locked drawer, cabinet, or panel of the kiosk you are using, if possible. If you are at a trade show or convention where you don't have the luxury of a lockable system, at least put everything except the monitor under a table, and try to make sure that someone is attending the booth at all times.

 Caution   Don't drape running computers with cloth or any other material that inhibits the airflow around them because it increases the risk of overheating.

In an unattended setting, the best way to protect your monitor from walking off is to place it behind a Plexiglas panel where nobody can touch it. Without such a barrier, you run the risk of some jokester turning off its power or turning down its contrast, and anyone who knows something about computers could walk right up and disconnect it and carry it away.

You can also buy various locking cables at computer stores and office supply centers. These lock down computer equipment to prevent it from being removed. They include steel cables with padlocks, metal locking brackets, and electronically controlled magnetic locks.

Making Sure the Presentation Continues to Run

I admit that I am guilty of disrupting other people's presentations. When I walk up to an unattended computer in a store, the first thing I do is abort whatever program is running and restart the system to check out its diagnostics and find out what kind of computer it is. It's a geek thing, but all geeks do it.

You will doubtless encounter such geeks wherever you set up your presentation, but especially at trade shows and conventions. (We geeks love trade shows and conventions.) Your mission must be to prevent them from stopping your presentation.

The best way to prevent someone from tinkering with your presentation is to get the input devices out of sight. Hide the CPU (the main box of the computer), the keyboard, and the mouse. You can't disconnect the keyboard and mouse from the PC, or an error message will appear, but you can hide them. Again, don't cover them with anything that might restrict the airflow, or you might end up with an overheated PC.

You can also set up the following security measures in your presentation file:

✦ Choose Slide Show ⇨ Set Up Show and make sure you have chosen Browsed at a kiosk. This disables the right-click menu while the slide show is running. This way, you can provide a mouse so passers-by can advance the slides (by clicking) manually if desired, without allowing the audience to abort the show or jump around. You can also turn these features off without using kiosk mode by choosing Tools ⇨ Options and deselecting their checkboxes on the View tab.

✦ Save the presentation as a PowerPoint Show (choose File ⇨ Save As) and give the presentation using the PowerPoint Viewer program rather than PowerPoint itself. That way, in case someone does manage to stop the presentation, that person cannot use PowerPoint to alter the presentation for their amusement (and your embarrassment).

✦ Set a startup password for your PC so that if people manage to reboot it, they won't get into your PC to tamper with its settings. This is usually set through the BIOS setup program. If you can't do that, set a Windows startup password (Start ⇨ Settings ⇨ Control Panel ⇨ Passwords).

Summary

In this chapter, you learned the ins and outs of preparing a presentation that can run unattended or without user interaction. You can probably think of some uses for such a show, and even more may occur to you later. In the next chapter, I show you how to create user-interactive presentations that allow people to make choices about the presentation content they see.

✦   ✦   ✦

Designing User-Interactive Presentations

In the preceding lesson, you learned how to create a self-running presentation. Self-running presentations do their thing without any intervention from the audience or from you. If a self-running presentation runs at a trade show and there is no one to hear it, it still runs nonetheless.

In contrast, user-interactive shows also lack a human facilitator or speaker, but they rely on an audience's attention. The audience presses buttons, clicks a mouse, or clicks graphics or hyperlinks onscreen to advance the show from one slide to the next, and they may even be able to control which content is displayed. (See the "Interactive Presentation Ideas" section at the end of this chapter for some usage ideas.)

What Is a Hyperlink?

The navigational controls you place in your presentation take various forms, but are all hyperlinks. A *hyperlink* is a bit of text or a graphic that you (or your audience) can click to jump somewhere else. When you click a hyperlink, you might jump to a different slide in the same presentation, to a different presentation, to another program on your computer, or even to an Internet Web page. (If you are jumping to a Web page, your Web browsing program, such as Internet Explorer, starts automatically.)

The most common type of hyperlink is underlined text. Hyperlink text is typically underlined and a different color than the rest of the text onscreen. In addition, *followed links* may be a different color from ones that you have not yet checked out, depending on the program. (In PowerPoint, they are two different colors unless you set them for the same color on the Format ⇨ Slide Color Scheme command's Custom tab.)

However, you are not limited to underlined bits of text for your hyperlinks. You can also use graphics or any other objects on your slides as hyperlinks. For example, PowerPoint provides some special-purpose graphics called action buttons that serve very well with hyperlinks. For example, you can assign a hyperlink to the next slide to the action button that looks like a right arrow, as you see in Figure 26-1 in the following section.

Navigational Control Choices

Figure 26-1 shows a slide with several types of navigational controls, any of which could be used in your own i.

✦ **Action buttons:** These graphics come with PowerPoint. You can set them up so that clicking them moves to a different slide in the presentation. The ones in Figure 26-1 move forward (to the next slide) and back (to the previous slide).

✦ **Hyperlink with helper text:** The text "Click here to learn more" in Figure 26-1, for example, provides built-in instructions for less technically sophisticated users. In this case, clicking the text might jump to a hidden slide containing more detailed information about the topic.

✦ **Hyperlink without helper text:** The text "Customer Satisfaction Survey Program" in Figure 26-1 is a hyperlink, but the audience must know enough about computers to know that clicking those words jumps to the slide containing more information.

✦ **Bare Internet hyperlink:** The Internet address in Figure 26-1 (`http://www.mysite.com/quality`) is also a hyperlink — in this case, to a Web page on the Internet. This kind of hyperlink can be intimidating for beginners who don't recognize Internet syntax, but it is very good for the advanced audience member because it lists the address up front. Viewers can jot it down for later exploration if they don't want to visit the page right now.

✦ **Instructions:** If you do not build specific navigation controls into the presentation, you may want to add instructions on the slide that tell the reader how to move forward and backward in the presentation. The instruction box at the bottom of Figure 26-1 does just that.

Choosing Appropriate Controls for Your Audience

Before you dive into building an interactive presentation, you must decide how the audience will navigate from slide to slide. There is no one best way; the right decision depends on your audience's comfort level with computers and with hyperlinks. Consider these points:

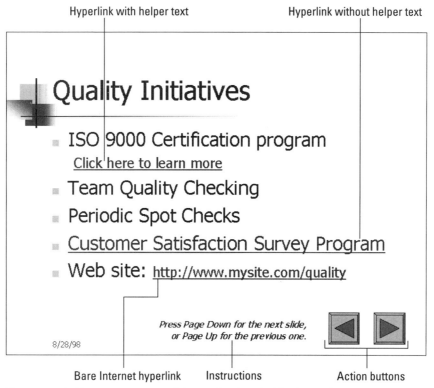

Figure 26-1: Use one or more of the navigational aids shown here.

✦ Is the audience technically savvy enough to know that they should press a key or click the mouse to advance the slide, or do you need to provide that instruction?

✦ Does your audience understand that the arrow action buttons mean forward and back, or do you need to explain that?

✦ Does your audience understand hyperlinks and Web addresses? If they see underlined text, do they know that they can click it to jump elsewhere?

✦ Is it enough to include some instructions on a slide at the beginning of the show, or do you need to repeat the instructions on every slide?

Think about your intended audience and their needs and come up with a plan. Here are some sample plans:

✦ **For a beginner-level audience:** Begin the presentation with an instructional slide explaining how to navigate. Place action buttons on the same place on each slide (using the Slide Master) to help them move forward and backward, and include a Help action button that they can click to jump to more detailed navigation instructions.

✦ **For an intermediate-level audience:** Place action buttons on the same place on each slide, along with a brief note on the first slide (such as the instruction in Figure 26-1) explaining how to use them.

✦ **For an advanced audience:** Include other action buttons on the slide that allow the user to jump around freely in the presentation—go to the beginning, to the end, to the beginning of certain sections, and so on. Advanced users are able to understand and take advantage of a more sophisticated system of action buttons.

Using Action Buttons

Action buttons, which you saw in Figure 26-1, are the simplest kind of user-interactivity controls. They enable your audience members to move from slide to slide in the presentation with a minimum of fuss. PowerPoint provides many preset action buttons that already have hyperlinks assigned to them, so all you have to do is place them on your slides.

 Tip Most people prefer to place action buttons on the Slide Master so that they appear in the same spot on every slide, rather than trying to place them manually.

The action buttons that come with PowerPoint are shown in Table 26-1, along with their preset hyperlinks. As you can see, some of them are all ready to go; others require you to specify where they jump to.

Table 26-1
Action Buttons

Button	Name	Hyperlinks to
	None	Nothing, by default. You can add text to the button to create custom buttons.
	Home	First slide in the presentation. (Home is where you started, and it's a picture of a house, get it?)
	Help	Nothing, by default, but you can point it toward a slide containing help.
	Information	Nothing, by default, but you can point it to a slide containing information.
	Back or Previous	Previous slide in the presentation (not necessarily the last slide viewed; compare to Return).
	Forward or Next	Next slide in the presentation.
	Beginning	First slide in the presentation.
	End	Last slide in the presentation.
	Return	Last slide viewed, regardless of normal order. This is useful to place on a hidden slide that the audience will jump to with another link (such as Help), to help them return to the main presentation when they are finished.
	Document	Nothing, by default, but you can set it to run a program that you specify.
	Sound	Plays a sound that you specify. If you don't choose a sound, it plays the first sound on PowerPoint's list of standard sounds (Applause).
	Movie	Nothing, by default, but you can set it to play a movie that you specify.

Setting Up Action Buttons

To place an action button, follow these steps:

1. If you want to place the button on the Slide Master, display it (View ➪ Master ➪ Slide Master).

Note Some action buttons are best placed on the Slide Master, such as Next and Previous; others, such as Return, are special-use buttons that are best placed on individual slides.

2. Choose Slide Show ➪ Action Buttons. A palette of buttons appears, corresponding to the buttons you saw in Table 26-1. See Figure 26-2.

3. Click the button that you want to place. Your mouse pointer turns into a crosshair.

4. To create a button of a specific size, drag on the slide (or Slide Master) where you want it to go. Or, to create a button of a default size, simply click once where you want it. You can resize the button at any time later, the same as you would any object.

5. The Action Settings dialog box appears. Make sure the Mouse Click tab is on top. See Figure 26-3.

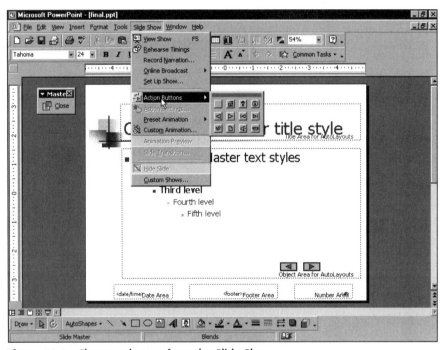

Figure 26-2: Choose a button from the Slide Show menu.

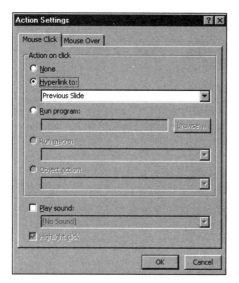

Figure 26-3: Specify what should happen when you click the action button.

6. Confirm or change the hyperlink set up there:

   • If the action button should take the reader to a specific location, make sure the correct slide appears in the Hyperlink to box. Refer to the right column in Table 26-1 to see the default setting for each action button. Table 26-2 lists the choices you can make and what they do.

   • If the action button should run a program, choose Run program and enter the program's name and path, or click Browse to locate it.

   • If the action button should play a sound, click None in the Action on click section, make sure the Play sound checkbox is marked, and choose the correct sound from the Play sound drop-down list.

7. Click OK. The button has been assigned the action you specified.

8. Add more action buttons as desired by repeating these steps.

9. If you are working in Slide Master view, exit it by clicking the Close button.

10. Test your action buttons in Slide Show view to make sure they jump where you want them to.

To edit a button's action, right-click it and choose Action Settings to reopen this dialog box at any time.

Table 26-2 Hyperlink to Choices in the Action Settings Dialog Box	
Drop-Down Menu Choice	*Result*
Previous Slide Next Slide First Slide Last Slide Last Slide Viewed	These choices all do just what their names say. These are the default actions assigned to certain buttons you learned about in Table 26-1.
End Show	Sets the button to stop the show when clicked.
Custom Show...	Opens a Link to Custom Show dialog box ,where you can choose a custom show to jump to when the button is clicked.
Slide...	Opens a Hyperlink to Slide dialog box, where you can choose any slide in the current presentation to jump to when the button is clicked.
URL...	Opens a Hyperlink to URL dialog box, where you can enter a Web address to jump to when the button is clicked.
Other PowerPoint Presentation...	Opens a Hyperlink to Other PowerPoint Presentation dialog box, where you can choose another PowerPoint presentation to display when the button is clicked.
Other File...	Opens a Hyperlink to Other File dialog box, where you can choose any file to open when the button is clicked. If the file requires a certain application, that application will open when needed. (To run another application without opening a specific file in it, use the Run Program option in the Action Settings dialog box instead of Hyperlink To.)

Adding Text to an Action Button

The blank action button you saw in Table 26-1 can be very useful. You can place several of them on a slide and then type text into them, creating your own set of buttons.

To type text into a blank button, follow these steps:

1. Place a blank action button on the slide.

2. Right-click the action button and choose Add Text. An insertion point appears in it.

3. Type your text. Format it as desired using the normal text formatting commands and buttons.

4. When you are finished, click outside of the button to stop.

5. Resize the button, if needed, to contain the text more neatly. You can drag a button's side selection handles to make it wider.

6. If you need to edit the text later, simply click the text to move the insertion point back into it, just as you would with any text box.

Figure 26-4 shows some examples of custom buttons you can create with your own text.

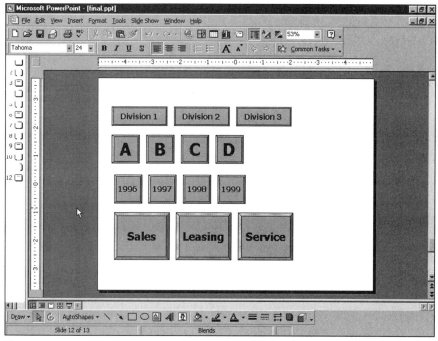

Figure 26-4: You can create any of these sets of action buttons by typing and formatting text on blank buttons.

Creating Your Own Action Buttons

You can create an action button out of any object on your slide: a drawn shape, a piece of clip art, a photograph, a text box — anything. To do so, just right-click the object and choose Action Settings. Then, set it to Hyperlink To, Run Program, or Play Sound, just as you did for the action buttons in the preceding sections.

Adding Text-Based Hyperlinks to Slides

Now that you know that hyperlinks are the key to user interactivity, it's time to add some to your presentation. Start with text-based hyperlinks since they're the easiest. You can either add them bare or with explanatory text.

Adding a Bare Hyperlink

The most basic kind of hyperlink is an Internet address, typed directly into a text box. When you enter text in any of the following formats, PowerPoint automatically converts it to a hyperlink:

✦ **Web addresses:** anything that begins with `http://`.

✦ **E-mail addresses:** any string of characters with no spaces and an @ sign in the middle somewhere.

✦ **FTP addresses:** anything that begins with `ftp://`.

You do not have to do anything special to create these hyperlinks; when you type them and press Enter or the space bar afterward, PowerPoint converts them. You know the conversion has taken place because the text becomes underlined and different-colored. (The exact color depends on the color scheme in use.)

Figure 26-5 shows some examples of bare hyperlinks. They are considered bare because they are exactly what the text says. The text `user@mysite.com` is a hyperlink that sends e-mail to that address. In contrast, a link that reads "Click here to send e-mail to me" and contains the same hyperlink address is not bare, because you do not see the address directly.

Note   FTP stands for File Transfer Protocol. It's a method of transferring files via the Internet. Up until a few years ago, FTP was a totally separate system from the Web, but nowadays, most Web browsers have FTP download capabilities built in, so anyone who has a Web browser can receive files via FTP. However, to send files via FTP, the user must have a separate FTP program.

Creating Text Hyperlinks

A text hyperlink is a hyperlink comprised of text, but not the bare address. For example, in Figure 26-1, "Click here to learn more" is a text hyperlink. So is "Customer Satisfaction Survey Program."

You can select already-entered text and make it a hyperlink, or you can enter new text. Either way, follow these steps.

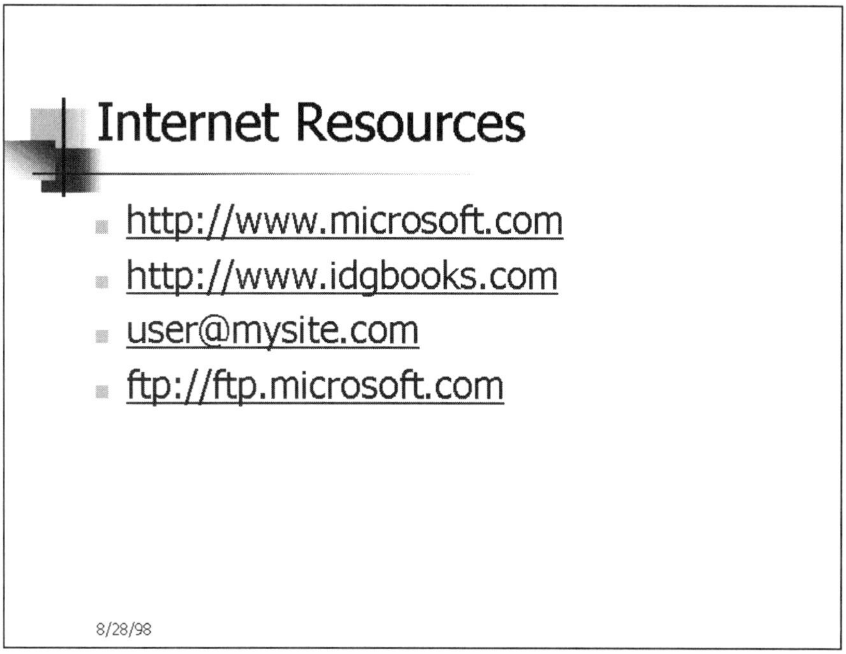

Internet Resources

- http://www.microsoft.com
- http://www.idgbooks.com
- user@mysite.com
- ftp://ftp.microsoft.com

8/28/98

Figure 26-5: Some examples of bare Internet hyperlinks.

Note

These steps take you through the process generically; see the sections in "Choosing a Hyperlink Address" later in the chapter for specific information about various kinds of hyperlinks you can create.

1. To use existing text, select the text. Otherwise, just position the insertion point where you want the hyperlink.

2. Choose Insert ➪ Hyperlink or press Ctrl+K. The Insert Hyperlink dialog box opens. See Figure 26-6.

3. In the Text to display field, type or edit the hyperlink text. This text is what will appear underlined on the slide.

4. Enter the hyperlink or select it from one of the available lists. (See the following section, "Choosing the Hyperlink Address," to learn about your options in this regard.)

5. (Optional) If you would like a ScreenTip to appear when the user points the mouse at the hyperlink, click the ScreenTip button. This can be handy to tell users where the hyperlink goes, so they don't have to click it to find out.

6. Enter the text for the ScreenTip. See Figure 26-7. Many people like to use the actual address for the ScreenTip; others enter a short description of the destination.

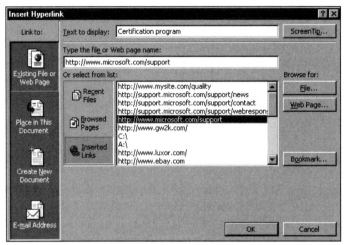

Figure 26-6: Insert a hyperlink by typing the text to display and choosing the address of the slide or other location to jump to.

Figure 26-7: Enter a custom ScreenTip if desired.

Caution   Internet Explorer 4.0 supports ScreenTips, but other browsers may not. This is not an issue if you plan to distribute the presentation in PowerPoint format, but if you plan to convert it to Web pages (see Chapter 27), it might make a difference because not everyone who views the presentation is likely to have Internet Explorer 4.0.

7. Click OK to close the Set Hyperlink ScreenTip dialog box.

8. Click OK to accept the newly created hyperlink.

Choosing the Hyperlink Address

You can use the Insert Hyperlink dialog box to create a hyperlink to any address that's accessible via the computer where the presentation will run. Although many people think of a hyperlink as an Internet address, it can actually be a link to any file, application, Internet location, or slide.

Caution　A hyperlink will not work if the person viewing the presentation does not have access to the needed files and programs or does not have the needed Internet or network connectivity. A hyperlink that may work fine on your own PC may not work after the presentation has been transferred to the end user's PC.

Possible addresses to hyperlink to include the following:

✦ Other slides in the current presentation

✦ Slides in other presentations (if you provide access to those presentations)

✦ Documents created in other applications (if the user has those applications installed and those document files available)

✦ Graphic files (if the user has access to an application that can display them)

✦ Internet Web pages (if the user has an Internet connection and a Web browser)

✦ E-mail addresses (if the user has an Internet connection and an e-mail program)

✦ FTP site addresses (if the user has an Internet connection and either a Web browser or an FTP program)

Creating a Link to a Slide in This Presentation

The most common kind of link is to another slide in the same presentation. There are lots of uses for this; you might, for example, hide several backup slides that contain extra information. You could then create hyperlinks on certain key slides that allow the user to jump to one of those hidden slides to peruse the extra facts. (Figure 26-1 has two such links.)

To create a link to another slide, follow these steps:

1. To use existing text, select the text. Otherwise, just position the insertion point where you want the hyperlink.

2. Choose Insert ➪ Hyperlink or press Ctrl+K. The Insert Hyperlink dialog box opens.

3. In the Text to display field, type or edit the hyperlink text. This text is what will appear underlined on the slide.

4. Click the Place in This Document button. The dialog box controls change to show a list of the slides in the presentation. See Figure 26-8.

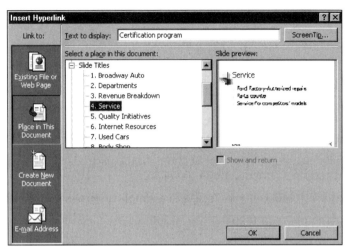

Figure 26-8: Select the slide that the hyperlink should refer to.

5. Select the slide you want.

6. (Optional) If you want the presentation to continue from the original spot after showing this slide, mark the Show and return checkbox. If you prefer that the presentation continue from the new location forward, leave it unmarked.

7. Click OK.

Creating a Link to an Existing File

You can also create a hyperlink to any file available on your PC's hard disk or on your local area network. This can be a PowerPoint file or a data file for any other program, such as a Word document or an Excel spreadsheet. Or, if you don't want to open a particular data file, you can hyperlink to the program file itself, so that the other application simply opens.

For example, perhaps you have some detailed documentation for your product in Adobe Acrobat format (PDF). This type of document requires the Adobe Acrobat reader. So you could create a hyperlink with the text "Click here to read the documentation" and link to the appropriate PDF file. When your audience member clicks that link, Adobe Acrobat Reader opens and the documentation displays.

To link to a file, follow these steps:

1. To use existing text, select the text. Otherwise, just position the insertion point where you want the hyperlink.

2. Choose Insert ➪ Hyperlink or press Ctrl+K. The Insert Hyperlink dialog box opens.

3. In the Text to display field, type or edit the hyperlink text. This text is what will appear underlined on the slide.

4. In the Insert Hyperlink dialog box, click the Existing File or Web Page button.

5. In the Or select from list area (see Figure 26-9), click Recent Files. A list of the files you have worked with most recently on this computer appears.

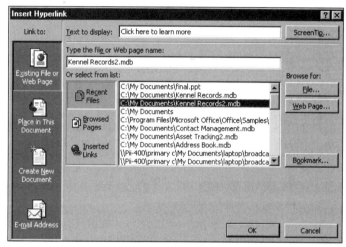

Figure 26-9: Choose a recently used file if appropriate, or click the File button to browse.

6. If you see the file you want on the list, click it and click OK. Otherwise, go on to Step 7.

7. Click the File button. The Link to File dialog box appears. See Figure 26-10.

8. Choose the file you want to link to. Do any of the following as needed to find it:

   • Navigate to a different drive and folder, as you learned in Chapter 4.

   • Change the file type from the Files of type drop-down list. The default is to display only Office data files, but you can choose All Files, Internet Files, or some other type.

9. Click OK to return to the Insert Hyperlink dialog box.

10. Click OK to insert the hyperlink.

Figure 26-10: Browse for the file you want to hyperlink to, just as you would select a file for opening with PowerPoint's File ➪ Open command.

Creating a Link to a Web or FTP Ssite

If you want to link to a Web or FTP site, as you learned earlier in the chapter, you can simply type the address directly into any text box. But if you want to be more elegant and have some different text displayed rather than the bare hyperlink, you must use the Insert Hyperlink dialog box instead.

1. To use existing text, select the text. Otherwise, just position the insertion point where you want the hyperlink.

2. Choose Insert ➪ Hyperlink or press Ctrl+K. The Insert Hyperlink dialog box opens.

3. In the Text to display field, type or edit the hyperlink text. This text is what will appear underlined on the slide.

4. From the Insert Hyperlink dialog box, click the Existing File or Web Page button.

5. If you know the exact Web or FTP address that you want to link to, type it in the Type the file or Web page name box. Then click OK. Otherwise, go to Step 6.

6. In the Or select from list area, click Browsed Pages to display a list of pages you have visited recently (including pages from PowerPoint's Help system), or click Inserted Links to show a list of addresses you have recently hyperlinked to. See Figure 26-11.

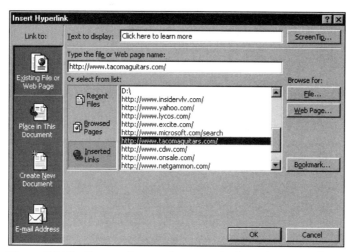

Figure 26-11: You can browse for recently viewed or recently inked files, or click Web Page to browse.

7. If the address you want appears as a result of Step 6, click it and click OK. Otherwise, go on to Step 8.

8. Click the Web Page button to browse for the page you want. Internet Explorer (or your default Web browser) opens.

9. If the Dial-Up Connection dialog box appears prompting you to connect to the Internet, enter your username and password, if needed, and then click Connect. See Figure 26-12.

Figure 26-12: You may be prompted to start your Internet connection; do so.

10. In Internet Explorer, navigate to the page that you want to hyperlink to. You can use your Favorites list or look up the page with a search site such as the one found at `http://www.yahoo.com`. See Figure 26-13.

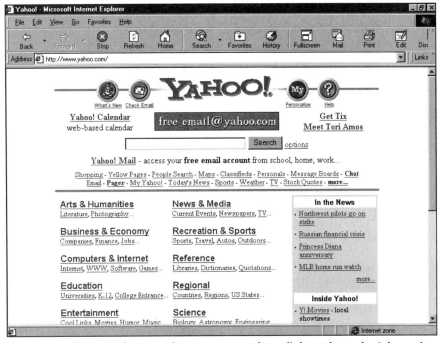

Figure 26-13: Locate the page that you want to hyperlink to. If you don't know its address, look it up at one of the many search sites like this one.

11. When you have arrived at the page you want, jump back to PowerPoint by clicking its button on your Windows taskbar. The page's address appears in the Type the file or Web page name text box.

12. Click OK to create the link.

Creating a Link to a New Document

Perhaps you want the audience to be able to create a new document by clicking a hyperlink. For example, perhaps you would like them to be able to type in information about their experience with your Customer Service department. One way to do this is to let them create a new document using a program that they have on their system, such as a word processor.

Caution

Be careful to set up a new document hyperlink to create a new document using a program that you are sure your audience members will have access to.

To create a link to a new document, follow these steps:

1. To use existing text, select the text. Otherwise, just position the insertion point where you want the hyperlink.

2. Choose Insert ➪ Hyperlink or press Ctrl+K. The Insert Hyperlink dialog box opens.

3. In the Text to display field, type or edit the hyperlink text. This text is what will appear underlined on the slide.

4. From the Insert Hyperlink dialog box, click Create New Document. The dialog box controls change, as shown in Figure 26-14.

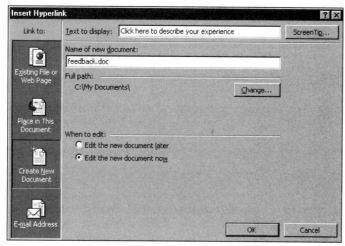

Figure 26-14: PowerPoint prompts you to enter the new document name and location.

5. Enter the name of the new document that you want to create. The type of document created depends on the extension you include. For example, to create a Word document, use the .doc extension. See Table 26-3 for other extensions.

6. If the path where it should be stored is not correct in the Full path area, click the Change button. Navigate to the desired location, and click OK to return.

7. Choose Edit the new document later.

8. Click OK.

The most important part about adding a link to create a new file is to make sure that you use an extension that corresponds to a program that users have installed on the PCs where they will be viewing the presentation. When a program is installed, it registers its *extension* (the three-character code after the period in a file's name) in the Windows Registry, so that any data files with that extension are associated with that program. For example, when you install Microsoft Word, it registers the extension .doc for itself. And PowerPoint registers .ppt for its own use. Table 26-3 lists some of the more common file types and their registered extensions on most PCs.

Table 26-3 Commonly Used Extensions for Popular Programs	
Extension	**Associated Program**
DOC	Microsoft Word, or WordPad if Word is not installed. Use for documents if you are not sure whether your audience has Word or not, but you are sure they at least have Windows 95.
WRI	Write, the predecessor to WordPad. WordPad and Word also open these if Write is not installed. Safest to use for documents if you do not know which version of Windows your audience will be using.
TXT	Notepad, a plain text editor. Creates text files without any formatting. Not my first choice for documents unless you specifically need them to be without formatting.
WPD	WordPerfect, a competitor to Word. Opens in Word if Word is installed but WordPerfect is not.
BMP	Microsoft Paint (which comes free with Windows), or some other more sophisticated graphics program if one is installed.
MDB	Microsoft Access, a database program.
MPP	Microsoft Project, a project management program.
PPT	Microsoft PowerPoint (you know what *that* is!).
XLS	Microsoft Excel, a spreadsheet program..

Creating a Link to an E-mail Address

You can also create a link that opens the audience's e-mail program and address an e-mail to a certain recipient. For example, perhaps you would like the audience to e-mail feedback to you about how they liked your presentation or send you requests for more information about your product.

To create an e-mail hyperlink, follow these steps:

1. To use existing text, select the text. Otherwise, just position the insertion point where you want the hyperlink.

2. Choose Insert ➪ Hyperlink or press Ctrl+K. The Insert Hyperlink dialog box opens.

3. In the Text to display field, type or edit the hyperlink text. This text is what will appear underlined on the slide.

4. From the Insert Hyperlink dialog box, click the E-mail Address button. The dialog box changes to show the controls in Figure 26-15.

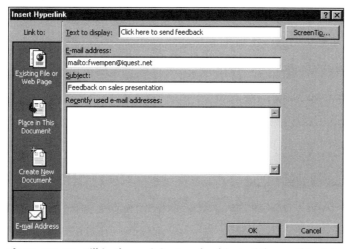

Figure 26-15: Fill in the recipient and subject of the mail-to link.

5. In the E-mail Address box, enter the e-mail address. PowerPoint automatically adds mailto: in front of it. (You can also select from one of the addresses on the Recently used e-mail addresses list if there are any.)

6. In the Subject field, enter the text that you want to be automatically filled in for the Subject line of each e-mail.

7. Click OK. The hyperlink appears on the slide.

Editing a Hyperlink

If you need to change the displayed text for the hyperlink, simply edit it. Move the insertion point into it and press Backspace or Delete to remove characters; then retype new ones. It's the same as with any other text.

If you need to change the link to which the hyperlink points, follow these steps:

1. Right-click the hyperlink.

2. On the shortcut menu that appears, choose Hyperlink ➪ Edit Hyperlink. The Edit Hyperlink dialog box appears. It is exactly the same as the Insert Hyperlink dialog box except for the name.

3. Make changes to the hyperlink. You can change the displayed text, the address it points to, and/or the ScreenTip.

4. Click OK.

Removing a Hyperlink

If you decide not to hyperlink in a particular spot, you can delete the displayed text, effectively deleting the hyperlink attached to it. But if you want to leave the displayed text intact and remove the hyperlink only, follow these steps:

1. Right-click the hyperlink.

2. On the shortcut menu that appears, choose Hyperlink ➪ Remove Hyperlink.

Creating Graphics-Based Hyperlinks

There are two ways to create a graphics-based hyperlink. Both involve skills that you have already learned in this chapter. Both work equally well, but you may find that you prefer one over the other. The Action Settings method is a little bit simpler, but the Insert Hyperlink method allows you to browse for Web addresses more easily.

Creating a Hyperlink with Action Settings

A graphics-based hyperlink is really no more than a graphic with an Action Setting attached to it. You set it up just as you did with the action buttons earlier in this chapter:

1. Place the graphic that you want to use for a hyperlink.

2. Right-click it and choose Action Settings.

3. Choose Hyperlink To.

4. Open the Hyperlink To drop-down list and choose URL to enter an Internet address, or choose one of the other options from Table 26-2 to link to some other location or object.

5. Click OK.

Now the graphic functions just like an action button in the presentation; the audience can click on it to jump to the specified location.

Creating a Hyperlink with Insert Hyperlink

If you would like to take advantage of the superior address-browsing capabilities of the Insert Hyperlink dialog box when setting up a graphical hyperlink, follow these steps instead of the preceding ones:

1. Place the graphic that you want to use for a hyperlink.

2. Right-click it and choose Hyperlink. The Insert Hyperlink dialog box appears.

3. Choose the location, as you learned earlier in this chapter for text-based hyperlinks. The only difference is that the Text to display box is unavailable because there is no text.

4. Click OK.

Interactive Presentation Ideas

You have probably thought of some good ideas for interactive presentations as you worked through this chapter. Here are some more:

✦ **Web resource listings:** Include a slide that lists Web page addresses that the user can visit for more information about various topics covered in your presentation. Or, include Web cross-references throughout the presentation at the bottom of pertinent slides.

✦ **Product information:** Create a basic presentation describing your products, with For More Information buttons for each product. Then, create hidden slides with the detailed information, and hyperlink those hidden slides to the For More Information buttons. Don't forget to put a Return button on each hidden slide so the user can easily return to the main presentation.

✦ **Access to custom shows:** If you have created custom shows, as described in Chapter 24, set up action buttons or hyperlinks that jump the user to them on request. Use the Action Settings dialog box's Hyperlink To command and choose Custom Show; then choose the custom show you want to link to.

✦ **Quizzes:** Create a presentation with a series of multiple-choice questions. Create custom action buttons for each answer. Depending on which answer the user clicks, set it up to jump either to a Congratulations, You're Right! slide or a Sorry, Try Again slide. From each of those, include a Return button to go on with the quiz.

✦ **Troubleshooting:** Ask the user a series of questions and include action buttons or hyperlinks for the answers. Set it up to jump to a slide that further narrows down the problem based on their answer, until they finally arrive at a slide that explains the exact problem and proposes a solution.

✦ **Directory:** Include a company directory with e-mail hyperlinks for various people or departments so that anyone reading the presentation can easily make contact.

Summary

In this chapter, you learned how to create action buttons and hyperlinks in your presentation that can help your audience jump to the information they want in a self-service fashion. Now you can design great-looking presentations that anyone can work their way through on their own, without assistance. In the next chapter, you learn how distribute these fine user-interactive presentations on the Internet.

✦   ✦   ✦

Preparing a Presentation for Online Distribution

PowerPoint is a rather specialized program. It helps you create presentations very well, but it is not the best choice for creating other business documents such as letters, databases, or spreadsheets. For those needs, you use other tools, such as word processors, database programs, and spreadsheet programs.

Similarly, PowerPoint is probably not the best choice for building your company's main Web site. There are other, better tools for building the traditional newsletter style of Web pages that are a staple of Internet life. Good, inexpensive programs include Microsoft FrontPage (under $100), FrontPage Express (free with PowerPoint), and even Microsoft Word (comes with Office 2000).

Even though you probably won't create a lot of stand-alone Web pages with PowerPoint, you may sometimes want to publish PowerPoint presentations on an existing Web site. You can do this in either of two ways: PowerPoint format and HTML format. Both have pros and cons:

✦ **PowerPoint format.** You can make the PowerPoint presentation file available for download from your Web site, just as you can make any other file available.

  • *Pros:* The audience sees the presentation exactly as you created it, including any embedded sounds, movies, transitions, and animation.

- *Cons:* Only people who own a copy of PowerPoint or who have downloaded the PowerPoint Viewer program can see it.

✦ **HTML (Web) format.** You can convert your PowerPoint presentation to HTML format with an easy-to-use converter included in PowerPoint.

- *Pros:* Anyone with a Web browser can view the presentation without any special preparation. It makes your work widely accessible.

- *Cons*: Some of the special effects in your presentation may not be visible to all users. PowerPoint 2000 has some very sophisticated saving abilities that enable you to create a Web presentation that is almost exactly like a PowerPoint one. Table 27-1 lists the effects that you lose when you view a Web presentation in a Web browser; as you can see, the losses are minimal. However, some of the Web-based versions of certain features, such as transitions and multimedia, work only if your audience is using Internet Explorer 4.0 or higher for a Web browser. With other browsers, your audience may miss out on animations, transitions, movies, sounds, or other goodies.

Note   *HTML* is a term you see a lot in this chapter. It stands for Hypertext Markup Language, and it is the file format used for Web pages, just as PPT is the format for PowerPoint presentation files. The terms *Web format* and *HTML format* are roughly interchangeable.

Table 27.1
Features Lost When Converting a Presentation to Web Format

Animations:

✦ You cannot introduce text using the By Word or By Letter options.

✦ The After Animation option that makes an AutoShape appear dimmed doesn't work.

✦ Chart animation effects don't work.

✦ A sound plays only for a single slide; it doesn't continue to play when you move to the next slide.

✦ Linked and embedded objects don't play.

✦ The following paragraph effects don't work: Spiral, Stretch, Swivel, and Zoom.

✦ Rotated text is not animated separately from an attached AutoShape.

✦ If you have set up automatic transitions, all mouse-click animations on the slide behave as automatic animations.

✦ Animated GIF pictures are not animated if they are grouped with other objects using the Group command.

Action Settings:

✦ The Run Macro option doesn't work.

✦ The Highlight Click and Highlight When Mouse Over checkboxes don't work.

✦ Object Action options don't work.

✦ A hyperlink to a custom show does not play that show.

✦ The Play Sound option doesn't play if the object is also formatted as a hyperlink.

✦ If a hyperlink on the Slide Master is covered by a placeholder (even an empty one), the hyperlink doesn't work.

Other Features:

✦ The right-click menu commands do not work when viewing the slide show.

✦ Not all of the slide show shortcut keys are supported.

✦ The Backspace key displays the last slide viewed, not necessarily the previous slide in the show.

✦ You can't run individual custom shows.

✦ The Update Automatically checkbox doesn't work for dates and times.

✦ Pressing F1 doesn't display help.

✦ The Shadow and Embossed font formatting effects don't work.

Considerations for Web Presentations

When you are creating a presentation that you think you might make available on the Internet, you need to keep some special considerations in mind. For one thing, of course, you want to make the presentation as friendly and user-interactive as possible, as you learned in Chapter 26. That means you should include action buttons, directions, and/or hyperlinks to help the user move through the slides.

You should also remember in what format you are planning to publish (as explained in the preceding section). If you are planning to save your work in HTML format, don't waste your time setting up animations and transitions, for example, because they'll be lost upon conversion.

Finally, you want to keep the presentation file as small as possible to minimize the time required to download the presentation to the users' PCs. That means avoiding gratuitous graphics, sounds, movies, transitions, and other elements, even if you are planning to distribute it in PowerPoint format where these elements will be usable.

Your Action Plan

As you just learned, you can either save the presentation as a Web page and then publish it on a Web server as you would any other Web pages, or you can transfer a normal PowerPoint file to the Web server and then create an introductory page to help the audience access it. You need to decide up front which method you want to use.

In most cases, it is best to save as a Web page. The only reason you might not want to choose that option is if the animations and other special effects in the presentation are a critical part of the message, and you are not sure that all of your audience members are using Internet Explorer 4.0 or higher. In such a case, publishing as a PowerPoint presentation and providing the PowerPoint Viewer might be better.

To learn how to save as a Web page, see the following section. If you are going to publish in PowerPoint format, you can skip it. However, no matter which format you choose, you need to learn how to transfer the presentation to the Internet server, explained in the "Transferring a Presentation to a Web Server" section later in this chapter.

If you are planning to publish in PowerPoint format, you need to create a Web page as a starting point. That Web page should contain a link that users can click to download the PowerPoint Viewer and a link that enables them to download the presentation itself. You learn to create such a page in the "Creating a Helper Page for Native PowerPoint Shows" section near the end of this chapter.

Saving As a Web Page

Saving a presentation as a Web page is almost as easy as saving it normally. You simply issue a command and provide a name; PowerPoint does the rest.

Caution   When you save as a Web page, the resulting presentation is in HTML format. That means that if you continue to work on the presentation onscreen after saving, any changes you make and save are saved to the HTML version. If you want to resave the original PowerPoint file, you must use File ⇨ Save As and choose PowerPoint as the file type.

Follow these steps to save as a Web page without setting any special options. (You learn about the available options in the following section.)

1. Choose File ⇨ Save As Web Page. The Save As dialog box appears, with Web Page chosen as the Save As type. See Figure 27-1.

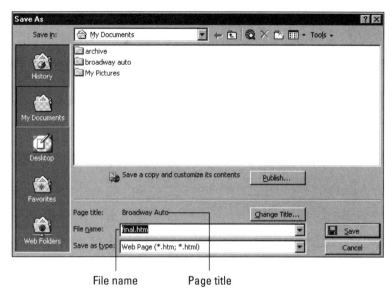

File name   Page title

Figure 27-1: When you save as a Web page, the Save As dialog box has a few special options.

2. The default name is the presentation name with .htm on the end. If you want a different name, type it in the File name box.

3. PowerPoint takes the default Page title (that is, the words that will appear in the Web browser title bar when the page displays) from the title of the first slide. If you want a different title, click the Change button, type a different title, and click OK.

4. If you want to save in a different location, navigate to the drive or folder you want. To save files directly to an FTP site on the Internet, see the "Saving in an FTP Location" section later in this chapter.

5. Click Save. PowerPoint saves the presentation in HTML format.

6. (Optional) check your work by opening the home page file in your Web browser. To learn how to do so, see the "Navigating a Presentation in a Browser" section later in this chapter. Figure 27-2 shows an example of how it might look.

Navigation Controls; users can click a page name to jump to it

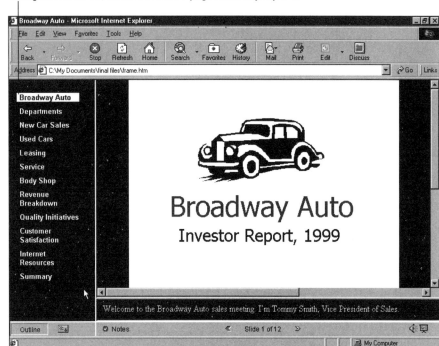

Figure 27-2: Here's a PowerPoint presentation saved in Web page format.

A saved HTML presentation is actually many files, not a single one. PowerPoint creates a home page (an entry point) with the same name as the original presentation. (This is the file you named when you chose a name in Step 2 above.) For example, if the presentation file is named Final.ppt, the home page is named final.htm. Then, PowerPoint creates a folder named {presentation name} Files (for example, Final Files) that contains all the other HTML, graphics, and other files needed to display the complete presentation.

If you are transferring the HTML presentation to another PC (which is very likely if you are going to make it available on the Internet through your company's server), you must be careful to transfer not only the lone HTML home page but also the entire associated folder.

Setting Publishing Options

When you save using the steps in the preceding section, you have very little control over how PowerPoint translates the presentation to HTML. For more control, click the Publish button in the Save As dialog box. When you do so, the Publish as Web Page dialog box appears. See Figure 27-3.

Figure 27-3: Use this dialog box to provide more input on how PowerPoint converts your work to HTML format.

Use this dialog box as a replacement for the Save As dialog box and set any of these options:

✦ **Publish what?** The default is complete presentation, but you can choose a range of slides or a custom show.

✦ **Display speaker notes.** The default is yes (checkbox marked), so that an icon on each page enables your readers to jump to that page's notes.

✦ **Browser support.** The default is Microsoft Internet Explorer 4.0 or later, which is the Web browser that comes with Windows 98. (Included in the *or later* is IE 5.0, which comes with PowerPoint 2000.) This format takes advantage of IE 4 and later's ability to process certain codes and run certain miniapplications. If you think some of your audience may not have this browser, choose one of the other options instead.

✦ **Publish a copy as.** These are the same controls as the ones in the Save As dialog box. You can change the page title with the Change button, or type a different name and/or location in the File name box.

✦ **Open published Web page in browser.** If you leave this checkbox marked, PowerPoint opens Internet Explorer and displays your presentation's first page automatically, as shown in Figure 27-2. This is a good way to check your work.

But wait! There's more! Notice the Web Options button in Figure 27-3. You can click it to display the Web Options dialog box, shown in Figure 27-4, where you have even more options to change regarding your presentation's conversion.

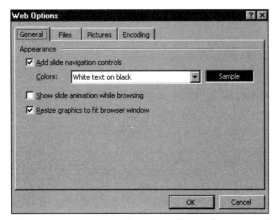

Figure 27-4: You can fine-tune the Web export of your presentation even more precisely with these options.

General Web Options

On the General tab, you can set the following:

✦ **Add slide navigation controls.** This option is turned on by default, and it results in the left pane shown in Figure 27-2 that lists the names of the slides. Users can click a slide's name to jump to it.

✦ **Colors.** Notice in Figure 27-2 that the aforementioned navigation area is black with white lettering. You can choose a different color scheme for that area from this Colors drop-down list. Choices include Browser colors (whatever default colors are set in the user's Web browser), Presentation colors (text color or accent color) taken from the presentation, or Black text on white.

✦ **Show slide animation while browsing.** If you have set any slide animations (see Chapter 20) and you want them to be a part of the Web show, mark this checkbox. It is unmarked by default because Web users may find animations annoying, rather than clever, because of their Internet connection's slowness.

✦ **Resize graphics to fit browser window.** This option is marked by default so that if users are running their browsers at less that full-screen size or using a different screen resolution, your content will not be cut off, but rather resized so that it fits the screen.

Files Web Options

On the Files tab, shown in Figure 27-5, you can set these options to control how your files are saved, named, organized, and updated:

✦ **Organize supporting files in a folder.** This option is the default, as you saw earlier. PowerPoint saves the needed files in a folder with the same name as the presentation home page. If you deselect this option, all the supporting files are saved in the same folder as the home page.

✦ **Use long file names whenever possible.** This option preserves the Windows 95/98/NT long filenames, which are usually more descriptive than the shorter 8-character names in DOS and Windows 3.1. If you need to transfer the presentation to a server that does not support long filenames, deselect this option.

✦ **Update links on save.** With this option marked, every time you save your presentation in Web format in PowerPoint, all the links are also saved.

✦ **Default editor.** Unmark the single checkbox in this section if you want to edit your Web pages in a third-party editing program (non-Office). For example, if you want to work on your exported PowerPoint show in a program like Microsoft Front Page, deselect this checkbox.

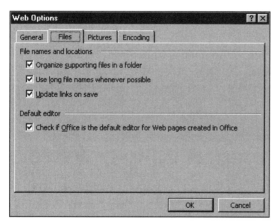

Figure 27-5: All these checkboxes are marked by default; deselect any of them as needed.

Pictures Web Options

On the Pictures tab, you can set these options to control how the images are saved and displayed:

✦ **Rely on VML for displaying graphics in browsers.** VML is an advanced format that enables content to be displayed more easily and accurately, but not all browsers support it. If your audience will all be using IE 5.0, mark this checkbox; otherwise, leave it blank.

✦ **Allow PNG as an output format.** PowerPoint 2000 can save in a special format called PNG instead of HTML that provides more features and helps stick closer to your original presentation when translating. However, not all browsers can read this format. Again, unless your entire audience will be using IE 5.0, leave this blank.

✦ **Target monitor.** Windows can run at several screen resolutions. The smallest is 640 x 480. (The numbers refer to the number of pixels, or individual dots, that make up the display.) Most people run Windows at 800 x 600 or higher, but people with old, small monitors may still be using 640 x 480. Choose the size that you want your presentation optimized for. In most cases, the default of 800 x 600 is the right choice.

Encoding Web Options

And finally, on the Encoding tab are a few settings that only multilingual offices will ever use:

✦ **Save this document as.** Choose a language character set here. For all English-speaking countries and countries that use the same alphabet as English, choose Western European.

✦ **Always save Web pages in the default encoding.** If you want PowerPoint to always rely on Windows' information about what kind of alphabet you are using, mark this checkbox, and you never have to worry about the character set again.

Transferring a Presentation to a Web Server

Publishing a presentation to the Web means transferring it to a server or other computer that has a direct, full-time Web connection. If you are an individual or small-business user, that server probably belongs to your local Internet service provider (ISP). If you work for a very large company that has its own Web site, there may be a server in-house that you should transfer your files to. Consult your company's network administrator or Webmaster to find out what you need to do.

Address Differences

There are a couple of ways to get the files from point A (your PC) to point B (the server): saving in an FTP location and using the Web Publishing Wizard. I outline each of these ways in the following sections.

The main difference between the two methods is the address that you enter to save your files to the server. A single location on a Web server has two distinct addresses: the FTP one and the Web one. Both addresses point to the same place; they are simply two different ways of describing that place. An FTP (File Transfer Protocol) address begins with ftp. A Web address begins with http. For example, the FTP address for the place you are to store your presentation might be `ftp.acme.net/user/fw/public_html`. If you are using an FTP transfer, that is the address you would enter. You use this type of address if you transfer using the steps in the "Saving in an FTP Location" section that follows.

But when people visit the Web site to view the page, they use the Web address, which might be `http://www.acme.net/~fwempen`. The Web Publishing Wizard program (which comes with Windows 98) understands this kind of address, so this is the kind of address you use if you transfer your files using the steps in the "Using the Web Publishing Wizard" section later in this chapter.

Saving in an FTP Location

If you have FTP access to the server where you want to store the presentation, you can save it directly there with the Save As dialog box. All you need is the FTP address of the Web server on the Internet and the path of the folder into which you should save. You can get this information from your company's Webmaster or network administrator.

You can save directly whether you are saving as a Web page or just as a regular presentation. Just follow these steps:

Note
The first time you perform the following steps, you must set up the FTP location with Add/Modify FTP Locations, as these steps document. In subsequent sessions, the FTP site you want appears on the Save In list and you can simply select it, skipping the rest of the setup.

1. Open the File menu and choose either Save As or Save As Web Page, depending on the format in which you are publishing.

2. Open the Save In drop-down list and choose Add/Modify FTP Locations. See Figure 27-6.

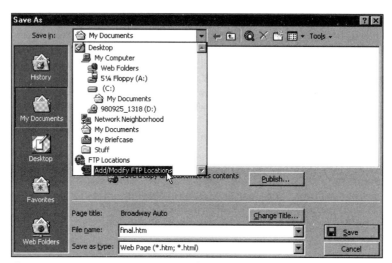

Figure 27-6: Use FTP Locations as the Save In location to save directly to the Internet server.

3. The Add/Modify FTP Locations dialog box appears. Enter the server's FTP address in the Name of FTP site box. See Figure 27-7.

Figure 27-7: Enter a name and address for the FTP location you want to add.

4. You are probably required to log in to the server. If so, click the User button and then type your username in the text box.

5. If you are required to log in, enter your login password in the Password box.

Tip   If you do not have to log in, you can enter anything you want in the Password box, but it is considered courteous to use your e-mail address for it, so the owner of the site you are visiting knows who you are.

6. Click OK. The available FTP locations appear.

7. Double-click the location you just created. If a connection box appears prompting you to connect to the Internet via modem, do so.

8. The top level of folders at the FTP site you specified appear. Double-click the folders to navigate through them to the spot where you are instructed to save your files.

9. When the correct folder appears in the Save In box, click Save.

10. It will take at least a few minutes to transfer the files. While you are waiting, a Transferring File dialog box appears, so you can monitor the progress.

11. When the files have transferred, disconnect your dial-up Internet connection if necessary. Then, check your work by accessing the files using a Web browser. See the "Navigating a Presentation in a Browser" section later in this chapter.

Using the Web Publishing Wizard

Another way to transfer files to a Web server is with the Web Publishing Wizard. This handy program comes free with Windows 98 and is also available for installation from the Office 2000 or PowerPoint 2000 CD-ROM.

Installing the Web Publishing Wizard

If the Web Publishing Wizard is not installed and you have Windows 98, follow these steps to install it:

1. In Windows 98, choose Start ➪ Settings ➪ Control Panel.

2. Double-click the Add/Remove Programs icon.

3. Click the Windows Setup tab.

4. Double-click Internet Tools. A list of Internet tools appears.

5. Click to place a checkmark next to Web Publishing Wizard. See Figure 27-8.

6. Click OK.

7. If prompted, insert the Windows 98 CD-ROM and click OK to continue. Windows installs the Web Publishing Wizard.

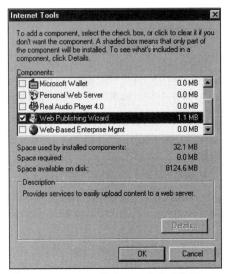

Figure 27-8: Install the Web Publishing Wizard from the Windows 98 CD-ROM, if needed.

If you do not have Windows 98, you can install the Web Publishing Wizard from the Office 2000 CD-ROM. Just rerun the Office 2000 setup program and choose Web Publishing to install from the Office Tools list. See Appendix A for details.

Using the Web Publishing Wizard

To use the Web Publishing Wizard to transfer your files, follow these steps:

1. Save the presentation as a Web page or as a regular presentation, depending on how you want to publish it. Make a note of the location where you save it.

2. In Windows, choose Start ➪ Programs ➪ Internet Explorer ➪ Web Publishing Wizard. Or, if the Web Publishing Wizard is not there, try Start ➪ Programs ➪ Accessories ➪ Internet Tools ➪ Web Publishing Wizard. The Web Publishing Wizard starts.

3. Click Next to begin.

4. On the Select a File or Folder screen, enter the name of the file or folder you want to transfer, or use the Browse Files or Browse Folders buttons to browse for it. See Figure 27-9.

You can transfer only one file or folder at a time. You probably have one file (the home page for your presentation) and one folder (the folder of the same name that contains all the other files), so you will probably have to work through the Web Publishing Wizard twice.

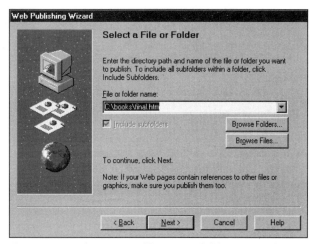

Figure 27-9: Choose one file or one folder to transfer at a time.

5. Click Next.

6. You're prompted for a descriptive name for the Web server. Use a name that you will recognize later, such as Acme Web Server. Then, click Next.

   Or, if you have already been through this process at least once, a drop-down list of servers appears at this point. Select the one you want from the list or click the New button to add one to the list.

7. If you typed a new server name in Step 6, fields appear where you can fill in information about this server. In the URL or Internet address field, enter the Web address that users will use to access the presentation, such as `http://www.mysite.net/PowerPoint`. If you chose an existing server in Step 6, skip to Step 10.

8. In the Local directory field, enter the path to the local folder on your hard disk that corresponds to this URL. This is the folder where you saved your PowerPoint work. See Figure 27-10.

9. Click Next to go on.

10. If prompted to connect to the Internet, do so.

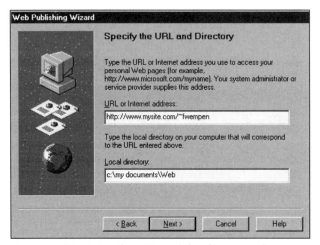

Figure 27-10: Enter the URL and the directory where your network administrator or Internet service provider has instructed you to save your work.

11. When you see a message that the Web Publishing Wizard is ready to publish your files, click Finish.

12. When you see a message that the wizard has successfully published your files, click OK.

13. Repeat the process from Step 2 to publish more files.

Navigating a Presentation in a Browser

Now that your presentation files have been transferred to the Web server, it's time to test them to make sure they work. To do that, you need to use a Web browser. Internet Explorer 5.0 comes with Office 2000 and works very well for this purpose. (It is probably already installed on your PC.) Other Web browsers, such as Netscape Navigator or Internet Explorer 4.0, work fine, too.

To test your work, follow these steps:

1. Open your Web browser. If you chose to install Internet Explorer when you installed Office 2000, or if you have Windows 98, you can start IE by clicking the Internet Explorer shortcut on your Windows desktop. If not, look for your browser on the Start ➪ Programs menu.

2. In the Address box, type the Web address of your presentation's home page. For example, it might be something like `http://www.acme.net/~fwempen/final.htm`. Then, press Enter.

3. The first page appears, as shown in Figure 27-11. Use any of the navigation methods pointed out in the following list to move to each slide, making sure there are no errors.

- Move to the next slide by clicking the > button at the bottom of the window.

- Click the Speaker button to pause or play the narration.

- Click the Full Screen button to switch to a full-screen view of the slide, just like in Slide Show view in PowerPoint. To return to the Web page view, press Esc.

- To jump to a specific slide, click its name in the left pane (the outline). To hide the outline, click the Outline button.

- To expand or collapse the outline, click the Expand/Collapse Outline button.

4. To end the show, close the browser or navigate to a different Web site.

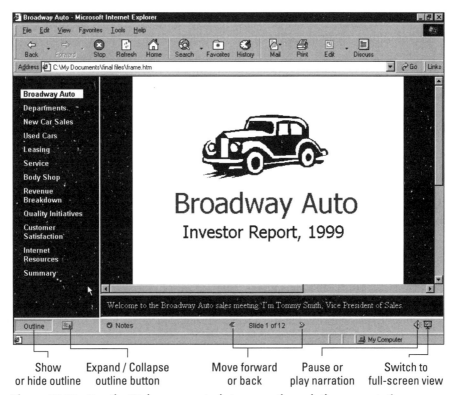

Figure 27-11: Use the Web page controls to move through the presentation.

Creating a Helper Page for Native PowerPoint Shows

If you plan to distribute the presentation as a regular PowerPoint presentation, you must do some extra work. You probably cannot assume that every member of your intended audience owns a copy of PowerPoint, so you should make the PowerPoint Viewer available to them. If you are distributing your presentation internally only (that is, only to people in your company), you can make the PowerPoint Viewer program available on your LAN. If, however, the presentation will be available to the entire Internet, you should create a Web page from which the audience can download the viewer and your presentation file.

Tip   If you are providing the presentation in PowerPoint format, you might want to save it as a PowerPoint Show rather than a regular PowerPoint file. A PowerPoint Show is the same thing as a normal PowerPoint file except it cannot be edited. Using this format prevents people from appropriating your work and making changes to it to make it their own.

You can use any Web page creation program to create this simple page. You can use PowerPoint (which has the advantage of being familiar to you already), FrontPage Express, or Microsoft Word. In this chapter, I show you how to do it with PowerPoint.

Installing the PowerPoint Viewer on Your PC

The PowerPoint Viewer is not installed by default when you install PowerPoint or Office 2000, but you can rerun the setup program and choose it specifically from the PowerPoint group of features (see Appendix A). You might want this viewer installed, for example, to test a PowerPoint file's ability to be shown with the viewer, or to become familiar with the viewer's controls so you can teach others to use it. After you install it, you can find it in the `Program Files\Microsoft Office\Office\Xlators` folder.

Copying the PowerPoint Viewer to the Server

You can use the Web Publishing Wizard, explained earlier in this chapter, to transfer the PowerPoint Viewer to your Web server. Install the PowerPoint Viewer on your own PC, as described in the preceding section. Then, start the Web Publishing Wizard and use it to transfer the file `ppview32.exe` to the same location on the Web server as your other files.

Creating the Starting Web Page

To create a single Web page in PowerPoint, start a new presentation with a single slide in it. Then, create instructions and hyperlinks on it to access the PowerPoint Viewer and your PowerPoint presentation, like the one in Figure 27-12.

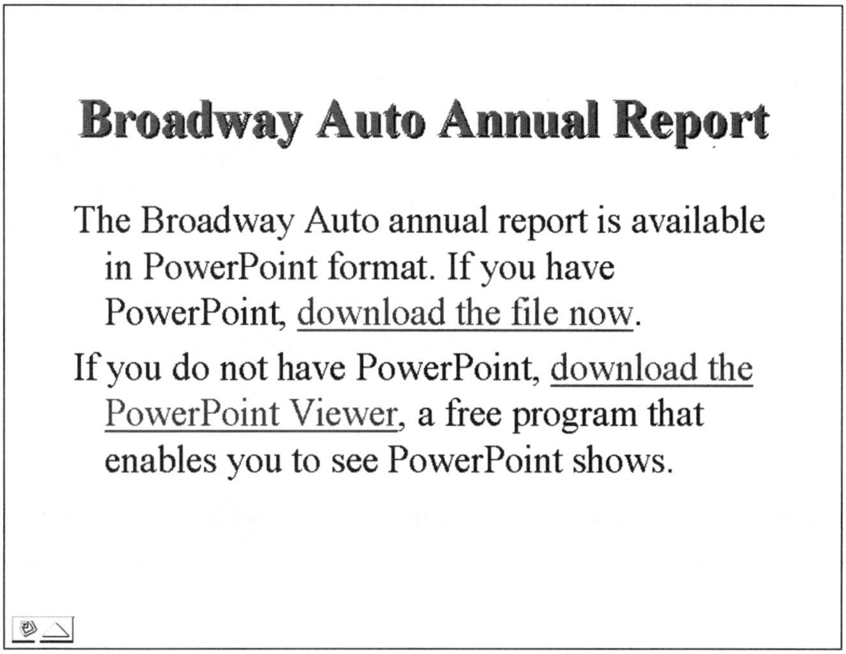

Broadway Auto Annual Report

The Broadway Auto annual report is available in PowerPoint format. If you have PowerPoint, <u>download the file now</u>.

If you do not have PowerPoint, <u>download the PowerPoint Viewer</u>, a free program that enables you to see PowerPoint shows.

Figure 27-12: An instruction page like this one provides links to the downloadable PowerPoint file as well as the PowerPoint Viewer program.

Follow these steps:

1. Start a new presentation. It can either be blank or based on a design template. Do not use the AutoContent Wizard.

2. In the New Slide dialog box, choose the Bulleted List layout. Then, click OK.

3. Add a title to the page in the Title box, replacing the placeholder.

4. Click in the body area, and then click the Bullet List button on the Formatting toolbar to turn off the bullets.

5. Type the instructions. Here's sample wording:

- The Broadway Auto annual report is available in PowerPoint format. If you have PowerPoint, download the file now.

- If you do not have PowerPoint, download the PowerPoint Viewer, a free program that enables you to see PowerPoint shows.

6. Select the text that you want to hyperlink to the presentation file itself. For example, in the sample text above, I might select *download the file now*.

7. Choose Insert ➪ Hyperlink. The Insert Hyperlink dialog box appears. (You probably remember this box from Chapter 26.)

8. Enter the path to the PowerPoint presentation on the server. For example, it might be something like `http://www.acme.net/~fwempen/final.ppt`.

9. Click OK.

10. Select the text that you want to hyperlink to the PowerPoint Viewer. In the sample text, for example, I might select *download the PowerPoint Viewer*.

11. Choose Insert ➪ Hyperlink.

12. Enter the path to the PowerPoint Viewer on the server. For example, it might be something like `http://www.acme.net/~fwempen/pptview32.exe`.

13. Click OK.

14. Choose File ➪ Save As Web Page. The Save As dialog box appears.

15. Enter a name for the starting page in the File name box.

16. If you want to save to an FTP location, select it, as you learned to do earlier.

17. Click Save.

18. If you did not save to an FTP location in Step 16, transfer the newly created page to your Web server with the Web Publishing Wizard, as you learned to do earlier in the chapter.

Working with the PowerPoint Viewer

If you expect your audience to use the PowerPoint Viewer, you should become familiar with it yourself so you can answer any questions that may arise.

The PowerPoint Viewer is a Windows-based program, but it does not create a shortcut for itself on the Start menu or your desktop. You may want to create either or both of these yourself, but you can almost as easily start the program from Windows Explorer or My Computer.

You must install the PowerPoint Viewer from the Office 2000 setup program. Rerun it if needed. See Appendix A.

After you install the PowerPoint Viewer from the Office 2000 or PowerPoint 2000 installation program, you can find the viewer in the following folder: `Program Files\Microsoft Office\Office\Xlators`. The file is called `ppview32.exe`. To run it, navigate to that folder using Windows Explorer or My Computer and double-click the file. See Figure 27-13.

Tip   To create a shortcut for the PowerPoint Viewer on the desktop, drag from the Windows Explorer window to the desktop.

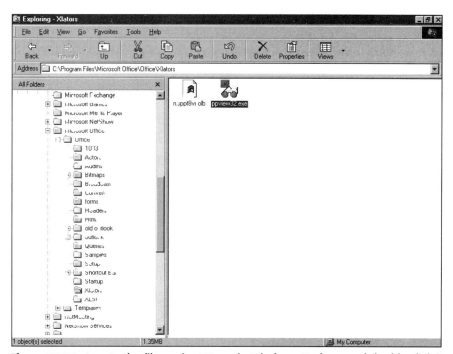

Figure 27-13: Locate the file ppview32.exe in Windows Explorer and double-click it.

The first thing you see when you start the PowerPoint Viewer is a dialog box prompting you to select the presentation to view. See Figure 27-14. From there, follow these steps:

1. Navigate to the folder containing the presentation.

2. Click the presentation's name to select it.

3. If you want to advance the slides manually, click the Manually button. If you want the built-in timings to operate, select Using Timings, if present.

4. Set any of the following options as needed before the show:

   • To print a copy of the slides, click the Print button to open the Print dialog box. From there, click OK to print.

   • To override any of the saved settings for the presentation, click the Options button and choose Override saved settings from the dialog box that appears. See Figure 27-15. Then, choose which settings you want to override and click OK.

   • To enable or disable viewer settings, such as the right-click pop-up menu, click the Options button and select or deselect checkboxes in the Viewer Settings area of the dialog box. Then, click OK.

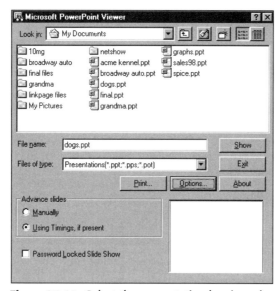

Figure 27-14: Select the presentation be viewed and set any options for it. Then click Show to see it.

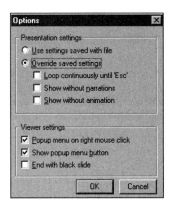

Figure 27-15: Choose any options before the show starts. Many of these are the same as options you have already learned to set in PowerPoint.

5. Click Show to begin the presentation.

6. View the show, controlling it using the same controls you learned about in Chapter 22. If you want to quit early, press Esc.

7. When the presentation is over, or when you press Esc, the Microsoft PowerPoint Viewer dialog box reappears (Figure 27-14). View another presentation or click Exit to leave.

Summary

In this chapter, you learned how to prepare a presentation for Internet distribution. This process involves not only designing the presentation thoughtfully with Internet users in mind, but also saving the file in HTML format or providing a PowerPoint Viewer for the audience's use. You can now save presentations as Web pages, transfer them to Internet servers online, and prepare introductory Web pages that contain links to presentations.

You've learned a lot in the last few chapters, and now it's time to take a break. The last section of this book, "Cutting Edge Power," helps you explore some more specialized and nontraditional topics related to PowerPoint and to public speaking.

The next chapter is all about the noncomputer aspects of giving a live presentation. Your presentation should be nearly perfect by this point, but what about you as a presenter? Are you also polished and ready? In the next chapter, you get some pointers for creating the very best possible impression on your audience.

✦   ✦   ✦

Cutting-Edge Power

What Makes a Great Presentation?

Wow! What a Great Presentation! That's what you want your audience to come away thinking, right?

Most people won't be nit-picky enough to pinpoint exactly what they loved about the experience. Nobody is likely to say, "Weren't the colors in that pie chart on slide 43 artfully chosen?" or "Did you see his tie? I wonder where I can buy one just like it." Instead, you'll leave your audience with an overall impression that they gather from a host of little details, from the color scheme on your slides to the anecdotes and jokes you tell.

In this chapter, you take a short break from the details of PowerPoint and learn about some of the little details that, collectively, can work toward making your audience pleased with their experience.

How to Create Great Slides

Since this is a book on PowerPoint, great slides are the top concern. Your slides should say to the audience, "I had you in mind when I created this," and "Relax; I'm a professional, and I know what I'm doing." Good-looking, appropriate slides can give the audience a sense of security, and can lend authority to your message. On the other hand, poorly done or inconsistent slides can tell the audience, "I just slapped this thing together at the last minute," or "I don't really know what I'm doing."

...g Appropriate Designs for the Occasion

...offers dozens of slide designs, as you've seen throughout this book.
...verse bunch because there are many different presentation situations.
...at some of the presentation design templates that PowerPoint offers
...at kind of message they send to the audience.

Table 28-1	
Design Templates and Suggested Uses	
Design Template	***Colors/Uses***
Blends	A white background, simple design, suitable for almost any situation, but not really a standout in any way. Use when you don't want the design to distract from the message, or when you don't want to make it look like you've gone to too much trouble.
Marble	Dark-green marble background, simple and elegant. Great for financial reports or for more conservative industries like banking.
Soaring	Blue background with a lighter-blue swoop. This design has a modern, open feel to it, and the dark background makes it work well for onscreen shows.
Ribbons	Despite its festive name, this dark-maroon design is really a nice balance of conservative color and font choices and whimsical ribbon background pattern.
Dad's Tie	This white background design has a striped bar with blues, greens, and shades of white/gray/black along the left side. Its bar adds a nice touch of color without looking too formal or fancy.
Factory	This dark-blue design has cogs on it, reminiscent of factory machinery, and its modern sans-serif fonts give a progressive feel. Great for use in any industrial setting.

Choosing Formatting That Matches Your Medium

Are you going to present transparencies on an old-time overhead projector? Or will
you use 35mm slides, or a computer screen? Thinking about the size and quality of
the image that the audience will see can help you make intelligent formatting
choices.

Overhead Projector

Using an overhead projector is never anyone's first choice, but sometimes it's all
that's available. If that's the case, you just have to be a good sport about it. You can
make transparencies by feeding transparency film into your computer's printer.

Caution Make sure you get the kind of transparencies designed specifically for your printer! The kind for ink jets, for example, melts inside a laser printer and ruins it.

An overhead projector image is medium-sized (probably about 36" x 36"), but often of poor quality. You will probably be fighting with room lighting, so your slides may appear washed out. Here are some tips for preparing slides to be shown with overhead projectors:

✦ **Fonts:** For headings, choose chunky block lettering, like Arial Black font, that can stand up to a certain amount of image distortion. For small type, choose clear, easy-to-read fonts like Arial or Times New Roman.

✦ **Text color:** Black letters on a light background stand out well. Avoid semidark lettering, like medium-blue; it can easily wash out under the powerful light of an overhead projector.

✦ **Background color:** Avoid dark backgrounds. You probably will not get each slide perfectly hand-positioned on the overhead projector, and the white space around the edges will be distracting if your transparencies have a dark background.

✦ **Content:** Keep it simple. Overheads are best when they are text-heavy, without a lot of fancy extras or clip art. The overhead projector is an old technology, and slides that are too dressy seem pretentious.

35mm Slides on a Slide Projector

Although 35mm slides are more expensive to create than overhead transparencies, the extra expense may be justifiable. The image size is generally a bit larger, and the image quality is improved. Slides transport well in carousels, and don't get out of order. You also don't have to fumble with placing them manually on the projector, and they don't have that annoying white space around the edges.

Note You can make 35mm slides by sending your PowerPoint file to a slide-making service. One of the largest services, Genigraphics, provides its own driver for PowerPoint, so you can print to a Genigraphics file. Find out from the slide-making service what format they want your slide file to be in.

Here are some guidelines for formatting slides destined to be 35mm slides.

✦ **Fonts:** You can use almost any readable font on 35mm slides. If your audience is going to be sitting far away from the screen, try to stick with plain fonts like Arial and Times New Roman for the body text.

✦ **Text color:** Try light text on a dark background. My personal favorite for 35mm slides is bright yellow text on a navy blue background.

✦ **Background color:** Keep it dark—but not black. Light colors make the screen too bright. Dark blue, dark green, and dark purple are all good choices. Stick with solid backgrounds to compensate for any image distortion onscreen. (Don't attempt patterned, shaded, or clip art backgrounds.)

✦ **Content:** You can use any combination of text and graphics with success, but it has to be static. Builds and transitions don't work with 35mm slides. For example, if you have a bulleted list, don't try to build the bulleted list one bullet at a time from slide to slide, as you learned in Chapter 20. It looks awkward.

Computer-Driven Presentations

If you are lucky enough to have access to a computer-based presentation system, you can show your slides on a PC monitor or TV screen. Some large meeting facilities even have projection TVs that let you project the image onto very large screens. Presenting from a computer is definitely the way to go if it's available because you have all of PowerPoint's presentation controls at hand, as you learned in Chapter 22. You also don't have to print, convert, or otherwise prepare your slides individually, because you can present from a single PowerPoint file.

Here are some guidelines for formatting for this medium:

✦ **Fonts:** The image on a computer screen is nice and sharp, so you can use any fonts you want. If you are presenting to a large group on a small screen, however, make sure you keep all the lettering rather large.

✦ **Text color:** As with 35mm slides, light text on a dark background works well.

✦ **Background color:** Dark backgrounds are best, like dark blue, green, or purple. You are also free to use gradients, shading, patterns, pictures, and other special backgrounds because all of these show up nicely on most monitors.

✦ **Content:** You can go all out with your content. Not only can you include both text and graphics, but also animations, transitions, sounds, and videos.

Strategies for Avoiding Information Overload

When presenting, you want to give the audience exactly the information they need and no more. You don't want them to leave clutching their heads saying, "Wow, that was too much to absorb!" But neither do you want them to leave saying, "What a waste of time!"

So, suppose you have a great deal of information that you need to convey to the audience in a very short time. You want to make sure they absorb it all without feeling overwhelmed. Here are a few ideas to help you accomplish that goal:

✦ Analyze your presentation closely before you give it to make sure that only the essential topics are covered. By trimming some nonessential topics, you make more room to cover the important themes in enough detail.

✦ Don't try to cram every detail on your slides. Use the slides for general talking points, and then fill in the discussion with your speech.

✦ Provide detailed handouts that elaborate on your slides, and make sure the audience receives them at the beginning of the presentation. Then, refer to the handouts throughout the presentation, letting them know that they can read all the details later. See Chapter 21.

✦ Summarize at the end of the presentation with a few simple slides that contain bullet points outlining what the audience should have learned. Chapter 24 covers creating summary slides.

Ten Qualities of an Effective Presentation

See how many of these qualities you can incorporate into your own presentation. An effective slide show:

1. Uses the right PowerPoint design, with colors and fonts chosen to reinforce the message of the presentation.

2. Is designed and formatted appropriately for the audience and the medium. Refer to Chapter 6 for planning help.

3. Is tightly focused on its subject, with extraneous facts trimmed away or hidden for backup use. See Chapter 24.

4. Includes the right amount of text on each slide, without overcrowding. See Chapter 8.

5. Uses artwork purposefully to convey information and create an overall visual impression. See Chapters 12 and 13.

6. Uses graphs and charts rather than raw columns of numbers to present financial or numeric information. See Chapter 14.

7. Employs sound and video to create interest where needed, but does not allow the effects to dominate the show. See Chapters 18 and 19.

8. Uses animations and transitions if appropriate for the audience and message, but does not allow them to dominate. See Chapter 20.

9. Offers the audience handouts that contain the information they will want to take with them. See Chapter 21.

10. Leaves time at the end for a question-and-answer session so the audience members can clarify any points they were confused about.

How to Be a Dynamic Speaker

No miracle cures here—some people are naturally better, more interesting speakers than others. But there are definite steps that all speakers can take to stack the odds in their favor when it comes to giving a successful live presentation. In the following sections, I tell you about some of them.

Choosing and Arranging the Room

If you have any say in it, make sure you get an appropriate size room for the presentation. A too-small room makes people feel uncomfortable and crowded, while a too-large one can create a false formality and distance that can cause people to lose focus easily. You also don't want to have to shout to be heard.

Caution   Along the lines of not shouting, make sure there is a working sound system, with microphone and amplifier available if necessary. Check this detail a few days ahead of time, if possible, to avoid scrambling for one at the last minute.

Next, make sure tables and chairs are set up appropriately. Figures 28-1 through 28-4 illustrate several setups, each appropriate for a certain kind of presentation:

✦ For a classroom setting where the attendees will take lots of notes, give them something to write on, as in Figure 28-1. This arrangement works well when the audience will be listening to and interacting with you, but not with one another.

✦ If you are giving a speech and the audience is not expected to take notes, consider an auditorium setup, as in Figure 28-2. This arrangement is also good for fitting a lot of people into a small room.

✦ If you want the audience to interact in small groups, set up groups where people can see each other and still see you, too. Figure 28-3 shows a small-group arrangement.

✦ To make it easier for the entire group to interact with one another as a whole, use a U-shape, as in Figure 28-4.

Presenter

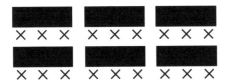

Figure 28-1: In a classroom arrangement, each audience member has plenty of room to write and work.

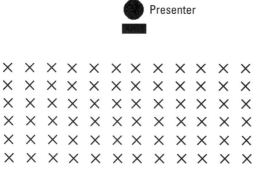

Figure 28-2: Auditorium-style seating fits lots of people into a small space; it's great for company meetings.

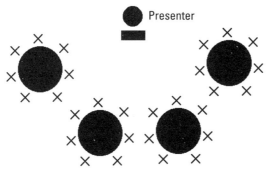

Figure 28-3: Having small groups clustered around tables encourages discussion and works well for presentations incorporating hands-on activities.

Figure 28-4: Arrange the room in a U-shape if you want participants to have discussions as a large group.

What to Wear

The outfit you choose for the presentation should depend on the expectations of the audience and the message you want to send to them. Before you decide what to wear, ask yourself, "What will the audience be wearing?" Choose one of these classifications:

✦ **Very informal:** Jeans, shorts, T-shirts

✦ **Informal:** Nice jeans, polo shirts

✦ **Business casual:** Dress slacks and oxfords, with or without a tie, for men; dress slacks or a skirt and a dressy casual shirt (sweater, silk blouse, vest) for women

✦ **Business:** Slacks and a shirt and tie, with or without a jacket for men; dress or skirt (blazer optional) for women

✦ **Business formal:** Suit and tie for men; suit or dress for women

Then, shape your own choice depending on the feeling you want to convey. To convey authority, dress one level above your audience. Use this dress any time your audience does not know who you are and you need to establish yourself as the leader or the expert. (Most teachers fall into this category.) For example, if your audience is dressed informally, you wear a dress shirt and tie (for men) or a skirt and sweater (for women). Try not to dress more than two levels above your audience, though; it makes them feel intimidated. For example, if you are presenting to factory workers dressed in very informal clothing, you should not wear a business suit.

To convey teamwork and approachability, dress at the same level as the audience or slightly (no more than one level) above. For example, if you are a CEO visiting a factory that you manage, the workers already know you are authoritative; you don't have to prove this. Instead, you want to appear approachable, so if they are wearing informal clothing, you might wear dress slacks and a dress shirt (but no tie) for a man, or slacks and a sweater for a woman.

Avoid dressing below the audience's level. This is almost never a good idea. If you do not know what the audience will be wearing, err on the side of formality. It is better to look a little stiff than it is to look less professional than your audience.

Keeping the Audience Interested

This is an age-old question: How do you keep the audience's attention? There is no one sure-fire trick, but this section includes some hints that you can pick and choose as appropriate for your situation.

Public Speaking Tips

Consider these speech techniques:

✦ *Plant your feet firmly; don't pace.* Pacing looks like nervousness, and people have to work to follow you with their eyes. But keep your upper body mobile; don't be afraid to use arm gestures.

✦ *Use gestures to support your voice.* If you are talking about three points, hold up fingers to illustrate one, two, and three points. If you are talking about bringing things together, bring your hands together in front of you to illustrate. Don't freeze your hands at your sides.

✦ *Don't memorize your speech.* If someone asks a question, it will throw you off and you'll forget where you were.

✦ *Conversely, don't read the speech word for word from your notes.* Notes should contain keywords and facts, but not the actual words that you will say.

✦ *Don't talk with your face in your notes.* Make eye contact with an audience member before you begin speaking.

✦ *Pick a few people in the audience, in different places in the room, and make direct eye contact with each of them, in turn, as you speak.* Talk directly to a single person for the duration of the point you are making and then move on. And don't forget to smile!

✦ *Don't be afraid to pause.* Speaking slowly, with pauses to look at your notes, is much more preferable than rushing through the presentation.

✦ *Emphasize verbs and action words in your presentation.* Remember that the verb is the most powerful element in the sentence.

Content Tips

Consider these content techniques:

✦ If the audience is not in a hurry and you are not rushed for time in your presentation, start with some kind of icebreaker, like an anecdote or joke.

Caution

Be careful with humor. Analyze the joke you plan to tell from all angles, making very sure it will not offend any race, ethnic group, gender, sexual orientation, or class of workers. It is much worse to tell an offensive joke than it is to tell none at all.

✦ Include the audience in interactive exercises that help firm up their understanding of the topic.

✦ Ask questions to see if the audience understood you, and give out small prizes to the people who give correct answers. Nothing energizes an audience into participation more than prizes, even if they are cheap giveaways like key chains and bandanas.

✦ If possible, split the presentation into two or more sessions, with a short break and question-and-answer period between each session.

✦ During the Q&A portion, turn off the slide projector, overhead, or computer screen so people will focus on you and on the question, not on the previous slide.

Managing Stage Fright

Even if you're comfortable with the PowerPoint slides you've created, you still might be a little nervous about the actual speech you're going to give. And that's normal. A study a few years ago showed that public speaking is the number-one fear among businesspeople. Fear of death came in second. That should tell you something.

It's okay to be a little bit nervous because it gives you extra energy and an edge that can actually make your presentation better. But if you're too nervous, it can make you seem less credible.

One way to overcome stage fright is to stop focusing on yourself, and instead focus on your audience. Ask yourself what the audience needs and how you are going to supply that need. Become their caretaker. Dedicate yourself to making the audience understand you. The more you think of others, the less you think of yourself.

Ten Tips for Being a Great Presenter

Need some pointers to quell that nervousness? Keep these things in mind:

1. Rehearse your presentation, including practice in using the audiovisual equipment. Do this well ahead of time to avoid rushing.

2. Dress appropriately for the presentation, based on what the audience will be wearing and how you want them to see you in relation to themselves.

3. Arrive early and check the logistics. Make sure your laptop will hook up to the projector, make sure there is a spare slide projector bulb, and so on. Formulate backup plans against bad luck.

4. Know your audience's needs and plan for how you are going to provide for them.

5. When speaking, speak deliberately, without rushing. Don't be afraid to pause to gather your thoughts or review your notes.

6. Use hand gestures; don't keep your arms glued to your sides.

7. Don't pace or fidget.

8. Do not speak into your notes. Make eye contact with several people in the audience in turn. Do not open your mouth unless you have eye contact with someone.

9. Explain difficult concepts with colorful examples and anecdotes that people will remember.

10. Be sure to leave time for questions at the end. Invite people to stay afterwards and ask more questions individually if there is time.

Summary

This chapter had little to do with PowerPoint, but lots to do with the successful presentations you will make using your PowerPoint slides as a tool. The information you learned here can help a beginning presenter look more experienced, or help an old pro polish his or her skills to perfection.

In the next chapter, you get back into PowerPoint and learn about one of PowerPoint 2000's most exciting new features — team collaboration.

✦   ✦   ✦

Team Collaboration on a Draft Presentation

Few people these days create a presentation with no input or feedback from another living soul. Every presentation usually goes through review cycle upon review cycle, and everybody gets to add his or her two cents about how to make the presentation slides stronger and more meaningful.

The old way of reviewing was to print out and distribute hard copies of a presentation and let everyone mark them up by hand. Then some poor assistant or junior executive would get assigned the task of deciphering all the handwritten notes (some of them directly conflicting with others!) and making the changes in PowerPoint.

Fortunately, PowerPoint 2000 offers many more appealing options for soliciting and receiving feedback on a presentation, as you learn in this chapter.

Sharing Your Presentation File on a Network

If your company has a local area network (LAN), you can copy the presentation file to a drive that everyone can access and let whoever is interested in seeing it take a look. Interested people can then either copy the presentation to their own PCs or view it directly from the network.

If not everyone has PowerPoint installed on their PCs, you might also want to place the PowerPoint Viewer program on the network too, so people without PowerPoint can review the show. You learned about the PowerPoint Viewer in Chapter 27.

Caution   Make sure you copy the presentation file to the network, rather than moving it there. That way, if something happens to the networked copy or the whole network server goes down, you still have access to your presentation.

Configuring Your PC to Share

In a large company, the network includes one or more servers, which are computers that do nothing except run the network and serve up common files that multiple people need. If your network includes a server, one of its hard disks is probably the best place to copy your presentation file. That's because everyone on the network already has access to the server, so no special setup is necessary. See your network administrator for details.

However, if your company uses peer-to-peer networking, there may not be a server to which you can copy the presentation. In that case, you must make one or more folders on your own hard disk accessible to other network users. This may be set up already, but in case it isn't, here are the steps for making it happen:

1. In Windows, choose Start ➪ Settings ➪ Control Panel.

2. Double-click the Network icon. A Network dialog box opens.

3. On the Configuration tab, click the File and Print Sharing button. A File and Print Sharing dialog box opens.

4. Make sure there is a checkmark in the I want to be able to give others access to my files checkbox. See Figure 29-1. Then click OK.

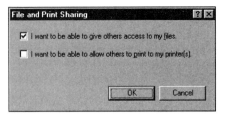

Figure 29-1: Elect to share files on your PC with others.

Note   Choosing to share files in Step 4 does not automatically make all files on your system accessible; you must specifically set up each folder or entire drive you want to share, as you do in the following steps.

5. Click OK again to close the Network dialog box. If prompted to restart your PC, do so.

Creating a Shared Folder

Now that your PC is set up to share files, you must create a folder to share. You can share your entire hard disk, but this is not prudent. You don't want everyone to have access to all your personal files! Instead, create a folder for the express purpose of sharing, and copy everything into it that you want to share.

Follow these steps to create and share a folder:

1. In Windows Explorer or My Computer, create a new folder that you want to share with network users. To do so, right-click and choose New ➪ Folder. Type a name for the new folder and press Enter.

2. Copy into the new folder all the presentation files and other files you want to offer to others. (Include the PowerPoint Viewer if you think someone might need it.)

3. Right-click that folder and choose Sharing from the shortcut menu.

4. In the Properties dialog box that appears, click the Shared As button.

5. Enter a Share Name for the folder, the name by which other network users will know it. See Figure 29-2. The name can be up to 12 characters long.

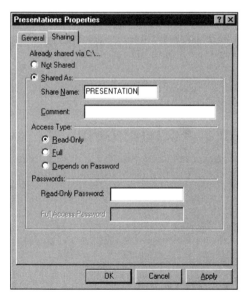

Figure 29-2: Mark Shared As and enter a network name for the folder.

6. If you want to provide a brief description of the folder, enter it in the Comment field.

Note

The comment that you enter appears whenever anyone is browsing the file using Details view (View ➪ Details) in Network Neighborhood.

7. Choose an access type:

- **Read-Only** allows people to view the folder content but not delete or change it.

- **Full** gives access to everyone.

- **Depends on Password** determines a user's access based on a password.

8. If you want read-only access to be password-protected, enter a password in the Read-Only Password box. This box is unavailable if you chose Full as the access type.

9. If you want full access to be password-protected, enter a password in the Full Access Password box. This box is unavailable if you chose Read-Only as the access type.

Note

You can use the passwords to set up multiple levels of access for the folder. If certain people should have read-only access and others full access, set the Access Type to Depends on Password, and assign different passwords to Read-Only and Full Access. Network Neighborhood will prompt for a password, and depending on which password the user enters, read-only or full access is granted.

10. Click OK. The folder is now shared. You can tell it is a shared folder because it has a picture of a hand under it, as shown in Figure 29-3.

Posting a Presentation to Exchange Folder

If your company uses a Microsoft Exchange server to share files, you can easily post a PowerPoint presentation there. (You can ignore this procedure if your company doesn't use Exchange.) To do so, follow these steps:

1. Open the presentation in PowerPoint.

2. Choose File ➪ Send To ➪ Exchange Folder. A list of folders appears.

3. Choose the folder you want to post the presentation to.

4. Click OK.

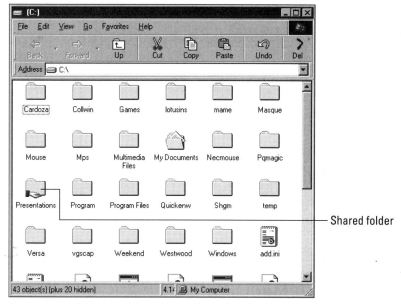

Shared folder

Figure 29-3: Shared folders show a hand beneath them, so you can easily keep track of which folders are shared.

Mailing a Presentation via E-mail

You can attach a PowerPoint presentation file to an e-mail message, just as you can attach any other file. If you use Outlook, for example, you can click the Insert File button on the toolbar to attach a file to an e-mail message you are creating. See Figure 29-4.

You can also send a presentation via e-mail directly from PowerPoint. To do so, follow these steps:

1. With the presentation open in PowerPoint, choose File ⇨ Send To ⇨ Mail Recipient (as Attachment). Your e-mail program opens, with the presentation file as an attachment. See Figure 29-5.

Note

If you have not configured your mail program yet, the Internet Connection Wizard appears at Step 1. If you see that, work through it, providing the information requested, and when you are finished, pick up at Step 2.

Insert File button

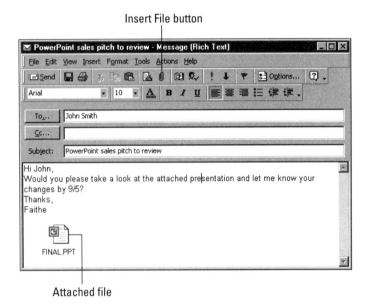

Attached file

Figure 29-4: Most e-mail programs, including Outlook, let you attach files to send along with e-mail messages.

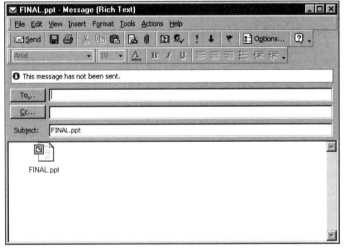

Figure 29-5: If you send a presentation by e-mail from within PowerPoint, the attachment and subject are preentered on the message form.

2. Enter a recipient (or multiple recipients) in the To box.

3. Enter any accompanying message you want in the body text area.

4. Send the e-mail. Outlook and many other mail programs have a Send button that you click to send the message, but your program may vary.

Routing a Presentation

E-mailing a presentation works well if only one person needs to review it or if several people need to review concurrently. But more often, you must follow a chain of review, with first one person reviewing, then another reviewing the original plus the first person's comments, and so on. For situations like this, PowerPoint's Routing feature comes in handy. With routing, the first person sends the presentation to the second, the second to the third, and so on, without it having to come back to you for remailing at each step.

Configuring a File for Routing

To route a presentation file, follow these steps:

1. Within the presentation, choose File ⇨ Send To ⇨ Routing Recipient.

2. If you see a Choose Profile dialog box, click the profile you want to use and click OK. This happens only if you have multiple Outlook or Microsoft Exchange profiles set up on your PC.

3. The Add Routing Slip dialog box opens. Click the Address button. Your address book appears.

4. Select a recipient (or recipients) and click the To button to move their names to the Message Recipients list. See Figure 29-6. Then click OK.

5. The names now appear in the Add Routing Slip dialog box. See Figure 29-7. If you need to rearrange the names on the list, use the Move up and down arrow buttons to move a name on the list.

6. If you want to change the subject in the Subject line, do so.

7. If you want to include comments, add them in the Message text area. I recommend that you give the reviewers a deadline, and possibly remind them about the Comments feature (explained later in this chapter).

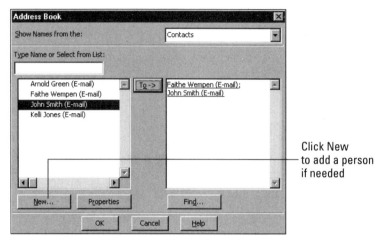

Figure 29-6: Select the routing recipients from your address book.

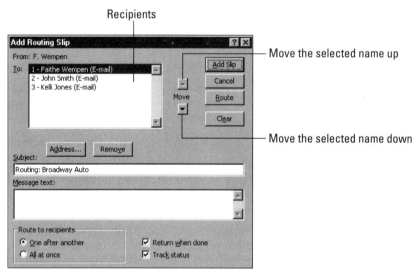

Figure 29-7: Rearrange the order of the recipients if needed.

Note

The following message is automatically sent with the routing, so you do not have to duplicate it in your comments:

The attached presentation has a routing slip. When you are done reviewing this presentation, choose Next Routing Recipient from the Send To menu on the File menu to continue routing.

8. In the Route to Recipients box, choose One after another or All at once to describe how you want the routing done. Use the former if it is important for each person to see the previous people's comments; use the latter if it is not.

9. Click Add Slip.

10. Choose File ➪ Send To ➪ Next Routing Recipient. A Send dialog box appears.

11. Click OK to send it. PowerPoint sends the routing to your e-mail program's Outbox, to be sent to the recipient the next time mail is sent.

When the recipient receives the e-mail message and opens the attachment in PowerPoint, it looks just like a normal presentation. He or she can make changes, save a copy, and perform all the normal PowerPoint activities.

Forwarding a routing to the Next Recipient

To send the presentation to the next routing recipient, the reviewer would then do the following:

1. Choose File ➪ Send To ➪ Next Routing Recipient.

2. When the Send dialog box appears, showing the name of the next recipient, click OK.

And it's on its way again to the next person.

When the routing is finished, the presentation returns to you, the sender, and you can check out the changes and suggestions that were made.

Working with Comments

As you are soliciting feedback from reviewers, you might not want them to make changes directly to the presentation. Instead, you might request that they use the Comments feature to provide their feedback and leave the actual changes to you.

Comments are like yellow sticky-notes that people reviewing the presentation can add, letting you know what they think about individual slides. You can see them in Normal view and also in Slide Show view.

Here are the steps for adding a comment:

1. Display the slide on which you want to add a comment.

2. Choose Insert ➪ Comment. A yellow box appears with your name in it.

Tip   If you have already inserted a comment, the Reviewing toolbar appears, and you can create an additional comment by clicking its Insert Comment button instead of using the menu command in Step 2.

   3. Type your comment. When you are finished typing, click outside the comment box.

When you insert a comment on a slide, the Reviewing toolbar appears. (It's shown in Figure 29-8.) The comment floats on the slide, just like any other object. You can drag it around, change its text formatting, change its size, and so on. You can even delete it — permanently — by selecting it and pressing Delete. But don't delete a comment if you merely wish to hide it temporarily. To hide comments, click the Show/Hide Comments button on the Reviewing toolbar.

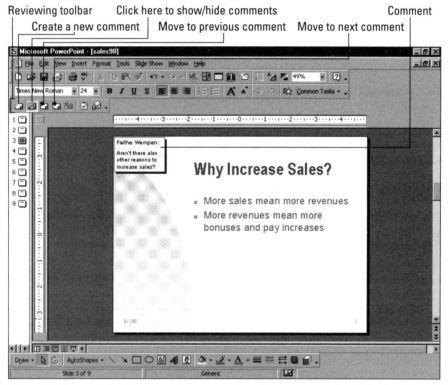

Figure 29-8: By default, comments appear in yellow boxes on the slide, just like sticky notes.

Tip   You can use any AutoShape for the comment boxes. To change a shape, select the comment. Then, click the Draw button on the Drawing toolbar, choose Change AutoShape ➪ Callouts, and then select the shape you want.

When you get a presentation back from a reviewer or from multiple reviewers, there will likely be many comments. You can page through the slides one by one, looking for comments, or you can use the Next Comment and Previous Comment buttons on the Reviewing toolbar to move quickly to the next or previous slide that contains a comment.

Online Collaboration

Microsoft NetMeeting is an online meeting application. It allows you to share information with people at different sites all over the world all at once. (It's sort of like the presentation broadcast you learned about in Chapter 23, but the audience gets to participate, not just watch.) NetMeeting is tightly integrated into PowerPoint (and all the Office 2000 applications), so you can share data from your applications during a meeting.

If you work for a large company, the company may have a NetMeeting server set up. If so, you specify that server name when scheduling the meeting. If not, you can meet online using one of Microsoft's NetMeeting servers.

Scheduling a NetMeeting

You can schedule a NetMeeting either from PowerPoint or from Outlook. (When you schedule in PowerPoint, PowerPoint goes through Outlook to send the messages if Outlook is installed, so you are indirectly using Outlook.)

People attending the meeting must be running NetMeeting when it's time for the meeting, so the e-mail that Outlook sends them serves as a reminder to start the NetMeeting program at the given time and to connect to the named server.

To schedule a NetMeeting through PowerPoint:

1. Open the presentation.
2. Choose Tools ➪ Online Collaboration ➪ Schedule Meeting. If you have not used NetMeeting before, an information box appears. Enter your information (name, e-mail address, and so on) and click OK. A meeting scheduling box from Outlook appears. See Figure 29-9.

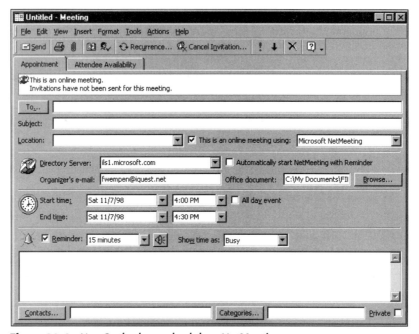

Figure 29-9: Use Outlook to schedule a NetMeeting.

3. Enter the meeting details (time, date, and so on). Make sure you include the directory server that you want to use for the meeting. Find out from your network administrator what directory server to use or use one of the Internet-based Microsoft servers listed on the server list.

4. Click Send. The Outlook message is sent to the participants.

Starting a NetMeeting

To start a NetMeeting from PowerPoint, follow these steps:

1. Open the presentation.

2. Start your online connection if you are using NetMeeting over the Internet. This is not necessary if you are using a NetMeeting server provided by your company over your LAN.

3. Choose Tools ➪ Online Collaboration ➪ Meet Now. The Place a Call dialog box appears.

4. Choose a directory from the Directory drop-down list. For example, to invite people who are already logged on to the NetMeeting server that you plan to use, choose it.

5. On the list of names, choose the name of the person you want to invite. See Figure 29-10. Or to invite a person not on the list, such as someone on your

LAN, click the Advanced button and enter a specific network address or computer name.

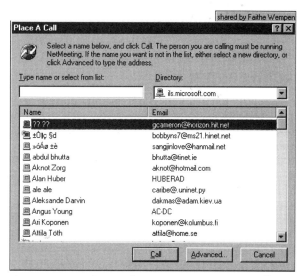

Figure 29-10: Choose the person you want to call from the directory.

6. Click the Call button. A window appears telling you that NetMeeting is trying to find the person.

   Meanwhile, on the other person's screen, an Incoming Call box appears. When the person clicks Accept, the window on your screen goes away and is replaced by the Online Meeting toolbar. The names of the people participating in the meeting appear in a small gray box above it. See Figure 29-11.

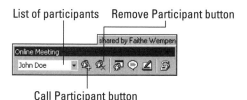

Figure 29-11: The Online Meeting toolbar indicates who has joined your meeting.

7. Now you're ready to meet! See the following section to learn how to control the meeting.

Controlling the Participant List

If you want to invite more people at any time, click the Call Participant button on the Online Meeting toolbar to reopen the Place a Call dialog box. To remove a participant, select him or her from the list of participants and then click Remove Participant.

Controlling a NetMeeting

The presentation appears on the participants' screens immediately. You can move through the presentation normally in any view. Slide Show view gives them the best view of the presentation, but other views, such as one that includes the notes pane, help them see the reasoning behind the choices you made.

Participants see everything you are doing in PowerPoint, and can comment on it using the Chat window described below. However, they cannot control the PowerPoint window in any way unless you cede control to them, as described later.

While the meeting is going on, the participants are not able to use their mouse pointers; they appear as a circle with a line through it. They can switch to other running applications on their systems with the taskbar, however, so they can leave the meeting temporarily to take care of other matters as needed.

Giving Another Participant Control

Only one person can have control of the meeting at a time. By default, this is the person who initiated the meeting. The person who has control can change views, show the presentation in Slide Show view, advance the slides, skip to other slides, and so on. Everyone else can only watch.

If you are holding a collaborative session, you might want to pass control to another meeting participant so he or she can make a point or show an example. You can always take control back later, as the meeting leader.

To let someone else control the presentation (temporarily), follow these steps:

1. Click the Allow Others to Edit button on the Online Meeting toolbar.

2. A warning message appears telling you not to leave the PC unattended while others are in control. (If another person can control your PC, he or she could make dangerous or malicious changes to it.) Click OK.

Note

To regain control at any time, the meeting leader can press Esc. This doesn't work for other meeting participants; they must wait until whoever is in control has ceded it before jumping in. If you are eager to gain control, you can make a comment to that effect using the Chat window, described in the following section.

Taking Control As a Participant

Someone else can take control on his or her own PC by following these steps:

1. Double-click the PowerPoint screen being displayed to take control.

2. A box appears explaining that you are beginning collaboration. Click OK.

3. Now your initials appear on the mouse pointer, and you can edit the PowerPoint presentation from the leader's PC right there on your own screen. Make any edits you like.

4. When you are ready to cede control to some other participant, jump to the NetMeeting window (use your taskbar) and click the Stop Collaborating button. See Figure 29-12.

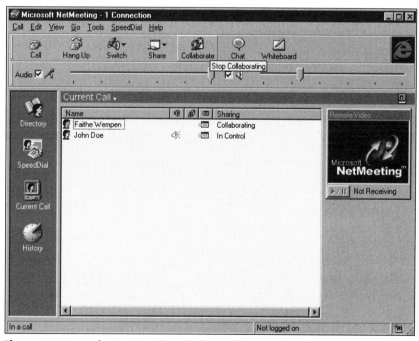

Figure 29-12: In the NetMeeting window, click Stop Collaborating.

5. A warning box appears asking you if you really want to stop collaborating. Click OK. Another participant can now take control.

Chatting with Other Participants

The Chat window is the main means of communication among participants. Open the Chat window by clicking the Display Chat Window button on the Online Meeting toolbar. Only the meeting leader can open the Chat window, but once it is open, everyone can use it on his or her own screen. See Figure 29-13.

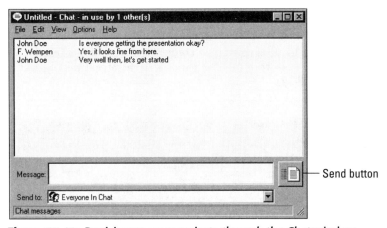

Figure 29-13: Participants communicate through the Chat window.

To send a message using the Chat window, follow these steps:

1. In the Chat window, choose a single recipient or Everyone in Chat from the Send to box.

2. Type your comment in the Message box.

3. Press Enter or click the Send button.

The Chat window has many options that each user can play with. The settings that each user picks do not affect the settings for the other users. These settings include the following:

✦ **File ➪ Save.** You can save the chat log as a text file for later reference.

✦ **File ➪ Print.** You can print the chat log.

✦ **Edit menu.** You can use the Cut, Copy, and Paste commands to move or copy text from the Chat window into another program.

✦ **Options ➪ Chat Format.** You can choose from several window formats that determine how text wraps on the screen and whether the people's names, the date, and the time appear with each comment.

✦ **Options ➪ Font.** You can change the font used to display the chat conversation.

Using the Whiteboard

Only the leader can use the Whiteboard feature, which provides a big blank space for drawing, just like in a regular presentation. To use the whiteboard, click the Whiteboard button on the Online Meeting toolbar. A Whiteboard window appears. It looks a lot like the Paint program that comes with Windows, but has some additional features. See Figure 29-14.

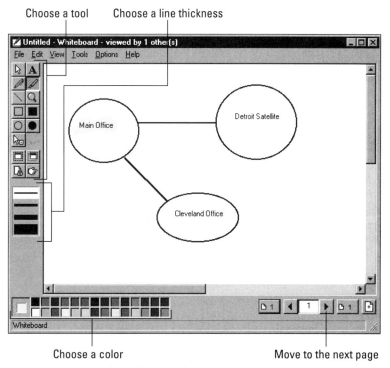

Figure 29-14: Use the Whiteboard program to draw conceptual diagrams during a meeting.

The Whiteboard is its own application, and there isn't space to cover it fully in this book. However, it is extremely intuitive to use, and you should not have any trouble with it. Select a tool from the palette on the left, and if applicable, select a line thickness from the thicknesses below the tools. Then, select a color from the color palette at the bottom. Finally, drag the mouse on the drawing area to create lines, shapes, text, or whatever.

For example, in Figure 29-14, I have drawn a diagram using three ovals and two straight lines. Then I used the Text tool (A) to type some descriptions of the ovals, and I used the Highlight tool to highlight the Main Office label.

You can have multiple pages of drawings and notes; to move to the next page, click the right arrow button in the bottom-right corner.

Tip Experiment with the tools on the Whiteboard ahead of time so you can use them with confidence during the meeting.

Ending a NetMeeting

Only the leader can end a NetMeeting, although individual participants can drop out by closing the NetMeeting program (File ➪ Exit).

To end a NetMeeting, click the End Meeting button on the Online Meeting toolbar. (Participants can leave the meeting by clicking Hang Up on the NetMeeting toolbar.) A message appears that you are in the middle of a meeting and asking whether you are sure you want to exit. Click Yes.

If any chatting took place, a box appears asking whether you want to save the current list of messages. If you do, click Yes, and enter a filename when prompted by the Save As dialog box. Otherwise, click No.

The NetMeeting window reappears. Close it by choosing Call ➪ Exit.

Note All participants need to close NetMeeting on their own PCs and are prompted to save the contents of the chat log, the Whiteboard, and any other elements you used. That way, each person can decide whether the materials from the meeting are worth saving.

Summary

In this chapter, you learned how to solicit feedback and collaboration on your presentation through e-mail, routing, and NetMeeting online meetings. This is pretty advanced stuff! You should be proud of yourself that you have mastered something that 99 percent of PowerPoint users don't know how to use.

In the next chapter, you continue this journey toward PowerPoint Master status by learning how to customize the program to meet your needs. You learn not only how to set simple options, but how to create your own menus and toolbars for total customization.

✦　　✦　　✦

Making PowerPoint Easier to Use

♦ ♦ ♦ ♦

In This Chapter

Changing the way
PowerPoint operates

Creating and
modifying toolbars

Creating and
modifying menus

Using the self-repair
feature

♦ ♦ ♦ ♦

This chapter focuses on tweaking PowerPoint to make it work the way you do. If you have ever said to yourself "I wish PowerPoint worked differently" this chapter is for you.

Changing PowerPoint's Program Options

PowerPoint contains an amazing array of customizable settings. Some of them make purely cosmetic changes, while others enable or disable timesaving or safety features.

In most cases throughout this book, I've been operating with the default options, and assumed that you're doing the same. If you change some of these program options, the steps in this book may not work the same way anymore. You may see more or fewer warning boxes, or the cursor might not behave the same way, or your screen might look different from the ones pictured. That's why I've saved this topic for the end of the book. Now that you understand PowerPoint, these changes won't throw you.

Here's the general procedure for changing an option:

1. Choose Tools ⇨ Options.

2. Click the tab you wish to display. (See the descriptions in the following sections.)

3. Select or deselect checkboxes, enter text, or choose from drop-down lists to state your preferences for a feature.

4. Click OK to apply your changes.

The program options fall into six categories, and each has its own tab in the Options dialog box. In the following sections, I tell you about each of the categories and explain your options within each one.

View Options

The View tab contains options that affect how PowerPoint appears onscreen. See Figure 30-1. They are divided into two types: the Show items, which control what PowerPoint elements appear onscreen as you are building the presentation, and the Slide Show items, which control the way an onscreen slide show behaves.

Figure 30-1: The View tab of the Options dialog box controls which elements are visible onscreen.

Here are explanations of the Show items:

✦ **Startup dialog.** Clear this checkbox if you do not want the PowerPoint dialog box to appear each time you start PowerPoint.

✦ **New slide dialog.** Clear this checkbox if you do not want the New Slide dialog box to appear each time you create a new slide. If you do so, you won't get to choose an AutoLayout for a new slide, so all new slides will be blank.

✦ **Status bar.** Clear this checkbox to suppress the display of the status bar.

✦ **Vertical ruler.** Clear this checkbox to suppress the display of the vertical ruler (when rulers are displayed at all). Remember, you can turn rulers on or off with the View ➪ Ruler command in PowerPoint.

✦ **Windows in taskbar.** If you want each presentation to appear as a separate taskbar item when multiple presentations are open, leave this marked. If you would prefer that PowerPoint work the old way, with a single taskbar item for PowerPoint, clear this box.

Here are explanations of the Slide Show items:

✦ **Popup menu on right mouse click.** Clear this checkbox if you do not want the person running the show to access the shortcut menu by right-clicking during the slide show.

✦ **Show popup menu button.** Clear this checkbox to suppress the arrow button and attached menu that normally appear when you move the mouse during a slide show.

✦ **End with black slide.** Deselect this if you do not want a black slide after the last slide in the show.

General Options

Most of the customization I do to PowerPoint comes from the General tab. See Figure 30-2. It contains the features that I most want to tinker with. This may be the case for you too! Take a look at what the General tab offers:

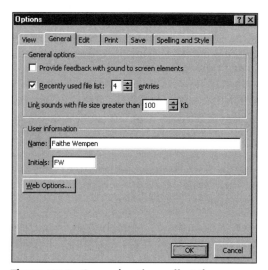

Figure 30-2: General options affect the way PowerPoint operates in general, rather than in a specific area.

✦ **Provide feedback with sound to screen elements.** When this feature is on, PowerPoint plays the sounds associated with various system events. (You set these up from the Windows Control Panel's Sound feature.) Most people find these annoying after the first 10 minutes and turn this feature back off again.

✦ **Recently used file list.** As you learned in Chapter 4, one way to open a file that you have recently used is to select it from the bottom of the File menu. The File menu, by default, lists the four most recently used files. To increase or decrease this number, change the number in this text box. Or, turn off the feature completely by deselecting the checkbox.

✦ **Link sounds with file size greater than.** When you place a sound file in a presentation, PowerPoint creates a link to it, rather than including it in the actual presentation file, if it is larger than the size you list here. This keeps the presentation file from growing too large. For sounds smaller than the listed size, PowerPoint embeds a copy of the sound right in the presentation.

✦ **Name and Initials.** Fill in your name and initials in these fields if they don't already appear. PowerPoint uses this information in several ways, including placing it on the Properties sheet (File ⇨ Properties) and filling it in on certain forms and templates.

✦ **Web Options.** Clicking this button opens the Web Options dialog box, where you can specify how PowerPoint exports presentations to HTML format. I explain this box thoroughly in Chapter 26, so I won't rehash it here.

Edit Options

On the Edit tab, you find a variety of options that affect the way PowerPoint works as you create and change objects on slides. See Figure 30-3. Setting these options the way you feel most comfortable can be a big time-saver and frustration-eliminator. Here are some examples:

✦ **Replace straight quotes with smart quotes.** If you leave this checkbox marked, PowerPoint replaces straight quotation marks (") with curly ones that face inward toward the text it modifies, like "this."

✦ **When selecting, automatically select entire word.** If this checkbox is marked, when you select part of a word, the entire word becomes selected, along with the white space after it.

✦ **Use smart cut and paste.** When this feature is enabled and you move things around with the Cut, Copy, and Paste commands, PowerPoint automatically removes excess spaces and adds spaces when needed.

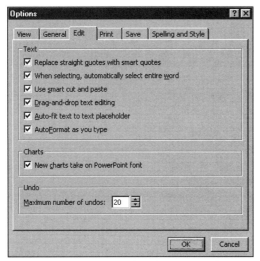

Figure 30-3: Use the Edit tab to set up how PowerPoint behaves when you enter and edit content.

✦ **Drag-and-drop text editing.** Drag and drop is a great feature that enables you to move text from place to place by dragging with the mouse. Most people leave this feature turned on; however, if you don't use the feature and find yourself accidentally moving things when you didn't mean to, turn off the feature.

✦ **Auto-fit text to text placeholder.** When this feature is on and you resize a placeholder text box so that the text no longer fits in it, the text resizes itself so that it doesn't overrun the edges of the box. Very handy!

✦ **AutoFormat as you type.** When this feature is enabled, PowerPoint helps format your text by applying AutoFormatting. For example, if you type a number followed by a period, a space, and some text, PowerPoint formats it as a numbered list item.

✦ **New charts take on PowerPoint font.** This option sets the font for inserted charts at 18-point Arial. Clear the checkbox to use the chart's own fonts.

✦ **Maximum number of undos.** This is the number of actions that PowerPoint remembers so you can undo them with the Edit ➪ Undo command or the Undo toolbar button. The higher the number, the more overhead used up by this remembering, so do not increase this number much past 20.

Print Options

PowerPoint can print a variety of handouts, notes, and other items, and the Print tab lets you fine-tune the printing process. See Figure 30-4.

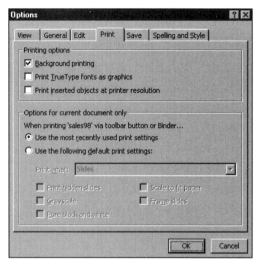

Figure 30-4: The Print tab controls determine how your printouts will print.

✦ **Background printing.** If you clear this checkbox, you won't be able to continue to use PowerPoint after issuing the Print command until the print job has been completely sent to the printer. I recommend that you leave this on.

✦ **Print TrueType fonts as graphics.** This option sends your presentation's TrueType fonts to the printer as pictures rather than as outline font images. If you are having trouble with your printer running out of memory during a print job, experiment with this setting; sometimes changing it can make a difference.

✦ **Print inserted objects at printer resolution.** If an inserted object has a higher graphic resolution than your printer supports, this option dumbs down the object to match the printer's capabilities, thereby decreasing the size of the print file and making it print faster.

✦ **When printing via toolbar button or Binder.** This option controls what happens when you click the Print button on the Standard toolbar. There are two choices here: Use the most recently used print settings, and Use the following default print settings. If you choose the latter, several additional controls become available at the bottom of the dialog box to enable you to specify your preferences. As the section title implies, these settings are applicable only for the active presentation.

Save Options

On the Save tab, you find a number of settings that specify what happens when you save your work in PowerPoint. See Figure 30-5.

Figure 30-5: The Save tab controls how your presentation is saved.

✦ **Allow fast saves.** Fast saves speed up the saving process by saving only the changes to the presentation each time you save. When you are ready to save the presentation for the final time, if you clear this checkbox temporarily, you get a full resave of the entire file, which may result in a smaller file size.

✦ **Prompt for file properties.** If this box is marked, the first time you save a file, the File Properties dialog box appears, prompting you to enter extra information about the file. Some organizations manage their presentation files based on this extra information; most people ignore it.

✦ **Save AutoRecover info every.** PowerPoint periodically saves your work in an AutoRecover file so that if the power goes out before you have saved your work, all is not be lost. You can specify the interval at which this occurs; 10 minutes is the default.

Caution

A lot of people misunderstand the AutoRecover feature. It does not save your work in the same sense that the Save command does. You cannot use it as a substitute for normal saving. Instead, it saves a hidden, temporary copy of your work that is not accessible by normal means. If PowerPoint terminates abnormally, the next time it starts, it reopens any AutoRecover-saved file that it finds. When you exit PowerPoint normally, all AutoRecover-saved files are deleted, as if they never existed.

✦ **Save PowerPoint files as.** You can save your PowerPoint files by default in any of several PowerPoint version formats. If you need to share presentation files with other people who use older versions of PowerPoint, you should set this to the oldest version that you have to exchange with. Newer versions can open older files, but not vice-versa.

✦ **Default file location.** By default, PowerPoint saves your work in the My Documents folder. You can change this setting by entering any drive and folder you want.

Spelling and Style Options

On the Spelling and Style Options tab, shown in Figure 30-6, you find settings that control the way the Spelling program runs in PowerPoint and that turn on/off and control the Style Checker. (Chapter 17 covers these features in detail.)

Figure 30-6: The Spelling and Style tab lets you fine-tune these two proofreading features.

✦ **Check spelling as you type.** This option does just what it says; deselect this box if you do not want PowerPoint to run a spelling check in the background as you work.

✦ **Hide spelling errors in this document.** Marking this checkbox suppresses the wavy red lines that indicate spelling errors on a slide.

✦ **Always suggest corrections.** This option controls whether PowerPoint offers spelling suggestions or not. If this option is turned off, you must click the Suggest button in the Spelling dialog box to see the suggestions. Turning this off can speed up the spell check somewhat on slower computers.

✦ **Ignore words in UPPERCASE.** When this checkbox is marked, all-uppercase words are not spell-checked.

✦ **Ignore words with numbers.** When this checkbox is marked, strings of letters that contain numbers are not spell-checked.

✦ **Check style.** This checkbox enables and disables the style checker.

✦ **Style Options.** Click this button to open the Style Options dialog box, described in Chapter 17, where you can configure how the Style Checker works.

Customizing Toolbars

As you know, the toolbars in PowerPoint change depending on what you're doing. For example, in Slide Sorter view, the Slide Sorter toolbar appears; it goes away when you switch to another view. And when you're working on a picture, the Picture toolbar appears. In Chapter 2, you learned that you can display and hide toolbars by right-clicking a toolbar and selecting from the pop-up list.

You can also customize a toolbar to show the buttons you want it to display. You might remove buttons that you never use, for example, or add buttons for features that you frequently use. You can even add entirely new toolbars of your own, and populate them with any buttons you like.

Changing What Buttons Appear on a Toolbar

Not all PowerPoint users use the program in the same way, and you may find that you frequently use a few commands for which there are no buttons on any of the toolbars. For example, perhaps you often apply the superscript attribute to text. Since there is no toolbar button for superscripting, each time you use it you must choose Format ➪ Font, click the Superscript checkbox, and then click OK. You could save yourself a lot of time by adding a Superscript button to the Formatting toolbar that toggles the superscript attribute on/off. (You could also create one for subscript if you also use it often.)

To add a new toolbar button, follow these steps:

1. Choose Tools ➪ Customize. The Customize dialog box opens.

2. Click the Commands tab.

3. Select a menu or toolbar from the Categories list. All the buttons, commands, and options available from that menu or toolbar appear on the Commands list to the right. See Figure 30-7. For example, many commands on the Format menu open dialog boxes full of options. When you select Format in the Categories list, a complete list of all the options from those dialog boxes appears on the Commands list.

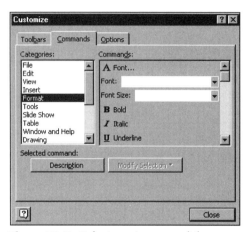

Figure 30-7: Select a category and then select a command within the category.

4. Scroll through the Commands list and select the command that you want to make into a toolbar button. Some of the commands listed have ellipses (…) after their names. If you choose one of these, the button you add to the toolbar will open a dialog box. Others (for example, Font in Figure 30-7) have a drop-down list after their names. Choosing one of these places a drop-down list on the toolbar.

5. Drag the command from the Commands list to a toolbar. As you drag onto a toolbar, your pointer becomes a bold vertical line that indicates where the new button will go. When you release the mouse button, the command becomes a button on that toolbar.

6. Repeat Steps 3 through 5 to add more buttons if you want.

7. If you want to remove any buttons from the toolbar, drag them away from the toolbar.

8. When you're finished, click Close.

As you saw in Step 7, when the Customize dialog box is open, you can not only add buttons, but you can also remove them. You can also rearrange buttons by dragging them from one toolbar to another or from one spot to another on the same toolbar.

Caution   When the Customize dialog box is open, none of the menu commands and tool-bars works normally; instead, they respond to your dragging them around. So don't try to use any of the menus when the Customize dialog box is open (for example, don't try Edit ⇨ Undo to reverse a button-dragging action), or you might accidentally make a change to the menu itself.

If you make mistakes in customizing one of PowerPoint's toolbars, you can undo your changes by selecting the toolbar from the Toolbars tab of the Customize dialog box and clicking the Reset button. This works only with the toolbars that come with PowerPoint, not toolbars you have created yourself (which you learn to do in the following section).

Creating New Toolbars

Sometimes a nip and tuck at an existing toolbar just isn't enough. Perhaps you need to add ten buttons — there won't be enough room for them on an existing toolbar! In cases like that, it's best to create a brand-new toolbar. For example, if you work a lot with multiple presentations, frequently arranging the panes for various purposes, you might want to create a window-arranging toolbar that contains buttons that cascade, arrange all, and so on.

To create a toolbar, follow these steps:

1. Choose Tools ➪ Customize.

2. Click the Toolbars tab. See Figure 30-8.

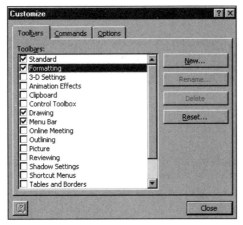

Figure 30-8: You can create your own toolbars from here.

3. Click the New button. The New Toolbar dialog box appears.

4. Type a name for the new toolbar in the Toolbar Name text box (for example, Window Control) and click OK. A little floating window appears alongside the Customize dialog box. This is your new toolbar. See Figure 30-9.

New toolbar

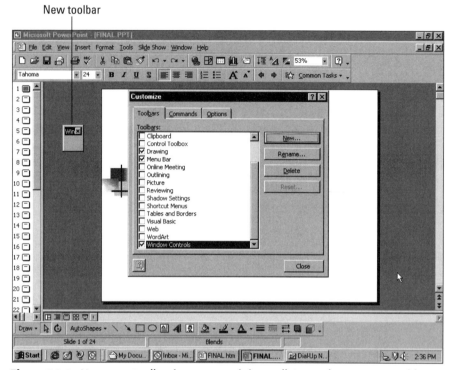

Figure 30-9: Your new toolbar is empty, so it is small. It gets larger as you add buttons.

Note If you don't see the new toolbar, drag the title bar of the dialog box to move it. The new toolbar might be behind it.

5. (Optional) If you want the new toolbar to be anchored at the top of the screen, like the other toolbars, drag its title bar up to the position where you want it. See Figure 30-10.

Tip If you plan to use the toolbar in its docked position at the top or bottom of the screen, drag it into place (Step 5) before you add buttons to it (Step 6). That way, you can gauge how many buttons can fit on the toolbar without running off the screen.

6. Add buttons to the new toolbar, as you learned in the preceding section.

7. When you are finished, click Close.

You can make a toolbar appear only when a certain template is in use if you like. Just open the template for editing (select File ➪ Open and then choose one of the templates). Then create the new toolbar and save the template. The toolbar is saved with it.

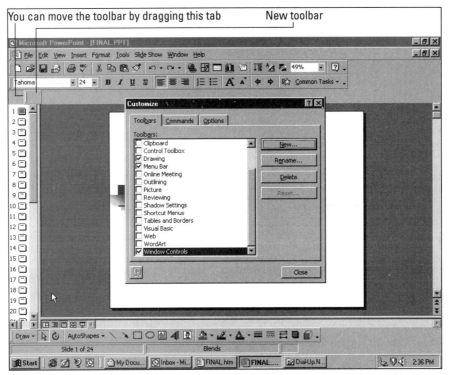

You can move the toolbar by dragging this tab   New toolbar

Figure 30-10: When the toolbar is anchored (docked), it no longer has a title bar.

Choosing Which Toolbars to Display

You have already learned how to display and hide toolbars—just right-click any toolbar and choose the one you want to display or hide from the shortcut menu. A checkmark means the toolbar is displayed.

Figure 30-10 shows another way to choose which toolbars to display or hide. Each toolbar listed on the Toolbars tab of the Customize dialog box has a checkbox beside it. Click to place or remove checkmarks to display or hide each toolbar.

Managing Your Toolbars

You cannot delete the toolbars that come with PowerPoint, but you can delete the custom toolbars you create yourself. To do so, click the checkbox next to the toolbar's name on the Toolbars tab and then click the Delete button.

Like deleting, renaming works only with toolbars you've created yourself. To rename a toolbar, select it from the Toolbars tab of the Customize dialog box and then click the Rename button. The Rename Toolbar dialog box appears. Type a new name in the Toolbar Name text box and click OK.

Customizing Menus

Customizing menus is a lot like customizing toolbars, but for some reason many people are more afraid of doing it. It's not complicated, really. When the Customize dialog box is open, the menus become customizable, just like the toolbars. With the Customize dialog box open, you can do the following:

✦ Drag a menu from one spot to another to rearrange the order in which menus appear.

✦ Drag a menu away from the menu bar to remove it (not recommended, because you won't have access to its commands anymore).

✦ Click a menu to open it and then drag a command to a different spot on the menu (or off the menu completely to remove it).

✦ Rename a menu by right-clicking it and typing a new name in the Name text box on the shortcut menu.

You can also create your own new menus and add commands to them. To create a new menu, follow these steps:

1. If the Customize dialog box is not open, open it (Tools ➪ Customize).

2. Click the Commands tab.

3. Choose New Menu at the bottom of the Categories list. See Figure 30-11.

Figure 30-11: Choose New Menu from the Categories list and then drag the words "New Menu" from the Commands list to the menu bar.

4. Drag the words "New Menu" from the Commands list to the spot on the menu bar where you want the new menu. The new menu appears with the name New Menu.

5. To change the menu name, right-click it and type a new name in the Name text box. Press Enter when you're finished.

6. To add commands to the menu, locate the command you want to add on the Commands list (after choosing the appropriate category) and drag it up to the new menu. When the mouse pointer touches the new menu, the menu opens, so you can drag the command onto it. Then release the mouse button.

7. Repeat Step 6, filling your new menu with the commands you want.

8. Click Close when finished.

If you right-click one of PowerPoint's default menu's names, you can see that the name of a menu has an ampersand (&) in it. The ampersand precedes the letter that should appear underlined. (Remember, the underlined letter can be pressed along with Alt to open a menu.) For example, F&ormat means the *o* will appear underlined. When you are naming menus that you create yourself, don't forget to add an ampersand in the name to indicate which letter should be underlined. Make sure you choose a letter that none of the other menu names is currently using as their underlined letter.

Setting Toolbar and Menu Options

While the Customize dialog box is open, take a quick look at its Options tab, shown in Figure 30-12. There are a few options here you might find useful:

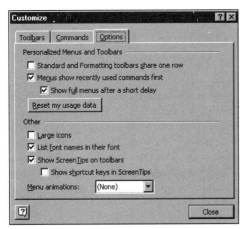

Figure 30-12: The Options tab in the Customize dialog box contains a few miscellaneous settings for menus and toolbars.

✦ **Standard and Formatting toolbars share one row.** You learned about this setting at the beginning of this book. By default, PowerPoint shows these two toolbars on a single row, but you can easily put them on separate rows either by deselecting this checkbox or by manually dragging one of the toolbars to a different row at any time.

✦ **Menus show recently used commands first.** This new feature in PowerPoint 2000 displays recently used commands on a menu when you first open it, and then the remaining commands a few seconds later. This option is on by default; to turn it off, deselect the checkbox.

✦ **Show full menus after a short delay.** This option works in conjunction with the above one. If you turn it off (not recommended), you will not be able to access the less-used commands from the menu system at all.

✦ **Reset my usage data.** PowerPoint watches you work to see which commands you use. After you use a command, it is placed on a Recently Used list and appears when the menu first opens. To reset the Recently Used list to the default list that comes with PowerPoint, click this button.

✦ **Large Icons.** This option makes the buttons on the toolbars larger. This feature is helpful if you have poor eyesight, but fewer icons fit on the screen at once.

✦ **Show ScreenTips on toolbars.** Deselect if you don't want ScreenTips popping up whenever you position your mouse pointer over a toolbar button.

✦ **Show shortcut keys in ScreenTips.** Select this checkbox if you want the ScreenTips to include any shortcut key equivalents for the button.

✦ **Menu animations.** Open this drop-down list and choose an animation type if you like. (The default is None.) This option makes the menus open with more of a flourish, but it may make slower computers run even more slowly.

Using the Self-Repair Feature

PowerPoint requires dozens of files to operate, and if any one of them is corrupted or missing, PowerPoint might not run properly.

A file can get corrupted or deleted in several ways. Try to avoid the following:

✦ Shutting down the computer while PowerPoint is running, either intentionally or as a result of a power outage. This can cause disk errors. Disk errors can be corrected with ScanDisk (Start ➪ Programs ➪ Accessories ➪ System Tools ➪ ScanDisk), but if the disk errors are allowed to remain, the errors can compound, causing problems with more and more files.

✦ Accidentally deleting some files. Not all the files that PowerPoint needs are stored in the Program Files folder; some of them are in the Windows folder. When you are doing a disk cleanup, you might press the Delete key at the wrong time and wipe out a needed file.

✦ Uninstalling a program that shares some files with PowerPoint and choosing to delete the shared files. The Uninstall utility may not inform you that PowerPoint needs the shared files; you won't have a clue until you try to run PowerPoint and it won't work.

✦ Introducing a virus. Some computer viruses can damage your hard disk's filing system, causing it to misplace or corrupt files. If you have recently detected and removed a virus and PowerPoint doesn't work, suspect this cause.

Whatever the reason for your problems, if PowerPoint doesn't run properly, you need to fix it. In previous versions of PowerPoint, your only recourse was to completely reinstall the application, but PowerPoint 2000 comes with a Detect and Repair feature that can find and fix missing or corrupted files without a full reinstallation.

To repair PowerPoint, follow these steps:

1. Make sure the PowerPoint 2000 or Office 2000 CD-ROM is in your drive.

Tip   If you put the Office 2000 CD in your CD-ROM drive, the installation program may start and you may see an option to Repair Office 2000. This option checks and repairs all your Office 2000 applications, not just PowerPoint. If PowerPoint can be opened at all, click Cancel to close this installation box and run the repair utility from within PowerPoint, as described in Step 2. If you cannot start PowerPoint, you have to run the repair utility from the CD.

2. In PowerPoint, choose Help ⇨ Detect and Repair. The Detect and Repair dialog box appears. See Figure 30-13.

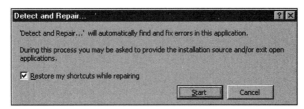

Figure 30-13: Click Start to begin repairing PowerPoint.

3. Wait for Windows to check PowerPoint. A dialog box appears telling you that the application is being checked. This takes a long time; be patient.

4. When you see a message that the application has been successfully repaired, click OK.

Summary

In this chapter, you learned how to make PowerPoint your very own by customizing its features, menus, and toolbars. Now there's no excuse for nonproductivity because you are free to make PowerPoint work just the way you want it to.

In the next, final chapter, you learn how to automate your work with macros. Macros are sets of recorded steps that you can play back to save time if you do the same lengthy procedures frequently.

✦   ✦   ✦

Writing Your Own Macros

Macros are recorded sets of steps that you can play back to perform tasks more easily. For example, suppose you frequently need to import your company logo, resize it, and move it to the top-left corner of a slide. You can create a macro that does that, and save yourself several steps.

Macro recording works a lot like tape recording. You click Record, and PowerPoint records all your actions until you click Stop. The recording is saved under a unique name, and you can play back the recording at any time to reperform the actions.

You can also write your own macros using the Visual Basic Editor provided in PowerPoint, but this gets a little tricky. To write macros, rather than record them, you must know something about Visual Basic programming, and most of us have never studied that. So most people find it much easier to record macros than to write them. However, if you need to make a minor change to a recorded macro, such as removing a command that you didn't mean to record, the Visual Basic Editor works well even for nontechies. You learn to work with the Visual Basic Editor later in this chapter.

Here are some ideas for using macros:

- ✦ Insert boilerplate text, such as disclaimers.
- ✦ Apply a complex set of formatting, such as text size, paragraph alignment, and line spacing.
- ✦ Insert the company logo.
- ✦ Set a default slide transition effect for the presentation.
- ✦ Create a graph from a selected table and place it on a slide.

Recording a Macro

Before you record a macro, THINK. Think about exactly what you want to record, and from what position you want to start. Keep in mind that everything you do after clicking Record will be recorded. For example, suppose you want to create a macro that applies certain formatting to text. You already know that before you can format text, you must select it, but you don't want the text selection to be part of the macro, because you will select different text each time. So select some text first, before you start recording. Along those same lines, if you want to record a macro to format graphics in a certain way, select a graphic before you start recording so that the graphic selection won't be part of the macro.

You also need to think about where you are going to store the macro. If the macro should be used only in the active presentation, record it while that presentation is open. If you want it to be available in every presentation based on a certain template, open that template. (Remember to delete any dummy content that you create in the process of recording the macro in the template so that content does not become part of the template.)

When you're sure you know what you need to do and you're sure you want to start recording, follow these steps:

1. Choose Tools ➪ Macro ➪ Record New Macro. The Record Macro dialog box opens.

2. Enter a name for the macro in the Macro name box. Be descriptive. For example, if you plan to record a macro that makes text bold, italic, and underlined, you might call it BoldItalicUnderline. See Figure 31-1.

Note Macro names must begin with a letter and can contain up to 80 characters. You can't use any spaces, and no symbols are allowed except the underscore character. You also can't use any Visual Basic keywords for the name, such as Private, Public, Integer, or Sub.

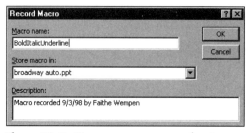

Figure 31-1: Name your macro, and enter a description for it if desired.

3. If you have more than one presentation or template open, choose the one in which you want to store the macro from the Store macro in drop-down list.

4. (Optional) Edit the description in the Description box, if desired. This is a good place to put an explanation of what the macro does if the name is not self-explanatory.

5. Click OK. A tiny floating toolbar appears with a square in it, as shown in Figure 31-2. That is the Macro toolbar, and that square is the Stop button. You can click it at any time to stop the recording.

Figure 31-2: The Macro toolbar provides a Stop button for stopping the recording.

6. Perform the steps that you want to record.

Caution

When you are recording, you can use the mouse to click commands and options, but any mouse movements in the Presentation window are ignored. For example, if you move the insertion point or select an object, that action isn't recorded. You must use the keyboard if you need to record such activities. Certain toolbar buttons' actions aren't recognized, either. For example, the Increase Font Size and Decrease Font Size buttons can't be recorded.

7. When you are finished, click the Stop button to stop recording.

When you finish the above steps, the Macro toolbar goes away, and it's as if nothing has happened. But don't be fooled; your macro is safely hidden away. Use the steps in the following section to play it back.

Playing a Macro

There are two ways to play a macro. The normal way is to use Tools ⇨ Macro ⇨ Macros, as outlined in the following section, but that's not terribly convenient. The alternative takes more setup, but is easier in the long run: assigning a macro to a button on a toolbar.

Playing the Macro from the Macro Dialog Box

Here's the most straightforward way to play a macro. It doesn't require any special setup.

1. Choose Tools ⇨ Macro ⇨ Macros or press Alt+F8. The Macro dialog box opens. See Figure 31-3.

Figure 31-3: Choose a macro and then click Run.

2. If the macro is not in the active presentation, open the Macro in drop-down list and choose All open presentations.

3. Select the macro from the Macro name list if more than one is listed.

4. Click Run. The macro runs.

If you're thinking "that's too much work!," see the following section for steps that make it easier to run that macro.

Note To play a macro from the Macro dialog box, the presentation or template in which you created it must be open. However, you can use a macro toolbar button regardless of which presentation is open. Therefore, it's a good idea to create a special Macros toolbar and place buttons for all your macros on it. That way, all macros are available in all presentations.

Assigning a Toolbar Button to a Macro

In Chapter 30, you learned how to modify toolbars by adding your own buttons for common commands. But you can add buttons for macros, too, and it's just as easy as adding any other button. Follow these steps:

1. Choose Tools ➪ Customize. The Customize dialog box appears.

2. Click the Commands tab.

3. Scroll down the Categories list and select Macros. A list of all the macros in the active presentation appears. See Figure 31-4.

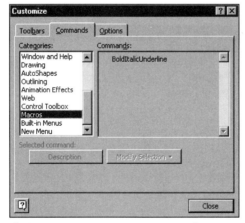

Figure 31-4: Drag a macro to a toolbar to create a button for it.

4. Drag the macro from the Commands box to a toolbar. (Create a new toolbar if you want, as explained in Chapter 30.)

5. (Optional) To change the button name, right-click the button and type a new name in the Name box. Or, to add a picture, right-click the button, choose Change Button Image, and then click one of the pictures displayed. See Figure 31-5.

Figure 31-5: Change the button's name or choose a picture to use instead of or in addition to a name.

6. (Optional) If you want to use the image alone (without the button text), right-click the button and choose Default Style.

7. When you have finished creating the button, click Close to close the Customize dialog box.

Editing a Macro with Visual Basic

When you're recording a macro, errors inevitably occur. Perhaps you meant to click the Bold button and hit the Italic button instead, so you had to turn italics back off again. Or maybe you opened the wrong menu.

If the macro performs its function, even with the errors, you might want to leave it alone. For example, it doesn't hurt anything if the macro turns Italics on and then off again, because the end result is that it's off. But if there are a lot of mistakes in a complex macro, it can take a little longer for the macro to run. Some people, too, are sticklers for efficiency and can't stand the thought of their macro being longer and more convoluted than necessary, regardless of the performance issues.

To edit a macro, you use the Visual Basic Editor. This is a scary-sounding program, but as long as you stick to editing with it, you should be fine.

Follow these steps to edit a macro:

1. Choose Tools ➪ Macro ➪ Macros or press Alt+F8. The Macro dialog box appears (refer back to Figure 31-3).

2. Click the macro you want to edit.

3. Click Edit. The Visual Basic Editor opens with your macro in it. See Figure 31-6. If you have more than one macro recorded in the same file, both macros appear in the Module1 window, regardless of which one you chose.

This is one macro . . .

. . . and this is another

Figure 31-6: The macros in your PowerPoint file open in the Visual Basic Editor.

4. To remove a line from the macro, highlight it and press Delete. You can figure out what a line does by reading it carefully. For example, this line turns the Bold attribute on by settings its value to True:

```
ActiveWindow.Selection.TextRange.Font.Bold = msoTrue
```

5. When you are finished editing the macro, choose File ➪ Close and Return to Microsoft PowerPoint or press Alt+Q. Your changes are automatically saved.

Deleting a Macro

To delete a macro, follow these steps:

1. Choose Tools ➪ Macro ➪ Macros to open the Macro dialog box.

2. Select the macro you want to delete.

3. Click Delete. A confirmation box appears.

4. Click Yes.

More About the Visual Basic Editor

Visual Basic is a rich programming language, and the version of it that works within Office applications (Visual Basic for Applications, or VBA) enables you to write complex macros and even build miniapplications with dialog boxes that run within PowerPoint. This is way beyond what most business users would ever consider doing, but you may nevertheless be curious about the Visual Basic Editor window that you saw in Figure 31-6.

The Visual Basic Editor is divided into three panes: Project, Properties, and Code. The Project window shows a hierarchy of the modules in the presentation. All of the macros you record are stored in Module1, so you don't have to worry about this much. The Properties panel shows the properties for the module. This pane is FYI only too, as far as beginners are concerned.

The main panel that you work with is the Code window, the big one. In it are the lines of programming code that make up your macro.

Here are some things to note about the code. Some example code appears in Figure 31-7.

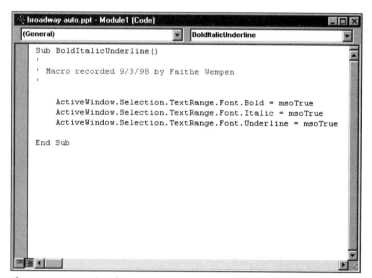

Figure 31-7: A simple macro's code. This macro makes text bold, italic, and underlined.

✦ Each macro begins with the word Sub, followed by the macro name.

✦ Each macro ends with the words End Sub.

✦ Each command of the macro is on its own line.

✦ Some lines begin with I symbols, such as the Macro recorded… line in Figure 31-7. These lines are comments and are ignored when the macro runs.

✦ Each command in the macro narrows down what's being done through a series of words separated by periods. For example, the first line of code in Figure 31-7 starts with Active Window (the active presentation), then narrows it down to Selection (that is, whatever is selected before you run the macro), then TextRange (it's a text range), then Font (what you want to control about the text), and then the attribute (Bold), and finally a value for that attribute (True).

If you want to experiment with Visual Basic, you owe it to yourself to install the online Help for it. This help is not installed by default. You can install it by clicking the Help button on the toolbar. A box appears asking whether you want to install the Answer Wizard. Follow the prompts to do so. (You need your PowerPoint or Office CD-ROM.) After you install the Help system, Rocky the Office Assistant and the entire Help system are at your disposal.

Don't think, however, that you can teach yourself Visual Basic programming from scratch just by reading the Help system. It's good, but the help there is slanted toward people who already know something about programming. You won't find many easy explanations of how programming works. If you want to write your own Visual Basic macros from scratch, take a Visual Basic class at your local community college.

Summary

In this chapter, you learned how to automate your work with macros. Macros aren't for everyone — they take some time to set up and may not be worth the trouble if you don't have tasks that you perform over and over the same way. But for those who need them, they can be a real time-saver.

This concludes the main part of the book. Appendix A explains how to install PowerPoint (which you doubtless have already done!), and Appendix B explores the content of the CD-ROM that accompanies this book.

✦   ✦   ✦

Installing PowerPoint

You can purchase PowerPoint by itself or as part of the Office 2000 suite. The latter is the more common way of acquiring it; Office 2000 is the best-selling business application suite in the world. PowerPoint 2000 comes on all versions of Office 2000 except the Small Business Edition.

Either way, it comes on a CD-ROM, and you must install it on your PC in order to use it. Installation involves several processes:

+ Copying files from the CD to your hard disk.
+ Decompressing files that have been compressed for shipping.
+ Adding information in your Windows configuration files to help Windows recognize PowerPoint.

All of this happens behind the scenes, however; all you do is issue the installation command, and the setup program does the rest.

Using the Setup Program

To start the Setup program, place the Office or PowerPoint CD in your CD-ROM drive. The program should start automatically. If it does not, open the My Computer window and double-click the CD-ROM drive icon.

The Setup program is fairly self-explanatory, except for a few areas. Rather than walk you through the many steps that are easy, I'll save my breath here for the hard stuff. In most cases, you simply follow the prompts, clicking Next to move to the next screen and entering the data requested.

User Information

The very first thing the Setup program asks for is user information. See Figure A-1. The CD key is the tricky thing here. The pre-entered CD key does not match the number on the back of your CD's jewel case. What's up? Well, the pre-entered key allows somebody who doesn't have the real one to use PowerPoint (or Office) on a trial basis for 25 uses. After 25 uses, you must enter a real CD key. If you enter the one from the CD's jewel case from the beginning, you're never bothered with this.

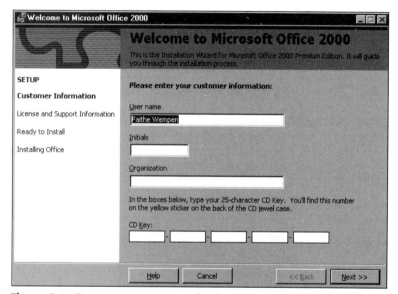

Figure A-1: Enter your name, organization, initials, and CD key.

End User License Agreement (EULA)

You must accept the license agreement before you can install. It's a contract that specifies how you can and can't use the software. This is boring legalese, but the crux of it is that you must not use the software on more than one PC or share it on a network without buying a multiuser license. Click I accept the terms in the License Agreement and then click Next to move on.

Customization

After the user info and the EULA, you can choose Install Now or Customize:

✦ **Install Now:** Runs the installation program using the default settings. Choose this option if you are a beginner who has plenty of hard disk space available for a full installation and if you don't mind the files being stored in the default folder (Program Files\Microsoft Office).

✦ **Customize:** Lets you make choices about file locations and features to be installed. Choose this option if you want to pick which Office (or PowerPoint) components are installed, or if you want to set up a different folder than the default one to hold the files.

If you choose Install Now, you can set this appendix down and follow along with whatever pops up on your screen because nothing else will be difficult for you.

If you choose Customize, however, hang in there a bit, because I have some things to tell you that you should know.

Program Location

Normally it's good to stick with the default program location: `Program Files\Microsoft Office` on the same drive as Windows is installed (usually C). However, if you are running out of hard disk space on that drive, you might want to change to a different drive.

At the Install Location screen in the Setup program, make note of the drives listed and the amount of available space. (Figure A-2 shows two drives.) If there is another drive on the list besides C: with more space available than C: has, you might decide to use it instead for the installation. To do so, click in the top text box to move an insertion point there, and then replace C: with D: or with the letter for the desired drive.

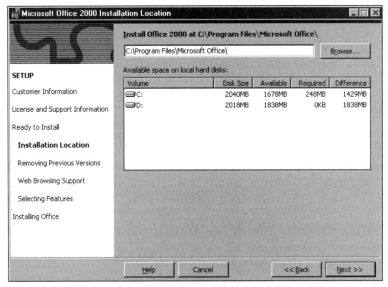

Figure A-2: Choose a different location if necessary.

Selecting Features

When you arrive at the Select Features part of the Setup program, you see all the programs in Office 2000 on a *tree*, like in Windows Explorer. See Figure A-3. (If you're installing from a PowerPoint, not Office, CD-ROM, your tree will look somewhat different.)

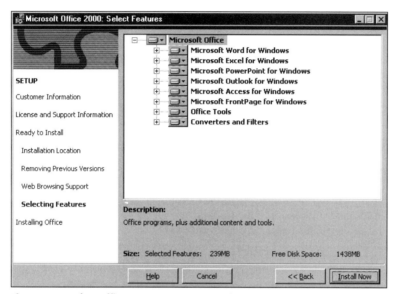

Figure A-3: The Office 2000 components in a tree structure.

By default, the Setup program installs all of the Office 2000 applications listed in Figure A-3. You can certainly install all these programs, but it will eat up a lot of your hard disk space (over 200 MB). That's fine if you have space to spare, or if you need all of the applications, but most people don't need all of them. You will probably want to deselect at least some of the programs or deselect some of their options.

To deselect an entire program, click the little down-pointing arrow next to its icon to open a drop-down list. Then choose one of these options:

✦ **Run from My Computer:**. This means install it. Leave this chosen for the programs you want to be installed.

✦ **Run All from My Computer:** This option sets not only the chosen item to run from your local PC, but also every item subordinate to it on the tree.

✦ **Run from CD:** This option enables you to run an application from the CD. A pointer to it is installed on your hard disk, but the actual application remains on CD, so that when you run it, the Office 2000 CD must be in your CD-ROM drive. The option is useful if you need an application but don't have enough free hard disk space.

✦ **Run All from CD:** This sets not only the chosen option to run from CD, but also every item subordinate to it.

✦ **Installed on First Use:** This sets up a link to the program on your hard disk, but does not install the program itself until you activate the link. That way the program is not installed until the last possible moment, so if you end up never needing it, it never takes up the space.

✦ **Not Available:** Choose this option if you don't want to install the application at all. For example, people who have no need for e-mail and scheduling might want to deselect Microsoft Outlook for Windows.

You don't have to select or reject an application as a whole; you can choose individual parts of it to have different installation settings. To do so, click the plus sign next to it to open a list on the tree. Then choose a setting for each individual item on that tree. See Figure A-4, for example, which shows PowerPoint components you can choose to install.

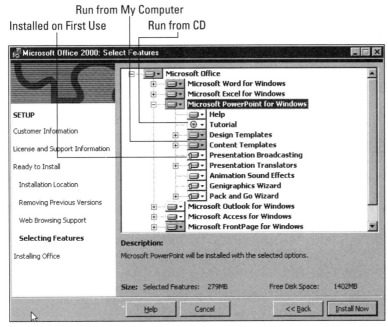

Figure A-4: Different components of PowerPoint you can install.

You may have noticed that besides the Office 2000 applications, there are two other big categories: Office Tools and Converters and Filters. Office Tools contains an assortment of add-in programs that work with more than one of the Office 2000 programs. It includes the Office Assistant, the Spelling Checker, Microsoft Organization Chart, and more. Converters and Filters provide utilities that convert files from one format to another and that enable the Office 2000 applications to use graphics.

When you are finished making your feature selections, click Install Now to start the file copying.

Copying the Files

While the file copying is taking place, there's nothing to do but be patient. This takes a long time (a half-hour or more on some systems, depending on what you are installing). You may not see any progress, and it may even seem like your PC has locked up. It hasn't. Just wait it out.

When you see a message that the installation completed successfully, click OK. If prompted to restart your PC, click Yes to do so. Even if you aren't prompted to restart, it's a good idea; choose Start ➪ Shut Down ➪ Restart.

✦   ✦   ✦

What's on the CD-ROM?

The CD-ROM that accompanies this book contains some great stuff! You'll find clip art, sound, and video samples, demo programs of flow charting programs and utilities, and lots more. The CD is organized into folders, with each company's offerings in its own folder. In this appendix, I'll tell you about each of the companies and their products and explain how to install the goodies.

Artbeats: Stock Video Footage

Location on CD: \Artbeats Software

Installation: Requires QuickTime, which you can install by running QuickTime30.exe in the Apple Computers folder.

View each clip from the CD by double-clicking it in Windows Explorer, or copy the clips to your hard disk for use. Place the clips in your PowerPoint presentation with Insert ➪ Movie ➪ From File.

Artbeats is a company that specializes in "stock footage": high-resolution movie and animation special effects clips. They have provided five high-resolution clips in QuickTime format on this book's CD for your unlimited use. These require a QuickTime player to view; to install one, run the file Qteasy32.exe in the Artbeats folder on the CD. You can buy a Starter Kit CD from Artbeats very inexpensively that includes these clips in Targa format too.

Note   There are two main video tape standards in the world today. NTSC is the video standard for the United States. It displays at 30 frames per second. PAL is a European format, at 25 frames per second. The movies included with this book are 30 frames per second, or NTSC. When you buy a video collection from Artbeats, you get both.

Compadre: Backgrounds and Images

Location on CD: \Compadre

Installation: In Windows Explorer, double-click CompDemo.exe.

Use: In PowerPoint, navigate to the folder Program Files\Microsoft Office\Office\Compadre Demo while choosing a clip.

Compadre is a really neat collection of backgrounds, buttons, sounds, and other clips that are specifically chosen for their appropriateness for PowerPoint. The sample pack on this CD provides a handful of items in each category; the full version that you can purchase offers more of everything.

Crystal Graphics: 3D Transition Add-In

Location on CD: \Crystal Graphics

Installation: Run the installation program 3ds1set.exe.

Use: Installing this program adds two user tools on PowerPoint's Slide Show menu. The Add 3D Transition tool creates cool 3D transitions, and then the View Show With 3D tool shows your 3D-enhanced presentation.

This program can pump up your presentations by providing very cool 3D transitions. The only quirk is that is requires you to have a 3D accelerated graphics card in your PC, so it might not work on older PCs (especially on an older or less powerful laptop; mine is less than a year old and it wouldn't work with).

DeMorgan Industries: Sample Images and Animation

Location on CD: \DeMorgan Industries\Animation Samples and \DeMorgan Industries\WebSpice®

Installation: Copy the files to a folder on your hard disk.

These are sample animations and images. To check them out, double-click on one of them from Windows Explorer. You can use them in PowerPoint the same as you do any other picture or movie.

Eyewire, Inc.: Sample Images

Location on CD: \Eyewire, Inc.

Installation: Copy the files to a folder on your hard disk.

Use: Here are some high-quality business images that you can use for backgrounds. Apply them in PowerPoint with the Format ➪ Background command.

IDG Books: Internet Directory from *The Internet Bible*

Location on CD: \Internet Bible

Installation: Run from the CD, or copy to your hard disk, as you please.

This file doesn't have anything to do with PowerPoint per se, but it's really cool. It provides almost 1000 Web site links, organized in about 140 categories. You can use it as an Internet directory to research topics that you want to know more about.

JASC Software: Paint Shop Pro Image Editor

Location on CD: \Jasc Software

Installation: Run psp501ev.exe.

Run Paint Shop Pro from the Windows Start menu. It's a stand-alone graphics program that you can use to create, capture, modify, and convert images for use in PowerPoint (or any other program).

Don't let the fact that this program is available as shareware fool you; it's great. It's one of the few shareware programs that I have ever been so impressed with that I bought the full version. You can use it to capture screenshots, to convert images from one format to another, to color-correct an image, and lots more that you may have not even thought of yet.

LiveImage: Image Map Editor

Location on CD: \LiveImage Corporation

Installation: Run LiveImg129Inst.exe.

This program helps you create image maps for use on Web pages. This can be useful if you want to distribute your PowerPoint presentation on the Internet. You have probably used image maps before while visiting other Web sites; when you click on different parts of the image, you are taken to different Web pages.

This program is a 14-day evaluation copy; you must buy the full version if you want to use it after that time.

MindSpring: Internet Services

Location on CD: \MindSpring

Installation: Run mspring308.exe.

MindSpring is an Internet Service Provider. If you don't have an Internet account, run this software to walk through a very easy process of getting one. Keep in mind that you will pay a monthly fee for MindSpring service, just as you would for any other Internet service.

Netscape: Netscape Communicator

Location on CD: \Netscape4.5\95_NT_32

Installation: Run Cc32e405.exe.

Netscape is a Web browser, a competitor to Microsoft's Internet Explorer. Lots of people prefer it to the Microsoft product, but personally I see very little difference between the capabilities of the two. You might as well give Netscape a try if you haven't before, seeing as it's absolutely free and it's right here on the CD.

Nova Development: Sounds, Pictures, and Animations

Location on CD: \Nova_Dev

Installation: Run the installation programs: Animation Explosion Sampler.exe, Clip Art Sampler.exe, and Kaboom! Sampler.exe. When you run each installation program, you are prompted for a folder name to store the clips. Make sure you provide a full path, including the hard drive letter (for example, C:\Clipart) and remember what name you choose!

Use the Insert menu commands to start inserting a sound, movie, or picture, and then navigate to the folder where you installed the demos.

You may not have heard of Nova Development, but you have probably heard of their products. They are the makers of the very popular Art Explosion, Animation Explosion, and Kaboom! collections of clip art, animation, and sounds, and they have provided some wonderful samplers of each of these three products for your enjoyment.

- ✦ Animation Sampler: Animated GIFs that look great in any presentation, including animated buttons, arrows, cartoon sequences, and more.
- ✦ Clip Art: all kinds of professionally-drawn clips that you won't find anywhere else, and all royalty free.
- ✦ Sounds: Both whimsical and practical sounds to enhance your presentations (and to use in other programs too!)

Retro Ad Art: 1930s Clip Art

Location on CD: \Retro Ad Art© Sampler

Installation: Copy the clips to a folder on your hard disk, or access them directly from the CD from within PowerPoint when needed.

In PowerPoint, place the images with Insert ⇨ Picture ⇨ From File.

This collection provides faithful reproductions of that classy, kitchy artwork of the 1930s through 1950s. The full collection offers over 1800 images, everything from cocktail signs from nightclubs to service station logos. On this book's CD are over 45 samples from the collection, ready for use. Even if you don't think you'll want to use these images in your presentation, go ahead and browse them—they'll make you smile.

RFFlow: Flow Charting Utility

Location on CD: \RFF Electronics\RFFlow

Installation: Run the installation program setup.exe.

Run from the Start menu in Windows. Create flow charts in RFFlow, and then select your work and use Edit ⇨ Copy and Edit ⇨ Paste to copy it to a PowerPoint slide. Or create a new RFF object on your slide in PowerPoint with Insert ⇨ Object.

The one thing that PowerPoint lacks, in my opinion, is a decent flow charting utility. RFFlow makes up for this by specializing in flow charting. In this program you can create great-looking flow charts, diagrams, and more; no more struggling with Microsoft Organization Chart to fudge your way through!

Symantec: WinFaxPro Trial

Location on CD: \Symantec, Inc.

Installation: Run Wftrybuy.exe.

WinFaxPro is my favorite faxing program. It does a great job sending and receiving faxes, broadcasting faxes, creating fax cover sheets, and more. You can use it to fax pages of your presentation to people who cannot attend one of your shows. This is a limited-time trial, so you can see whether it fits your needs.

UniTech: Font Management Utilities

Location on CD: \UniTech\MyFonts and \UniTech\TrueType Font Namer

Installation: Run the Setup.exe programs in each of the folders.

There are two utilities provided in this folder: Font Namer helps you easily rename fonts in Windows (which can be great if you have some cryptic name five-word name for a font), while MyFonts helps you add, remove, and organize fonts.

✦   ✦   ✦

Index

B

Continued

M

Continued

IDG BOOKS WORLDWIDE, INC.
END-USER LICENSE AGREEMENT

4. **Restrictions on Use of Individual Programs.** You must follow the individual requirements and restrictions detailed for each individual program in Appendix B, "What's on the CD-ROM," of this Book. These limitations are also contained in the individual license agreements recorded on the Software Media. These limitations may include a requirement that after using the program for a specified period of time, the user must pay a registration fee or discontinue use. By opening the Software packet(s), you will be agreeing to abide by the licenses and restrictions for these individual programs that are detailed in Appendix B, "What's on the CD-ROM," and on the Software Media. None of the material on this Software Media or listed in this Book may ever be redistributed, in original or modified form, for commercial purposes.

5. **Limited Warranty.**

   (a) IDGB warrants that the Software and Software Media are free from defects in materials and workmanship under normal use for a period of sixty (60) days from the date of purchase of this Book. If IDGB receives notification within the warranty period of defects in materials or workmanship, IDGB will replace the defective Software Media.

   (b) **IDGB AND THE AUTHOR OF THE BOOK DISCLAIM ALL OTHER WARRANTIES, EXPRESS OR IMPLIED, INCLUDING WITHOUT LIMITATION IMPLIED WARRANTIES OF MERCHANTABILITY AND FITNESS FOR A PARTICULAR PURPOSE, WITH RESPECT TO THE SOFTWARE, THE PROGRAMS, THE SOURCE CODE CONTAINED THEREIN, AND/OR THE TECHNIQUES DESCRIBED IN THIS BOOK. IDGB DOES NOT WARRANT THAT THE FUNCTIONS CONTAINED IN THE SOFTWARE WILL MEET YOUR REQUIREMENTS OR THAT THE OPERATION OF THE SOFTWARE WILL BE ERROR FREE.**

   (c) This limited warranty gives you specific legal rights, and you may have other rights that vary from jurisdiction to jurisdiction.

6. **Remedies.**

   (a) IDGB's entire liability and your exclusive remedy for defects in materials and workmanship shall be limited to replacement of the Software Media, which may be returned to IDGB with a copy of your receipt at the following address: Software Media Fulfillment Department, Attn.: *Microsoft PowerPoint 2000 Bible*, IDG Books Worldwide, Inc., 7260 Shadeland Station, Ste. 100, Indianapolis, IN 46256, or call 1-800-762-2974. Please allow three to four weeks for delivery. This Limited Warranty is void if failure of the Software Media has resulted from accident, abuse, or misapplication. Any replacement Software Media will be warranted for the remainder of the original warranty period or thirty (30) days, whichever is longer.

(b) In no event shall IDGB or the authors be liable for any damages whatsoever (including without limitation damages for loss of business profits, business interruption, loss of business information, or any other pecuniary loss) arising from the use of or inability to use the Book or the Software, even if IDGB has been advised of the possibility of such damages.

(c) Because some jurisdictions do not allow the exclusion or limitation of liability for consequential or incidental damages, the above limitation or exclusion may not apply to you.

7. <u>U.S. Government Restricted Rights</u>. Use, duplication, or disclosure of the Software by the U.S. Government is subject to restrictions stated in paragraph (c)(1)(ii) of the Rights in Technical Data and Computer Software clause of DFARS 252.227-7013, and in subparagraphs (a) through (d) of the Commercial Computer — Restricted Rights clause at FAR 52.227-19, and in similar clauses in the NASA FAR supplement, when applicable.

8. <u>General</u>. This Agreement constitutes the entire understanding of the parties and revokes and supersedes all prior agreements, oral or written, between them and may not be modified or amended except in a writing signed by both parties hereto that specifically refers to this Agreement. This Agreement shall take precedence over any other documents that may be in conflict herewith. If any one or more provisions contained in this Agreement are held by any court or tribunal to be invalid, illegal, or otherwise unenforceable, each and every other provision shall remain in full force and effect.

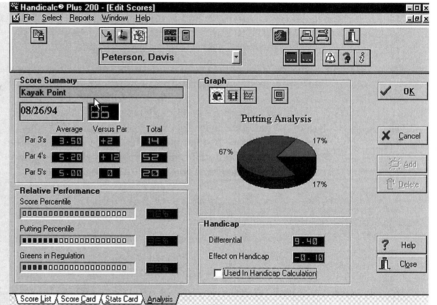

Over 1,800 authentic hi-rez B&W ad cuts from the '30s, '40s & '50s on one cross-platform CD-ROM.

For more info: call
1-800-830-1212

Here's looking at you

Drive in
THEATRE

HI THERE!

Let's
HAVE ONE

Only
$179
for the
complete
package

RECORDS

SAVE
25%

Only **$134.**²⁵
with this coupon!